Make Getting a
with Programs Like These.

Math/Science

At Denison University in Granville, Ohio, the Wells Scholarship in Science is awarded for outstanding academic performance/potential by students who plan to major in science or math. It covers three-quarters of tuition.

Creative/Visual Arts

Clarion University of Pennsylvania awards scholarships to twenty-five to thirty high school students who have exhibited high interest and achievement particularly in the areas of art, music, and intercollegiate athletics. Awards of $200 to $500 are paid each semester as a tuition credit.

Music

Students who show promise and talent in music may qualify for the William P. Foster Scholarship award at Florida A&M University. The award is made annually to senior majors in choral and instrumental music. A faculty committee of the Music Department makes the decision on the recipient based on performance, achievement, academic record, leadership, and organizational membership.

Languages/Literature/Humanities

Eastern New Mexico University offers scholarships for students interested in studying modern languages, literature, or science fiction. Awards are based on academic achievement and other criteria.

General

The U.S. Bank Multicultural Scholarship ($1,000 to $4,000) is awarded at Washington State University to African-American and other minority students who meet certain criteria.

ERLENE B. WILSON has been writing college-related literature for almost a decade, including an advice column for college women in *Glamour* magazine. She is the co-founder of Creative Planners, a college marketing firm targeting African-American students, and the author of *The 100 Best Colleges for African-Americans* (Plume). She lives in Randallstown, Maryland.

MONEY FOR COLLEGE

A Guide to Financial Aid for African-American Students

Erlene B. Wilson

A PLUME BOOK

PLUME

Published by the Penguin Group
Penguin Books USA Inc., 375 Hudson Street, New York, New York 10014, U.S.A.
Penguin Books Ltd, 27 Wrights Lane, London W8 5TZ, England
Penguin Books Australia Ltd, Ringwood, Victoria, Australia
Penguin Books Canada Ltd, 10 Alcorn Avenue, Toronto, Ontario, Canada M4V 3B2
Penguin Books (N.Z.) Ltd, 182–190 Wairau Road, Auckland 10, New Zealand

Penguin Books Ltd, Registered Offices:
Harmondsworth, Middlesex, England

First published by Plume, an imprint of Dutton Signet, a division of Penguin Books
USA Inc.

First Printing, May, 1996
10 9 8 7 6 5 4 3 2 1

 REGISTERED TRADEMARK—MARCA REGISTRADA

LIBRARY OF CONGRESS CATALOGING-IN-PUBLICATION DATA:
Wilson, Erlene B.
    Money for college : a guide to financial aid for African-American students / Erlene
Wilson.
        p.   cm.
    Includes indexes.
    ISBN 0-452-27276-9
    1. Student aid—United States.   2. Afro-American college students—Scholarships,
fellowships, etc.   I. Title.
LB2337.4.W55   1993
378.3'089'96073—dc20   95-43155
                                                                                            CIP

Printed in the United States of America
Set in New Baskerville
Designed by Jesse Cohen

BOOKS ARE AVAILABLE AT QUANTITY DISCOUNTS WHEN USED TO PROMOTE PRODUCTS OR
SERVICES. FOR INFORMATION PLEASE WRITE TO PREMIUM MARKETING DIVISION, PENGUIN
BOOKS USA INC., 375 HUDSON STREET, NEW YORK, NEW YORK 10014.

 **Merrill Lynch**

Darnell D. Jackson
Vice President
Senior Financial Consultant

Toria A. Herold
Registered Administrative
Assistant

Private Client Group

200 Renaissance Center
Suite 3000
Detroit, Michigan 48243
313 446 1277
800 777 9413 Toll Free
FAX 313 446 1199

Enclosed is the paperwork we discussed.

Please sign and return as soon as possible.

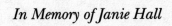

In Memory of Janie Hall

ACKNOWLEDGMENTS

The completion of this project is owed, in large part, to the patience, understanding, and love of many people. Top on my list is my mother, Esther Berry, who literally took care of me and my family as I secluded myself writing all day and sometimes into late hours at night. Thanks, Mom! I also want to thank my son, Charlie, who, I believe, is learning through my writing about the sacrifice and joy of taking a dream or idea from conception to completion. Keep on dreaming, Charlie, and don't be afraid to think big! My immediate and extended family have all contributed to this work through their words of encouragement and support. Special thanks to Guy, Karen, Maisha, Angel, especially Pierre, and Ariel Douyon for all their hard work!

Finally, I want to thank all of the colleges and universities, and corporate, private, and nonprofit organizations that contributed grant and scholarship information to this book.

CONTENTS

x **Contents**

HOW TO USE THIS BOOK

The first section of this book outlines the realities of financing a college education and discusses strategies and savings programs that students and parents can use to pay for college. It contains information on recent trends in college financing that affect college enrollment, particularly of African-American students, including a federal court ruling declaring a race-based scholarship program at the University of Maryland—College Park to be illegal. The U.S. Supreme Court refused to review the decision, which affects race-based scholarships in Maryland, North Carolina, South Carolina, Virginia, and West Virginia. It remains unclear how the decision will affect other public and private scholarship programs targeted to African-American students, since it does not rule out race-specific scholarships in all situations. Many programs currently consider ethnicity along with other criteria; other programs probably will be altered to withstand legal challenge. Regardless of this decision, numerous colleges and universities remain committed to creating more culturally diverse student bodies on their campuses. Given this more inclusive climate, students are well advised to make use of the many educational and financial aid programs that have been created for them. The opportunities do exist.

This section also discusses financial aid programs offered by colleges and universities, the government, and corporations, as well as the military and private and nonprofit organizations.

Section II takes readers through the process of applying for financial aid including how to work with high school guidance counselors and how to research scholarships.

Section III lists grant and scholarship programs by field of study. A special listing of minority/race-specific programs is included in this section. This subject listing provides a description of the aid program, amount awarded, and application deadline.

Section IV provides information on academic, athletic, and other scholarship offerings at colleges and universities.

Section V contains profiles of private, corporate, and nonprofit grant and scholarship opportunities by subject. The majority of these programs target and/or encourage African-American applicants. Included in each profile is a description of the program, amount of award, application deadline, and where to write or call for application information.

Readers will find where to write or call for applications and more information in the section on Financial Aid by Institutions. Also included in this section is the total financial aid budget for each school, undergraduate enrollment, percentage of African-American students enrolled, and the percent who received financial aid as well as the average financial aid award amount for these students. In addition, a list of college ROTC programs is included in Appendix A.

Many different financing patterns exist in colleges and universities around the nation. In the absence of information about a particular school, readers are advised to use the topics in this book as a guide for asking questions about grant and scholarship programs at the specific schools that interest them. Many schools have policies that favor minorities in the allocation of financial aid. For example, nearly all states have established grant programs (aid that does not have to be repaid) for their residents. Like federal Pell Grants, these programs often are used as the foundation of financial aid packages, particularly for minority students. Some of these programs may be even used to study at out-of-state schools. Information about aid programs in your state may be obtained through individual colleges and universities or by contacting the higher education commission in your home state. A list of these commissions nationwide is included in Appendix B of this book.

Other resources in this book include a listing of African-American fraternal and professional organizations (Appendix C). Students would do well to contact these organizations. Many of them provide scholarships, internships, and career information specifically for African-Americans.

HOW THE SCHOOLS WERE SELECTED

Money for College: A Guide to Financial Aid for African-American Students profiles a small sampling of schools nationwide. As in the case of my previous book, *The 100 Best Colleges for African-American Students*, top-ranked schools nationwide were mailed a detailed survey requesting information on financial aid assistance available at their institutions for African-American students. Not all were willing to share this information. Also, the [varying] methods of recording and retrieving information at individual schools sometimes make it difficult to ferret out financial aid opportunities for African-Americans. Still, care was taken to include a full range of colleges and universities—public, private, predominantly African-American, and Ivy League.

INTRODUCTION

This is a good time for African-Americans to pursue higher education. Indeed, after years of discouraging news about African-American college enrollment, finally there is good news to report. Government figures show that the number of African-Americans enrolled in college is inching up again. According to estimates by the National Center for Education Statistics, the number of African-Americans enrolled in college increased from 1.1 million in 1980 to 1.3 million in 1990. The current increase in no way replicates the surge in college enrollments of the 1970s and early 80s, when the African-American undergraduate enrollment increased nearly 100 percent, but it puts African-Americans in sync with the total college enrollment figures, projected to increase from about 13.9 million in 1990 to 15.7 million in the year 2000.

To the African-American community, increases in college enrollment are welcome antidotes to grimmer reports of increased poverty, illiteracy, and violence. However, the continued success of African-Americans in obtaining a college education will depend upon access to information about college attendance as well as community, parental, governmental, and institutional support for higher education. A trend toward greater racial diversity on campus through the use of race-sensitive scholarship and grant programs has created opportunities for many African-American students to attend college. Fortunately, many institutions remain committed to creating more racially balanced campuses, even in the face of legal challenges to race-based scholarship programs for helping African-American students.

Those willing to invest the time, effort, and resources will find that numerous financing opportunities exist, including college savings plans, loans, scholarships, grants, and tuition payment plans. Whatever strategy a family selects, the key is to make informed decisions about college selection and financing and—most important—to start early.

Information on college financing is available from libraries, schools, bookstores, financial institutions, the federal government, and now through computer databases and other services, much of it at no cost.

I encourage you to be persistent and resourceful in your quest to locate financial aid for college, and to follow a simple rule—the more you look, the more you will find!

Good luck and remember to keep your eyes on the prize.

SECTION I: COLLEGE FINANCING FOR AFRICAN-AMERICAN STUDENTS

With college tuitions steadily increasing, most students have become cost conscious and are seeking financial aid. This means that students from middle-class families compete alongside economically disadvantaged students for financial aid. Indeed many families have been caught off guard. The cost of college today can give parents sticker shock and have them recalling "the good old days" when the entire cost of a college education equaled that of one semester at many schools today.

For many African-Americans, obtaining financial aid is a major factor in selecting a college. According to government statistics, nearly half of all undergraduate students receive some financial assistance and more than 70 percent of African-Americans receive financial aid. The availability of aid may not only determine whether a student attends college but may also dictate the type of institution a student will attend. U.S. Department of Education statistics show that the average cost of attendance at public institutions was $8,109 in 1990, while the average price tag at private not-for-profit colleges and universities was $13,689. At the same time, the average financial aid award, including grants and loans, at private nonprofit institutions was $8,662. It is no surprise then that more than 75 percent of all undergraduate students attend public institutions. While these figures have implications for all students, African-Americans who rely heavily on aid often are forced to attend public institutions or other less expensive institutions such as predominantly Black colleges and universities. Even those fortunate enough to attend a private college or university will need to have substantial personal savings or receive full scholarships to attend.

In their search for college funding, African-American students will, for once, be at an advantage on account of their minority status. Today, numerous corporations, foundations, religious organizations, social organizations, unions, and veterans groups target minorities for awards. Many of these scholarship programs are well known—the Thurgood Marshall Scholarship Fund and Coca-Cola Scholars Program, for example—but others, such as the National Association of Black Journalists Scholarship, the American Geological Institute Minority Participation Program Scholarship, and the Presbyterian Church Student Opportunity Minority Scholarship have received less publicity. Students will have to commit time, energy, and resourcefulness to unearthing these scholarships, but the effort can have favorable results. The Coca-Cola Scholars program, for example, awards 50 four-year college scholarships of $20,000 each and 100 scholarships of $4,000 each, which may be used at any school. The National Association of Black Journalists Scholarship awards eight scholarships of $2,500 annually to African-American students, and the Presbyterian Church Student Opportunity Minority Scholarship makes more than 125 awards annually of $100 to $1,400 to minority students who are members of the Presbyterian Church. Like many other private scholarships, those specifically targeted to minorities are generally for small amounts ranging from $100 to $1,500, and they usually have very specific stipulations and requirements such as religious affiliation, career interest (such as engineering, accounting, or the arts), local residency, or professional affiliation. Once again, however, the benefits of obtaining these scholarships far outweigh the effort of searching and applying for consideration to receive them.

It is a student's dream to attend college on a fully paid scholarship. However, most students will wind up paying for college through a combination of funding sources, including *Scholarships,* which are financial awards that support studies at the undergraduate level and do not have to be repaid; *Grants,* which provide financial support to undergraduate education, special projects, travel, or other educational efforts and which do not have to be repaid; *Loans,* which are borrowed money that must be repaid with interest; and self-help programs such as *College Work-Study,* which provide students an opportunity to work and earn money to pay for college.

The federal government is the largest provider of college financial aid, administering billions of dollars annually through five federal aid programs. Awards made under these federal programs are race-blind; that is, they are given to students without regard to their race, gender, or ethnic background. To qualify, a student must be a U.S. citizen or eligible noncitizen, have a high school diploma or a General Education Development (GED) certificate, be enrolled in a degree program in an accredited school, and have financial need. A recipient also must have a Social Security number, and a young man must register with the Selective Service. The programs are:

Federal Pell Grants. The Pell Grant program, which provides aid to over 4 million students, is among the largest and most popular federal grant programs. A Pell Grant is an award that provides a "base" or "foundation" of financial aid to which aid from other federal and nonfederal sources may be added. These grant awards generally are provided to students from low-income families. Eligibility for a Pell Grant is determined by a U.S. Department of Education standard formula established by Congress. The formula produces an Expected Family Contribution (EFC) number. The amount of each student award varies depending on the EFC, the cost of education at the school one attends, and whether the student attends for a full academic year or less. It also depends on the amount of program funds available. The maximum award is $2,300 per eligible student.

Federal Supplemental Educational Opportunity Grant (FSEOG). The Federal Supplemental Educational Opportunity Grant (FSEOG) program also provides funds to students with exceptional financial need, or students with the lowest EFC's who are also Federal Pell Grant recipients. These grants can be as high as $4,000 ($4,400 if costs abroad exceed the cost of education at home), and do not have to be repaid.

Federal Work-Study. While the Federal Work-Study program is not considered "gift-aid," it does provide students in financial need an opportunity to earn money to help pay for educational expenses. Many students work at on-campus jobs. Off-campus jobs are generally at private non-profit organizations or local, state, or federal public agencies, and the work performed must be in the public interest. Some schools also have agreements with private employers to provide Federal Work-Study jobs related to a student's course of study. Work-Study students earn at least minimum wage and may earn more, depending on the type of work and skills required to perform the job.

Perkins Loans. This is a low-interest loan to help undergraduate and graduate students pay for their education. These must be paid back. The program is administered through participating schools, which set the deadlines and determine the amount of funding depending on your need and other sources of aid you are receiving.

PLUS Loans/Supplemental Loans. PLUS loans allow parents to borrow money for your education, whereas Supplemental loans are for student borrowers. Each of these loans is made by a private lender such as a bank, credit union, or savings and loan association. You can apply for these loans in the same way you do Stafford loans. The difference is that you do not have to show need to obtain a loan, although you may have to submit to a credit check. For information on any of the federal financial programs outlined here, write to: Federal Student Aid Information Center, P.O. Box 84, Washington, D.C. 20044.

Federal Direct Student Loans Program (available at **some** *schools).* The FDSLP is a new program that offers a low-interest loan of 4 percent to students or parents to pay for college. It consists of Federal Direct Stafford Loans (subsidized and unsubsidized) and Federal Direct PLUS loans. These loans are basically the same as the Stafford and PLUS loans. The difference is that the U.S. Department of Education is the lender (rather than a bank or credit union) and that loan proceeds are delivered through your school. You (or your parents, if they have a Federal Direct PLUS loan for you) will send all your loan repayments to the Department of Education rather than to several lenders.

The FDSLP was instituted under President Clinton as a way to simplify the complex third-party lending process for students that existed under programs administered by the Student Loan Marketing Corporation (Sallie Mae). There was also compelling evidence that the federal government could administer the program more cost effectively and save billions in taxpayer dollars over time. Because the Department of Education is the lender, students and parents do not have to find a bank or other financial institution willing to make them a loan and funds are sent directly to the college.

The first Direct Loans were made for periods of enrollment beginning on or after July 1, 1994. However, only a small number of schools will be participating in the Federal Direct Student Loan Program for 1994–95, so check with the school(s) you're interested in to see if it participates. If it does not, you can apply for a Federal Direct Stafford Loan simply by filling out a Free Application for Federal Student Aid (FAFSA) or a Renewal Application, which is a shorter version of the FAFSA. Your parents will have to complete a separate application for a Direct PLUS loan, which may be obtained from your school.

In addition to FDSLP loans, students may now opt to refinance other loans that are currently being repaid to private sources through the federal government's loan consolidation program. You may want to consider this option if the government repayment terms and options are better than those you received from your private lender. Among other things, the government program has an extended repayment plan, which reduces your monthly payments by stretching them over a longer period of time. It also offers a graduated repayment plan and income contingent plan that considers your income in setting the amount of monthly payments. For more information on how to do this, call the toll-free federal hotline at 1-800-4-FED AID (1-800-433-3243).

APPLYING FOR FEDERAL AID

To apply for federal student aid, you must complete the Free Application for Federal Student Aid (FAFSA). There is no fee for this form. The U.S. Department of Education offers a free publication, *The Student Guide,* which provides advice in applying for federal aid. The FAFSA and *The Student Guide* may be obtained from your school, local library, or by calling the Federal Student Aid Information Center (listed at the end of this section). The FAFSA should be filed as soon as possible after January 1. Students and parents are advised to take great care in completing this form accurately, promptly, and honestly. It takes about four weeks for your federal application to be processed. If you have to confirm or correct any information provided, it will take another two to three weeks. A student must have a Social Security number to apply for federal aid; an application will not be processed without this number.

In addition to the FAFSA form, some colleges also require that you complete the Financial Aid Form (FAF) and pay a small processing fee. The FAF provides additional information about family finances, which colleges use to determine eligibility for their own funds. Schools that use the ACT (American College Testing) admissions test may stipulate that students complete the Family Financial Statement. In addition, individual states may require a student to complete additional forms to compete for aid.

OTHER WAYS TO FINANCE YOUR EDUCATION

Even though it may take years actually to get a degree, many students may find that working their way through college is the most realistic way to pay for college education. Single women who are the heads of household, children from large families, and children from poor families often have to work to help support their families. Such circumstances are real obstacles to obtaining a college degree but need not stop motivated students from going to college.

Recognizing the constraints of many potential students, some community and public colleges now offer evening and weekend programs. Increasingly, too, employers are developing cooperative relationships with local colleges and universities to provide training and other job skills to their employees. These institutions are happy to oblige and have begun to design curriculums that will provide employers a more qualified workforce. The local community or public colleges in your state can provide information on programs that may meet your specific needs and tell you whether financial assistance is available. In addition, many government programs provide financial assistance to disadvantaged or nontraditional students. The Head Start Program, for example, provides educational stipends to single mothers who have children in their program. For more information about Head Start Stipends, contact Head Start, 330 "C" Street, S.W., P.O. Box 1182, Washington, D.C. 20013, 202-245-0572.

THE NATIONAL SERVICE PROGRAM

In fulfillment of his campaign promise to resurrect national service in a Peace Corps–type effort, President Clinton signed into law the National and Community Service Trust Act in fall 1993 and established the Corporation for National and Community Service and AmeriCorps to administer the effort nationwide. Through this effort, the President hopes to engage youth in addressing social problems nationwide through community service, while allowing them to earn an educational stipend that can be used to defray college costs or repay college loan debt. The newly established Corporation for National and Community Service builds on the efforts and programs currently funded by the federal domestic volunteer programs ACTION, VISTA, and the National Senior Volunteer Corps. The AmeriCorps initiative, however, specifically targets youth to work in programs designed to address the nation's critical educational, human, public safety, and environmental needs at the community level.

AmeriCorps directs, administers, and manages the national service effort, providing funding and technical assistance to more than 450 community-based programs nationwide that meet a variety of criteria. AmeriCorps also serves as a clearinghouse for national service programs and a referral service for participants, matching them to provide service to programs that meet their skills and area of interest. To be eligible to serve in AmeriCorps programs, you must be a U.S. citizen or a legal resident alien, age 17 or older. Members must be high school graduates or agree to achieve their General Education Diploma (GED) prior to receiving their educational awards. They must also agree to serve 1,700 service hours in the program. Applicants to AmeriCorps will have an assessment made of their leadership abilities, skills, and area of interest for service. This information will be compiled and entered into an AmeriCorps computer database that matches volunteers and programs.

Currently, the National Civilian Community Corps (NCCC) is the only residential program being run by AmeriCorps. NCCC trains and mobilizes youth to work in teams to address critical needs in urban and rural communities. The program draws on methods used in our civilian service projects as well as the motivational training methods used in the military to train recruits. Applicants must be at least 17 years of age, U.S. citizens or legal resident aliens, and be high school graduates or have obtained their GED prior to receiving their educational award. Selections are based on individual skill, leadership potential, and commitment to service. Those selected live dormitory style and train together at military bases. Training is focused on leadership, team building, citizenship, and physical conditioning. Corps members work in teams and will be trained in specific project areas. Assignments will be in a variety of settings such as nonprofit community organizations, campus-based service programs, public safety programs, youth programs and the like.

NCCC Corps members receive housing, meals, uniforms, health care, child care, and earn a small wage amounting to about $8,000 a year. They also receive an educational award of $4,725 per year, for each year of service, for a maximum of two years. Part-time members can earn an award worth half that amount. The educational award may be used as a scholarship for college or vocational training, or to pay back college loans. Corps members have up to seven years to claim their award, which will be sent directly to the college or vocational school they decide to attend. While the educational award may be used to help pay back a loan, participating in the national service program is not a loan deferment program. Members still have an obligation to pay back the total amount of any student loan made through their bank or school. If a corps member so chooses, a cash award of $2,362 can be provided in lieu of the educational award.

The national service program may hold special appeal for young people who have not decided whether to attend college right after high school. Open to anyone who meets the age, service, and educational requirements, AmeriCorps participants may be students, single parents, disabled, or recipients of government assistance, although the programs in its network can select candidates based on its own criteria and needs. Participants can expect to earn only the equivalent of a minimum wage, although the real-life work experience, health care, and child care benefits may prove worthwhile. The educational stipend is small—the maximum educational award of $9,450, for example, will fund only about two years of college costs at a public institution and is well below the yearly cost of tuition and room and board at a private university. Still, the national service program represents a fine opportunity to find oneself, earn an educational stipend, and give back something to needy communities and individuals in the process.

To find out more about AmeriCorps, call 1-800-4-FED-AID. For more information about the National Civilian Community Corps program, contact NCCC, 1100 Vermont Avenue, N.W., Washington, D.C. 20525, 1-800-94-ACORPS or 202-606-5000.

FINANCING YOUR EDUCATION THROUGH THE MILITARY

Today's high-tech military requires its recruits to be better educated and more diverse. No longer a last-resort option to the disenfranchised, the military has become an alternative way to finance and obtain education and training beyond high school. It even supplements many who currently have careers through its Reserve Program.

In recent years, the military has engaged in a multimillion-dollar advertising and recruitment program to attract highly motivated and talented recruits into its employ. Many of these advertisements are specifically targeted at the African-American community, and we are responding; statistics indicate that a growing number of African-Americans enroll in military education programs each year. The military's intense recruitment and retention efforts have made it an attractive option for many African-Americans who want to obtain a good education or a marketable skill after high school. Some of the programs not only pay for educational costs but provide an income as well. This government-financed plan is most attractive to African-Americans from families whose financial situation cannot support the kind of education obtainable through the military.

Striking a bargain with the military sounds simple enough. You give several years of service in exchange for an opportunity to obtain a college education, financed by the government, which you do not have to pay back. If these offers seem too good to be true, consider the price. When the military pays for your education, it requires you to perform active military service for no less than two years. During peacetime, this may look like a good deal. If war breaks out, the military option may not seem as sweet. During the Persian Gulf War large numbers of African-American soldiers were called into action, and we heard time and again that they'd never thought they would have to go to war; that they played soldier to make extra money or get a college education, not really considering the consequences or possibility of war. If you decide in favor of the military option, be sure you understand what you're getting into. Here are some of the educational programs the military offers to college-bound students:

Air Force ROTC. Through this program a student can obtain a two- to four-year fully paid scholarship covering tuition, fees, expenses, and a $100 nontaxable allowance each month, as well as earn an officer's commission in the Air Force. Scholarships are awarded on a competitive basis and are open to men and women. For applications (DD Form 1893) for four-year scholarships, write for the brochure "Scholarship Applicant Booklet," Air Force ROTC, Selections Division, Maxwell AFB, Alabama 36112. The deadline for submitting these applications is December 1. If you're interested in two- or three-year scholarships, write to the Professor of Aerospace at the college to which you're applying, or write to Air Force ROTC, Recruiting Division, Maxwell AFB, Alabama 36112.

College Degree Program (CDP). This program provides selected Marine officers an opportunity to complete their baccalaureate degrees by attending a college or university as full-time students for up to two years.

Marine Corps Enlisted Commissioning Education Program (MECEP). This program is for enlisted Marines and gives them an opportunity to obtain a four-year college degree as full-time students and become commissioned officers.

Marine Corps Tuition Assistance Program. This is a financial assistance program for Marines who want to take college courses during their off-duty time toward a degree or other postsecondary education. The Marine Corps may pay 75 to 100 percent of the cost of tuition for approved college courses, depending on the status of the applicant.

Naval ROTC. The Navy offers students an opportunity to earn a commission as ensign, U.S. Navy, or second lieutenant, U.S. Marine Corps, by successfully completing the NROTC Navy–Marine Corps Scholarship Program at one of the sixty-five colleges and universities nationwide that offer the program. Students may receive two-year or four-year scholarships, which cover full tuition, fees, books, uniforms, and a $100 nontaxable allowance each month (for up to forty months). To obtain an application for the four-year scholarship program, contact your local Navy or Marine Corps recruiting station or high school guidance counselor, or write to NROTC units and the Commander, Navy Recruiting Command (Code 314), 4015 Wilson Boulevard, Arlington, VA 22203. Be sure to apply between March 1 and December 1 of the year before your college enrollment. Two-year scholarship program applicants can obtain information in the same way but must enter one of the sixty-five host institutions with junior status at the time of enrollment in the program.

New Mexico Military Institute Regent Scholarship, North Hill, Roswell, NM 88201. Scholarship awards of $300, $500, and $1,000 are available through this program to the New Mexico Military Institute. The scholarships are conditional on attending NMMI and entering the Advance Course of Senior Army ROTC leading to a commission as second lieutenant.

U.S. Coast Guard Academy. The Coast Guard also provides an opportunity for a student to obtain a four-year college education and become commissioned as an ensign in the Coast Guard through an annual nationwide competition based on the SAT or ACT test. For more information on the program, write to Director of Admissions, U.S. Coast Guard Academy, New London, CT 06320. To qualify, submit your application before December 15.

A number of colleges and universities across the country either "host" or have agreements with host institutions that allow students to take part in its ROTC campus-based program. Those with such agreements are considered "cross-enrollment" institutions. A list of colleges and universities nationwide that either have ROTC or cross-enrollment programs may be found in Appendix A.

DEVELOPING A FINANCIAL AID STRATEGY

Many students and parents are surprised to find that their selection of a college is an important first step in devising a financial aid strategy. With some thought and planning, you should be able to get into a college that will not only satisfy your academic interests but either provide the financial aid needed or cost no more than you and your family can afford. Families are still advised to begin planning for college as early in their child's life as possible, because the earlier one starts, the more money there will be for college and the less debt the student will have upon graduation.

African-American high school students who have done well in academics or sports will find that generous financial assistance and/or scholarships may be available to them from colleges as well as private foundations and organizations. Students with less impressive records but who are well rounded in academics and social life also have good chances of landing race-based scholarships and grants, thanks to the effort that many colleges and universities are making to achieve racially diverse campuses.

Some schools are more generous than others in the amount of money they provide through scholarships and grants, depending on the financial ability of the college and/or their commitment to using financial aid as a tool to recruit African-Americans. These school-based funds are often less restrictive than government funds and lend prestige to a college or university. Indeed, it is through this source that many colleges and universities provide race-based scholarship and grant funds to attract and retain African-American and other minority students to their campuses. Schools that are well endowed through private and corporate funds are generally in an even better position to provide minority scholarships, since they have more money to work with than many less well-off colleges and universities.

But students should be careful not to fall into the trap of selecting a college solely upon the financial aid and scholarship award a school offers. Many bright African-American students have compromised their interests for lucrative financial aid packages, only to find the school they chose did not live up to their expectations. A student may even be forced to drop out because of an inability to meet the academic or athletic criteria needed to maintain the financial awards that lured them to the campus in the first place. Besides, if a student needs to "buy time" to save additional funds or is hesitant to commit to a four-year college program, attending a community college for a year or two is an opportunity that is available to almost any student. Many of the students who have dropped out of college often land at community colleges anyway, so if you are unsure about your college future, you may get ahead of the game by first enrolling in a community college for a while until you decide what kind of school is best for you.

A determined student willing to give time and effort to planning will find many ways of financing a college education. A good place to begin is to ask yourself a few questions:

- What kind of student are you? Do you get above-average grades, or are you an average student?

- Do you have a particular career in mind? If so, have you worked in that field either as a volunteer or paid employee or been involved in it through professional organizations?

- Have you worked as a volunteer or paid employee in any field?

- Do you excel in a sport?

- Have you undertaken any projects in which you have played a leadership role?

- Do you have any special talents or interests such as the visual or performing arts or music? Have you attained any special achievements in these fields?

- Aside from a career, what do you want to achieve in life?

What should emerge from this self-assessment is a profile of your particular talents and interests as well as some of your goals in life. Such an assessment will be helpful in determining whether you "stack up" against the competition for scholarships and grants offered in a particular area.

Many professional organizations and corporations designate scholarship and internship opportunities for African-Americans as a way to increase their numbers in career fields in which they are underrepresented such as engineering, science, journalism, business, health care, and the technology fields. Indeed, despite doomsday reports of a still-slow economy, there continues to be high demand for qualified applicants in selected fields, and experts predict that those demands will continue to grow through at least the next decade. African-American students would be wise to consider exploring opportunities in fields where these scholarships are being offered. With reports of declining wages even for the college-educated, African-American students will especially need to be in touch with where the opportunities for growth lie.

Researching and applying for scholarships and grants is a time-consuming process, and students and parents may wonder if the time investment is worthwhile. The short answer to this question is a resounding *Yes!* A fair number of these awards come from the colleges and universities themselves and from the federal government. Be prepared, however, to spend a great deal of time gathering pertinent information and completing arduous application forms. Also, be aware that many programs require you to submit an essay, recommendations from teachers or administrators, academic transcripts, and samples of your work.

Keep in mind that it takes as much effort to apply for a $100 scholarship as it does for one worth thousands of dollars, so maximize your efforts by choosing carefully the scholarships for which you apply. Though many scholarships and grants are awarded in small amounts, students who have made a thorough self-assessment of their talents and skills and who are diligent in their search can identify many programs that are worthwhile. A rule of thumb to follow is the more you look, the more you will find, so leave no stone unturned.

SAVING FOR COLLEGE

Having some savings for college will reduce the amount of money a student will have to borrow for college and may improve his or her chance of receiving a lucrative financial aid award. Indeed, colleges usually insist that families pay a portion of student expenses as a condition of receiving financial aid.

By beginning a regular plan of saving for college early, parents can make time work for them and ease their anxiety about the increasing cost of a college education. "Saving fifty dollars a month over fifteen years at 8 percent, for example, can yield as much as seventeen thousand dollars in a planned college fund program," says Sabrina Warren, a stockbroker at Chapman Company, a Black-owned brokerage company in Baltimore, Maryland. "The earlier in your child's life you begin saving, the more aggressive you can be in your saving strategy, utilizing investments with higher risk early on in your savings plan that generally pay a higher yield." Although most parents know they should start saving money for college when their children are young, many put off saving for college until they are within a few years of a child's going off to college. It's an all-too-familiar story and one that can be costly. "By the time a child has reached fourteen years of age," says Warren, "a family has lost the advantage of time and will have to save more to obtain the same return on a smaller investment that was allowed to grow over time."

For college saving, Warren recommends investing in growth-stock mutual funds, many of which can be started with a small investment. According to Warren, stocks have outperformed other investments over time and provide a greater return. In addition, mutual-fund growth stocks are fairly low-risk and user-friendly investments. "Many of these growth-stock mutual funds have made it relatively painless to invest in them," says Warren. "With a small investment of, say, one hundred dollars and deposits of about fifty dollars a month, you can open a custodial account for your child's education." Another investment tool that Warren recommends is the zero coupon bond. An almost risk-free type of zero coupon bond is the familiar Series EE U.S. Savings Bond, although there are many others on the market. She cautions, however, that U.S. Savings Bonds are a very inefficient method of saving for college, since the return on investment is so low.

In addition to traditional investment plans, a number of specialized investment strategies have emerged in the marketplace. Indeed, the high cost of college has spawned a cottage industry of college savings plans as banks, brokerage houses, and other financial institutions compete for investment dollars. One plan that is touted as being most innovative is a certificate of deposit with interest rates tied directly to the total cost of college (tuition, fees, room and board). The CollegeSure CD, which is sold in units equal to one full year of average college costs, is guaranteed to keep abreast of college costs. Each unit at maturity is equal to one full year's average college costs at a four-year private college. The units are sold much like zero coupon bonds, with the cost lower than the face value of the CD, which matures over time. For more information about the CollegeSure CD, contact the College Savings Bank at 1-800-888-2723.

Not to be left out of the opportunity to market themselves and shore up their own financial future, colleges themselves have gotten into the act, offering a variety of payment plans and investment strategies. Some schools aggressively promote their own prepaid tuition plans, which they offer at discounted rates. Parents should review these plans, which allow them to pay for a child's tuition in advance, very carefully and consider their options. Is it wise, for example, to invest in such plans which estimate college costs in the future against current economic conditions? Once again, as Warren points out, parents have more investment choices when time is on their side and should weigh the financial benefits of any investment plan they decide to undertake.

Since saving for college today is tantamount to saving for a home or other major investment, it is not always so easy to determine the best strategy. Add to this the ever-changing tax laws and college financial aid regulations, and it is understandable why some parents may want to consider utilizing the services of a financial planner or broker to assist them in deciding the best investment strategy to use in saving for college. Although any plan of regular savings is better than none at all, a professional planner or broker can help you get the best return on your investment and demystify the financial world. By doing so, families will be introduced to the numerous options available for investment beyond a passbook savings account and other traditional vehicles. The challenge is to find a planner/broker who is right for you and with whom you are comfortable. As with finding other professionals such as attorneys or doctors, often the best source is word-of-mouth recommendation. In fact, you may be surprised to find that people you know and trust currently work with a planner or broker, so it's a good idea to begin your search by asking friends, relatives, or associates for a recommendation. Armed with a few names, you will then want to do some research. Start by calling and asking questions about the services the planner/broker offers and how he or she works with clients. It's also probably a good idea to ask for a face-to-face meeting. Inquire about fees up front and whether the planner/broker works on an hourly or fixed rate and what the fee includes. Expect the planner/broker to ask you questions—your objectives, financial information, and what you feel you can afford to do in the way of investing. A good planner/broker is interested in serving your needs rather than selling a particular product or service. Most of all, pay attention to and trust your instincts—if something doesn't seem right it probably is not. Keep in mind that this will be an ongoing relationship you develop with a planner/broker and that you need to be comfortable with the person you select. Organizations such as the National Association of Securities Dealers can tell you whether any formal complaint has been levied against a stockbroker, and any reputable financial planner should be registered with the Securities and Exchange Commission in Washington, D.C., and state securities commissions.

Whether you decide to use a professional planner/broker or choose one of many established plans, you should be aware of the current tax rules that affect college saving. For example, under the so-called "kiddie tax," the first $600 in interest or dividend income earned by a child under age 14 is tax-free, the second $600 is taxed at the child's rate of 15 percent, and amounts over that are taxed at the parent's rate. At age 14, income is taxed at the child's rate of 15 percent. Clearly, age 14 is a pivotal point in a college savings strategy. If you have invested college savings in your name, you may now want to consider placing investments in your child's name, since his or her tax rate of 15 percent is likely much lower than your own. Parents should also be aware that the tax rules for gifts of up to $10,000 to each child are tax-free. On the face of it, one would assume the more savings the better to ensure a child's education. Again, however, parents will need to consider the tax implications of such a gift, since college financial aid formulas weigh more heavily against the child's savings rather than family finances. The money placed in the parents' name may be a better strategy if the family plans to apply for college financial aid.

Many colleges and financial institutions now offer tuition payment plans that allow families to pay for college on an installment plan. Colleges and universities that offer this service will provide you the name and contact information of the company or agency they work with to provide this service.

SECTION II: THE FINANCIAL AID PROCESS

Today, many students qualify for financial aid, but to get your fair share you will need to begin preparing while in high school. Start by asking your guidance counselor about federal and local government aid programs as well as scholarship and other aid programs for which you may qualify. Counselors may also help devise and implement financial aid strategies to meet particular needs. Many counselors routinely work with students in college selection and financial aid; some even have access to computer databases to help students in their search. Your counselor may be helpful, for example, in advising you on career fields for which there is ample scholarship money or tell you about colleges that provide substantial financial aid to African-American students as a means of improving racial diversity on their campuses. Counselors often know about scholarship and aid programs that are not listed in guidebooks and other publications. In addition, your counselor may help you "package" yourself to colleges and grant-making organizations, advising you how to improve your grade point average, to take a preparation course to improve your SAT scores, or encourage you to participate in certain extracurricular or athletic activities that may lead to scholarship opportunities. Counselors also can help you get focused on your life goals. As you clarify what you want to do in life, the field of schools and financial aid opportunities narrows, allowing you to make clearer decisions about where to focus your search.

A guidance counselor may be a virtual wellspring of information on college admission and financial aid. Just don't fall into the trap of believing it is only the counselor's responsibility to help you with college admissions and financial aid. Students and parents must be ready to work with each other and to seek other advisers, too. Not every guidance counselor has the resources, skill, or interest to provide the assistance a student may need. Indeed, most are overworked and overwhelmed by the number of students for which they are responsible, no matter what size the school, to give individual attention to each student's needs. As in all of life, you will occasionally find a counselor who has little interest in doing more than the absolute minimum. Yet, the large majority of counselors will bend over backward to ensure that a student is admitted to a good school and finds adequate financial aid. The rule of thumb to follow is that there is no rule. You should expect the amount of assistance you receive to vary depending on the school you attend, as well as on your own persistence about obtaining its help. Keep in mind that the saying "the squeaky wheel gets the grease" applies to this overworked lot. If you are fortunate enough to have the support and time of a counselor to work with you on college admissions and financial aid, by all means take advantage. The advice of a good high school counselor is invaluable and, best of all, it's free!

TIPS ON WORKING WITH YOUR GUIDANCE COUNSELOR

- Make an appointment to meet the counselor in your junior year of high school.

- Be prepared to talk openly about your academic record and your interests, including hobbies, volunteer work, athletics, and participation in cultural and artistic activities, such as theatrical performances, art contests or exhibits, and any musical training or experience in singing in a group or choir or playing an instrument. These talents make you stand out to colleges and may qualify you for scholarships or other aid.

- Research colleges ahead of time. Be prepared to tell the counselor about ten to twenty that you are considering and ask if he or she has any special relationship with financial aid or admissions officials at these schools. Keep in mind that some colleges have special relationships with local high schools to recruit their African-American graduates, and many have special admission and financial aid programs to encourage such students to apply.

- Ask about dates of upcoming college fairs in your area. This is an opportunity to talk to officials from colleges and universities in your region and to learn about any financial aid opportunities or special programs they have for African-American students.

- Ask the counselor for guidance on how to "package" yourself to colleges to improve your chances of obtaining scholarships and grants. Also, ask about scholarships and grants from private foundations, corporations, or organizations for African-American students.

- Ask for a Free Application for Federal Student Aid (FAFSA) or Financial Aid Form (FAF) and any state financial aid forms that are required to apply for federal and local aid programs. The Free Application for Federal Student Aid (FAFSA) is used to establish eligibility for all federal aid. The FAFSA and FAF are available in November and state financial aid forms are available in the spring. You are not required to complete these forms until your senior year in high school, but it is a good idea to become familiar in advance with the information needed to complete them accurately. Some of these forms are quite complex. They ask for many details about family finances. The FAFSA, for example, has fewer than fifty questions, yet to complete it an applicant has to wade through more than ten pages of instructions and include detailed tax information months before the Internal Revenue Service's April 15 filing deadline. Knowing ahead of time what's on them may save you the agony of gathering information under pressure of a deadline.

- Find out if there are college foundations and other organizations in your community that provide counseling, ongoing support, or financial assistance to qualified high school students. Your guidance counselor, teachers, church, local legislator, or other community leaders may know of such programs.

- Finally, use this opportunity to establish an ongoing dialogue with your guidance counselor. Share your goals and dreams of an "ideal job or career"; talk about your family and lifestyle; discuss your opinions about local and national events. Help your counselor take a personal interest in you by being enthusiastic as well as persistent in your search for financial aid. At the same time, be mindful of the limited time that can be spent on your individual needs. Chances are, the more you do for yourself, the more others will want to help you succeed.

Your state council on higher education has information about financial aid programs offered to residents. A list of higher-education councils by state may be found in Appendix B of this book. In addition, you may find a number of financial aid opportunities easily within reach. Here are some tips to help you locate them:

- If you're interested in becoming a teacher, you may qualify for the Paul Douglas Teacher Scholarship Program, which provides up to $5,000 a year to high school students who graduate in the top 10 percent of their class and meet other criteria. The financial aid office at the college you plan to attend or the state council on higher education can tell you how to apply for this program.

- Your high school counselor or state council on higher education can tell you about the Robert C. Byrd Honors Scholarship Program, the National Science Scholars Program (NSSP), and the National Achievement Scholarship Program for Outstanding Negro Students. The Byrd Program awards $1,500 to students who demonstrate outstanding academic achievement, and the NSSP Program awards up to $5,000 to students who demonstrate excellence in the physical, life, or computer sciences, mathematics, or engineering. The National Merit Scholarship Program offers awards to African-American students who compete for scholarships underwritten by corporations, foundations, colleges, and individuals. To enter the competition, you must take the Preliminary Scholastic Aptitude Test/National Merit Scholarship Qualifying Test (PSAT/NMSQT) in high school and meet other eligibility requirements. For more information, write the National Achievement Scholarship Program for Outstanding Negro Students, One Rotary Center, 1560 Sherman Avenue, Evanston, IL 60201.

- The NAACP offers a number of scholarships to African-American students who are winners in its local NAACP Afro Academic, Cultural,

Technological, and Scientific Olympics (ACT-SO) program. There are twenty-four categories, including the performing arts, humanities, visual arts, and sciences, and awards range from $500 to $1,000. Contact your local NAACP branch to obtain information on how you can apply.

The NAACP also offers the Roy Wilkins Scholarship, which awards scholarships up to $1,000 to needy African-American students in their senior year of high school or first year of college. For more information, write: NAACP Youth and College Division, 4805 Mt. Hope Drive, Baltimore, MD 21212-3297.

- Contact professional organizations, especially those in fields that you have an interest in studying—business, computer science, education, engineering, journalism, medicine, law, to name a few. Many of these organizations are listed in the U.S. Department of Labor's *Occupational Outlook Handbook* and can also be found in directories of associations in your local library. To obtain a copy, write to: Chief, Division of Occupational Outlook, Bureau of Labor Statistics, U.S. Department of Labor, Washington, D.C. 20212. A list of national African-American professional and fraternal organizations that provide educational aid is also listed in Appendix C.

- If you've chosen a historically Black college, the United Negro College Fund, 500 62nd Street, New York, NY 10021 can supply information about the financial aid programs at its member schools.

- Many African-American sororities and fraternities, such as the Delta Sigma Theta sorority and the Omega Psi Phi fraternity, offer scholarships to young people through their local chapters. Contact the chapter in your area for information on financial aid and other programs for college-bound students. Check the yellow pages under "Associations" or "Organizations" for a local chapter, or use the *Directory of Associations* in the reference section of your library.

- Veterans or their family members may qualify for financial assistance. Check with your local Department of Veterans Affairs office to see whether you qualify.

- Numerous churches, social groups, civic organizations, and foundations provide funds for college to the children of its membership, or those who live within its area of service. Some major ones to investigate are the local NAACP, Urban League, Girl Scouts and Boy Scouts, YMCA, 4-H clubs, and Jaycees.

- Parents' employers or labor unions may have a program to help finance your education. The personnel office can usually provide this information.

COMPUTERIZED SEARCH SERVICES

If you are unwilling or unable to do the legwork required to locate scholarships and grants, you may choose to have a private company provide the information from their computerized database or matching service for a fee. Companies that offer these services promise to locate grant and scholarship programs for a nominal fee usually ranging between $45 and $60. Students are asked to complete a general questionnaire form, which will be matched against a database of scholarships and grants. Students are then supplied with a list of scholarships and grant opportunities, including application information and deadlines.

On the face of it, these computerized services appear to provide accurate, state-of-the-art solutions to locating funds for college. In fact, the grants and scholarships identified are generally for small amounts ranging from $100 to $2,500, and information about many of them is widely available through foundation directories or other reference books available free in your local or school library.

Given a little "sweat equity" in the form of time spent in the library researching, anyone can locate a sizeable number of scholarship and grant opportunities at no cost other than time spent looking. The benefits of using this strategy more than outweigh the investment of time and energy spent unearthing a few scholarship gems. For one thing, you will feel the sense of achievement and satisfaction that comes with being recognized for your talents and skills by receiving an award of money. Receiving a scholarship or grant is prestigious and is an impressive addition to your college admissions application and job résumé. Winning a scholarship or grant through your own effort is a boost to your self-esteem and gives you a level of confidence that a computer program can't buy! Finally, as any student or professor will tell you, knowing how to do research is an invaluable skill to have in college. Which brings me to another valuable source of information for locating financial aid—your school and local library.

LIBRARIES—A FREE RESOURCE

School and local librarians are virtually walking encyclopedias of information, and they are usually more than willing to share that information with students or anyone else who asks. Librarians can suggest grant and scholarship directories for you to review as well as other references to check for available funds. A community library is often aware of local organizations and companies that offer scholarship opportunities for college-bound students as well. Like high school guidance counselors and college financial aid officers, librarians can offer advice that can help you toward your goal of locating a college that is right for you and financing to help you pay for your education.

Generally, scholarship and grant directories and reference books are organized in a similar fashion, each typically providing a description of the grant program, qualifications needed to be considered, the number of awards given annually, an average dollar amount or range of the award, and the name of a contact person with the address and deadline for applying. A sample profile of past awardees is sometimes included as well to help applicants decide if they may qualify. Here are some suggestions to help you get the most from your research:

RESEARCH TIPS

- Plan to spend several hours reviewing directories and other resources in the library. Books such as the *Foundation Directory* and *Directory of Associations* are kept in the reference section and cannot be checked out of the library. In addition, these voluminous books contain hundreds of programs for which you may qualify. Maximizing their use requires a great deal of time reviewing and recording the application information on each scholarship or grant program for which you want to apply.

- Make sure you have the most current information. Check the date of directories and other reference books to be sure you have the most current edition. Many are revised annually. Be sure, too, that any scholarship lists you use are the most recent.

- Get organized! Purchase a spiral notebook to use exclusively for recording scholarship and grant application information. Use it each time you do research in the library and to record other aid programs for which you receive information. Having all scholarship information in one place will save time and effort when you begin the application process and will help you avoid duplicating entries.

- Finally, check with the sponsor to make sure that the scholarship is still being offered. You don't want to spend a lot of time preparing a proposal and application without first confirming this. A telephone call or postcard to the contact address will usually do the trick.

OTHER RESOURCES

Here are some of the commonly referred-to directories and references for scholarships and grants you may want to check, including some specifically for minorities:

- *American Institute of Architects Information Poster & Booklet.* American Institute of Architects, 1735 New York Avenue NW, Washington, D.C. 20006. This is a free booklet and poster that lists accredited professional programs of architecture as well as career information.

- *College Funding Made Easy: How to Save for College While Maintaining Eligibility for Financial Aid* by J. Grady Cash. Betterway Publications, Inc., White Hall, VA. An easy-to-understand guide to financing college from the perspective of a certified financial planner. Provides specific long-term savings and investment strategies to pay for college costs.

- *Directory of Financial Aids for Minorities* by Gail A. Schlacter. ABC-CLIO Information Services, 2040 Alameda Padre Serra, Box 4397, Santa Barbara,

CA 93103. A comprehensive resource book that lists more than 1,500 financial aid opportunities for minorities including African-Americans, Hispanics, Asians, and Native-Americans. The book contains references to scholarships, fellowships, loans, grants, and awards and is indexed by program, sponsor, geographic location, subject, and deadline date.

- *Exploring Careers in Music* by Paul Bjorneberg. Music Educators National Conference, 1902 Association Drive, Reston, VA 22091. A free booklet that provides information on careers in the performing arts, including music education, the commercial music business, the recording industry, and related fields.

- *Financial Aid for Minorities for Students with Any Major.* Garrett Park Press, P.O. Box 190F, Garrett Park, MD 20896. This book lists sources of financial aid, including application information.

- *Financing a College Education: The Essential Guide for the '90s* by Judith B. Margolin. Plenum Press. A thorough review of college financing strategies for parents and students.

- *Finding Money for College* by John Bear. Ten Speed Press, Berkeley, CA. A well-researched guide on searching for sources of financial aid as well as helpful hints on how to pursue them.

- *Fleming's One Thousand: Top College Merit Scholarships* by Robert A. Fleming. A comprehensive guide to scholarships based not on need but on the student's merit—academics, leadership, school/community involvement.

- *Foundation Grants to Individuals.* The Foundation Center, 79 5th Avenue, New York, NY 10003. Contains over 1,000 aid opportunities from grant-making foundations in categories including educational support, arts and cultural support, grants to foreign individuals, awards, prizes and grants. Many of these funds are restricted by geographical and other limitations and should be so noted when reviewing these aid opportunities. Available in most major libraries.

- *Fund Your Way Through College: Uncovering 1,700 Great Opportunities in Undergraduate Financial Aid* by Debra M. Kirby. Visible Ink Press, Detroit, MI. A comprehensive directory of undergraduate financial aid including scholarships, grants, loans, internships, work-study programs, awards and prizes in particular fields as well as other forms of financial assistance.

- *How to Get Into the College of Your Choice and How to Finance It* by Jayme Stewart. Morrow. A guidebook to college admissions and financial aid which includes helpful case studies and worksheets.

- *Journalism Career Guide for Minorities.* Dow Jones Newspaper Fund, Inc., P.O. Box 300, Princeton, NJ 08543-0300. A free guide for students interested in careers in newspaper reporting and editing. This comprehensive guide lists newspaper recruiters, career information, salaries, internships, and related information.

- *Paying Less for College.* Peterson's Guides, Princeton, NJ. Profiles current facts and statistics on more than 1,600 colleges and universities nationwide including college costs, undergraduate financial aid resources, data on need-based and non-need awards for freshmen and a listing of money-saving options offered by the institution.

- *Putting Your Kids Through College* by Scott Edelstein and the Editors of Consumer Reports Books, Consumer Union, Mount Vernon, NY. A definitive guide to all aspects of the financial aid process.

- *The College Board* has a number of publications and software packages to assist you in locating colleges and universities that meet your needs and in determining college costs and how to pay for them. The College Cost Explorer Fund Finder software package provides you with potential financial aid packages utilizing information from a database of numerous private scholarship and loan sources. This service is available at no charge or can be used for a small fee at many high schools and college financial aid offices. Check with your school before purchasing the program. For more information, contact College Board Publications, Department R05, Box 886, New York, NY 10101-0886 or call 212-713-8165.

- *The Foundation Directory.* Foundation Center, 79 5th Avenue, Dept. DC, New York, NY 10003. Provides detailed information on more than 5,000 foundations in the United States; available in most libraries.

- *The Scholarship Book* by Daniel J. Cassidy and Michael J. Alves. Prentice Hall, Englewood Cliffs, NJ 07632. Contains a listing of more than 1,700 financial aid references including some unusual scholarships like the Evans Scholarship Program, which provides full tuition and housing for high school seniors in the top 25 percent of their class who have been caddies for two years or more. Aid programs include an index for Ethnic Background.

FINANCIAL AID OFFICERS

Getting to know the college financial aid officer is another strategy you may want to use in your search for locating dollars for college. As the keepers of an institution's scholarships and grants funds, financial aid officers are in a position to get you a larger financial aid award, or negotiate a better award structure in favor of more grants and college work-study, instead of a heavy loan debt. In addition, their years of experience and numerous contacts can prove invaluable in your search for financial aid, as they may know about other scholarships for which a student may qualify.

To obtain their assistance, students only need to ask. Most financial aid officers are willing to provide you the benefit of their knowledge and experience, particularly if you have demonstrated a sincere interest in helping yourself as well. For your part, supplying them with information about yourself such as hobbies, career goals, religious affiliation, and other activities will help them help you locate needed funding. It's advisable to use this time-consuming strategy with the schools that you are confident you will gain admission to.

Applying for financial aid will take a great deal of time, organization and patience. To help you through the process here some valuable tips:

Apply Early. As the saying goes, "the early bird gets the worm." If you think you want to go to college, start planning for it in your junior year in high school. Starting earlier will put you even further ahead in your college selection and financing, but if you're like most, the junior year is a more realistic goal to achieve. If your grades are not the best, this is the time to improve your grades, and otherwise begin a campaign to improve your chances of getting into college. Get involved in extracurricular activities, take advantage of summer job opportunities or just volunteer your time toward some worthy cause. Doing so helps to create a positive image of yourself as a well-rounded individual with a variety of interests— qualities many colleges look for in the students they admit into their institutions. The more of these appealing qualities you have, the greater your chances of being admitted and getting the financial aid you need to attend.

Meet All Deadlines. It is important that students meet all deadlines, especially if they are applying for financial aid. These dollars are already limited at most institutions and after the school has made certain allowances for awards to very disadvantaged students, it usually awards money on a first-come, first-served basis. So if you're not in line to receive money because you haven't applied, chances are you're not going to get any. Also, don't be lulled into a false sense of security about obtaining a college scholarship because of your academic achievement, a high score on the SAT or your racial heritage. Colleges want students who are enthusiastic and sincere as well as academically and socially prepared to succeed at their school. Indeed, the manner in which you handle applying for admission and financial aid will provide as good a picture of your individual character as a college essay, maybe even more.

Be Honest. Any and all of the information supplied on financial aid forms may be checked, so be sure that you answer all questions correctly and honestly to the best of your ability. If you are caught falsifying information on the financial aid form you could be subject to a fine and/or jail sentence and your application for aid will be disqualified. It's just not worth the risk!

Retain Copies. It is a good idea to make and retain photocopies of the entire financial aid form and any attachments in the event that your form is lost or there are questions or discrepancies in the processing of your application.

Do the Legwork. Write a draft of the letters of recommendation you are requesting from teachers, coaches, community leaders, or other adult leaders. Often these people are overwhelmed with such requests and will appreciate your initiative and consideration, further convinced that you are, indeed, worthy of the award.

Inquire about Other Aid. Be aware that to be considered for *nonfederal* aid such as institutional and/or state aid, you may have to complete an additional application and pay a fee to have it processed. Schools have supplies of these applications, as well as libraries and your state commission on higher education. *There is no charge to apply for federal student aid.*

You Must Reapply Each Year! Remember that your financial aid is not guaranteed each year and that you must reapply for federal aid each year! Also, if you change schools, your federal financial aid does not necessarily go with you. Check with the financial aid office at your new school to determine what steps you need to take.

Have the Records You Need to Apply. You will need to have certain records to apply for financial aid. They are:

- Your and your parents' U.S. income tax return from the previous year. This is the most important record because you must use exact numbers from specific lines on the tax return to apply.

- W-2 forms, business/farm records, and bank statements are also useful records that may be referred to when you are applying.

Ask Questions. If you are not sure how to complete the standard government financial aid forms or complete an application from the college to which you are applying, don't be afraid to call and ask for help. The U.S. Department of Education has a toll-free number you can call with questions about completing the FAFSA. The number is 1-800-433-3243. If you have questions about a college aid form, contact the school's financial aid department directly. Even if you don't have any questions, you may want to follow up with the college within two weeks of submitting your financial aid application to make sure it has been received.

Telephone Numbers You May Need When Applying. The Federal Student Aid Information Center can answer questions you have about the financial aid process. The Center is open between 9:00 A.M. and 5:30 P.M. (Eastern Time), Monday through Friday:

1-800-4-FED AID (1-800-433-3243) is a toll-free number which provides information on:

- questions you have regarding applying for financial aid;

- determining whether a school takes part in the federal student aid program;

- explaining student eligibility requirements for receiving financial aid;

- explaining the process of determining financial aid awards;

- mailing publications on federal student aid.

1-301-722-9200 is the number at the Information Center to find out if your "Free Application for Federal Student Aid" (FAFSA) or your "Renewal Application" has been processed, or to request a copy of your Student Aid Report (SAR). *This is not a toll-free number and you will have to pay for this call.*

1-800-730-8913 is a toll-free TDD number for the hearing-impaired.

1-800-MIS-USED (1-800-647-8733) is a toll-free hotline number to report any suspected fraud, waste, or abuse involving federal student aid funds. This number will reach the U.S. Department of Education's Inspector General's office directly, and you do not have to give your name.

SECTION III: COLLEGE SCHOLARSHIPS BY FIELD

=:=

Agriculture

Florida A&M University
Tallahassee, FL 32307

Description: Grants and scholarships are available to students interested in majoring in agriculture and related fields through the College of Science and Technology.

Amount: Various

Deadline: April 1

University of Illinois at Urbana—Champaign
Champaign, IL

Type: Scholarships

Description: Students interested in majoring in agriculture and related fields may qualify for grant and scholarship awards.

Amount: Various

Deadline: March 15

University of Maryland—College Park
College Park, MD

Type: Grants/Scholarships

Description: Grants and scholarship awards available to students with an interest in agriculture and related fields.

Amount: Various

Deadline: February 15

Agriculture—Animal Science

California State Polytechnic University
Pomona, CA

Type: Scholarships

Description: Scholarships for students majoring in animal and veterinary sciences.

Scholarship awards include: Arabian Horse Association of Southern California Scholarship, Biotech Nutrition Scholarship, California Cattle Women Scholarship, Chicago Mercantile Exchange Beef and Pork Industry Scholarships, Coast Grain and Milling Co., Inc., Award, Homer D. Fausch Scholarship, Dr. Antonio A. Jimenez Memorial Award, Eugene K. Keating Horse Show and Rodeo Club Scholarship, Mack H. Kennington Memorial Scholarship, O. H. Kruse Grain and Milling, Inc., Award, Harry B. McLaughlin Scholarship, Monsanto Agricultural Company Scholarships, Moorman's Mfg. Company Dairy Beef Scholarships, Outstanding Freshman Scholarship, San Diego County Cowbelles Memorial Scholarship.

Amount: $500–$2,500

Deadline: Various

Write: Animal & Veterinary Sciences Department
             Building 2, Room 123
             Cal Poly University
             Pomona, CA 91768–4008

Agriculture—Horticulture

**California State Polytechnic University
Pomona, CA**

Type: Scholarships

Description: Scholarships available to students majoring in horticulture, natural resource management, and related fields.

             Scholarship awards include: Armstrong Garden Centers Award, Bandini Horticulture Award, Calif. Assn. of Nurserymen Award, James L. Degen Award, Environmental Industries Award, Glendale Chrysanthemum Society, Los Angeles County Grange #37 Scholarship, National Agronomy Student Recognition Program, Nor-Am Chemical Award, Theodore Payne Foundation Award, Street Tree Seminar Award, Ueberroth/Jim Hastie Memorial Scholarship.

Amount: $100–$2,500

Deadline: Various

Write: Horticulture/Plant & Soil Science Department
             Building 2, Room 209
             Cal Poly University
             Pomona, CA 91768–4008

Florida A&M University
Tallahassee, FL 32307

Description: Grants and scholarships are available to students interested in majoring in agriculture and related fields through the College of Science and Technology.

Amount: Various

Deadline: April 1

Biological Sciences

Antioch College
Yellow Springs, OH

Type: Grants/Scholarships

Description: Hughes Science Scholarships are offered to new students with financial need pursuing studies in the biological, biomedical or related sciences.

Amount: Up to $8,000

Description: J. D. Dawson Science Scholarships are available to first-year students in the sciences.

Amount: $5,000

Description: Evan Spalt Scholarships for Science and Math are awarded to first-year students in math and the sciences.

Amount: $2,000

Deadline: February 15

Bard College
Annandale, NY

Type: Scholarships

Description: Students who excel academically in the sciences and are interested in continuing their studies in the science field may be eligible for one of 35 merit awards through the Distinguished Scientists program.

Amount: $19,624

Deadline: March 15

Centenary College of Louisiana
Shreveport, LA

Type: Grants/Scholarships

Description: College offers scholarships to students interested in pursuing undergraduate studies in the biological sciences.

Amount: Various

Deadline: March 15

Denison University
Granville, OH

Type: Grants/Scholarships

Description: Scholarships are awarded to students majoring in the biological sciences and who meet academic and other criteria.

Amount: Various

Deadline: April 19

Frostburg State University
Frostburg, MD

Type: Grants/Scholarships

Description: Scholarship awards to students interested in pursuing undergraduate studies in the biological sciences. Some awards require students to meet academic and other criteria.

Amount: Various

Deadline: April 1

King's College
Wilkes-Barre, PA

Type: Grants/Scholarships

Description: College offers scholarship awards to students interested in pursuing undergraduate studies in the biological sciences. Academic and other criteria may be required.

Amount: Various

Deadline: March 1

Lebanon Valley College
Annville, PA

Type: Grants/Scholarships

Description: College offers scholarships for students interested in majoring in the biological sciences.

Deadline: Before April 1 (for the fall semester)

St. Mary's College
St. Mary's City, MD

Type: Grants/Scholarships

Description: Students interested in studying biology may qualify for the Izaak Walton Scholarship.

Amount: Various

Deadline: March 1

Tuskegee University
Tuskegee, AL

Type of Aid: Scholarships

Description: Students interested in pursuing undergraduate studies in the
                 biological sciences may be eligible for scholarship awards; some
                 based on academics.

Amount: Various

Deadline: April 15

Xavier University
New Orleans, LA

Type: Grants/Scholarships

Description: Students majoring in biology, chemistry, physics/engineering,
                 pharmacy, mathematics or computer science may receive
                 scholarships through several programs including E. E. Just
                 Scholars, M.A.R.C. Biomedical Fellows, M.B.R.S. Research Ap-
                 prentices, O.N.R. Future Scientists, and the RCMS Program.

Amount: Various

Deadline: Various

Business

Appalachian State University
Boone, NC

Type: Grants/Scholarships

Description: The College of Business awards three African-American
                 Scholarships each year.

Amount: $100–$1,000

Deadline: January 1

Centenary College of Louisiana
Shreveport, LA

Type: Grants/Scholarships

Description: College offers scholarships to students interested in pursuing
                 undergraduate studies in business administration and related
                 fields.

Amount: Various

Deadline: March 15

Florida A&M University
Tallahassee, FL

Description: Grants and scholarships are available to students interested in majoring in business administration and related fields through the School of Business and Industry.

Amount: Various

Deadline: April 1

Southern Methodist University
Dallas, TX

Type: Grants/Scholarships

Description: The Edwin L. Cox School of Business provides scholarship assistance to junior and senior business students who have demonstrated academic excellence, outstanding leadership, and/or community service.

Amount: Various

Deadline: February 1

University of Alabama at Birmingham
Birmingham, AL

Type of Aid: Scholarships

Description: Students planning to major in business and related fields may qualify for grants and scholarships based on academics and other criteria.

Amount: Various

Deadline: May 1

University of Maryland—College Park
College Park, MD

Type: Grants/Scholarships

Description: Scholarships awarded to students interested in majoring in business administration and related fields.

Amount: Various

Deadline: February 15

Virginia Polytechnic Institute & State University
Blacksburg, VA

Type: Grants/Scholarships

Description: Grants and scholarships are available through the colleges of engineering, agriculture and life sciences, business, and the departments of art, mathematics, music and theatre arts.

Amount:	Various
Deadline:	February 15

**Washington State University
Pullman, WA**

Type:	Grants/Scholarships
Description:	Transfer students may qualify for one of 70 awards through the College of Business and Economics.
Amount:	$1,000
Description:	U.S. Bank Multicultural Scholarship awarded to African-Americans and other minority students who meet certain criteria.
Amount:	$1,000–$4,000
Deadline:	March 1

Business—Accounting

**California State Polytechnic University
Pomona, CA**

Type:	Scholarships
Description:	Scholarships are available to students majoring in accounting and business administration.
	Scholarship awards include: Accounting Alumni Association Award, Accounting Department Scholarships, Arthur Andersen & Company Award, C.F.M.A. (Construction Financial Management Assn.) Award, Coopers & Lybrand Award, Deloitte & Touche Award, Ernst & Young Award, Frazer & Torbet Award, Frito Lay Scholarship, International Center Scholarship, KPMG Peat Marwick Award, Kenneth Leventhal & Co. Award.
Amount:	Varies
Deadline:	January 1
Write:	Accounting Department
Building 94-252
Cal Poly University
Pomona, CA 91768-4008
909-869-2365

Eastern New Mexico University
Portales, NM

Type: Scholarships

Description: ENMU offers a number of scholarships for students interested
                 in pursuing undergraduate training in various areas of busi-
                 ness. They include: Arthur Andersen & Company Scholarship,
                 Governor John Burroughs Endowed Scholarship, Cattle Baron
                 Scholarship, College of Business Student Organizations Schol-
                 arship, Conoco Business Scholarship, Data Processing Manage-
                 ment Association Scholarship, Dollar Rent-a-Car Endowed
                 Scholarship, The Hanrahan Family Award, Gilbert May En-
                 dowed Scholarship, Myrtle Moore Women in Business Scholar-
                 ship, New Mexico Claims Association Endowed Scholarship,
                 New Mexico Society of Certified Public Accountants Scholar-
                 ship, New Mexico Society of Public Accountants Scholarship,
                 Ronald K. Payne/KPMG Peat Marwick Scholarship Fund, Pe-
                 troleum Accountants' Society of New Mexico Scholarship in
                 Accounting, Baron M. Stuart Endowed Scholarship, Garland
                 Tilley Memorial Scholarship in Business, J. Henry Young En-
                 dowed Scholarship.

Amount: Various, up to full college costs

Deadline: March 1

Business—Banking & Finance

California State Polytechnic University
Pomona, CA

Type: Scholarships

Description: Scholarships available to students majoring in business ad-
                 ministration, finance, real estate. Scholarship awards include:
                 American Institute of Real Estate Appraisers Scholarship,
                 C.A.R. Scholarship Foundation Trustees Scholarship, Delta
                 Mu Delta Scholarship, Inland Empire Mortgage Bankers Assn.
                 Scholarship, Lambda Alpha Scholarship.

Amount: $500–$1,500

Deadline: Various

Write: Finance, Real Estate & Law Department
                 Building 66-213
                 Cal Poly University
                 Pomona, CA 91768-4008
                 909-869-2350

Seattle University
Seattle, WA

Type: Grants/Scholarships

Description: Seafirst Bank Minority Scholarship awards ten scholarships to full-time juniors who have established financial need and are majoring in the field of business. The scholarship is renewable if student maintains a 3.33 GPA.

Amount: $1,000

Description: The Robert Truex Scholarship provides funds to minority students majoring in business. Scholarship is renewable.

Amount: Various

Description: The U.S. Bank Business Scholarship awards ten scholarships annually to minority students in the Albers School of Business and Economics.

Amount: $3,000

Deadline: February 15

Business—Business Administration

California State Polytechnic University
Pomona, CA

Type: Scholarships

Description: The IREM Foundation Minority Scholarship Program awards two scholarships to eligible African-American and other minority students who are real estate, business, finance, and marketing majors with an emphasis on real estate.

Amount: $1,000

Deadline: March 15

Write: Financial Aid Office *or*
                 IREM Foundation Coordinator
                 Institute of Real Estate Management Foundation
                 P.O. Box 109025
                 Chicago, IL 60610-9025
                 312-329-6008

Description: Twenty scholarships are available to eligible first- or second-year African-American graduate students in business administration or management programs through the Coca-Cola Company. Apply to your college financial aid office.

Amount: $3,000

Deadline: March 27

Pittsburg State University
Pittsburg, KS

Type: Scholarships

Description: Incoming freshman students with financial need may qualify for awards through the Gladys A. Kelce School of Business. Residency requirements may exist for some awards.

Amount: $100–$500

Deadline: March 1

Business—Management

California State Polytechnic University
Pomona, CA

Type: Scholarships

Description: Scholarships available to students majoring in business and contracting management. Scholarship awards include: National Contracting Management Association Scholarship, Phi Kappa Phi Scholarship.

Amount: $200–$6,000

Deadline: Various

Write: College of Business Administration
Building 6-215
Cal Poly University
Pomona, CA 91768-4008
909-869-2400

Business—Real Estate

California State Polytechnic University
Pomona, CA

Type: Scholarships

Description: The IREM Foundation Minority Scholarship Program awards two scholarships to eligible African-American and other minority students who are real estate, business, finance and marketing majors with an emphasis on real estate.

Amount: $1,000

Deadline: March 15

Write: Financial Aid Office *or*
IREM Foundation Coordinator
Institute of Real Estate Management Foundation

P.O. Box 109025
Chicago, IL 60610-9025
312-329-6008

Description:	20 scholarships are available to eligible first- or second-year African-American graduate students in business administration or management programs through the Coca-Cola Company. Apply to your college financial aid office.
Amount:	$3,000
Deadline:	March 27

Communications

Richard Stockton College of New Jersey
Pomona, NJ

Type:	Grants/Scholarships
Description:	Awards scholarships to students interested in pursuing a career in journalism and related fields.
Amount:	Various
Deadline:	March 1

Seattle University
Seattle, WA

Type:	Grants/Scholarships
Description:	KING-5 Television Scholarships provide three annual awards to minorities who are juniors majoring in communications.
Amount:	Various
Deadline:	February 15

Communications—Journalism

Bemidji State University
Bemidji, MN

Type:	Grants/Scholarships
Description:	College offers two McMahon Scholarships each year for students with an interest in studying journalism.
Amount:	Various
Deadline:	May 15

Chapman University
Orange, CA

Type:	Scholarships
Description:	Chapman offers scholarship awards to students pursuing undergraduate training in communications and related fields.
Amount:	Various
Deadline:	March 2

Murray State University
Murray, KY

Type:	Grants/Scholarships
Description:	The John Fetterman Minority Journalism Scholarship annually to one minority student in the department of journalism with a grade point average of 2.5.
Amount:	Various
Description:	The Paducah Sun Minority Scholarships are awarded to full-time minority students who are preparing for a career in the field of newspaper journalism. Applicants must have a GPA of 2.75. Recipients will also receive a summer internship with the *Paducah Sun* newspaper.
Amount:	Various
Deadline:	April 1

Southern Methodist University
Dallas, TX

Type:	Scholarships
Description:	Undergraduate scholarships in communications and related fields are awarded to students based on academics and a variety of other criteria.
Amount:	Various
Deadline:	February 1

University of Northern Colorado
Greeley, CO

Type:	Scholarships
Description:	The College of Arts and Sciences offers scholarships for journalism, mass communications, speech and writing.
Amount:	Various
Deadline:	March 1

Communications—Radio and Television Broadcasting

Eastern New Mexico University
Portales, NM

Type: Scholarships

Description: ENMU offers scholarships for students interested in pursuing undergraduate training in various areas of the communications field. Dr. and Mrs. P. M. Baily Scholarship in Communications, Debate-Forensics Participation Scholarship, Gordon Greaves Memorial Scholarship in Journalism, New Mexico Broadcasters Assn. Scholarship, Roger and Millie Pattison Scholarship Fund for Speech and Hearing Clinic.

Amount: Various, average award $250

Deadline: March 1

University of Maryland—College Park
College Park, MD

Type: Grants/Scholarships

Description: Departmental awards with various academic or other criteria include the Knight-Ridder Minority Public Affairs Assistantship, Arizona Daily Star Scholarship for Minorities, Leonard M. Perryman Communications Scholarship for Ethnic Minority Students, Los Angeles Chapter SPJ, SDX Minority Award, National Association of Black Journalists Award, National Newspaper Publishers Association Scholarship Committee Award.

Amount: Various

Deadline: February 15

Communications—Speech

Austin Peay State University
Clarksville, TN

Type: Grants/Scholarships

Description: The Center for Creative Arts awards scholarships in disciplines including Art, Music, Speech, Communication & Theatre, Creative Writing; various athletic, department, private and military scholarships and grants.

Amount: Various

Deadline: April 1

Eastern New Mexico University
Portales, NM

Type: Scholarships

Description: ENMU offers scholarships for students interested in pursuing
               undergraduate training in various areas of the communica-
               tions field. Dr. and Mrs. P. M. Baily Scholarship in Communi-
               cations, Debate-Forensics Participation Scholarship, Gordon
               Greaves Memorial Scholarship in Journalism, New Mexico
               Broadcasters Assn. Scholarship, Roger and Millie Pattison
               Scholarship Fund for Speech and Hearing Clinic.

Amount: Various, average award $250

Deadline: March 1

University of Northern Colorado
Greeley, CO

Type: Scholarships

Description: The College of Arts and Sciences offers scholarships for jour-
               nalism, mass communications, speech and writing.

Amount: Various

Deadline: March 1

Computer Science and Mathematics

Antioch College
Yellow Springs, OH

Type: Grants/Scholarships

Description: Evan Spalt Scholarship for Science and Math are awarded to
               first-year students in math and the sciences.

Amount: $2,000

Deadline: February 15

Denison University
Granville, OH

Type: Grants/Scholarships

Description: Wells Scholarship in Science is awarded for outstanding aca-
               demic performance/potential by students who plan to major
               in science or math.

Amount: Three-quarters tuition

Deadline: April 1

Eastern New Mexico University
Portales, NM

Type: Scholarships

Description: ENMU offers scholarships for students interested in studying
                 mathematics. Candidates must have at least a 3.0 GPA in
                 mathematics and demonstrate academic excellence and in-
                 terest in math. Open to students at junior or senior level.

Amount: $300–$400 per academic year

Deadline: March 1

Georgetown University
Washington, D.C.

Type: Scholarships

Description: The University awards National Science Scholarships to stu-
                 dents who excel in achievement in the math, physical, life,
                 and computer sciences.

Amount: Up to $5,000 per year for four years

Deadline: January 1

Winthrop University
Rock Hill, SC

Type: Grants/Scholarships

Description: S.C. Governor's School of Science and Mathematics Scholar-
                 ship are awarded to graduates of the Governor's School and
                 have a minimum SAT of 1100 (ACT of 26). Renewable for
                 eight semesters.

Amount: Full tuition

Deadline: May 1

Xavier University
New Orleans, LA

Type: Grants/Scholarships

Description: Students majoring in biology, chemistry, physics/engineering,
                 pharmacy, mathematics or computer science may receive
                 scholarships through several programs including E. E. Just
                 Scholars, M.A.R.C. Biomedical Fellows, M.B.R.S. Research Ap-
                 prentices, O.N.R. Future Scientists, and the RCMS Program.

Amount: Various

Deadline: Various

Computer Science and Mathematics—Mathematics

Virginia Polytechnic Institute & State University
Blacksburg, VA

Type: Grants/Scholarships

Description: Grants and scholarships are available through the colleges of engineering, agriculture and life sciences, business, and the departments of art, mathematics, music and theatre arts.

Amount: Various

Deadline: February 15

Computer Science and Mathematics—Technology

Florida A&M University
Tallahassee, FL

Description: Grants and scholarships are available to students interested in majoring in technology and related fields through the College of Science and Technology.

Amount: Various

Deadline: April 1

Pittsburg State University
Pittsburg, KS

Description: Students majoring in technology or applied science may qualify for scholarships in various amounts through the School of Technology and Applied Science.

Amount: Various

Deadline: March 1

Creative/Visual/Performing Arts

Austin Peay State University
Clarksville, TN

Type: Grants/Scholarships

Description: The Center for Creative Arts awards scholarships in disciplines including art, music, speech, communication & theatre, creative writing; various athletic, department, private, and military scholarships and grants.

Amount:	Various
Deadline:	April 1

Chapman University
Orange, CA

Type:	Scholarships
Description:	Chapman offers Master Talent and Talent Service Awards to students with exceptional talent and achievement in the visual, performing and communications arts.
Amount:	Various
Deadline:	March 2

Clarion University of Pennsylvania
Clarion, PA

Type:	Grants/Scholarships
Description:	Clarence & Janet Lesser Scholarships make awards to 25 to 30 high school students who have exhibited a high interest and achievement particularly in the areas of art, music and inter-collegiate athletics. Awards are paid each semester as tuition credit. Contact the financial aid office for information.
Amount:	$200–$500
Deadline:	January 1

Cornell College
Mount Vernon, IA

Type:	Scholarships
Description:	A number of academic, music and art scholarships are awarded to outstanding students each year.
Amount:	$4,000–$7,000
Deadline:	March 1

Eastern New Mexico University
Portales, NM

Type:	Scholarships
Description:	ENMU offers scholarships for students interested in pursuing undergraduate training in various areas of the arts. They include: E. P. Compton Endowed Scholarship in Theatre, University Theatre Center Endowed Scholarship in Technical Theatre, Harry Barton Scholarship in Music, Gillian Director's Award, Shirley A. Hamilton Memorial Music Scholarship, Paul Muench Scholarship for Piano Majors, Mary L. Peed Scholarship in Music, Presser Foundation Scholarship in Music, Lorraine Schula Scholarship in Music, Floren and Mary

Thompson Instrumental Scholarship, University Symphony League Scholarship, Arthur Welker Strings Scholarship Fund.

Amount: Various, up to $2,500

Deadline: March 1

Huntingdon College
Montgomery, AL

Type: Scholarships

Description: Available to students studying the performing arts including dance, drama, musical theatre and music. Selections based on departmental committee judgement in an annual competition.

Amount: $500–$4,000 per year, renewable

Description: Visual Arts Scholarship available to students based on departmental judgement.

Amount: $500–$4,000 per year, renewable

Deadline: May 1

Southern Methodist University
Dallas, TX

Type: Grants/Scholarships

Description: Scholarship awards are provided to students majoring in dance, music, and theatre, based upon an evaluation of their artistic competence and potential. Visual and fine arts awards are evaluated on the basis of a portfolio review.

Amount: Partial and full tuition

Deadline: February 1

United States International University
San Diego, CA

Type: Scholarships

Description: School of Performing and Visual Arts (SPVA) Talent Award for outstanding talent in the arts.

Amount: $9,000

Deadline: January 1

University of Northern Colorado
Greeley, CO

Type: Scholarships

Description: Scholarships are available for students interested in studying music and music composition, theatre, dance, visual arts, theatre design and technology through the College of Performing and Visual Arts.

Amount: $100–$2,200

Deadline: March 1

Virginia Polytechnic Institute & State University
Blacksburg, VA

Type: Grants/Scholarships

Description: Grants and scholarships are also available through the colleges of engineering, agriculture and life sciences, business, and the departments of art, mathematics, music, and theatre arts.

Amount: Various

Deadline: February 15

Winthrop University
Rock Hill, SC

Type: Grants/Scholarships

Description: One-time freshman award of Dean's Merit Scholarship available to students with artistic ability and academic achievement.

Amount: Up to $1,000

Description: Art/Visual General Scholarship available upon portfolio review. Renewable for up to eight semesters.

Amount: Up to $1,200, renewable

Description: Dance General Scholarship available upon an audition. Renewable for up to eight semesters.

Amount: $500

Description: Interior Design General Scholarship available upon portfolio review. Renewable for up to eight semesters.

Amount: Up to $1,200

Description: Music Scholarship available upon audition. Renewable for up to eight semesters.

Amount: Up to $1,200

Description: Theatre Firstnighter Scholarship available upon audition. Renewable for up to eight semesters.

Amount: Up to $1,000

Deadline: May 1

Xavier University
New Orleans, LA

Type: Grants/Scholarships

Description: Every student who applies to Xavier is automatically consid-
                ered for an Xavier University Scholarship based on academic
                achievement or talent in art, music, or athletics.

Amount: Various

Description: Students with demonstrated talent in the visual and perform-
                ing arts may qualify for the Mother McAuly Scholarship, Na-
                tional Scholastic Art Scholarship or Performing Arts Grants.

Amount: Various

Deadline: Various

Creative/Visual/Performing Arts— Architecture/Landscape Architecture

California State Polytechnic University
Pomona, CA

Type: Scholarships

Description: Scholarships available to students majoring in architecture
                and related fields.

                Scholarship awards include: AIA/AAF Foundation Scholar-
                ship, AWA, Assn. of Women in Architecture Award, Charles
                DuBose Scholarship, Mel Ferris Scholarship, Inland Empire
                Chapter, AIA, LAF/Class Fund Scholarship Awards, Albert C.
                Martin Associates Scholarship, Pomona Valley NAWAIC/
                Nat'l Assn. of Women in Construction, RTKL Traveling
                Scholarship, Santa Clara Valley Chapter, AIA, Scholastic All
                American Scholarship, Skidmore Owings & Merrill Founda-
                tion Award, Harry S. Truman Scholarship.

Amount: $400–$9,000

Deadline: Various

Write: College of Environmental Design
                Architecture Department
                Building 7-210
                Cal Poly University
                Pomona, CA 91768-4008
                909-869-3508

Type: Scholarships

Description: The LAF/Class Fund Scholarship Minority Program awards two scholarships to African-American and other minorities who are full-time students with majors in landscape architecture or ornamental horticulture.

Amount: $1,500

Deadline: January 1

Description: African-American and other minority students majoring in architecture may be eligible to receive an Albert C. Martin Associates Scholarship. Students must be enrolled full-time and be third-year students in architecture. The award also comes with a 500-hour paid internship and is renewable.

Amount: $1,000

Deadline: December 11

Creative/Visual/Performing Arts— Drama

Northwest Nazarene College
Nampa, ID

Type: Scholarships

Description: College awards include Nazarene Youth International Awards for drama and debating.

Amount: Various

Deadline: March 1

Creative/Visual/Performing Arts— Fine Arts

Birmingham—Southern College
Birmingham, AL

Type: Scholarships

Description: Students interested in studying the arts may qualify for a Fine Arts Scholarship. Selection is made on the basis of an audition or portfolio with interview and audition.

Amount: $3,000–$4,000 per year, renewable

Deadline: March 15

Marietta College
Marietta, OH

Type: Grants/Scholarships

Description: Talent Scholarships in Fine Arts are awarded on the basis of the student's performance in a college-sponsored competition in art, music, and theatre.

Amount: 25 percent of tuition

Deadline: March 1

Minneapolis College of Art and Design
Minneapolis, MN

Type: Grants/Scholarships

Description: Portfolio Scholarships, Abbey Weed Grey Scholarships, and Admissions Scholarships are available to new students based on portfolio review and academic performance.

Amount: $6,000

Description: ARTS Scholarships are awarded to a high school senior selected by the Art Recognition and Talent Search competition.

Amount: $1,000

Description: Scholastic Art Awards are awarded to a high school senior selected by the Scholastic Art Award jury.

Amount: $1,000

Description: Scholarships are awarded in the senior year to MCAD juniors with 3.0 grade point average through the Shirley and Fitterman Scholarship, Virginia M. Binger Scholarship, and Wanda Gag Scholarship programs.

Amount: Full tuition

Deadline: April 1

Rosemont College
Rosemont, PA

Type: Grants/Scholarships

Description: The Revere Scholarship provides scholarships to a student planning to major in art. Faculty members from the Arts Division select the recipient based on a portfolio review.

Amount: One full-tuition (or two half-tuition)

Deadline: March 1

Creative/Visual/Performing Arts— Music

Agnes Scott College
Decatur, GA

Type: Scholarships

Description: Students planning to major in music may compete for Nannette Hopkins Scholarships in Music. These scholarships are renewable and are awarded on the basis of student auditions.

Amount: $2,000

Deadline: January 1

Bemidji State University
Bemidji, MN

Type: Grants/Scholarships

Description: College offers 12 scholarships each year for students with an interest in studying music.

Amount: Various

Deadline: May 15

Centenary College of Louisiana
Shreveport, LA

Type: Grants/Scholarships

Description: Music scholarships available to students who have demonstrated talent in music.

Amount: $1,000–$6,000

Deadline: March 15

Concordia College
Moorhead, MN

Type: Grants/Scholarships

Description: 30 Music Scholarships and two annual Theatre and Forensics Scholarships.

Amount: $1,750, renewable

Deadline: May 1

Denison University
Granville, OH

Type: Grants/Scholarships

Description: Flora Dodson Skipp Scholarship is awarded to students who demonstrate special talent in music.

Description: Marimac Scholarships are awarded to students who demonstrate promise in a performing or visual art.

Amount: $500–$2,000

Description: Estelle King Van Beuren Scholarships are awarded to students who demonstrate special talent in music.

Amount: $1,000–$2,000

Deadline: April 1

Florida A&M University
Tallahassee, FL

Description: Students who show promise and talent in music may qualify for the William P. Foster Scholarship award. The award is made annually to senior majors in choral and instrumental music. A faculty committee of the Music Department makes the decision on the recipient based on performance, achievement, academic record, leadership and organizational membership.

Amount: $1,000

Deadline: April 1

Northwestern College
St. Paul, MN

Type: Grants/Scholarships

Description: Students with interest and talent in music and the performing arts may qualify to receive Bronson String Scholarships and music performance grants.

Amount: Various

Deadline: April 1

Ohio Wesleyan University
Delaware, OH

Type: Grants/Scholarships

Description: University offers grants and scholarships to students majoring in music.

Amount: Various

Deadline: Various

Pittsburg State University
Pittsburg, KS

Type:	Scholarships
Description:	Students majoring in music may qualify for scholarship awards through the Music Department. Residency requirements may exist for some awards.
Amount:	$200–$1,000
Deadline:	March 1

Scripps College
Claremont, CA

Type:	Grants/Scholarships
Description:	Students with demonstrated music talent and interest may qualify for Alice Shapiro Awards or Jaqua Harden Awards.
Amount:	Various
Deadline:	February 1

University of San Diego
San Diego, CA

Type:	Scholarships
Description:	Choral Scholars are selected to receive awards through the University of San Diego Department of Fine Arts on the basis of an audition.
Amount:	Over 50 percent of tuition
Deadline:	February 20

William Paterson College of New Jersey
Wayne, NJ

Type:	Grants/Scholarships
Description:	Students with demonstrated music ability may qualify for a Music Department Talent Scholarship.
Amount:	Full tuition (in-state)
Description:	Students with music talent may also qualify for Music Department Awards.
Amount:	$300–$500
Deadline:	April 1

Creative/Visual/Performing Arts—Theatre

Bemidji State University
Bemidji, MN

Type: Grants/Scholarships

Description: College offers two scholarships each year for students with an interest in studying theatre.

Amount: Various

Deadline: May 15

Concordia College
Moorhead, MN

Type: Grants/Scholarships

Description: 30 Music Scholarships and two annual Theatre and Forensics Scholarships.

Amount: $1,750, renewable

Deadline: May 1

Ohio Wesleyan University
Delaware, OH

Type: Grants/Scholarships

Description: University offers grants and scholarships to students majoring in theatre.

Amount: Various

Deadline: Various

Creative/Visual/Performing Arts—Visual Arts

Denison University
Granville, OH

Type: Grants/Scholarships

Description: Marimac Scholarships are awarded to students who demonstrate promise in a performing or visual art.

Amount: $500–$2,000

Deadline: April 1

Education

Eckerd College
St. Petersburg, FL

Type: Grants/Scholarships

Description: Paul Douglas Teacher Scholarships and Robert C. Byrd Honors Scholarships are available to students who meet certain academic requirements.

Amount: $1,500–$5,000

Deadline: March 1

Morgan State University
Baltimore, MD

Type: Grants/Scholarships

Description: Teacher Education Distinguished Scholar Awards

Amount: $3,000

Description: Sharon Christa McAuliffe Educational Awards

Amount: Tuition, fees, room and board

Description: Paul Douglas Teachers' Scholarships

Amount: Up to $5,000

Deadline: March 1

Northeast Missouri State University
Kirksville, MO

Type: Grants/Scholarships

Description: Over 50 Vocational Rehabilitation grants are awarded to students who meet certain criteria.

Amount: $656–$4,736

Description: Nearly 650 teachers' scholarships including Paul Douglas Teachers' Scholarships and Missouri Teachers' Scholarships are awarded annually.

Amount: $2,000–$5,000

Description: University awards over 20 athletic scholarships in various men's and women's sports.

Amount: $198–$7,416

Deadline: April 1

University of Illinois at Urbana-Champaign
Champaign, IL

Type: Scholarships

Description: University participates in the Paul Douglas Teachers' Scholarship program which provides awards to Illinois residents who graduate in the top 10 percent of their high school class and have high academic achievement.

Amount: $5,000

Description: Minority students interested in pursuing a teaching career may also receive funds through the Minority Teachers' Scholarship program. Applicants must be Illinois residents.

Amount: Up to $5,000

Deadline: March 15

University of Northern Colorado
Greeley, CO

Type: Grants/Scholarships

Description: Local scholarship programs include the Macallister Teacher Education Scholarship.

Amount $2,500

Description: Project Teacher Find

Amount: $1,000

Deadline: March 1

University of Southern Indiana
Evansville, IN

Type: Scholarships

Description: The Minority Teachers' Scholarship is awarded to African-American and/or Hispanic students who are enrolled in a program leading to Indiana Teacher certification who plan to teach full-time in Indiana following graduation.

Amount: $1,000 per academic year

Deadline: March 1

Western Illinois University
Macomb, IL

Type: Scholarships

Description: Students interested in teaching may qualify for the Paul Douglas Teachers' Scholarship program with average awards of $4,167 to eligible students.

| Amount: | Various, average award $4,167 |

Description: Teacher Shortage Scholarships
Amount: $1,099

Description: Special Education Tuition Waivers
Amount: $2,071

Description: African-American and other minorities may qualify for Women & Minorities in Educational Administration Awards and Minority Teacher Incentive Grants.

Amount: $1,620–$4,178
Deadline: March 1

Winthrop University
Rock Hill, SC

Type: Grants/Scholarships

Description: Teacher Cadet Scholarship available to Teacher Cadet Program participants who demonstrate commitment to teaching, leadership, and high academic achievement.

Amount: $1,000

Description: One-time freshman award of Werts Scholarship available to Teacher Cadet Program participants.

Amount: $500
Deadline: May 1

Xavier University
New Orleans, LA

Type: Grants/Scholarships

Description: The Sisters of the Blessed Sacrament Teacher Education Grant is awarded annually to incoming freshmen majoring in education.

Amount: $2,500, renewable for four years

Description: Paul Douglas Teachers' Scholarships are awarded to students interested in a career in teaching.

Amount: Various
Deadline: Various

Education—Elementary/Secondary Education

Birmingham—Southern College
Birmingham, AL

Type: Scholarship

Description: Students interested in becoming teachers of math and science at the secondary level in Alabama may qualify for a B.B. Comer Teacher Education Scholarship. Selection is made on the basis of academic record, test scores, and an interview.

Amount: $2,500 per year, renewable

Deadline: March 15

Pittsburg State University
Pittsburg, KS

Type: Scholarships

Description: Students majoring in education may qualify for Paul Douglas Teachers' Scholarships and Kansas Teacher Scholarships, or a number of departmental scholarships available through the School of Education.

Amount: Various, average award $5,000

Deadline: March 1

University of San Diego
San Diego, CA

Type: Scholarships

Description: Duchesne Scholarships are offered through the School of Education to ethnic minority students interested in becoming elementary and secondary teachers.

Amount: Up to $3,000

Deadline: February 20

Education—Special Education

Western Illinois University
Macomb, IL

Type: Scholarships

Description: Students interested in teaching may qualify for the Paul Douglas Teachers' Scholarship program with average awards of $4,167 to eligible students.

Amount:	Various, average award $4,167

Description:	Teacher Shortage Scholarships
Amount:	$1,099

Description:	Special Education Tuition Waivers
Amount:	$2,071

Description:	African-American and other minorities may qualify for Women & Minorities in Educational Administration Awards and Minority Teacher Incentive Grants.
Amount:	$1,620–$4,178
Deadline:	March 1

Engineering

Auburn University
Auburn University, AL

Type:	Grants and Scholarships
Description:	African-American and other minority students interested in studying engineering may qualify for Sonat Minority Engineering Scholarships.
Amount:	$2,000

Description:	E.I. duPont deNemours Scholarships are available to students who meet certain academic and other criteria.
Amount:	$5,000

Description:	BCM Engineers, Inc., Scholarships and chemical engineering scholarships
Amount:	Various
Deadline:	April 15

Georgetown University
Washington, D.C.

Type:	Scholarships
Description:	The University also awards National Science Scholarships to students who excel in achievement in math and engineering.
Amount:	Up to $5,000 per year for four years
Deadline:	January 1

Menlo College
Atherton, CA

Type: Scholarships

Description: Students who are from racially ethnic backgrounds that are underrepresented in the field of engineering may qualify for awards from the National Action Council for Minorities in Engineering. Applicants must have a 2.5 grade point average and have financial need.

Amount: $500–$3,000

Deadline: March 2

Pittsburg State University
Pittsburg, KS

Type: Scholarships

Description: African-American and female students majoring in engineering technology may qualify for a Female/Minority Engineering Technology or Plastics Technology Scholarship, sponsored by Phillips Petroleum.

Amount: Various

Deadline: March 1

Seattle University
Seattle, WA

Type: Grants/Scholarships

Description: The Alliant Techsystems Engineering Scholarship is designed to encourage diversity in the field of engineering. The scholarship is renewable.

Amount: $2,000

Description: Boeing Company Corporate Scholarship is awarded to a minority entering the junior or senior year. The scholarship is not renewable.

Amount: $6,000

Deadline: February 15

Southern Illinois University at Carbondale
Carbondale, IL

Type: Grants/Scholarships

Description: African-American and other minority students interested in pursuing undergraduate training in engineering may qualify for Minority Engineering Scholarships.

Amount: Up to cost of tuition, fees, books, room and board

Deadline: February 1

Southern Methodist University
Dallas, TX

Type: Scholarships

Description: Undergraduate scholarships in engineering are based on aca-
                   demic achievement, leadership, and a range of personal ac-
                   complishments.

Amount: Various

Deadline: February 1

Tuskegee University
Tuskegee, AL

Type: Scholarship

Description: Incoming freshmen in engineering may qualify for one of ten
                   engineering technologies awards. Recipients are typically in
                   the top 10 percent of the pre-summer program.

Amount: $500–$3,000

Deadline: April 15

University of Alabama at Birmingham
Birmingham, AL

Type: Scholarships

Description: African-Americans planning to major in engineering at the
                   University of Alabama at Birmingham may qualify for Rust
                   Engineering Scholarships.

Amount: Full tuition, fees, and a stipend

Deadline: May 1

University of Illinois at Urbana-Champaign
Champaign, IL

Type: Scholarships

Description: University participates in the National Action Council for Mi-
                   norities in Engineering, which provides scholarship awards to
                   eligible students.

Amount: $250–$1,000

Deadline: March 15

University of Pittsburgh
Pittsburgh, PA

Type:	Grants/Scholarships
Description:	Engineering Honors Scholarships
Amount:	$500–$9,000
Deadline:	March 1

University of Virginia
Charlottesville, VA

Type: Grants/Scholarships

Description: The School of Engineering and Applied Science offers annual renewable scholarships based on academic excellence and leadership to qualified African-American students both from Virginia and outside the state.

Amount: Various

Deadline: March 1

Virginia Polytechnic Institute & State University
Blacksburg, VA

Type: Grants/Scholarships

Description: Grants and scholarships are also available through the colleges of engineering, agriculture and life sciences, business, and the departments of art, mathematics, music and theatre arts.

Amount: Various

Deadline: February 15

Xavier University
New Orleans, LA

Type: Grants/Scholarships

Description: Students majoring in biology, chemistry, physics/engineering, pharmacy, mathematics or computer science may receive scholarships through several programs including E. E. Just Scholars, M.A.R.C. Biomedical Fellows, M.B.R.S. Research Apprentices, O.N.R. Future Scientists, and the RCMS Program.

Amount: Various

Deadline: Various

Engineering—Agricultural Engineering

**California State Polytechnic University
Pomona, CA**

Description:	Scholarship awards in Agricultural Engineering available to all grade levels through the Cal-Poly Agricultural Engineering/ Landscape Irrigation Science Department. Students must have a minimum grade point average of 2.5 to apply, have an interest in agricultural engineering/water and irrigation, be involved in extracurricular and leadership activities and have work experience related to agricultural engineering.
Amount:	$500
Deadline:	February 15
Description:	American Society of Irrigation Consultants awards two scholarships to eligible students.
Amount:	$1,000
Deadline:	January 1
Description:	Association of California Water Agencies offers six awards to students who have completed sophomore work in engineering, agricultural and/or urban water supply, environmental studies. Minimum 3.0 GPA required.
Amount:	$1,000
Deadline:	January 1
Description:	Six Landscape Irrigation Design awards are made to undergraduates in agricultural engineering, ornamental horticulture, landscape architecture majors or landscape irrigation design minors.
Amount:	$500
Deadline:	October
Write:	Agricultural Engineering/Landscape Irrigation Science Department Building 45, Room 104 California State Polytechnic University Pomona, CA 91768 909-869-2220

Virginia Polytechnic Institute & State University
Blacksburg, VA

Type:	Grants/Scholarships
Description:	Grants and scholarships are also available through the colleges of engineering, agriculture and life sciences, business, and the departments of art, mathematics, music and theatre arts.
Amount:	Various
Deadline:	February 15

Engineering—Chemical, Civil, Electrical, and Mechanical Engineering

California State Polytechnic University
Pomona, CA

Type:	Scholarships
Description:	African-American and other minorities accepted to the university engineering program may receive awards from the Minority Engineering Scholarship and Incentive Grant Program. Awards are made on the basis of academic record, leadership and participation in school and community activities, work experience, statement of educational and career goals, personal essay, unique circumstances, and recommendation.
Amount:	$250–$1,500
Deadline:	January 1
Description:	African-American and other minority students may also receive an award through the Fluor Daniel Engineering Scholarship Program for Minorities and Women. Applicants must be full-time students in chemical, civil, electrical or mechanical engineering and be U.S. citizens. Students may apply through the university's College of Engineering.
Amount:	$2,000
Deadline:	March 1
Description:	A money award is available to African-American students and other minorities through the Lockheed Leadership Fund Fellowship. Awards are based on a student's academic record. Students may apply through the College of Engineering.
Amount:	Up to $5,000
Deadline:	October 1

Florida A&M University
Tallahassee, FL

Description: Grants and scholarships are available to students interested in majoring in engineering and related fields through the College of Science and Technology.

Amount: Various

Deadline: April 1

Health—Nursing

Pittsburg State University
Pittsburg, KS

Type: Scholarships

Description: Students majoring in nursing may qualify for scholarship awards through the Nursing Department.

Amount: Various

Deadline: March 1

University of Northern Colorado
Greeley, CO

Type: Scholarships

Description: Scholarships in various amounts are available for students interested in studying nursing, food, nutrition, and dietetics, and human rehabilitation through the College of Health and Human Sciences.

Amount: Various

Deadline: March 1

Health—Pharmacy

Florida A&M University
Tallahassee, FL

Description: Grants and scholarships are available to students interested in pursuing a career in pharmacy and related fields through the School of Pharmacy.

Amount: Various

Deadline: April 1

Washington State University
Pullman, WA

Type: Grants/Scholarships

Description: Students who wish to study pharmacy may qualify for scholar-
                   ships through the Multicultural Scholarship program at the
                   College of Pharmacy.

Amount: $1,000 awards to up to one-half tuition

Deadline: March 1

Xavier University
New Orleans, LA

Type: Grants/Scholarships

Description: Students majoring in biology, chemistry, physics/engineering,
                   pharmacy, mathematics or computer science may receive
                   scholarships through several programs including E. E. Just
                   Scholars, M.A.R.C. Biomedical Fellows, M.B.R.S. Research Ap-
                   prentices, O.N.R. Future Scientists, and the RCMS Program.

Amount: Various

Deadline: Various

Language/Literature/Humanities

Antioch College
Yellow Springs, OH

Type: Grants/Scholarships

Description: J. B. Tripp Humanities Scholarship for one year only is open
                   to first-year humanities students.

Amount: $1,250

Deadline: February 15

Denison University
Granville, OH

Type: Grants/Scholarships

Description: Merit scholarships include Denison Scholarship in the Hu-
                   manities, which is awarded based on outstanding academic
                   performance/potential in the humanities major.

Amount: Three-quarters tuition

Deadline: April 1

Eastern New Mexico University
Portales, NM

Type:	Scholarships
Description:	ENMU offers scholarships for students interested in studying modern languages, literature, or science fiction. Awards based on academic achievement and other criteria.
Amount:	$1,000
Deadline:	March 1

Southern Methodist University
Dallas, TX

Type:	Scholarships
Description:	Undergraduate scholarships available to students in the humanities and related fields through the Dedman College at SMU.
Amount:	Various
Deadline:	February 1

Language/Literature/Humanities— English

Florida A&M University
Tallahassee, FL

Description:	Grants and scholarships are available to students majoring in English. Students must have a GPA of 3.00 or above to qualify for the English Literary Guild Scholarship program.
Amount:	$250
Deadline:	April 1

Language/Literature/Humanities— Writing

Austin Peay State University
Clarksville, TN

Type:	Grants/Scholarships
Description:	The Center for Creative Arts awards scholarships in disciplines including art, music, speech, communication & theatre, creative writing; various athletic, department, private, and military scholarships and grants.

Amount: Various

Deadline: April 1

Physical Sciences

Bard College
Annandale, NY

Type: Scholarships

Description: Students who excel academically in the sciences and are in-
               terested in continuing their studies in the science field may
               be eligible for one of 35 merit awards through the Distin-
               guished Scientists program.

Amount: $19,624

Deadline: March 15

Cornell College
Mount Vernon, IA

Type: Grants/Scholarships

Description: College offers nearly 1,000 need- and non-need-based scholar-
               ships and grants including a number of academic and science
               scholarships. In addition, the college offers Distinguished Honor
               Scholarships and awards in the physical and natural sciences.

Amount: $4,000–$7,000

Deadline: March 1

Georgetown University
Washington, D.C.

Type: Scholarships

Description: The University awards National Science Scholarships to stu-
               dents who excel in achievement in the math, physical, life,
               and computer sciences.

Amount: Up to $5,000 per year for four years

Deadline: January 1

Xavier University
New Orleans, LA

Type: Grants/Scholarships

Description: Students majoring in biology, chemistry, physics/engineering,
               pharmacy, mathematics or computer science may receive
               scholarships through several programs including E. E. Just
               Scholars, M.A.R.C. Biomedical Fellows, M.B.R.S. Research Ap-
               prentices, O.N.R. Future Scientists, and the RCMS Program.

Amount: Various

Deadline: Various

Social Science—Public Administration

Antioch College
Yellow Springs, OH

Type: Grants/Scholarships

Description: Arthur Morgan Public Service Scholarships are awarded to first-year students with academic promise and interest in public/community service.

Amount: $5,000

Deadline: February 15

Social Science—Social Work

Antioch College
Yellow Springs, OH

Type: Grants/Scholarships

Description: Arthur Morgan Public Service Scholarships are awarded to first-year students with academic promise and interest in public/community service.

Amount: $5,000

Description: Beatrice Kotas Social Service/Work Scholarships are available to first-year students interested in a career in social work or social services.

Amount: $1,000

Description: E. Y. "Yip" Harburg Scholarship for African-American Men are available to male African-American students who show evidence of social concern, and have graduated from high school with at least a C average.

Amount: $1,500

Deadline: February 15

SECTION IV: ACADEMIC, ATHLETIC, AND OTHER SCHOLARSHIPS

Academic

Agnes Scott College
Decatur, GA

Type: Scholarships

Description: Presidential Scholarships are awarded to students with out-
                standing academic achievement. The scholarship is renewable
                for four years.

Amount: Full tuition, room and board

Description: Honor Scholarships are awarded to students who have demon-
                strated high levels of academic achievement and leadership.

Amount: $6,000–$12,000 per year

Description: Agnes Scott College National Merit Scholarships are awarded
                to National Merit semifinalists.

Amount: $500–$2,000

Description: Governor's Scholarships are available to Georgia residents at-
                tending an eligible college or university.

Amount: $1,540

Deadline: January 1

Alabama A&M University
Normal, AL

Type: Scholarships

Description: As a predominantly Black university, a majority of aid is pro-
                vided to African-American students. Students may qualify for
                one of over 125 academic achievement scholarship programs.

Amount: Various

Deadline: June 1

Allegheny College
Meadville, PA

Type: Grants/Scholarships

Description: Presidential Scholar Awards are offered to students with excep-
                     tional academic credentials.

Amount: $7,500 per year for four years

Description: Students with strong academic records and achievements in
                     other areas, or in teaching, may qualify for Dean's Achieve-
                     ment Awards.

Amount: $5,000 per year for four years

Description: National Merit Scholarships may be granted to eligible students.

Amount: Up to $2,000 per year

Description: The Allegheny Minority Scholarship for Research Careers in Sci-
                     ence is awarded to African-Americans and other minorities who
                     are interested in science or math and have high academic
                     achievement in these areas. Selected students receive an award
                     each academic year, regardless of the student's financial circum-
                     stances. Students who receive this award may also be eligible to
                     receive Allegheny's Presidential Scholarship of up to $7,500 each
                     year or the Dean's Achievement Award of up to $5,000 per year.

Amount: $5,000

Deadline: February 15

Allentown College of Saint Francis de Sales
Center Valley, PA

Type: Grants/Scholarships

Description: College offers approximately 15 Presidential Scholar awards
                     annually to incoming freshmen. To be considered, applicants
                     must be in the top 5 percent of their class and have a com-
                     bined SAT score of at least 1250 or an ACT score of 29.

Amount: Full tuition

Description: Allentown College offers approximately 40 Trustee Scholar-
                     ships annually to incoming freshmen. Applicants must be in
                     the top 15 percent of their class and have a combined SAT
                     score of at least 1100 or an ACT score of 27.

Amount: $5000, renewable annually

Description: De Sales Grants are offered to incoming freshmen who rank
                     in the top 30 percent of their class and have SAT scores of at
                     least 1000.

Amount: $3,500, renewable annually

Description: High School Teaching Scholarships are available through a competition offered in February for entering students who are in the teaching certification program. Accepted students who have at least a B average and minimum SAT scores of 1000 are invited to compete for these scholarships.

Amount: $1,000–$2,000, renewable annually

Deadline: February 15

Description: Departmental Scholarships are offered through each academic department to students interested in their majors. The awards are competitive, and are made on the basis of outstanding academic achievement, demonstrated talent in the respective field, and participation in a special Scholarship Day on December 5 for each major except theatre and dance. These competitions take place on December 11.

Amount: Various

Deadline: December 5 and 11

Antioch College
Yellow Springs, OH

Type: Grants/Scholarships

Description: Horace Mann Presidential Scholarships are awarded to first-year students with academic promise and commitment to humanitarian values such as peace, civil rights, or environmental issues.

Amount: $5,000

Description: Arthur Morgan Public Service Scholarships are awarded to first-year students with academic promise and interest in public/community service.

Amount: $5,000

Description: Dean's Scholarships are available to students who have demonstrated academic abilities.

Amount: Up to $3,000

Description: Dean Philip Nash Scholarships are available to all first-year students with strong academic promise and financial need.

Amount: $1,250

Description: Dorothy E. Mooney Scholarship for one year only is open to all first-year students with strong academic promise and financial need.

Amount: $2,500

Description: Antioch Regional Scholarships are offered to students with academic promise based on residency requirements.

Amount: Up to $3,000

Description: Hughes Science Scholarships are offered to new students with financial need pursuing studies in the biological, biomedical or related sciences.

Amount: Up to $8,000

Description: J. D. Dawson Science Scholarships are available to first-year students in the sciences.

Amount: $5,000

Description: Evan Spalt Scholarships for Science and Math are awarded to first-year students in math and the sciences.

Amount: $2,000

Description: International Student Scholarships available to first-year foreign students with excellent academics.

Amount: Up to $3,000

Description: Alfred Hampton Memorial Scholarships are available to first-year African-Americans and other minority students with strong academics.

Amount: Up to $5,000

Description: E. Y. "Yip" Harburg Scholarships for African-American Men are available to male African-American students who show evidence of social concern and have graduated from high school with at least a C average.

Amount: $1,500

Description: Upward Bound Scholarships are available to students who have participated in an Upward Bound–type program.

Amount: Up to $3,000

Deadline: February 15

Appalachian State University
Boone, NC

Type: Grants/Scholarships

Description: More than 115 awards of North Carolina Student Incentive Grants are made to students each year.

Amount: $100–$2,500

Description:	More than 85 Chancellor's Scholarships are awarded to students annually.
Amount:	$3,500
Description:	50 Academic Scholarships are awarded to students who meet certain academic and other requirements.
Amount:	$100–$2,100
Deadline:	January 1

Ashland University
Ashland, OH

Type:	Grants/Scholarships
Description:	The Achievement Scholarship
Amount:	$800
Description:	The Ashbrook Scholarship
Amount:	$2,000
Description:	Talent Scholarships are awarded to students who demonstrate talent in selected fields.
Amount:	$500–$4,000
Description:	Ashland University Scholar Awards provide awards to students who meet certain criteria.
Amount:	$500–$12,000
Deadline:	Various

Auburn University
Auburn, AL

Type:	Scholarships
Description:	Over 800 non-need scholarships available with an average award amount of $1,100. Academic achievement awards include: Alumni Academic Scholarships, Blount Presidential Scholarships, Dudley Academic Scholarships, Dudley Opportunity Scholarships, License to Learn Scholarships, McWane Foundation Scholarships, Presidential Opportunity Scholarships, Comer Foundation Scholarships, James H. Hall Scholarships, Albert L. Thomas Scholarships, Estes H. Hargis Scholarships, ALFA Scholarships, Yetta G. Samford Scholarships, Charles N. Fortenberry Scholarships, Brook and Marion Moore Scholarships, Morris W. Savage Scholarships, R. Y. Bailey Scholarships, Michael A. Nobles Scholarships, Samuel E. Upchurch Scholarships, Atlanta Auburn Club Scholarships.

Write: Mr. Clark Aldridge
                          Director of Financial Aid
                          Auburn University
                          203 Martin Hall
                          Auburn University, AL 38849
                          205-844-4723

Austin Peay State University
Clarksville, TN

Type: Grants/Scholarships

Description: University offers several academic scholarships including Academic Honors.

Amount: Up to $2,000 annually

Description: The Presidential Scholarship

Amount: $1,000 annually

Description: The Martin Luther King, Jr., Scholarship

Amount: $2,000

Description: Community College Honors

Amount: Up to $2,000 annually

Description: The President's Community College Award and the Emory and Martha Beaumont Kimbrough Scholarship

Amount: Various, average $1,600

Deadline: April 1

Bard College
Annandale, NY

Type: Scholarships

Description: Students who meet academic and other criteria may qualify for one of 160 Excellence and Equal Cost merit scholarships awarded each year.

Amount: $13,624–$25,970

Description: Students who excel academically in the sciences and are interested in continuing their studies in the science field may be eligible for one of 35 merit awards through the Distinguished Scientists program.

Amount: $19,624

Deadline: March 15

Benedictine College
Atchison, KS

Type: Scholarships

Description: Ten Presidential Scholarships are awarded through competitive process to admitted students who have a 3.00 cumulative high school GPA and who have scored a minimum of 27 on the ACT or 1100 on the SAT. Recipients must maintain a GPA of 3.30 and may renew the scholarship for four years.

Amount: Full tuition paid

Description: First-time full-time freshmen may qualify for a Dean's Scholarship. Applicants must achieve a minimum score of 29 on the ACT and 1200 on the SAT or rank first academically or second in the high school graduating class.

Amount: $4,000 a year; renewable for up to four years

Description: A number of Academic Scholarships are awarded to freshmen who have achieved a score of 24–28 on the ACT or 940–1140 on the SAT, or who rank in the top 15 percent of their high school graduating class.

Amount: $8,000–$11,200 over a four-year period.

Description: Raven Recognition Scholarships are awarded to freshmen who have scored 20–23 on the ACT or 780–930 on the SAT or rank from the top 25th to 16th percentile in their high school graduating class.

Amount: $4,800–$7,200 for up to four years.

Deadline: March 1

Bethany College
Bethany, WV

Type: Grants/Scholarships

Description: College offers Academic Scholarships to students who meet academic and other criteria.

Amount: $1,000 to full tuition

Description: Leadership Awards are available to students who meet academic and other criteria.

Amount: $1,000–$4,000

Description: Disciples Awards and Bethany Grants are available to all eligible students.

Amount: $500–$9,000

Deadline: March 15

Birmingham—Southern College
Birmingham, AL

Type:	Scholarships
Description:	Students may qualify for Blount-Monaghan Honors Scholarships, Goodrich Scholarships, McWane Honors Awards, Neal and Anne Berte Honors Scholarships, Phi Beta Kappa Scholarships, William Rushton Scholarships. Recipients typically have 3.0 or better grade point average and 28 or better on the ACT and 1150 or more on the SAT.
Amount:	Full tuition to over $75,000 over four years
Deadline:	March 15

Boston College
Chestnut Hill, MA

Type:	Grants/Scholarships
Description:	Boston College Scholarship awards made on the basis of academic promise and financial need.
Amount:	Up to full tuition
Description:	Boston College grants are made on the basis of academics and financial need.
Amount:	Partial tuition
Description:	Presidential Scholars Program offers awards to students who are academically in the top 1–2 percent of the freshman applicant pool. Recipients also receive additional funding to meet their complete financial need, including summer programs.
Amount:	Half tuition
Deadline:	February 1

Bowie State University
Bowie, MD

Type:	Scholarships
Description:	African-Americans and other minority students may be eligible for one of more than 45 High Ability Scholarships. Awards based on academic achievement and other criteria.
Amount:	Tuition and fees
Description:	African-American and other minority students may be eligible for one of more than 45 private scholarships offered by the university, some with academic and other criteria.
Amount:	$250–$2,000
Deadline:	April 1

California State Polytechnic University
Pomona, CA

Type: Grants/Scholarships

Description: The CSU Scholarship Program for African-American Students and the Cal Poly Black Faculty & Staff Association Academic Incentive Awards provide scholarship and grant awards to African-American students each year.

Amount: Grants range from $100–$550; scholarships $1,000

Deadline: January 1

Campbellsville College
Campbellsville, KY

Type: Grants/Scholarships

Description: College offers academic scholarships to students who meet certain academic requirements.

Amount: $500–$9,130

Description: College offers church scholarships to students who meet certain criteria.

Amount: $100–$6,060

Deadline: March 1

Centenary College of Louisiana
Shreveport, LA

Type: Grants/Scholarships

Description: College offers Institutional Academic grants and scholarships to students who meet certain academic and other criteria.

Amount: $2,200 to full tuition

Description: Institutional Need grants are awarded to students with demonstrated financial need.

Amount: $600–$2,000

Description: Music scholarships available to students who have demonstrated talent in music.

Amount: $1,000–$6,000

Description: Church Careers scholarships and Methodist Minister's Dependent scholarships available to students who meet certain criteria.

Amount: $1,000–$1,500

Description: Institutional Endowment scholarships

Amount: $200–$1,500

Description: The college awards three Endowment Scholarships to African-American students.

Amount: $300–$500

Description: College offers awards to full tuition to athletes in Men's and Women's Cross Country, Tennis, Riflery, Soccer, Men's Basketball and Golf, and Women's Softball, Volleyball, and Gymnastics.

Amount: Various, average award $500

Deadline: March 15

Chadron State College
Chadron, NE

Type: Grants/Scholarships

Description: College participates in federal and state aid programs and offers numerous institutional scholarships and grants, many of which have residency or academic criteria. Programs include Board of Trustees Scholarships, which provide scholarships for students graduating from Nebraska high schools.

Amount: Full tuition, renewable

Description: Numerous scholarships are available from the Elizabeth and Bertha Braddock Memorial Scholarship program. Students are selected on the basis of academics, activities, and character.

Amount: $500–$1,000

Description: The college also offers a number of departmental scholarships, and awards in various major fields of interest.

Amount: Various

Type: Tuition waivers

Description: First-time freshmen may qualify for Dean's Scholarships awarded in the form of waivers.

Amount: One half of the in-state tuition for one year

Description: Presidential Scholarships are available to first-time freshmen with demonstrated talent, high academics, and leader abilities.

Amount: A waiver of the in-state portion of tuition

Deadline: Various

Chapman University
Orange, CA

Type:	Scholarships

Description: Presidential Scholars provide awards to entering full-time freshmen who demonstrate exceptional academic ability.

Amount: 55–100 percent tuition

Description: Provost's Scholars awards are available to entering full-time students with GPA's of 3.40 and above.

Amount: 40–50 percent tuition

Description: Dean's Scholars awards are offered to entering full-time students with GPA's of 3.00 to 3.39.

Amount: 15–25 percent tuition

Description: Students with SAT scores of 1000 or greater may receive a University Scholars' award in an amount equal to their SAT score.

Amount: Various

Description: Dependents of Chapman alumni may receive money awards.

Amount: $1,000

Description: Full-time undergraduate students who have demonstrated financial need may receive Chapman Grants.

Amount: Up to $11,054

Description: Thurgood Marshall Awards are available to minority students in the top 10 percent of their high school graduating class.

Amount: 50 percent of tuition

Deadline: March 2

Clarion University of Pennsylvania
Clarion, PA

Type: Grants/Scholarships

Description: The Clarion University Alumni Association Scholarship provides ten tuition credit awards annually to students who have completed at least 16 credits at Clarion. Applications are available in September, and awards are made during October. Recipients are selected by a committee of the Alumni Association. Contact Mr. Ron Wilshire, Director of University Relations, for information and applications.

Amount: $300

Description:	The Mary/Martha Colegrove Educational Foundation Scholarship is awarded to two women from McKean County attending Clarion University. Renewable if the student remains in attendance and maintains a GPA of 3.0. Contact the Dean of Enrollment Management and Academic Records or McKean County High Schools guidance counselors for more information.
Amount:	$3,500
Description:	The Clarion University Foundation makes available 32 departmental scholarships to sophomore- and junior-level students in the form of tuition credits. Application is made during the Spring Semester to individual department committees.
Amount:	$500
Description:	Foundation Honors Scholarships are awarded to academically talented students at Clarion University who participate in the Honors Program. These annual scholarships are awarded on the basis of academic achievement and are renewable for four years provided students maintain the academic standards required. Contact the director of the Honors Program for more information.
Amount:	$650
Description:	State Board of Governors Scholarship awards are made each semester to minority students. Candidates must possess a minimum 3.0 GPA. This tuition-based scholarship may vary in amount, depending on the student's need. Applications may be obtained in the Admissions Office.
Amount:	Various
Deadline:	January 1
Description:	Walter L. Hart Scholarships are awarded annually to incoming freshmen, with special consideration given to students who rank in the top 10 percent of their graduating class with SAT scores in excess of 1,000. Interested students are encouraged to submit a letter of application along with three letters of recommendation to the Dean of Enrollment Management and Academic Records.
Amount:	$2,000
Deadline:	Before March 30
Description:	Four Presidential Scholarships are made annually to incoming freshman and transfer students. Special emphasis is placed on outstanding academic achievement, demonstrated leadership, and involvement in extracurricular activities. The scholarships are paid as a tuition credit each semester. Completed applications, an essay, and three letters of recommen-

dation must be submitted to the Dean of Enrollment Management and Academic Records.

Amount: $1,000

Deadline: Before March 30

Description: Several Dana S. Still Scholarships are awarded annually to incoming students based on financial need. An application must be submitted for this one-year award. Contact the Dean of Enrollment Management and Academic Records.

Amount: $200

Deadline: March 30

Clemson University
Clemson, SC

Type: Grants/Scholarships

Description: College participates in federal and state aid programs as well as institutional grants and scholarships including Clemson Alumni, Faculty and Staff Scholarships, IPTAY Scholarships, Alumni Presidential Scholarships.

Amount: Various

Description: General university scholarships are awarded to students who meet academic and other criteria.

Amount: $250–$6,000

Deadline: April 1

Columbia College
Columbia, MO

Type: Grants/Scholarships

Description: College offers a number of institutional, academic, and departmental scholarships and grants, including the Columbia College Scholars Program for entering first-time freshmen who have a 3.6 grade point average or better and a score of 1200 on the SAT or 27 on the ACT. Applicants must have leadership skills and four recommendations.

Amount: Full tuition and room

Deadline: January 31

Description: The Achieving Curricular Excellence (ACE) Scholarship is for entering freshmen with a 3.3 grade point average and ACT score of 24 or better.

Amount: 50-percent tuition reduction, renewable

Deadline: March 15

Description: Leadership Award offered to a first-time freshman who has demonstrated leadership ability in at least three high school, community, or church activities.

Amount: $1,000, renewable

Deadline: March 15

Description: The Young Women of America competition makes several awards to students who meet certain criteria.

Amount: $500–$4,000 for tuition and $1,500 for housing

Description: A limited number of matching grant awards are made to state residents through the NAACP Matching Fund program.

Amount: Up to $750

Deadline: March 15

Denison University
Granville, OH

Type: Grants/Scholarships

Description: Merit scholarships include Denison Scholarship in the Humanities which is awarded based on outstanding academic performance/potential in the humanities major.

Amount: Three-quarters tuition

Description: Faculty Scholarship for Achievements are awarded to the Valedictorian or Salutatorian from an Ohio high school. Up to 35 are awarded each year.

Amount: Full tuition

Description: Heritage Scholarships are awarded to students who have outstanding academic performance or potential. Up to 200 are awarded annually.

Amount: Half tuition

Description: National Merit Founders Scholarships are awarded and combined with National Merit stipends to students with outstanding performance on the College Board PSAT/NMSQT.

Amount: Half tuition

Description: National Achievement Scholarship awarded to students for outstanding test performance.

Amount: Half tuition

Description: Scholarships based on special talents or circumstances include: Battelle Memorial Institute Foundation Scholarship which provides awards to students with demonstrated potential for superior academic work and outstanding leadership qualities.

Amount: Half tuition

Description: Park National Bank Scholarship is awarded for superior academic performance/potential.

Amount: $2,000

Description: Tyree Scholarship is awarded for outstanding academic performance/potential.

Amount: Half tuition

Description: Fisher & Meredith Scholarships and Bob & Nancy Good Scholarships are awarded to students with strong academic performance.

Amount: $1,500–$6,000

Description: I Know I Can Scholarships, Honda Scholarships, Thomas Ewart Scholarships, Elizabeth Platt Clements Scholarships, Frederick P. & Mary T. Beaver Scholarships, John W. Beattie Scholarships, and Bricker Family Scholarships are awarded for outstanding academic performance/potential.

Amount: $500–$2,000

Description: Elizabeth Trembley Swisher Scholarships are awarded for superior academic/personal contributions.

Amount: $500–$2,000

Description: Alpha Phi Scholarship is awarded for outstanding academic performance/potential.

Amount: $7,000

Description: Faculty Scholarships for Achievement
Amount: $2,000 to full tuition

Description: African-American students may qualify for the Black Achievers Scholarship which is awarded to participants of the YMCA Black Achievers program for strong academic performance.

Amount: Half tuition
Deadline: April 1

Eastern New Mexico University
Portales, NM

Type:	Scholarships
Description:	ENMU offers a number of academic scholarships for residents and nonresidents. Students are automatically considered for these awards upon admission to the University. Resident awards include: Honors Scholarships, New Mexico Scholars, Presidential Academic Scholarships, Silver Scholarships, Zia Scholarships, 4.0 Scholarships. Awards are based on academic and other criteria.
Amount:	Various, average award $500
Description:	ENMU nonresident academic scholarships include Chaparral Presidential Scholarship, Chaparral Scholarship, Chaparral Scholarship for Transfer Students, Chaparral Zia Scholarship, Chaparral Zia Scholarship for Transfer Students. Nonresident students who apply for admission are automatically considered for these awards. Selections are based on academic and other criteria.
Amount:	Various, average award $500
Deadline:	March 1

Eckerd College
St. Petersburg, FL

Type:	Grants/Scholarships
Description:	College-sponsored programs include Presidential Scholarships, Church and Campus Scholarships, and Special Talent Scholarships.
Amount:	$1,500–$8,000
Description:	Special Honors Program
Amount:	Up to full tuition
Deadline:	March 1

Emory University
Atlanta, GA

Type:	Grants/Scholarships
Description:	The Emory College Grant (ECG) is need-based gift assistance funded by the college.
Amount:	Varies, average award $8,600
Description:	National Merit finalists may also receive Emory Merit Scholarship program.
Amount:	$750–$2,000
Deadline:	February 15

Description: A number of merit scholarships are awarded annually through Emory University's Scholars Program. Recipients receive scholarships which are renewable for four years of undergraduate study, provided they maintain high standards of personal and academic excellence. Most of the scholarships require a student be nominated by appropriate officials of their high school or by a nominating committee. All scholarships are awarded solely on the basis of outstanding merit without regard to financial need, race, color, religion, sex, age, handicap, or national origin.

Amount: Various

Deadline: November 15

Faulkner University
Montgomery, AL

Type: Scholarship

Description: Students with high academic achievement may qualify for a number of academic scholarships including: Academic Excellence Award, Leadership Award, Presidential Academic Award, Lads to Leaders Award, President's List, Dean's List, Honors List Award, and Transfer and Junior College Graduate Scholarships. Selection is based on academic record, test scores and other criteria.

Amount: $600 to full tuition per year

Deadline: June 1

Write: Joe Wiginton, Director of Admissions
Faulkner University
5345 Atlanta Highway
Montgomery, AL 36109-3398
205-272-5820

Florida A&M University
Tallahassee, FL

Type: Scholarships

Description: FAMU offers President's Scholars Awards to students who have demonstrated outstanding academic achievement and special talents in high school or community college. Awards are based on scholastic achievement and leadership skills, not financial need. Selection is by committee.

Amount: $1,000 per academic year

Deadline: April 1

Write: Presidential Scholars Award Committee
P.O. Box 599
Florida A&M University
Tallahassee, FL 32307

Description:	University also participates in the National Achievement Scholars for Negro Students and the National Merit Scholars Award.
Amount:	Up to a four-year scholarship
Description:	Departmental, private, and corporate scholarships are also available, including the Alethia A. Lesesne Howard Award Fund; Joe Awkard, Sr., Psychology Award; American Foundation Pharmaceutical Education Award; William P. Foster Scholarship Award; Martin Luther King, Jr., Memorial Scholarship; Owens-Corning Fiberglass Corporation Scholarships; Greyhound Corporation and Armour-Dial Company Scholarships; General Motors Endowed Scholarship Program; William G. Selby and Marie Selby Scholarships.
Amount:	Various, $400–$1,000
Deadline:	April 1

Florida Institute of Technology
Melbourne, FL

Type:	Scholarships
Description:	Florida Institute of Technology offers the following scholarships to students: Selby Foundation Scholarship, Brecht Scholarship, Astronaut Scholarship, Army ROTC Scholarship, Numerical Control Society Scholarship, Supplemental Scholarship, National Merit Scholarship, Walter D. & Paula LaCler Wood, Warren Foster, Hughes Scholarship, Sun Bank Scholarship, Barnett Bank Scholarship, Reliance Bank Scholarship, C&S Bank Scholarship, Christopher S. Neese Scholarship, Southern Bell Scholarship.
Amount:	Various
Description:	Scholarship opportunities available to minority students include Presidential Scholarships, Faculty Scholarships, Articulation Scholarships, Merit Scholarships, National Merit Academic Scholarships, National Achievement Scholarships, Robert C. Byrd Honors Scholarships, Chappie James Most Promising Teacher Scholarships, and Paul Douglas Scholarships.
Amount:	$1,500–$7,500
Deadline:	March 1

Frostburg State University
Frostburg, MD

Type:	Grants/Scholarships
Description:	Academic awards include FSU Outstanding Scholar Awards, Dailey Scholarship, N. Rose Atwood Award, HPER Scholarship

(for physical education), Leila Brady Suter French Memorial Award, and a number of merit achievement awards. College also offers creative arts and performance awards and a Governor's Handicapped Award, Diehl Alumni Scholarships, McDonald's Scholarships (for employees), and Westvaco Scholarships (for employees).

Amount: Various

Deadline: April 1

Georgetown University
Washington, D.C.

Type: Scholarships

Description: The John Carroll Scholarship program, named for the founder of the University, provides scholarships to students from particular cities, states, or regions. Awards are based on need and academic merit.

The Bellarmine and Ignatian Scholarship program offers scholarships based on need up to a maximum grant equal to the full cost of tuition. Bellarmine awards are made to students nominated by their Jesuit high school who ranked first in their class. Ignatian scholarships are offered to students nominated by their Jesuit high school who ranked in the top 5 percent of their class.

Amount: $500 to more than $20,000, depending on a student's financial need.

Description: Robert C. Byrd Honors Scholarships are available to high school graduates who demonstrate outstanding academic achievement. The awards are nonrenewable.

Amount: $1,500

Deadline: January 1

George Washington University
Washington, D.C.

Type: Scholarships

Description: Alumni Scholarships, Presidential Academic Scholarships, and Valedictorian Awards available to students who meet certain criteria.

Amount: Various

Deadline: Various

Georgian Court College
Lakewood, NJ

Type:	Grants/Scholarships
Description:	College offers scholarship and grant programs including Mother Marie Anna Awards, Trenton Alumnae Awards to state and local students, Marguerite McCarty Awards, Dean's Scholarships, Board of Trustee Scholarships, Charlotte Campbell Scholarships, Sisters of Mercy Scholarships for New Jersey Sisters of Mercy High School graduates, President's Scholarships, Alumnae Scholarships, M. Greco Zarrelli Scholarships, Joseph McGovern Scholarships, Mother Mary Cecilia Scholarships, Mother Mary John Scholarships, Sivade Scholarships, Reynolds Fund Scholarships for local residents, and Georgian Court College Scholarships.
Amount:	Various
Description:	The Delores Parron Scholarship is available to an entering freshman undergraduate minority woman student in the top 10 percent of her high school graduating class, who has a combined SAT score of 1,000. The scholarship is renewable annually provided recipient maintains a 3.0 cumulative grade point average.
Amount:	Full tuition
Deadline:	October 1

Hamline University
St. Paul, MN

Type:	Grants/Scholarships
Description:	University offers a number of scholarships and grant programs including Hamline University Need-Based Grants.
Amount:	Up to $8,000
Description:	Hamline University Academic Scholarships are provided to students based on academic merit.
Amount:	Up to full tuition
Description:	Minnesota State Grants awarded to students based on need and residency.
Amount:	$5,000
Description:	Minority Education Project (MEP) awards to students who reside in St. Paul, Minnesota; based on need.
Amount:	Up to $5,000
Deadline:	March 15

**Hood College
Frederick, MD**

Type: Scholarships

Description: Some of the non-need-based scholarships include the Beneficial-Hodson Scholarship for Academic Excellence, offering awards to students with outstanding academic records.

Amount: Up to $7,500 per year

Description: Students with a strong academic record and 1050 or better on the SAT or 25 or more on the ACT may receive a Trustee Scholarship.

Amount: Up to $7,500 per year

Description: Transfer students who have above-average academic records and who have strong leadership skills may qualify for a Presidential Leadership Scholarship.

Amount: Up to $3,000 per year

Description: Students with good academics and low family contribution may qualify for a Bonner Scholars award.

Amount: $1,870 per year

Description: The Maryland Distinguished Scholar Award provides an award amount which Hood matches. Students' academics and SAT scores are considered.

Amount: $3,000–$6,000

Description: Maryland residents may qualify for Maryland General State Scholarships and Senatorial and Delegate Scholarship awards. These awards are made by Maryland State Senators and Delegates.

Amount: $200–$2,500 per year—Senatorial Awards
                $200–$1,500 per year—Delegate Awards

Description: Need-based awards include Hood Grants and Scholarships.
Amount: $100–$10,000

Description: African-American students with academic potential/achievement may qualify for an Opportunity Award. These awards are academically competitive and not need-based.

Amount: One-half tuition

Description: Three one-year scholarships are awarded to underrepresented minorities each year.

Amount: $5,000

Deadline: March 1

Howard University
Washington, D.C.

Type: Grants/Scholarships

Description: Howard University provides Trustee Scholarships, which are granted based on academics; University Grants, which provide tuition to recipients; Special Talent Grants-in-Aid and National Competitive Scholarships which are awarded only to undergraduate freshmen on the basis of academic achievement in high school, SAT scores, and other indicators of leadership potential.

Amount: Various

Deadline: April 1

Huntingdon College
Montgomery, AL

Type: Scholarships

Description: Students with high academic achievement may qualify for a number of academic scholarships including: Alabama Private School Scholarships, Endowed Scholarships, Huntingdon College Leadership Scholarships, Junior College Transfer Scholarships, Academic Scholarship Program Awards. Selection is based on academic record, test scores, and various other criteria.

Amount: $100 to full tuition, room and board per year

Deadline: May 1

Jacksonville State University
Jacksonville, AL

Type: Scholarships

Description: Students with high academic achievement may qualify for Faculty Scholars Awards, Leadership Scholarships, and Endowed Scholarships. Selection is based on academic record, test scores, and various other criteria.

Amount: Up to full tuition

Deadline: April 1

Kent State University
Kent, OH

Type: Grants/Scholarships

Description: Oscar Ritchie Scholarships are awarded to academically tal-
               ented African-Americans and other minority students.

Amount: $1,500–full tuition, fees, room and board

Deadline: Spring of junior year in high school

Description: The Founders Scholars Program makes awards to incom-
               ing freshmen each year. Scholarships are based on academic
               record and competitive exam. Candidates are eligible by invi-
               tation only.

Amount: Up to full tuition, fees, room and board

Deadline: December 1

Description: Minority Incentive Scholarships are offered to African-
               Americans and other minority students based on academic
               achievement. Awards are made to high school seniors who do
               not participate in or were not awarded a scholarship from the
               Oscar Ritchie Memorial Scholarship program. Students must
               have a GPA of 2.75 to qualify.

Amount: $2,000–$3,500, renewable

Deadline: May 1

Description: Scholarships for Excellence are awarded to incoming fresh-
               man valedictorians of Ohio high schools.

Amount: $1,000

Deadline: Various

Description: Honors Scholarships are offered to students based on aca-
               demic achievement and ACT or SAT scores.

Amount: $800 up to full tuition

Deadline: Various

Description: University Scholarships are awarded to Ohio residents based
               on academic record and SAT or ACT scores.

Amount: $500

Deadline: February 15

Kenyon College
Gambier, OH

Type: Scholarships

Description: The Kenyon Honor and Science Scholarship is awarded annu-
               ally to approximately 15 outstanding students who have typi-
               cally ranked in the top 3 percent of their secondary school
               classes and earned SAT or ACT scores that place them in the
               top 3 percent nationally. Interested students may contact the
               college financial aid office for an application.

Amount: $9,500–$19,000

Deadline: January 5

Description: National Merit Scholarships are awarded to students who are
               selected by the National Merit Corporation as finalists in that
               competition.

Amount: $500–$2,000

Description: The Kenyon African-American/Latino Scholarship is awarded
               to approximately ten academically outstanding African-
               American and Latino students who are also involved in school
               and community activities and who have achieved at honors-
               level at their secondary school.

Amount: $9,500–$19,000

Deadline: February 15

King's College
Wilkes-Barre, PA

Type: Grants/Scholarships

Description: College offers academic, merit, and other grant awards to stu-
               dents. Students who rank in the top 5 percent of their high
               school graduating class, have attained a score of 1200 or
               higher on the SAT, and who plan to attend full-time may com-
               pete for a Presidential Scholarship. Recipients must maintain
               at least a 3.25 GPA at the College.

Amount: Various, up to full tuition

Description: Students who rank in the top 10 percent of their high school
               class and plan to attend full-time may compete for the Moreau
               Scholarship, named for the Very Reverend Basil Anthony
               Moreau, C.S.C., founder of the Holy Cross Fathers and Broth-
               ers. The award may be combined with federal and state grants
               not to exceed annual tuition.

Amount: Various, minimum $3,000

Description: Students who are high academic achievers may be eligible for various Academic Scholarships. Recipients maintain at least a 3.00 GPA.

Amount: Various, minimum $1,500 per year for four years

Description: Merit Scholarships are awarded to students who have demonstrated the ability to maintain an above average academic record while being involved in extracurricular, leadership, and/or community service activities. Recipients must maintain at least a 2.5 GPA.

Amount: Various, minimum award $1,500

Description: Grants-in-Aid may be awarded to students who have financial need and who have exhausted all possibilities of receiving grant assistance from outside sources and who are active in campus activities. Recipients must maintain a 2.0 GPA. Holy Cross Fathers Scholarships are awarded to students who demonstrate extreme financial need. Recipients are selected by the Holy Cross Fathers.

Amount: Various

Deadline: March 1

Lebanon Valley College
Annville, PA

Type: Grants/Scholarships

Description: College offers a number of need-based as well as non-need-based scholarship and grant awards to students, some with restrictions.

Amount: Various

Description: Academic scholarships are available through the Presidential Scholarship Program. Awards include the Vickroy Scholarship, open to high school seniors who rank in the top 10 percent of their class.

Amount: One-half tuition

Description: Leadership Awards are offered to high school seniors who rank in the top 20 percent of their class.

Amount: One-third tuition

Description: Achievement Awards are offered to high school seniors who rank in the top 30 percent of their class. All scholarships are renewable for four years.

Amount: One-fourth tuition

Deadline: Before April 1 (for the fall semester)

Loras College
Dubuque, IA

Type:	Grants
Description:	State of Iowa Scholarships may be awarded to students with high academic potential.
Amount:	$100–$400
Description:	The college also offers Sibling/Family Grants to families with two or more full-time dependent undergraduate family members attending the college at the same time.
Amount:	$1,000 per family member enrolled
Description:	Alumni Grants are awarded to children of alumni.
Amount:	$1,000
Description:	Diversity Grants are available to African-Americans and other minorities who enroll as full-time students.
Amount:	Various
Deadline:	April 15

Loyola College in Maryland
Baltimore, MD

Type:	Grants/Scholarships
Description:	College offers numerous scholarship and grant opportunities in addition to federal and state aid programs. More than 100 Presidential Scholarships are awarded annually to students with a 3.5 average, SAT score of 1200, and a ranking in the upper one-fifth of their class.
Amount:	$5,000 to full tuition for four years
Description:	50 Loyola College Scholarships are awarded to freshmen based on high school average, SAT results, and rank in class.
Amount:	$3,000 per year for four years
Description:	Freshman commuter students may qualify for Sellinger Scholarships based on their academic achievement and demonstrated financial need.
Amount:	$1,000 per year for four years
Description:	Freshman Catholic students residing in the Archdiocese of Baltimore with a minimum 3.75 average and minimum SAT score of 1250 may be considered for a Marion Burk Knott Scholarship.
Amount:	Full tuition for four years

Description:	African-American students may qualify for Claver Scholarships. Applicants are considered based on academic potential and evidence of community service and involvement.
Amount:	$3,000 to full tuition per year for four years
Description:	Claver Grants are also available to African-American undergraduates with exceptional financial need.
Amount:	Award amount varies depending on need
Description:	Maryland residents may qualify for Senatorial and Delegate Scholarships based on financial need.
Amount:	$200–$2,500
Description:	Maryland high school juniors who have maintained a 3.7 average during their high school years may compete in the Distinguished Scholar Program.
Amount:	$3,000 grants, renewable each year
Deadline:	March 1

Marietta College
Marietta, OH

Type:	Grants/Scholarships
Description:	Marietta also offers numerous endowment and other awards to eligible students including the Ohio Academic Scholars Program which awards one scholarship to each high school in Ohio.
Amount:	$1,000
Description:	The Ohio Student Choice Grant (OSCG) provides grants to Ohio residents.
Amount:	Various
Description:	The Ohio Instructional Grant (OIG) provides grants to residents whose family income does not exceed $27,000.
Amount:	Various
Description:	The Presidential and Dean's Scholarship Program provides tuition assistance to eligible students. Recipients are selected by a faculty committee, based on the strength of their application for admission.
Amount:	75–100 percent of tuition
Description:	Talent Scholarships in Fine Arts are awarded on the basis of the student's performance in a college-sponsored competition in art, music, and theatre.

Amount: 25 percent of tuition

Description: Marietta College Grants consist of college funds awarded on the basis of need to students enrolled full-time.

Amount: Various

Description: Endowment and Gift Scholarships are awarded to students on the basis of financial need.

Amount: Various

Deadline: March 1

Mary Baldwin College
Staunton, VA

Type: Grants/Scholarships

Description: College meets 100 percent of student financial need and offers institution scholarships and grants including Wilson/Baldwin Scholarships to students who meet academic and other criteria.

Amounts: $2,000–$6,000

Description: Bailey Scholarships and daughters of ministers awards are made to qualifying students as well as awards to sisters of current students.

Amount: Various

Description: African-Americans and other minority students may qualify for Minority Scholarships.

Amount: $2,000

Deadline: January 1

Minneapolis College of Art and Design
Minneapolis, MN

Type: Grants/Scholarships

Description: MCAD Scholarships are awarded on the basis of academic merit and financial need.

Amount: Various

Description: Portfolio Scholarships, Abbey Weed Grey Scholarships, and Admissions Scholarships are available to new students based on portfolio review and academic performance.

Amount: $6,000

Description: ARTS Scholarships are awarded to a high school senior selected by the Art Recognition and Talent Search competition.

Amount: $1,000

Description: Scholastic Art Awards are awarded to a high school senior selected by the Scholastic Art Award jury.

Amount: $1,000

Description: Scholarships are awarded in the senior year to MCAD juniors with 3.0 grade point average through the Shirley and Fitterman Scholarship, Virginia M. Binger Scholarship, and Wanda Gag Scholarship programs.

Amount: Full tuition

Description: State residents with demonstrated financial need may qualify for Minnesota State Grants.

Amount: $100–$5,464

Description: Students with demonstrated financial need may also qualify for awards through the Charles and Ellora Allis Foundation Grant program.

Amount: $500–$4,000

Deadline: April 1

Morehouse College
Atlanta, GA

Type: Grants/Scholarships

Description: Nearly 100 academic scholarships are offered to students who exceed admissions requirements and stand out as citizens and leaders.

Amount: Various

Deadline: February 15

Murray State University
Murray, KY

Type: Grants/Scholarships

Description: College offers a number of merit, athletic, and need-based scholarship and grant programs as well as departmental scholarships for students.

Amount: Various

Description: Marvin D. Mills scholarship program to African-American freshmen or full-time transfer students who are residents of

Kentucky, have a composite score of 21 on the ACT, rank in the top 25 percent of their class (if transferring, have completed 12 semester hours with a GPA of 2.75), and have exhibited leadership abilities in school, church, job, or other related organizations. Applicants must submit a 200-word essay on a current event or public topic of choice as well as a recent official transcript.

Amount: Full tuition

Description: The John Fetterman Minority Journalism Scholarship is awarded annually to one minority student in the department of journalism with a grade point average of 2.5.

Amount: Various

Description: The J. J. Roberts Upward Bound Scholarship awards a small stipend of at least $50 a year to an Upward Bound graduate who has earned at least a 2.8 in high school and maintained a minimum of 2.5 on at least 24 credit hours per year.

Amount: Various, average award $50

Description: The Paducah Sun Minority Scholarships are awarded to full-time minority students who are preparing for a career in the field of newspaper journalism. Applicants must have a GPA of 2.75. Recipients will also receive a summer internship with the *Paducah Sun* newspaper.

Amount: Various

Deadline: April 1

New York University
New York, NY

Type: Grants/Scholarships

Description: All eligible incoming freshmen are automatically reviewed for New York University need-based and merit scholarships and grants, including Trustees Scholarships, Presidential Scholarships, Merit & Achievement Scholarships, and the Martin Luther King, Jr., Scholarship Program.

Amount: Various

Deadline: February 15

Northeast Missouri State University
Kirksville, MO

Type: Grants/Scholarships

Description: More than 630 Higher Education–Bright Flight grants are awarded annually to two African-American students.

Amount: $2,000

Description:	Ten Byrd Scholarships and 17 Missouri Grants are awarded annually to students who meet certain criteria.
Amount:	$1,118–$1,500
Description:	Nearly 650 teachers' scholarships including Paul Douglas Teachers' Scholarships and Missouri Teachers' Scholarships are awarded annually.
Amount:	$2,000–$5,000
Description:	More than 600 Private scholarships are awarded to students each year who meet certain criteria.
Amount:	$50–$7,694
Description:	Over 2,500 NMSU scholarships are awarded annually to students who meet certain criteria.
Amount:	$100–$7,416
Description:	Seventy-eight Minority Scholarships including nine President's Honorary Grants and 30 various Northeast Awards
Amount:	$459–$7,416—Northeast Awards $2,728–$7,516—President's Honorary Grants
Deadline:	April 1

Northwestern College
St. Paul, MN

Type:	Grants/Scholarships
Description:	Honor Scholarships available to students who meet certain academic and other criteria.
Amount:	$200–$1,500
Description:	Academic Tuition Benefits are available to students who meet certain criteria.
Amount:	$390–$2,000
Description:	The college offers non-need awards, including Presidential Scholarships and STEP Scholarships.
Amount:	Various
Deadline:	April 1

Northwest Nazarene College
Nampa, ID

Type:	Scholarships
Description:	Awards include the Presidential Scholarships, NNC Recognition Scholarships, Creative Arts and Performance Awards,

American Legion Awards for Leadership, the Professional Allowance Awards for relatives of clergy, and Nazarene Youth International Awards for drama and debating.

Amount: Various

Description: Nine grant awards were made to minorities in 1993–1994.

Amount: $100–$2,300

Deadline: March 1

Nova University
Fort Lauderdale, FL

Type: Grants/Scholarships/Tuition Vouchers

Description: University offers a number of scholarship and grant awards, some with restrictions. Includes academic, athletic, and need-based award programs such as the Florida Student Assistant Grants; State Tuition Vouchers; NSU Honor Awards; NSU Scholars Awards; and general Financial Aid Grants.

Amount: $500–$2,000

Deadline: April 1

Ohio Wesleyan University
Delaware, OH

Type: Grants/Scholarships

Description: University offers grants and scholarships to students who meet certain criteria. Programs include Wesleyan Scholars Awards, Presidential Scholarships, Faculty and Trustee Scholarships.

Amount: $500–$20,000

Deadline: Various

Oklahoma City University
Oklahoma City, OK

Type: Grants/Scholarships

Description: Provides over 1,600 need- and non-need-based scholarships each year. Academic awards include Freshmen Academic Achievement Awards, Petree Scholarships, and religious leadership awards.

Amount: $25–$12,467

Description: Nearly 800 institutional and departmental awards are available to eligible students.

Amount: Various

Description: More than 150 athletic awards are available in men's baseball, basketball, golf, tennis and soccer, and women's basketball, tennis, soccer, and softball.

Amount: $150–$12,467

Deadline: Various

Pittsburg State University
Pittsburg, KS

Type: Scholarships

Description: Institutional scholarship and grant programs are available for currently enrolled as well as incoming students. Some awards are based entirely on merit.

Amount: $100–$1,500 per year

Description: Presidential Scholarships are awarded on the basis of academic achievement.

Amount: Full tuition and fees, room and board, and books; renewable for three years

Description: University Scholarships awarded on the basis of academics.

Amount: Tuition and fees; renewable for three years

Description: Honors College Community College Transfer Scholarships are for community college transfer students who have a 3.75 grade point average or better and have at least 40 hours completed at the time of application.

Amount: Various; renewable

Description: Ethnic Minority Scholarship provides financial assistance to needy African-Americans and other minorities who have strong academics with a GPA of 3.0, and ACT score of 21 or SAT score of 816, and/or meet a number of other requirements. African-American and female students majoring in engineering technology may qualify for a Female/Minority Engineering Technology or Plastics Technology Scholarship sponsored by Phillips Petroleum. These awards are disseminated by the Engineering Technology department.

Amount: Various

Deadline: March 1

Potsdam College of the State University of New York
Potsdam, NY

Type: Grants/Scholarships

Description: College offers approximately 49 New York State TAP Grants to African-American students each year.

Amount: $100–$2,650

Description: College awards 30 New York State Educational Opportunity Program Grants to eligible students.

Amount: $200–$1,800

Description: Four New York State SUSTA awards are made to African-American students.

Amount: $50–$200

Description: Potsdam Scholarships are awarded to eligible students. 250 awards are made annually.

Amount: $100–$2,000

Description: The college also offers special financial aid opportunities to African-Americans and other minority students through the New York State Educational Opportunity Program (EOP). 30 grants are awarded each year to African-American students through this program.

Amount: $200–$1,800

Deadline: March 1

Providence College
Providence, RI

Type: Grants/Scholarships

Description: Five William & Doris Davis Scholarships are awarded each year.

Amount: Half tuition

Description: Four Margaret Brent-Plona Scholarships are awarded to cover the cost of books.

Amount: $400

Deadline: February 15

Rosemont College
Rosemont, PA

Type: Grants/Scholarships

Description: Up to ten scholarships are awarded annually to academically talented freshmen through the Rosemont Scholars Scholarship. Students must achieve a minimum of 1200 combined score on the SAT, have a B+ average, and graduate in the top 10 percent of their high school class.

Amount:	$1,500–$10,700, up to full tuition

Description: Two Connelly Scholarships are awarded annually to graduates of the Philadelphia Archdiocesan High Schools. They are based on academic excellence and financial need. Candidates must be nominated by a teacher or counselor, rank in the top 20 percent of their class, and have strong SAT scores.

Amount: Full tuition

Description: The McShain Scholarship program awards two scholarships on the basis of academic merit and financial need. Candidates must be in the top two-fifths of their class and have a combined score of at least 1000 on the SAT.

Amount: Full tuition

Description: A number of Trustee Scholarships are awarded to residents of Bucks, Chester, Delaware, Montgomery, or Philadelphia counties. Candidates must rank in the top two-fifths of their class and have a combined score of at least 1000 on the SAT.

Amount: Half tuition

Description: The Alumnae Scholarship provides one new scholarship annually based on academic merit and involvement in extracurricular activities.

Amount: $1,500

Description: One Presidential Scholarship is awarded annually competitively on academic excellence.

Amount: Full tuition

Description: Rosemont Academic Scholarships are offered to students based on academic merit and financial need. Recipients must rank in the top two-fifths of their class and have at least 500 on each section of the SAT.

Amount: Up to half tuition

Description: A limited number of W. W. Smith Scholarships are awarded to candidates in good academic standing with financial need.

Amount: Various

Description: One Sherman Scholarship is awarded to a commuter student based on academic standing and financial need.

Amount: Various

Deadline: March 1

St. John's College
Annapolis, MD

Type: Grants

Description: College offers St. John's Grants and State Grants for students with financial need who meet certain criteria.

Amount: $1,000–$15,000—St. John's Grants
                 $500–$2,500—State Grants

Deadline: March 1

St. John's College—New Mexico
Santa Fe, NM

Type: Grants/Scholarships

Description: The New Mexico Student Choice Grant is also available to students who meet certain criteria.

Amount: Various, average award $4,200 per year

Description: The New Mexico Scholars Program and the New Mexico Scholars/St. John's Match program are available based on a variety of criteria.

Amount: Various, average award $1,800 per year

Description: St. John's College Grants

Amount: $400–$16,000

Description: Endowed Grants

Amount: $400–$10,000 per year

Deadline: March 1

St. John Fisher College
Rochester, NY

Type: Grants/Scholarships

Description: More than 200 awards are made through the President's Scholarship program each year.

Amount: $1,000 to half tuition

Description: Entering students may be eligible to receive one of 600 St. John Fisher Grants.

Amount: $500–$5,000

Description: Each year 30 scholarship awards are made through the Trustee Scholarship program.

Amount: Half to full tuition

Description: African-Americans and other minority students may be eligible to receive one of 20 Cultural Diversity awards made each year.

Amount: Half to full tuition

Description: African-American and other minority students may be eligible to receive an Urban League Scholarship.

Amount: Half to full tuition

Deadline: March 1

St. John's University
Jamaica, NY

Type: Grants/Scholarships

Description: Awards scholarships and grants on the basis of academic achievement. Presidential Scholarships are awarded to entering freshmen with a 95 percent average and a 1200 combined score on the SAT.

Amount: Full tuition, less Tuition Assistance Program award

Description: Scholastic Excellence Scholarships are awarded to entering freshmen with a 92 percent average and an 1100 combined score on the SAT.

Amount: One-half tuition per year

Description: St. Vincent de Paul Scholarships are awarded to entering freshmen not eligible for the Presidential or Scholastic Excellence Scholarships. Students must have an average of at least 85–89 percent with at least an 1100 combined score on the SAT.

Amount: One-quarter tuition

Description: University Transfer Scholarships are awarded to any accepted new transfer student with a transfer index of at least 3.25 based on a minimum of one year or 24 credits of college-level study.

Amount: One-quarter–one-half tuition

Description: Competitive Scholarships are available to high school seniors with an 85 percent average and who take a competitive examination on the campus of St. John's University. The exam is held in the fall. One hundred scholarships are awarded annually through this program.

Amount: $2,500

Deadline: Various

Description: Daniel J. Tracy Scholarship is available to children of New York City firefighters with an 80 percent high school grade point average who compete in an examination. The exam is held in the spring each year in high schools.

Amount: $2,500–full tuition

Deadline: May

Description: African-American Catholic students may be eligible for a scholarship, based on academic achievement and other criteria.

Amount: Full tuition

Deadline: April 1

St. Paul's College
Lawrenceville, VA

Type: Grants/Scholarships

Description: College awards over 300 Virginia State Tuition Assistance Grants, over 70 College Scholarship Assistance Grants, five Presidential Scholarships, and ten Academic Scholarships.

Amount: $200–$1,500

Deadline: April 15

Samford University
Birmingham, AL

Type: Scholarships

Description: Students may qualify for one of 20 Presidential Scholarships available to students with proven leadership skills, a high grade point average (recipients have an average GPA of 4.0 and a 31.5 ACT or 1350 SAT score).

Amount: Various, average $4,000 up to full tuition

Description: National Merit Awards available to finalists.

Amount: Various

Description: Samford Scholarships available to students who meet certain academic criteria.

Amount: Various

Deadline: March 1

San Diego State University
San Diego, CA

Type: Grants/Scholarships

Description: University offers state grant programs including the Cal Grant
                 A, which provides financial assistance to residents who meet
                 the grade point average requirements and have exceptional
                 financial need; the Cal Grant B, which provides financial as-
                 sistance to continuing students who meet grade point aver-
                 age requirements and have financial need.

Amount: $1,196–$4,452

Deadline: March 1

Seattle University
Seattle, WA

Type: Grants/Scholarships

Description: Presidential Scholarships

Amount: $7,200

Description: Trustee Scholarships and Ignatian Scholarships

Amount: $4,200–$5,400

Description: The Seattle University Grant and Educational Opportunity
                 Grants are awarded to students who meet certain criteria.

Amount: $300–$8,000

Description: Seafirst Bank Minority Scholarship awards ten scholarships to
                 full-time juniors who have established financial need and are
                 majoring in the field of business. The scholarship is renewable
                 if the student maintains a 3.33 GPA.

Amount: $1,000

Description: The Robert Truex Scholarship provides funds to minority stu-
                 dents majoring in business. Scholarship is renewable.

Amount: Various

Description: The U.S. Bank Business Scholarship awards ten scholarships
                 annually to minority students in the Albers School of Business
                 and Economics.

Amount: $3,000

Description: KING-5 Television Scholarships provide three annual awards
                 to minorities who are juniors majoring in communications.

Amount: Various

Deadline: February 15

Smith College
Northampton, MA

Type: Grants/Scholarships

Description: College offers over $15.1 million in institutional grants to stu-
                 dents. All aid is need-based and average awards for students
                 nearly match tuition costs. Smith College Trust Grants for
                 Northampton residents are available to all eligible students in-
                 cluding minorities.

Amount: Various

Deadline: January 1

Sonoma State University
Rohnert Park, CA

Type: Grants/Scholarships

Description: California State residents who have demonstrated financial
                 need may qualify for State University Grants, Educational Op-
                 portunity Grants, Cal Grant A and Cal Grant B.

Amount: Various: average University award $960; average Educational
                 Opportunity Grant award $540; average California Grant A
                 award $1,440; California Grant B award $2,820

Deadline: March 2

Description: The SSU Scholarship Program provides approximately 150
                 scholarship awards annually to students who have demon-
                 strated academic excellence. Students with financial need may
                 be considered as well, but some restrictions may apply such as
                 residency or major field of interest. Incoming freshmen as well
                 as undergraduate students are eligible. Students may apply in
                 November of each year, and submit a completed application
                 package by March 1 of the following year. Awards for the suc-
                 ceeding Fall and Spring semesters are announced in June.

Amount: $250–$2,500 per year

Deadline: March 1

Southern Methodist University
Dallas, TX

Type: Grants/Scholarships

Description: Over $8 million in merit and leadership scholarships to stu-
                 dents, including the President's Scholar Award, which is avail-
                 able to 20 entering first-year students to SMU. Recipients must
                 have completed 17 academic units, score 1300 on the SAT or
                 31 on the ACT, be in the top 10 percent of their graduating
                 class and demonstrate leadership ability. Award renewable to
                 students in good standing and who maintain a 3.3 GPA.

Amount: Full tuition and transportation for a semester or full year abroad to one of SMU's International Programs

Deadline: On-campus interview of finalists by faculty committee in March, notification in April

Description: Dean's Scholar Award available to students who score 1300 on the SAT or 31 on the ACT, are in the top 10 percent of their graduating class, and demonstrate leadership potential. Award renewable with students who maintain a 3.3 GPA.

Amount: Half tuition for four years

Deadline: On-campus interview of finalists by faculty committee in March, notification in April

Description: Nancy Ann and Ray L. Hunt Leadership Scholars Program for up to 25 entering first-year students who have demonstrated extraordinary leadership. Students must have completed at least 16 academic units, scored 1100 on the SAT or 28 on the ACT, and been in the top 25 percent of their graduating class. Award is renewable to students who maintain a 3.0 GPA.

Amount: Full tuition and fees and tuition and transportation for a semester or full year abroad to one of SMU's International Programs

Deadline: Applicants must complete and return admission application by January 15, including an additional, separate essay, clearly labeled with student's name and "Hunt," on one of three assigned topics, be an admission recommendation leader, and be interviewed in March. Notification of winners in early April.

Description: Lawrence R. Herkimer–SMU Alumni Scholars offers awards for up to ten first-year students who have demonstrated strong leadership qualities, involvement, and high academic achievement. Recipients must be nominated by an SMU alumnus/ alumna.

Amount: $3,000 annually

Deadline: Nomination form must be completed by December 15, and scholarship application and admission application by January 15. Winners notified in April.

Description: Students with a strong academic background and a well-rounded extracurricular profile may qualify for the University Scholars program.

Amount: $3,000 per year for four years

Description: The Alumni Award annually awards scholarships to students with solid academic achievement records and well-rounded extracurricular profiles.

Amount:	$1,000 for four years

Description: SMU Mothers' Club and Dads' Club Awards provide scholarships in varying numbers and amounts to continuing students who have demonstrated financial need and high academic achievement.

Amount: Various

Description: The University provides a number of full-tuition Diversity Scholarships and Diversity Awards to students who have demonstrated leadership potential and exceptional academic achievement. Diversity Awards are also available to minority students in the middle range of scholastic ability who show a promising academic future. Awards have specific requirements and restrictions depending on the scholarship program.

Amount: $3,000 per year for four years up to full tuition

Description: The University is also a program sponsor of the National Achievement Scholarships for African-American Scholars. Any Achievement Finalist who indicates Southern Methodist University as a first college choice and who satisfies all admission requirements will be considered for a scholarship award.

Amount: Minimum of half tuition

Deadline: February 1

Southern Nazarene University
Bethany, OK

Type: Grants/Scholarships

Description: Nearly 200 Dean's Scholarships are awarded to students who meet academic and other criteria.

Amount: $800

Description: More than 100 Presidential Scholarships are awarded to students for academic achievement.

Amount: $1,600

Description: About 40 Honors Scholarships are available to students each year.

Amount: $3,420–$8,500

Description: Other awards include the Parman Foundation Scholarship, Church Matching Scholarship, District Matching Scholarship, 15 awards from the Oklahoma State Regents and nearly 100 miscellaneous local church scholarships.

Amount: $66–$3,500

Deadline: April 15

Southwestern University
Georgetown, TX

Type: Grants/Scholarships

Description: University awards more than $4 million in grants and scholarships from its own funds, not including federal, state and private scholarship and grant programs. Most aid awarded is based on financial need. Merit scholarships are primarily based on academic achievement.

Amount: $1,000–full tuition

Description: The Presidential Scholarship program awards two entering African-American and two entering Hispanic students with scholarships which are renewable for four years. Recipients must rank in the top 10 percent of their high school graduating class and score 1100 on the SAT or 25 on the ACT.

Amount: Full tuition

Deadline: March 15

Southwest Missouri State University
Springfield, MO

Type: Grants/Scholarships

Description: Alumni Scholarship awards to about 25 entering freshmen who rank in the upper 20 percent of their class, have an ACT score of 23 or above and demonstrate involvement in school and community. Financial need is required.

Amount: $1,550, renewable

Description: Freshmen Regents Scholarship awards to a number of entering freshmen with various levels of academic achievement.

Amount: $1,550, renewable

Description: GED Regents Scholarship is awarded to a number of entering freshmen who are admitted with a minimum GED score of 286.

Amount: $1,550, renewable

Description: Presidential Scholarships awarded to entering freshmen who rank in the top 10 percent of their class and have an ACT score of 30 or above, or an SAT score of 1240, or are National Merit Semifinalists.

Amount: Tuition, room and board, and a $400 University bookstore allowance, renewable

Description: University Scholarship is awarded to entering freshmen who meet the same class rank and test scores for the Presidential Scholarship.

Amount: Tuition and a $400 University bookstore allowance, renewable

Description: African-American and other minority students may be eligible for Minority Leadership Scholarships awarded to entering students who graduate in the upper one-half of their class and demonstrate leadership in the minority community.

Amount: In-state tuition and fees, renewable

Deadline: March 31

Spelman College
Atlanta, GA

Type: Scholarships

Description: In addition to federal and state aid programs, Spelman provides a number of academic scholarships to students each year, as well as Dean's Merit Scholarships, Honors Scholarships, DeWitt Wallace Awards, Presidential Scholarships, and departmental and other institutional awards.

Amount: Various

Deadline: February 1

State University College at Oneonta
Oneonta, NY

Type: Grants/Scholarships

Description: College offers a number of scholarship and grant programs including College Foundation Scholarships which are awarded to incoming students on the basis of academic achievement. Other awards are based on need.

Amount: Up to $1,000 per year, renewable

Description: Alumni Association Centennial Scholarship Endowment awards are awarded to students who have demonstrated strong academic achievement, leadership, and involvement in their school and community.

Amount: Up to $1,000 a year, renewable for four years

Description: Oneonta Scholar Awards are merit-based scholarships and are awarded to students who have demonstrated academic excellence.

Amount: Various, renewable for four years

Description: Presidential Scholarships are awarded to students based on a combination of academic performance and financial need. Students who maintain a B average may be considered for renewal.

Amount: $400 a year, renewable

Description: Alumni Association also funds scholarships and sponsors a number of annual internships.

Amount: Up to $1,000 per year

Description: Oneonta's Student Association also awards scholarships to students who are members of the Student Association.

Amount: Various

Description: Graduates of Alexandria Bay Central School, Lewis, Jefferson, St. Lawrence, and other eligible New York schools may qualify for John N. Conant Scholarships, which award up to the full need of eligible students.

Amount: Various

Description: African-American and other minority students may qualify for Oneonta Minority Honors Scholarships. Students must demonstrate superior academic achievement represented by a B average or better.

Amount: Up to $1,000 per year, renewable

Description: Minority students may also qualify for a Scott-Jenkins Fund Scholarship. Eligible students must be "needy and worthy" and maintain at least a C or better academic record. Students must apply annually to receive the awards.

Amount: Various

Deadline: April 15

Thomas More College
Crestview Hills, KY

Type: Grants/Scholarships

Description: Thomas More Scholarships/Awards are awarded through alumni organizations, endowment funds, and gifts. All eligible students who submit the Thomas More College Application for Scholarships and Financial Aid are considered for all scholarships, grants, and loans.

Amount: Various

Description: Thomas More Academic Scholarships are based upon class rank, grade point average, and ACT/SAT scores.

Amount: $500–full tuition, renewable; must apply each year

Description: Students who have had a high level of involvement in extracurricular activities may qualify for an Outstanding Service Award. Students must complete the Outstanding Service Award Application and submit a résumé with financial aid application.

Amount: $500

Description: Students who present a letter of recommendation from a priest, sister, or brother in the Catholic church may be eligible to receive a Religious Tuition Grant. Letters of recommendation must specifically state "Religious Tuition Grant" and be submitted by the deadline.

Amount: $500

Description: Students who participate in an internationally recognized seminar, "Principle-Centered Leadership for Young Adults," may compete for a renewable Leadership Grant. The program is a three-and-one-half-day on-campus experience available to high school juniors and seniors who demonstrate leadership skills.

Amount: $500

Description: African-American and other minority students may be eligible for a Minority Grant. Recipients must reapply each year.

Amount: $2,500 per year

Deadline: March 1

Towson State University
Towson, MD

Type: Grants/Scholarships

Description: Commonwealth Awards provide funding to eligible students who have attended Baltimore City public schools and participated in the Commonwealth program.

Amount: Full tuition and fees

Description: Helen Aletta Linthicum Scholarships are awarded to selected valedictorians from Maryland's high schools. Award is nonrenewable and can be applied only to the freshman year.

Amount: $1,000

Description: Presidential Scholarships, which provide tuition and fees to recipients, are awarded to entering freshmen who are Maryland residents with 3.50 grade point average and 1200+ score on the SAT.

Amount: Various

Description: Regent's Tuition Grants in various amounts are available to entering freshmen who are Maryland residents with a grade point average of 3.25 and SAT score of 1125 or higher.

Amount: Various

Description: Alumni Distinguished Scholar Award is awarded to a son or daughter of a Towson State University alumnus.

Amount: $1,500

Description: Outstanding Man and Woman Award is annually available to current full-time students with a 3.0 grade point average with at least one year of classes left before graduation.

Amount: $1,000

Description: University offers a number of departmental grants and scholarships—some with academic or residency requirements.

Amount: Various

Description: African-American students may qualify for a Minority Award for Academic Excellence which is available to U.S. minority citizens based on academic achievement and leadership potential.

Amount: $1,000 to full tuition and fees

Description: Residents of Maryland may also qualify for Undergraduate Other Race Grants.

Amount: Various

Description: Grants and scholarships available in various sports include: Richard Bartos Memorial Scholarship Endowment, B. Melvin Cole Endowment, Joe McMullen Athletic Scholarship, Rachuba Enterprises Scholarship Endowment, Carroll Stephen & George Thomas Rankin Endowment on rotating basis with football, men's basketball, and baseball.

Amount: Up to $2,500

Deadline: March 15

Trenton State College
Trenton, NJ

Type: Grants/Scholarships

Description: College participates in all federal and state aid programs and offers private and institutional grants and scholarships including Alumni Scholarships, Distinguished Scholar Supplement Awards, and departmental awards.

Amount: Various

Description: African-American students may qualify for Presidential Scholar awards.

Amount: $3,000

Description: African-Americans and other students may qualify for Trenton State College Scholar awards.

Amount: $1,500

Deadline: May 1

Troy State University
Troy, AL

Type: Scholarships

Description: Students may qualify for one of the Alumni Scholarships awarded to entering freshmen each year. Recipients have a minimum of 23 on the ACT or 1000 on SAT and a grade point average of 3.3.

Amount: One-half of current tuition for four years; seven scholarships awarded

Description: George C. Wallace Excellence in Leadership Scholarship is awarded to a student with 20 ACT or 800 SAT and 3.0 grade point average.

Amount: One-half to full tuition

Description: Chancellor's Awards are made to students with a score of 26 on the ACT or SAT equivalent, and 3.5 grade point average.

Amount: Full tuition

Description: Scholar's Award is made to students with 30+ on the ACT or SAT equivalent, 3.7 grade point average, or National Merit Finalist.

Amount: Full tuition, room and board

Deadline: May 1

United States International University
San Diego, CA

Type: Scholarships

Description: University offers Presidential Scholar award based on outstanding academic achievement.

Amount: $12,000 for four years

Description: University Scholar award is awarded based on scholarly achievement and demonstration of leadership in school and/or community activities.

Amount: $9,600 for four years

Description: USIU Scholarship and Grant awarded annually based on financial need.

Amount: Up to $2,400 per year

Description: ACT Scholarship offers a one-time award to eligible students.

Amount: $1,000

Deadline: January 1

Description: Business and Industry Tuition Assistance program provides assistance to students who meet certain criteria.

Amount: Up to 25 percent of tuition

Deadline: January 1

University of Florida
Gainesville, FL

Type: Scholarships

Description: Alfred I. duPont Scholarship awarded annually to students with demonstrated financial need who show high academic achievement.

Amount: Various, average award $450

Description: James K. Steiner Scholarship awarded annually to an incoming freshman with financial need, good academic background, and a strong interest in service to others.

Amount: $2,500

Description: University of Florida Student Memorial Scholarships awarded annually to undergraduates with a 3.5 or better grade point average with demonstrated financial need.

Amount: $1,000

Description: Honors Minority Undergraduate Transfer Scholarships for African-American Students awarded to entering transfer students with at least a 3.0 grade point average.

Amount: $1,500

Description: Honors Minority Scholarships for African-American Beginning Freshmen awarded for one year only to students with at least a 3.0 high school grade point average.

Amount: $2,000

Description: Presidential Minority Scholarships for African-American Beginning Freshmen awarded to students with at least a 3.0 high school grade point average and a score of 1000 or above on the SAT or 24 or above on the ACT.

Amount:　　　$2,000

Description:　　Howard and Susan Kaskel Minority Scholarships awarded to minority students from South Florida, with priority given to African-American students who are designated finalists in the National Merit Scholarship program.

Amount:　　　$1,000

Deadline:　　　April 15

University of Idaho
Moscow, ID

Type:　　　　Scholarships

Description:　　Private and institutional grants and scholarships are available to students, some with academic and/or residency requirements.

Amount:　　　Various

Deadline:　　　February 15

University of Illinois at Urbana-Champaign
Champaign, IL

Type:　　　　Scholarships

Description:　　University provides numerous grant and scholarship awards through its endowment and other financing programs.

Amount:　　　Various, based on financial need

Description:　　University participates in the Paul Douglas Teachers' Scholarship which provides awards to Illinois residents who graduate in the top 10 percent of their high school class and have high academic achievement.

Amount:　　　$5,000

Deadline:　　　March 15

University of Maryland—College Park
College Park, MD

Type:　　　　Grants/Scholarships

Description:　　Maryland residents may qualify for State programs including Senatorial Scholarships and Delegate Scholarships.

Amount:　　　$200 or more—House of Delegate Scholarships
　　　　　　　$400–$2,000—Senatorial Scholarships

Description: Distinguished Scholars awards
Amount: $3,000

Description: Francis Scott Key Scholarship
Amount: Full tuition, room and board

Description: Honors Scholarships
Amount: $750

Description: Transfer Merit Scholarships
Amount: Full tuition

Description: Full University Scholarship
Amount: Tuition, room and board

Description: Regents Scholarship and National Merit Scholarships
Amount: $750–$2,000

Description: Benjamin Banneker Scholarships
Amount: Full tuition, room and board

Description: Frederick Douglass Grants
Amount: Various, average award $1,500

Description: Presidential Minority Scholarships
Amount: $750–$2,000

Description: Project Excellence Scholarships
Amount: Full tuition, room and board

Description: Departmental awards with various academic or other criteria include the Thiokol Corporation Scholarship Fund for minorities or females, The NUS Corporation Scholarship Fund for African-Americans and/or Hispanics, James A. Yorke Minority Scholarship, Knight-Ridder Minority Public Affairs Assistantship. Outside scholarship resources include the Arizona Daily Star Scholarship for Minorities, Leonard M. Perryman Communications Scholarship for Ethnic Minority Students, Los Angeles Chapter SPJ, SDX Minority Award, National Association of Black Journalists Award, National Newspaper Publishers Association Scholarship Committee Award, Delta Sigma Theta Sorority, Inc., Award.

Amount: Various
Deadline: February 15

University of Miami
Coral Gables, FL

Type:	Scholarships
Description:	Henry King Stanford & Jay F. W. Pearson Scholarships make awards to freshmen and transfer students. Recipients must have excellent academic credentials, follow a college preparatory curriculum in high school, and demonstrate involvement in school and community activities. The scholarships are renewable annually.
Amount:	Up to half tuition
Description:	The Isaac Bashevis Singer Scholarships are the premier and most competitive scholarships awarded to the top 1 percent of enrolled freshmen.
Amount:	Full tuition
Description:	University of Miami Grants are awarded to African-American and other minority students who meet certain criteria.
Amount:	Various
Description:	The John F. Kennedy/Martin Luther King Scholarship makes awards based on demonstrated financial need and academic promise.
Amount:	$1,900
Description:	The Golden Drum/Ronald A. Hammond Scholarship provides awards to exceptionally well-qualified African-American high school seniors.
Amount:	Full tuition scholarship
Deadline:	March 1

University of Missouri—Columbia
Columbia, MO

Type:	Grants/Scholarships
Description:	University awards over 5,000 federal grants each year and more than 2,000 University grants.
Amount:	$200–$1,500
Description:	Thirty Brooks Grants are awarded to minorities each year.
Amount:	$7,000–$12,625
Description:	The African-American Achievement Award provides financial assistance to eligible students.

Amount: $3,000–$9,000

Deadline: March 1

University of Missouri—St. Louis
St. Louis, MO

Type: Grants/Scholarships

Description: University awards over 2,300 federal grants, nearly 100 Missouri Grants, and over 1,000 scholarships from various sources.

Amount: $1,255—Grants
                    $300–$3,000—Scholarships

Description: Minority students receive more than $320,000 in scholarship and grant awards including 35 awards from the Margaret Bush Wilson Scholarship, five awards from the Marian Oldham Scholarship, three Monsanto Scholarship awards, three Mark Twain Scholarships, 15 awards from the Interco Scholarship, four Monxmode Scholarship awards, and 64 awards from the Center for Academic Development.

Amount: $1,500–$6,800

Deadline: April 1

University of Northern Colorado
Greeley, CO

Type: Grants/Scholarships

Description: Colorado Student Grants and Student Incentive Grants

Amount: $800

Description: President's Honor Scholarship for freshmen who are Colorado residents and meet certain academic criteria.

Amount: $1,500

Description: Provost's Scholarship Program for entering freshmen with an ACT score of 24 or SAT score of 950 and 3.0 grade point average or rank in upper one third of their class.

Amount: $500

Description: Nonresident Awards to entering freshmen in top 20 percent of junior class with ACT score of 25 or SAT score of 1000.

Amount: $1,000

Description: Other local scholarship programs include the Macallister Teacher Education Scholarship.

Amount: $2,500

Description: Ledall Scholarships in Business

Amount: $3,000

Description: Project Teacher Find

Amount: $1,000

Description: African-Americans and other minority students may qualify for Colorado Diversity Grants.

Amount: $800

Description: President's Honor Cultural Diversity Scholarships

Amount: $1,500

Description: Presidential Cultural Diversity Transfer Scholarships

Amount: $500

Description: Local scholarships include the UNC-Boettcher Minority Scholarship.

Amount: $2,500

Deadline: March 1

University of Pittsburgh
Pittsburgh, PA

Type: Grants/Scholarships

Description: Chancellor's Scholarships

Amount: Tuition, room and board

Description: University Scholarships

Amount: $500–$6,000

Description: Engineering Honors Scholarships

Amount: $500–$9,000

Description: One Valedictorian Scholarship is awarded each year.

Amount: $500

Deadline: March 1

University of San Diego
San Diego, CA

Type: Scholarships

Description: Trustee Scholarships are available to entering freshmen with a grade point average of at least 3.8 in high school academic subjects and high SAT scores.

Amount: Up to $8,000

Description: Presidential Scholars awards are made to entering freshmen with at least a 3.5 grade point average and strong SAT scores.

Amount: Up to $6,500

Description: Provost Scholars awards are made to underrepresented students of high achievement who have financial need.

Amount: Up to full tuition

Description: Dean's Scholars awards are made to freshmen with at least a 3.4 grade point average and strong SAT scores.

Amount: Up to $5,000

Description: Choral Scholars are selected for awards through the Department of Fine Arts on the basis of an audition.

Amount: Over 50 percent of tuition

Description: University of San Diego Scholarships are awarded to new and continuing students on basis of academics and financial need.

Amount: Up to $5,600

Description: University of San Diego Grants are awarded on the basis of financial need.

Amount: Various

Description: Bishop Manher Catholic Leadership Scholarships are awarded on the basis of financial need, academic performance, and demonstrated leadership ability.

Amount: $200–$3,000 per year

Description: Duchesne Scholarships are offered through the School of Education to ethnic minority students interested in becoming elementary and secondary teachers.

Amount: Up to $3,000

Description: Cal Grants are offered through the State of California to residents who have demonstrated academic achievement and financial need.

Amount: $1,410–$6,660

Description: Cultural Diversity Grants are offered to students with demonstrated financial need whose experience, background, and culture will add diversity to the University environment.

Amount: Up to $2,000 per year

Deadline: February 20

University of Southern Indiana
Evansville, IN

Type: Scholarships

Description: The Scholastic Excellence Award is offered to students in the top 10 percent of their high school graduating class who earn a 3.6 GPA or better. This award is limited to first-time applicants (both freshman and junior college graduates).

Amount: One-half tuition waiver

Description: USI Honors Week Scholarships are available to currently enrolled students in early spring. Contact the school of your major within the University for application information.

Amount: Various

Description: The Herschel Moore Memorial Scholarship is available to an enrolled single African-American woman (preference given to a single parent) who has demonstrated outstanding academic achievement and financial need.

Amount: $1,500, renewable for up to three years

Description: The Rolland M. Eckels Scholarship Award provides an award annually to an outstanding African-American high school senior graduating from Vanderburgh, Gibson, Posey, or Warrick Counties in Indiana.

Amount: $500

Description: The John Edgar George Memorial Scholarship provides an award annually to an outstanding African-American high school senior with a minimum GPA of 2.5 (preference is given to North High School [Indiana] graduates).

Amount: Up to $2,000

Deadline: March 1

Description: USI Foundation Scholarships are awarded annually to graduating high school seniors.

Amount: $400–$1,600

Deadline: Apply through your high school guidance counselor before February 15.

University of Virginia
Charlottesville, VA

Type: Grants/Scholarships

Description: UVA participates in federal and state grant and scholarship programs and offers institutional and private scholarships as well. Over 20 percent of all students on campus receive some type of financial assistance.

Amount: Various

Description: University awards five Jerome Holland Scholarships to out-of-state African-American students. Stipend is renewable. Students are selected on academic achievement and their ability to demonstrate genuine interest in learning.

Amount: $10,000, renewable

Description: 50 University Achievement Awards are granted annually to the top-rated first-year African-American students from the Commonwealth of Virginia. Award is renewable.

Amount: Full tuition and fees, renewable

Description: The School of Engineering and Applied Science offers annual renewable scholarships based on academic excellence and leadership to qualified African-American students both from Virginia and outside the state.

Amount: Various

Deadline: March 1

Vanderbilt University
Nashville, TN

Type: Grants/Scholarships

Description: Nearly 2,000 need-based and 300 non-need-based scholarship and grant funds totaling over $20 million are made available to students annually. These aid programs include Harold S. Vanderbilt Awards, James Stewart awards in engineering, George Peabody scholarships in education, Engineering School Honors Awards, Dean's Select Scholarships in arts and sciences, the Windrow Honor Scholarships, Memphis-Vanderbilt Scholarships, Paul Harrawood Scholarships, National Merit Scholarship awards, and numerous other awards.

Amount: Various

Deadline: February 15

Virginia Polytechnic Institute & State University
Blacksburg, VA

Type: Grants/Scholarships

Description: Presidential Scholarships, the University's most prestigious award. In addition to the scholarship award, recipients are assigned the university president as their faculty adviser. Four awards are made each year.

Amount: Full tuition, room and board, fees, books for four years, and a personal computer

Description: National Merit Scholarships are awarded to up to 75 students. Candidates are National Merit finalists who have named Virginia Tech as their first-choice school.

Amount: $2,000 per year for four years and a personal computer

Description: National Achievement Scholarships, up to 20 awards each year.

Amount: $3,000 for four years and a personal computer

Description: National Achievement Scholarships are awarded to African-American finalists who name Virginia Tech as their first-choice school.

Amount: Various

Description: Alumni Presidential and Distinguished University Scholars awards.

Amount: $3,000 per year for four years

Description: College Scholarships are awarded to 35 freshmen each year.

Amount: $1,000

Deadline: February 15

Washington State University
Pullman, WA

Type: Grants/Scholarships

Description: More than 1,600 state grants are awarded to students who meet criteria such as academic achievement and residency requirements.

Amount: Various, average $975

Description: Alumni Leadership Awards, Glen Terrell Presidential Scholarships, Provost Waivers, and departmental scholarships are available to students who meet certain criteria.

Amount: Various

Description: Refco Minority Scholarships awarded to students who meet certain criteria.

Amount: Full tuition

Deadline: March 1

Wayne State College
Wayne, NE

Type: Grants/Scholarships

Description: College offers need-based, non-need-based, academic and institutional grant and scholarship programs including over 1,600 need-based grants.

Amount: $200–$2,300

Description: College awards more than 400 academic scholarships annually.

Amount: $40–$2,752

Description: College provides students with over 250 Annual and Endowed Foundation Scholarships.

Amount: $60–$2,500

Deadline: May 1

Western Illinois University
Macomb, IL

Type: Grants/Scholarships

Description: University participates in the Paul Douglas Teachers' Scholarship program with eligible students.

Amount: Various, average award $4,167

Description: Illinois State Monetary Award Program (MAP)

Amount: $1,666

Description: National Guard Scholarships

Amount: $1,489

Description: Policemen/Firemen Dependents Scholarships

Amount: $1,757

Description: Merit Recognition Scholarships

Amount: $982

Description: Teacher Shortage Scholarships
Amount: $1,099

Description: Special Education Tuition Waivers
Amount: $2,071

Description: Vocational Rehabilitation Grants
Amount: $1,238

Description: Scholarships for Dependents of POW/MIAs
Amount: $1,554

Description: General Assembly Tuition Waivers
Amount: $1,751

Description: Children & Family Services Tuition Waivers
Amount: $2,374

Description: General Scholarships awards
Amount: Various, average award $1,415

Description: State programs for African-Americans and other minorities include Women & Minorities in Educational Administration awards and Minority Teacher Incentive Grants.
Amount: $1,620–$4,178
Deadline: March 1

Winthrop University
Rock Hill, SC

Type: Grants/Scholarships

Description: Trustee's Scholarships are awarded to students with a minimum SAT of 1300 (ACT of 31) who rank in the top 10 percent of their high school class. Awards are renewable for eight semesters.

Amount: Full tuition, room and board, renewable

Description: The Founder's Scholarship is awarded to students with a minimum SAT of 1300 (ACT 31) who rank in the top 10 percent of their high school class. Awards renewable for eight semesters.

Amount: Full tuition and room, renewable

Description: Winthrop Scholars Award provides scholarship to South Carolina residents who are: top ranked in a South Carolina high

Description:	One-time freshman award of Dean's Merit Scholarship available to students with artistic ability and academic achievement.
Amount:	Up to $1,000
Description:	One-time freshman award of Art/Visual General Scholarship available upon portfolio review. Renewable for up to eight semesters.
Amount:	Up to $1,200, renewable
Description:	Dance General Scholarship available upon an audition. Renewable for up to eight semesters.
Amount:	$500, renewable
Description:	President's Scholar Award available based on academic achievement and student ability to bring a variety of experiences, backgrounds, and cultures to the Winthrop community.
Amount:	Half tuition
Deadline:	May 1

Xavier University
New Orleans, LA

Type:	Grants/Scholarships
Description:	Every student who applies to Xavier is automatically considered for an Xavier University Scholarship based on academic achievement or talent in art, music, and athletics.
Amount:	Various
Description:	Honor Scholarships, Presidential Scholarships, and Trustee Scholarships are awarded to students based on academic and other criteria.
Amount:	Various
Description:	As a member of the United Negro College Fund, Xavier may nominate students for UNCF Scholarships. Students must have a GPA of 3.0 or higher to qualify.
Amount:	Various
Description:	General Motors Scholarships are awarded to minorities and women according to academic ability. Preference is given to dependents of General Motors employees.
Amount:	Various
Description:	Xavier University also participates in the National Merit Achievement Scholarship Program.

school with a minimum SAT of 1100 (ACT of 26); the
African-Americans and other minority graduates with a m
mum SAT of 950 (ACT of 23); Palmetto Fellows; South (
olina National Merit Semifinalists with a minimum SAT
1100 (ACT 26) who rank in the top 25 percent of their hi
school class; South Carolina National Achievement Semifin
ists with a minimum SAT of 950 (ACT 23) who rank in the t
25 percent of their high school class. Other applicants are co
sidered on the basis of their academic record, SAT/AC
scores, and extracurricular activities.

Amount: Full tuition

Description: S.C. Governor's School of Science and Mathematics Scholar
               ships are awarded to graduates of the Governor's School who
               have a minimum SAT of 1100 (ACT of 26). Renewable for
               eight semesters.

Amount: Full tuition, renewable

Description: International Baccalaureate Scholarship candidates must have
               an International Baccalaureate Diploma, minimum SAT of
               1100 (ACT 26), and admission to Winthrop University. Renew-
               able for eight semesters of undergraduate study.

Amount: Full tuition, renewable

Description: President's Scholar Award recipients are selected on the basis
               of their academic accomplishments and ability to bring a varie-
               ty of experiences, backgrounds, and cultures to the Winthrop
               community. Renewable for eight semesters.

Amount: Half tuition, renewable

Description: Alumni Honor Awards made to South Carolina residents with
               a minimum SAT of 1000 (ACT 24) who rank in the top 25 per-
               cent of their high school class.

Amount: Half tuition

Description: Out-of-State Scholars Award available to out-of-state students
               with a minimum SAT of 1000 (ACT 24) who rank in the top 25
               percent of their high school class. Renewable for eight semes-
               ters.

Amount: Out-of-state fees

Description: Teacher Cadet Scholarship available to Teacher Cadet Pro-
               gram participants who demonstrate commitment to teaching,
               leadership, and high academic achievement.

Amount: $1,000

Amount: Various

Deadline: Various

Academic—Religion

Agnes Scott College
Decatur, GA

Type: Scholarships

Description: Agnes Scott participates in the National Presbyterian Scholarship Program, cosponsoring renewable annual awards. Recipients must demonstrate financial need and be Presbyterian Church (U.S.A.) members.

Amount: $1,400

Deadline: December 1

Write: National Presbyterian College Scholarship
                 Presbyterian Church (U.S.A.)
                 Financial Aid for Students
                 Mezzanine, 100 Witherspoon Street
                 Louisville, KY 40202-1396
                 Or
                 Agnes Scott College Office of Financial Aid

Benedictine College
Atchison, KS

Type: Scholarships

Description: Young men interested in further study for Catholic priesthood may qualify for a Priesthood Scholarship as well as a number of Endowed Scholarship programs available through the college. Information about these programs is available through the college financial aid office.

Amount: Varies

Deadline: March 1

Campbellsville College
Campbellsville, KY

Type: Grants/Scholarships

Description: College offers church scholarships to students who meet certain criteria.

Amount: $100–$6,060

Description: African-American Christian Ministry Scholarships are awarded to African-American students who are committed to a Christian ministry vocation. Scholarship may be renewed for up to eight semesters.

Amount: Up to one-half tuition

Deadline: March 1

Centenary College of Louisiana
Shreveport, LA

Type: Scholarships

Description: Church Careers scholarships and Methodist Minister's Dependent scholarships available to students who meet certain criteria.

Amount: $1,000–$1,500

Deadline: March 15

Chapman University
Orange, CA

Type: Scholarships

Description: Students who are members of the Christian Church (Disciplines of Christ) may receive scholarship awards.

Amount: $500–50 percent of tuition

Deadline: March 2

Emory University
Atlanta, GA

Type: Scholarships

Description: Sons or daughters of active United Methodist ministers or missionaries may receive awards through the Methodist Ministerial Scholarship program.

Amount: 45 percent of tuition

Deadline: February 15

Thomas More College
Crestview Hills, KY

Type: Grants/Scholarships

Description: Students who present a letter of recommendation from a priest, sister, or brother in the Catholic church may be eligible to receive a Religious Tuition Grant. Letters of recommendation must specifically state "Religious Tuition Grant" and be submitted by the deadline.

Amount: $500

Deadline: March 1

Athletic

Ashland University
Ashland, OH

Type:	Grants/Scholarships
Description:	Athletic Scholarships are awarded to students with athletic ability in a variety of sports.
Amount:	$500 to full tuition
Deadline:	Various

Austin Peay State University
Clarksville, TN

Type:	Grants/Scholarships
Description:	University offers athletic scholarships in men's basketball, football, baseball, golf, cross-country, tennis and women's basketball, softball, volleyball, cross-country, tennis, cheerleading.
Amount:	$125–$8,900
Deadline:	April 1

Campbellsville College
Campbellsville, KY

Type:	Grants/Scholarships
Description:	College offers awards to athletes in baseball, basketball, cross-country, golf, tennis, swimming, soccer, softball, and volleyball.
Amount:	$400–$9,130
Deadline:	March 1

Chadron State College
Chadron, NE

Type:	Grants/Scholarships
Description:	A number of tuition remission waivers and grants are awarded to men and women participating in college athletics. Information may be obtained by contacting the Director of Athletics. In addition, the college offers a number of individual athletic scholarships for students who meet certain athletic and/or academic criteria.
Amount:	$100–$2,000
Deadline:	Various

Clarion University of Pennsylvania
Clarion, PA

Type: Grants/Scholarships

Description: College offers the Ernest W. Johnson Memorial Baseball Scholarship, which provides an award to a member of the Clarion University baseball team who is a resident of Pennsylvania.

Amount: $700

Description: A Fran Shope Scholarship is awarded to a junior or senior woman who has made outstanding contributions to the school's athletics.

Amount: $300

Description: A George W. Williams Memorial Wrestling Scholarship and W. S. Tippin Scholarships for men and women are available to athletes who compete on intercollegiate teams at Clarion. Contact the athletic department for information.

Amount: Various, average $2,000

Deadline: January 1

Clemson University
Clemson, SC

Type: Grants/Scholarships

Description: Athletic awards are available in basketball, cross-country, swimming and diving, track and field, golf, soccer, football, and volleyball.

Amount: $100–full tuition

Deadline: April 1

Lander University
Greenwood, SC

Type: Grants/Scholarships

Description: College offers more than 60 athletic scholarships, including 13 men's basketball, 11 women's basketball, ten men's tennis, four women's tennis, 11 men's soccer and 15 men's and women's cross-country scholarship awards.

Amount: Men's—$500–$6,300
                 Women's—$500–$5,626

Deadline: January 1

Northeast Missouri State University
Kirksville, MO

Type: Grants/Scholarships

Description: University awards over 20 athletic scholarships in various men's and women's sports.

Amount: $198–$7,416

Deadline: April 1

Oklahoma City University
Oklahoma City, OK

Type: Grants/Scholarships

Description: More than 150 athletic awards are available in men's baseball, basketball, golf, tennis, and soccer; and women's basketball, tennis, soccer, and softball.

Amount: $150–$12,467

Deadline: Various

Providence College
Providence, RI

Type: Grants/Scholarships

Description: The College awards 160 to 180 athletic scholarships annually to all students including African-Americans.

Amount: $1,000–$20,000

Deadline: February 15

St. Paul's College
Lawrenceville, VA

Type: Grants/Scholarships

Description: College offers athletic scholarships, including 8 men's and 3 women's basketball awards, one women's tennis award; 3 softball awards, 2 volleyball awards, and 5 track and field awards.

Amount: $500–$9,371

Deadline: April 15

Seattle University
Seattle, WA

Type: Grants/Scholarships

Description: Athletic Need Grants and Athletic Talent Scholarships are available in various amounts. Athletic Room awards are also available to eligible student athletes in basketball, soccer, and tennis.

Amount:	Various
Deadline:	February 15

Stonehill College
North Easton, MA

Type:	Grants/Scholarships
Description:	College offers basketball scholarships to talented athletes.
Amount:	Up to $18,800, includes tuition, room and board, fees and books
Deadline:	February 15

The Citadel
Charleston, SC

Type:	Grants/Scholarships
Description:	145 scholarships are awarded to eligible athletes in a variety of sports.
Amount:	$500–full tuition
Deadline:	March 15

Towson State University
Towson, MD

Type:	Grants/Scholarships
Description:	Grants and scholarships available in various sports include: Richard Bartos Memorial Scholarship Endowment, B. Melvin Cole Endowment, Joe McMullen Athletic Scholarship, Rachuba Enterprises Scholarship Endowment, Carroll Stephen & George Thomas Rankin Endowment on rotating basis with football, men's basketball, and baseball.
Amount:	Up to $2,500
Deadline:	March 15

University of Missouri—Columbia
Columbia, MO

Type:	Grants/Scholarships
Description:	University awards nearly 200 athletic scholarships in various men's sports including football, basketball, baseball, golf, swimming, track, and wrestling.
Amount:	$500–$11,529
Description:	89 athletic scholarships are also awarded to women in sports including basketball, gymnastics, volleyball, golf, swimming, and track.

Amount: $200–$11,529

Deadline: March 1

University of Missouri—St. Louis
St. Louis, MO

Type: Grants/Scholarships

Description: College offers more than 120 athletic scholarships, including 14 men's and women's basketball, three men's and women's tennis, nine men's soccer and 23 women's soccer, 23 men's baseball, 26 men's golf, 11 men's swimming, nine women's softball, and 11 volleyball scholarship awards.

Amount: $318–$5,493

Deadline: April 1

University of North Dakota
Grand Forks, ND

Type: Scholarships

Description: Athletic scholarships are offered to upperclass-level students (none awarded to freshmen) in men's baseball, football, ice hockey, wrestling, women's softball, swimming, volleyball, and men's and women's basketball, track.

Amount: $150–$8,290

Deadline: April 15

Vanderbilt University
Nashville, TN

Type: Grants/Scholarships

Description: 194 grants/scholarships are awarded to eligible athletes in a variety of sports.

Amount: $500–$22,472

Deadline: February 15

Virginia Polytechnic Institute & State University
Blacksburg, VA

Type: Grants/Scholarships

Description: Athletic scholarships are awarded in a variety of sports based on the regulations of the Metro Conference and the NCAA.

Amount: Up to the cost of attendance

Deadline: February 15

Washington State University
Pullman, WA

Type: Grants/Scholarships

Description: Over 100 scholarships are awarded to women athletes and about 120 scholarships are awarded to men in a variety of sports.

Amount: $500–$12,000

Deadline: March 1

City/County/State

Agnes Scott College
Decatur, GA

Type: Scholarships/Grants

Description: Paul Douglas Teachers' Scholarships are available to Georgia residents planning to teach.

Amount: Up to $5,000

Description: Georgia Tuition Equalization Grants are available to Georgia residents attending eligible private colleges and universities.

Amount: $1,000

Description: Georgia HOPE Grants are awarded to first-year and sophomore residents from the Georgia HOPE (Helping Outstanding Pupils Educationally) Program.

Amount: $500

Description: The Middle Income Assistance Program awards grants on the basis of a combination of admission and financial criteria. The program is designed to help students who do not qualify for significant need-based assistance, but for whom the price of a private higher education is out of reach.

Amount: $3,000–$5,000

Deadline: January 1

Antioch College
Yellow Springs, OH

Type: Grants/Scholarships

Description: Antioch Regional Scholarships are offered to students with academic promise based on residency requirements.

Amount: Up to $3,000

Description:	Mumford/Michigan/Ohio Scholarship for one year only is available to first-year students from Ohio or Michigan with financial need.
Amount:	$1,000
Deadline:	February 15

Appalachian State University
Boone, NC

Type:	Grants/Scholarships
Description:	University offers over 870 North Carolina Need-Based Grants.
Amount:	$100–$500
Description:	More than 115 awards of North Carolina Student Incentive Grants are made to students each year.
Amount:	$100–$2,500
Deadline:	January 1

Benedictine College
Atchison, KS

Type:	Grants/Scholarships
Description:	The State Scholarship Program provides an award to eligible students who were designated as "state scholars." Students must demonstrate financial need and have a 3.0 GPA. The award is renewable.
Amount:	Up to $1,000
Description:	Students may receive assistance through a number of grant and scholarship programs including the Kansas Tuition Grant for state residents. Information about these programs is available through the college financial aid office.
Amount:	Varies
Deadline:	March 1

Bowie State University
Bowie, MD

Type:	Grants/Scholarships
Description:	Maryland residents may be eligible to receive one of nearly 30 State Student Incentive Grants awarded annually to qualified students.
Amount:	$500–$1,000
Description:	More than 330 state scholarships are awarded to students each year, many with residency and academic criteria.

Amount: $300–$1,800

Description: Residents may be eligible to receive one of more than 240 Senatorial scholarships awarded annually.

Amount: $200–$1,200

Deadline: April 1

Campbellsville College
Campbellsville, KY

Type: Grants/Scholarships

Description: College offers Kentucky Tuition Grants to students who meet certain criteria.

Amount: $1,200

Deadline: March 1

Chapman University
Orange, CA

Type: Grants

Description: Residents of California who meet the grade point average requirements and have exceptional financial need may qualify for a Cal Grant A or Cal Grant B, which provides awards to undergraduate freshmen for living costs.

Amount: Up to $4,452—Cal Grant A
                 $1,196—Cal Grant B

Deadline: March 2

Clarion University of Pennsylvania
Clarion, PA

Type: Grants/Scholarships

Description: Mary/Martha Colegrove Educational Foundation Scholarship awards two women from McKean County attending Clarion University. The award is renewable if student remains in attendance and maintains a GPA of 3.0. Contact the Dean of Enrollment Management and Academic Records or McKean County High Schools guidance counselors.

Amount: $3,500, renewable

Description: State Board of Governors Scholarship awards are made each semester to minority students. Candidates must possess a minimum 3.0 GPA. This tuition-based scholarship may vary in amount depending on the student's need. Applications may be obtained in the Admissions Office.

Amount: Various

Description: College offers the Ernest W. Johnson Memorial Baseball Scholarship, which provides an award to a member of the Clarion University baseball team who is a resident of Pennsylvania.

Amount: $700

Deadline: January 1

Denison University
Granville, OH

Type: Grants/Scholarships

Description: Faculty Scholarships for Achievement are awarded to the valedictorian or salutatorian from an Ohio high school. Up to 35 are awarded each year.

Amount: Full tuition

Description: Ohio Instructional Grants and Ohio Student Choice Grants for Ohio residents.

Amount: $588–$3,463

Description: I Know I Can Scholarships are available to graduates of a Columbus, Ohio, public high school.

Amount: $1,500

Deadline: April 1

East Carolina University
Greenville, NC

Type: Grants/Scholarships

Description: African-American students and other minority students may qualify for Minority Presence Grants for North Carolina residents.

Amount: $1,500 per year for four years

Deadline: April 15

Eastern New Mexico University
Portales, NM

Type: Scholarships

Description: ENMU offers a number of academic scholarships for residents and nonresidents. Students are automatically considered for these awards upon admission to the University. Resident awards include: Honors Scholarships, New Mexico Scholars, Presidential Academic Scholarships, Silver Scholarships, Zia Scholarships, 4.0 Scholarships. Awards are based on academic and other criteria.

Amount: Various, average award $500

Description: Dollar Rent-a-Car Endowed Scholarship awarded to a graduate
                      of a Roosevelt County high school majoring in business
                      administration. Preference given to students with strong aca-
                      demic records (approximately 3.0 GPA) who have financial
                      need.

Amount: $500

Deadline: March 1

Eckerd College
St. Petersburg, FL

Type: Grants/Scholarships

Description: Florida residents may qualify for Florida Student Assistance
                      Grants, Florida Tuition Vouchers for up to $1,100, Florida
                      Undergraduate Scholars Fund, and the Florida Work Experi-
                      ence Program.

Amount: $1,100–$2,500

Deadline: March 1

Emory University
Atlanta, GA

Type: Grants

Description: Georgia residents who demonstrate financial need may qual-
                      ify for Student Incentive Grants and/or Georgia Tuition
                      Equalization Grants (GTEG), which are awarded to eligible
                      residents regardless of need.

Amount: Various

Deadline: February 15

Florida A&M University
Tallahassee, FL

Type: Scholarships

Description: Florida Student Assistance Grants available to residents who
                      meet certain criteria.

Amount: $200–$1,200

Description: Florida Undergraduate Scholars' Fund offers merit scholar-
                      ships to state residents. The scholarship was created to encour-
                      age Florida's outstanding high school graduates to attend
                      Florida's postsecondary institutions.

Amount: $1,000–$2,500 per academic year; renewable up to four years

Deadline: April 1

Hamline University
St. Paul, MN

Type: Grants/Scholarships

Description: Minnesota State Grants are awarded to students based on need and residency.

Amount: $5,000

Description: Minority Education Project (MEP) awards to students who reside in St. Paul, Minnesota, based on need.

Amount: Up to $5,000

Deadline: March 15

Howard University
Washington, D.C.

Type: Grants

Description: Howard provides State grants to eligible students with demonstrated financial need.

Amount: $200–$2,400 per year

Deadline: April 1

Kent State University
Kent, OH

Type: Grants/Scholarships

Description: Scholarships for Excellence are awarded to incoming freshmen, valedictorians of an Ohio high school; academics are also considered.

Amount: $1,000

Deadline: Various

Description: University Scholarships are awarded to Ohio residents based on academic record and SAT or ACT scores.

Amount: $500

Deadline: February 15

Description: President's Grants are available to incoming freshmen, children of Kent alumni, and non-Ohio residents.

Amount: $3,740

Deadline: April 1

Description: Ohio Instructional Grants are offered to residents with demonstrated financial need.

Amount: $228–$1,392

Loras College
Dubuque, IA

Type: Grants

Description: Iowa Tuition Grants are available to residents who attend state colleges and universities.

Amount: The maximum grant is $2,650

Description: Iowa Grants are awarded to residents on the basis of financial need.

Amount: $1,000

Description: State of Iowa Scholarships may be awarded to students with high academic potential.

Amount: $100–$400

Deadline: April 15

Lynn University
Boca Raton, FL

Type: Tuition Vouchers/Grants/Scholarships

Description: Dependent students whose parents are residents of Florida or independent students who are residents may qualify for Florida Tuition Vouchers from the State of Florida.

Amount: Up to $950 per year

Description: Students with financial need may also qualify for a University Grant or State Grant.

Amount: Various

Description: Students may qualify for Florida Student Assistance Grants and other institutional grant and scholarship programs. Residency and other criteria may apply.

Amount: Various

Deadline: February 15

Marietta College
Marietta, OH

Type: Grants/Scholarships

Description: Marietta also offers numerous endowments and other awards to eligible students, including the Ohio Academic Scholars Program, which awards one scholarship to each high school in Ohio.

Amount: $1,000

Description: The Ohio Student Choice Grant (OSCG) provides grants to Ohio residents.

Amount: Various

Description: The Ohio Instructional Grant (OIG) provides grants to residents whose family income does not exceed $27,000.

Amount: Various

Deadline: March 1

Minneapolis College of Art and Design
Minneapolis, MN

Type: Grants/Scholarships

Description: State residents with demonstrated financial need may qualify for Minnesota State Grants.

Amount: $100–$5,464

Deadline: April 1

Morehouse College
Atlanta, GA

Type: Grants/Scholarships

Description: Georgia residents may qualify for Georgia Incentive Scholarships and/or Georgia Tuition Equalization Grants.

Amount: Various

Deadline: February 15

Northwestern College
St. Paul, MN

Type: Grants/Scholarships

Description: State residents may qualify for Minnesota State Grants.

Amount: $100–$5,889

Deadline: April 1

Nova University
Fort Lauderdale, FL

Type: Grants/Tuition Vouchers

Description: Florida Student Assistant Grants and State Tuition Vouchers are available to Florida residents.

Amount: Grants—$1,020
Tuition Vouchers—$1,090

Deadline: April 1

Purchase College of the State of New York
Purchase, NY

Type:	Grants/Scholarships
Description:	A quarter of a million dollars is given annually to students for scholarships with amounts varying depending on the program and its eligibility requirements. The Tuition Assistance Program (TAP) provides awards to state residents.
Amount:	Up to $2,600 per year
Description:	The Economic Opportunity Program provides awards to residents of New York State.
Amount:	Up to $1,250 per year
Description:	Residents may also receive a grant through the SUNY Tuition Assistance program.
Amount:	$200 per year
Type:	Work aid
Description:	Residents may also be eligible for assistance through the Aid for Part-Time Study program.
Amount:	Various
Deadline:	February 15

Rosemont College
Rosemont, PA

Type:	Grants/Scholarships
Description:	Two Connelly Scholarships are awarded annually to graduates of the Philadelphia Archdiocesan High Schools. They are based on academic excellence and financial need. Candidates must be nominated by a teacher or counselor, rank in the top 20 percent of their class, and have strong SAT scores.
Amount:	Full tuition
Description:	A number of Trustee Scholarships are awarded to residents of Bucks, Chester, Delaware, Montgomery, or Philadelphia counties. Candidates must rank in the top two-fifths of their class and have a combined score of at least 1000 on the SAT.
Amount:	Half tuition
Description:	One Sherman Scholarship is awarded to a commuter student based on academic standing and financial need.
Amount:	Various

Description: Several Community and Junior College Scholarships are awarded to highly qualified graduates of surrounding area junior and community colleges.

Amount: Various

Deadline: March 1

St. John's University
Jamaica, NY

Type: Grants/Scholarships

Description: Daniel J. Tracy Scholarship is available to children of New York City firefighters. Candidates with a high school grade point average in the top 80 percentile and who compete in an examination may qualify. The exam is held in the spring each year in high schools.

Amount: $2,500–full tuition

Deadline: May

St. Mary's College
St. Mary's City, MD

Type: Grants/Scholarships

Description: College offers state grants and scholarships to Maryland residents.

Amount: $500–$2,100

Deadline: March 1

St. Paul's College
Lawrenceville, VA

Type: Grants/Scholarships

Description: College awards over three hundred Virginia State Tuition Assistance Grants, over seventy College Scholarship Assistance Grants, five Presidential Scholarships, and ten Academic Scholarships.

Amount: $200–$1,500

Deadline: April 15

San Diego State University
San Diego, CA

Type: Grants/Scholarships

Description: University offers state grant programs including the Cal Grant A, which is available to residents who meet grade point average requirements and have exceptional financial need; the Cal Grant B, which provides financial assistance to continuing students who meet grade point average requirements and have financial need.

Amount: $1,196–$4,452

Deadline: March 1

Sarah Lawrence College
Bronxville, NY

Type: Grants/Scholarships

Description: Scholarship and grant opportunities for minority students include Sarah Lawrence Gifts, Supplemental Grants, State Grant programs, and various other public and private grant awards.

Amount: Various

Deadline: February 1

Seattle University
Seattle, WA

Type: Grants/Scholarships

Description: Students may qualify for grants including the Washington State Need Grant.

Amount: $300–$2,625

Description: The Regents' Scholarship and the Central Area Scholarship programs providing scholarships for 11 students from Seattle's central area are two of a number of scholarships the University has available for ethnic American students.

Amount: $2,000

Deadline: February 15

Sonoma State University
Rohnert Park, CA

Type: Grants/Scholarships

Description: California State residents who have demonstrated financial need may qualify for State University Grants, Educational Opportunity Grants, Cal Grant A and Cal Grant B.

Amount: $540–$2,820 each year

Deadline: March 2

Description: The SSU Scholarship Program provides approximately 150 scholarship awards to students who have demonstrated academic excellence. Students with financial need may be considered as well but some restrictions may apply such as residency, or major field of interest. Incoming freshmen and undergraduates are eligible.

Amount: $250–$2,000 annually

Deadline: Students may apply in November of each year, and submit a completed application package by March 1 of the following year. Awards for the succeeding Fall and Spring semesters are announced in June.

Write: For information and an application contact: Sonoma State University, Scholarship Office, Rohnert Park, CA 94928; or call the Scholarship Coordinator at 707-664-2261.

Southern Nazarene University
Bethany, OK

Type: Grants/Scholarships

Description: Oklahoma Tuition Aid Grants provide awards to students who meet need, residency, and other criteria.

Amount: $1,000

Description: Other awards include the Parman Foundation Scholarship, Church Matching Scholarship, District Matching Scholarship, 15 awards from the Oklahoma State Regents, and nearly 100 miscellaneous local church scholarships.

Amount: $66–$3,500

Deadline: April 15

Stanford University
Stanford, CA

Type: Grants/Scholarships

Description: California residents may qualify for Cal Grant A and Cal Grant B awards.

Amount: $600–$5,250

Deadline: February 1

State University College at Oneonta
Oneonta, NY

Type: Grants/Scholarships

Description: Graduates of Alexandria Bay Central School, Lewis, Jefferson, St. Lawrence, and other eligible New York schools may qualify for John N. Conant Scholarships, which award up to the full need of eligible students. Contact the financial aid office for more details.

Amount: Various

Deadline: April 15

Stonehill College
North Easton, MA

Type:	Grants/Scholarships
Description:	Stonehill Scholarship awards are available to students who meet certain criteria.
Amount:	$1,500–$12,170 (full tuition)
Description:	State Scholarships
Amount:	$300–$2,500
Deadline:	February 15

Syracuse University
Syracuse, NY

Type:	Grants/Scholarships
Description:	New York State Tuition Assistance program awards are available to students who qualify.
Amount:	Various, average award $2,500
Deadline:	March 1

Towson State University
Towson, MD

Type:	Grants/Scholarships
Description:	Commonwealth Awards provide funding to eligible students who have attended Baltimore City public schools and participated in the Commonwealth program.
Amount:	Full tuition and fees
Description:	Helen Aletta Linthicum Scholarships are awarded to selected valedictorians from Maryland's high schools. Award is nonrenewable and can be applied only to the freshman year.
Amount:	$1,000
Description:	Presidential Scholarships, which provide tuition and fees to recipients, are awarded to entering freshmen who are Maryland residents with 3.50 grade point average and 1200+ score on the SAT.
Amount:	Various
Description:	Regent's Tuition Grants in various amounts are available to entering freshmen who are Maryland residents with a grade point average of 3.25 and SAT score of 1125 or higher.
Amount:	Various

Description: University offers a number of departmental grants and scholar-
                    ships—some with academic or residency requirements.

Amount: Various

Description: Residents of Maryland may also qualify for Undergraduate
                    Other Race Grants.

Amount: Various

Deadline: March 15

University of Illinois at Urbana-Champaign
Champaign, IL

Type: Scholarships

Description: Monetary Award Program for Illinois residents.

Amount: $400–$3,325

Description: University participates in the National Action Council for Mi-
                    norities in Engineering, which provides scholarship awards to
                    eligible students.

Amount: $250–$1,000

Description: University participates in the Paul Douglas Teachers' Scholar-
                    ship, which provides awards to Illinois residents who graduate
                    in the top 10 percent of their high school class and have high
                    academic achievement.

Amount: $5,000

Description: Minority students interested in pursuing a teaching career may
                    also receive funds through the Minority Teachers Scholarship
                    program. Applicants must be Illinois residents.

Amount: Up to $5,000

Deadline: March 15

University of Maryland—College Park
College Park, MD

Type: Grants/Scholarships

Description: Maryland residents may qualify for State programs including
                    Senatorial Scholarships and Delegate Scholarships.

Amount: $200 or more—House of Delegates Scholarships
                    $400–$2,000—Senatorial Scholarships

Deadline: February 15

University of San Diego
San Diego, CA

Type: Scholarships

Description: Cal Grants are offered through the State of California to residents who have demonstrated academic achievement and financial need.

Amount: $1,410–$6,660

Deadline: February 20

University of Southern Indiana
Evansville, IN

Type: Scholarships

Description: The Rolland M. Eckels Scholarship Award provides an award annually to an outstanding African-American high school senior graduating from Vanderburgh, Gibson, Posey, or Warrick counties in Indiana.

Amount: $500

Description: The John Edgar George Memorial Scholarship provides an award annually to an outstanding African-American high school senior with a minimum GPA of 2.5 (preference is given to North High School [Indiana] graduates).

Amount: Up to $2,000

Deadline: March 1

University of Virginia
Charlottesville, VA

Type: Grants/Scholarships

Description: 50 University Achievement Awards are granted annually to the top-rated first-year African-American students from the Commonwealth of Virginia. Award is renewable.

Amount: Full tuition and fees, renewable

Description: The School of Engineering and Applied Science offers annual renewable scholarships based on academic excellence and leadership to qualified African-American students both from Virginia and outside the state.

Amount: Various

Deadline: March 1

University of Wisconsin—Whitewater
Whitewater, WI

Type: Grants/Scholarships

Description: Wisconsin Higher Educational Grants are available to Wisconsin residents.

Amount: Up to $1,350

Description: Wisconsin Talent Incentive Program provides awards to Wisconsin resident students in extreme financial need who meet specific requirements.

Amount: Up to $1,800

Description: Nonresidential Tuition Remission Grants are available to out-of-state students who demonstrate financial need and high academic achievement.

Amount: Various

Description: African-Americans may qualify to receive a Lawton Undergraduate Minority Retention Grant for Wisconsin residents.

Amount: $100–$2,100

Deadline: April 15

Virginia Polytechnic Institute & State University
Blacksburg, VA

Type: Grants/Scholarships

Description: Virginia residents may qualify for other aid programs including College Scholarship Assistance for students with high levels of demonstrated financial need.

Amount: Up to $2,000

Description: Virginia Tech Grants are awarded to Virginia residents with demonstrated financial need.

Amount: Up to $2,000

Description: Virginia Scholars Program provides merit-based scholarships to Virginia residents.

Amount: $3,000 per year

Deadline: February 15

Washington State University
Pullman, WA

Type: Grants/Scholarships

Description: More than 1,600 state grants are awarded to students who meet criteria such as academic achievement and residency requirements.

Amount: Various, average $975

Deadline: March 1

Type: Scholarship Service/Support Services

Description: College Knowledge for the Mind (CKM) multicultural program targets middle and high school students and their parents to encourage higher education among minority students.

Wells College
Aurora, NY

Type: Grants/Scholarships

Description: College offers, among other programs, New York State (TAP) Grants.

Amount: $100–$4,050

Deadline: February 15

Winthrop University
Rock Hill, SC

Type: Grants/Scholarships

Description: Winthrop Scholars Award provides scholarships to South Carolina residents who are: top ranked in a South Carolina high school with a minimum SAT of 1100 (ACT of 26); the top African-Americans and other minority graduates with a minimum SAT of 950 (ACT of 23); Palmetto Fellows; South Carolina National Merit Semifinalists with a minimum SAT of 1100 (ACT 26) who rank in the top 25 percent of their high school class; or South Carolina National Achievement Semifinalists with a minimum SAT of 950 (ACT 23) who rank in the top 25 percent of their high school class. Other applicants are considered on the basis of their academic record, SAT/ACT scores, and extracurricular activities.

Amount: Full tuition

Description: Alumni Honor Awards made to South Carolina residents with a minimum SAT of 1000 (ACT 24) who rank in the top 25 percent of their high school class.

Amount: Half tuition

Description: Out-of-State Scholars Award available to out-of-state students with a minimum SAT of 1000 (ACT 24) who rank in the top 25 percent of their high school class. Renewable for eight semesters.

Amount: Out-of-state fees

Deadline: May 1

General

Adrian College
Adrian, MI

Type: Grants/Scholarships

Description: College offers several scholarship and grant programs, including the Michigan State Scholarship.

Amount: Up to $1,900

Description: Adrian Academic Scholarship, for students who meet certain requirements.

Amount: Up to $8,000

Description: The Adrian Grant provides awards to students who meet certain requirements.

Amount: Up to $10,000

Description: Leadership Scholarships are available to students who demonstrate leadership in the area of diversity, multiculturalism, and civil rights.

Amount: 75 percent of tuition paid or $1,000 annually, renewable

Deadline: March 15

Antioch College
Yellow Springs, OH

Type: Grants/Scholarships

Description: College offers numerous grants and scholarships, including Antioch Grants, which supplement other financial aid and are based upon need.

Amount: Various

Description: Horace Mann Presidential Scholarships are awarded to first-year students with academic promise and commitment to humanitarian values such as peace, civil rights, or environmental issues.

Amount: $5,000

Description: Arthur Morgan Public Service Scholarships are awarded to first-year students with academic promise and interest in public/community service.

Amount: $5,000

Description: Dean's Scholarships are available to students who have demonstrated academic abilities.

Amount: Up to $3,000

Description: Dean Philip Nash Scholarships are available to all first-year students with strong academic promise and financial need.

Amount: $1,250

Description: Dorothy E. Mooney Scholarships for one year only are open to all first-year students with strong academic promise and financial need.

Amount: $2,500

Description: Antioch Regional Scholarships are offered to students with academic promise based on residency requirements.

Amount: Up to $3,000

Description: Hughes Science Scholarships are offered to new students with financial need pursuing studies in the biological, biomedical or related sciences.

Amount: Up to $8,000

Description: J. D. Dawson Science Scholarships are available to first-year students in the sciences.

Amount: $5,000

Description: Evan Spalt Scholarships for Science and Math are awarded to first-year students in math and the sciences.

Amount: $2,000

Description: Beatrice Kotas Social Service/Work Scholarships are available to first-year students interested in a career in social work or social services.

Amount: $1,000

Description: Foreign Exchange Student Scholarships are open to first-year students who have spent time living and/or working abroad in an American Field Service or other foreign student exchange program.

Amount: Up to $3,000

Description:	International Student Scholarships are available to first-year foreign students with excellent academics.
Amount:	Up to $3,000

Description:	J. B. Tripp Humanities Scholarships for one year only are open to first-year humanities students.
Amount:	$1,250

Description:	Mumford/Michigan/Ohio Scholarships for one year only available to first-year students from Ohio or Michigan with financial need.
Amount:	$1,000

Description:	Alfred Hampton Memorial Scholarships are available to first-year African-Americans and other minority students with strong academics.
Amount:	Up to $5,000

Description:	E. Y. "Yip" Harburg Scholarships for African-American Men are available to male African-American students who show evidence of social concern, and have graduated from high school with at least a C average.
Amount:	$1,500

Description:	Upward Bound Scholarships are available to students who have participated in an Upward Bound–type program.
Amount:	Up to $3,000

Description:	Paula Carlson Scholarships are available to first-year female students.
Amount:	$2,000
Deadline:	February 15

Appalachian State University
Boone, NC

Type:	Grants/Scholarships
Description:	University offers over 870 North Carolina Need-Based Grants.
Amount:	$100–$500

Description:	More than 115 awards of North Carolina Student Incentive Grants are made to students each year.
Amount:	$100–$2,500

Description: More than 85 Chancellor's Scholarships are awarded to students annually.

Amount: $3,500

Description: 50 Academic Scholarships are awarded to students who meet certain academic and other requirements.

Amount: $100–$2,100

Description: 53 North Carolina Minority Presence Grants are awarded to eligible African-Americans and other minority students.

Amount: $100–$1,500

Description: 34 African-American Scholarships are awarded to eligible students each year.

Amount: $100–$1,000

Description: The College of Business awards three African-American Scholarships each year.

Amount: $100–$1,000

Deadline: January 1

Ashland University
Ashland, OH

Type: Grants/Scholarships

Description: University offers more than 2,000 need- and non-need-based scholarships, including the Presidential Award.

Amount: $2,000–$6,000

Description: The Achievement Scholarships.

Amount: $800

Description: The Ashbrook Scholarships.

Amount: $2,000

Description: Talent Scholarships are awarded to students who demonstrate talent in selected fields.

Amount: $500–$4,000

Description: Ashland University Scholar Awards provide awards to students who meet certain criteria.

Amount: $500–$12,000

Description: Athletic Scholarships are awarded to students with athletic ability in a variety of sports.

Amount: $500 to full tuition

Description: The University offers financial support to African-American students and other minorities through several programs including the Society Scholarship, National City Bank Scholarship, and the Hearst Scholarship programs.

Amount: $500–$3,375

Deadline: Various

Austin Peay State University
Clarksville, TN

Type: Grants/Scholarships

Description: University offers several academic scholarships, including Academic Honors.

Amount: Up to $2,000 annually

Description: The Presidential Scholarship

Amount: $1,000 annually

Description: The Martin Luther King Scholarship

Amount: $2,000

Description: Community College Honors

Amount: Up to $2,000 annually

Description: The President's Community College award and the Emory and Martha Beaumont Kimbrough Scholarship.

Amount: Various, average $1,600

Description: The College also offers the President's Emerging Leaders Program (PELP). For information, call Director, Emerging Leaders Program, 615-648-7876.

Amount: $1,500

Description: The Center for Creative Arts awards scholarships in disciplines including art, music, speech, communication & theatre, creative writing, and various athletic, department, private and military scholarships and grants.

Amount: Various

Description: Martin Luther King, MAAPS Multicultural Scholarship awards.

Amount: $500–$2,000

Description: University offers athletic scholarships in men's basketball, football, baseball, golf, cross-country, tennis and women's basketball, softball, volleyball, cross-country, tennis, cheerleading.

Amount: $125–$8,900

Description: The Delta Sigma Theta awards four annual awards to African-American students.

Amount: $200–$500

Description: The Alpha Kappa Alpha makes six annual awards to African-American students.

Amount: $500–$1,200

Deadline: April 1

Barber-Scotia College
Concord, NC

Type: Grants/Scholarships

Description: University offers over 400 grant and scholarship awards each year including federal, state, and private awards.

Amount: $4,000–$7,000

Deadline: April 15

Bard College
Annandale, NY

Type: Scholarships

Description: The College awards 500 Bard Scholarships each year based on a variety of criteria.

Amount: $500–$17,000

Description: Students who meet academic and other criteria may qualify for one of 160 Excellence and Equal Cost merit scholarships awarded each year.

Amount: $13,624–$25,970

Description: Students who excel academically in the sciences and are interested in continuing their studies in the science field may be eligible for one of 35 merit awards through the Distinguished Scientists program.

Amount: $19,624

Deadline: March 15

Bates College
Lewiston, ME

Type: Grants/Scholarships

Description: There are over 400 endowed scholarship funds at Bates, from
                 which grants are awarded annually to needy students. The ac-
                 tual amount of scholarship awarded depends upon the stu-
                 dent's demonstrated financial need.

Amount: $500–$22,400

Description: Bates appoints several African-American students each year to
                 be Mays Scholars. The program is named in honor of Dr. Ben-
                 jamin E. Mays, a 1920 alumnus of Bates who later served as
                 President of Morehouse College for more than 20 years. Mays
                 Scholars are selected on the basis of scholarship, leadership,
                 and character.

Amount: Various

Description: The Admissions and Financial Aid Offices at Bates work to-
                 gether to ensure that eligible African-Americans and other
                 multicultural students receive financial aid packages which will
                 meet their needs.

Amount: Various

Deadline: February 11

Bemidji State University
Bemidji, MN

Type: Grants/Scholarships

Description: College offers over $7.2 million in need- and non-need-based
                 awards, including: Presidential Scholarships, Faculty Scholar-
                 ships, Troppman Scholarships, Alumni Scholarships, Hartz
                 Foundation Awards, University Honor Scholarships, Naylor
                 Scholarships, Patterson Memorial Awards, McMahon Schol-
                 arships in Journalism, Calder Scholarships in Business, Otter-
                 tail Power Company Scholarships, Minority Scholarships, and
                 other awards.

Amount: Various

Deadline: May 15

Berea College
Berea, KY

Type: Grants/Scholarships

Description: Berea is committed to providing a high-quality education at a
                 low cost. Students admitted to Berea pay no tuition from their
                 own resources. And since financial need is a requirement for
                 admission, the college provides what is needed to meet basic

costs. Grants and scholarships are also available from a variety of sources including private, public, and institutional programs.

Students and their families are, however, expected to contribute toward the cost of room, board, and fees. But if they cannot pay these expenses, financial aid is available to help meet these costs. Students are also required to help themselves by earning at least $700 from summer savings in a college work program and all freshmen work a minimum of ten hours per week in Berea's Labor Program. Funds from these efforts can be applied toward college costs.

Amount: Various

Deadline: May

Bethany College
Bethany, WV

Type: Grants/Scholarships

Description: College offers Academic Scholarships to students who meet academic and other criteria.

Amount: $1,000–full tuition

Description: Leadership Awards are available to students who meet academic and other criteria.

Amount: $1,000–$4,000

Description: Disciples Awards and Bethany Grants are available to all eligible students.

Amount: $500–$9,000

Description: African-American students may qualify for Multicultural Awards.

Amount: $1,000–$3,000

Deadline: March 15

Bowdoin College
Brunswick, ME

Type: Grants/Scholarships

Description: All financial aid at Bowdoin is need-based and relies on Institutional Methodology. The College offers a number of federal, state, private, and institutional scholarships and grants.

Amount: Various

Type: Loan

Description: Russwurm Scholars, named for journalist and publisher John Brown Russwurm, an alumnus of Bowdoin. The program provides loans to selected African-American students.

Amount: $500

Deadline: March 1

Bowie State University
Bowie, MD

Type: Grants/Scholarships

Description: Maryland residents may be eligible to receive one of nearly 30 State Student Incentive Grants awarded annually to qualified students.

Amount: $500–$1,000

Description: More than 330 state scholarships are awarded to students each year, many with residency and academic criteria.

Amount: $300–$1,800

Description: Residents may be eligible to receive one of more than 240 Senatorial scholarships awarded annually.

Amount: $200–$1,200

Description: African-Americans and other minority students may be eligible for one of more than 45 High Ability Scholarships. Awards based on academic achievement and other criteria.

Amount: Tuition and fees

Description: African-Americans and other minority students may be eligible for one of more than 45 private scholarships offered by the University, some with academic and other criteria.

Amount: $250–$2,000

Deadline: April 1

Bucknell University
Lewisburg, PA

Type: Grants/Scholarships

Description: Bucknell offers more than $17 million in aid to students. More than $10 million of that amount consists of scholarships and grants. Priority is often given to African-Americans and other minority students in extending financial aid. Twenty-five percent of the university financial aid budget is directed toward underrepresented minorities at Bucknell.

Amount: Various

Deadline: February 1

Campbellsville College
Campbellsville, KY

Type: Grants/Scholarships

Description: College offers Kentucky Tuition Grants to students who meet certain criteria.

Amount: $1,200

Description: College offers academic scholarships to students who meet certain academic requirements.

Amount: $500–$9,130

Description: College offers church scholarships to students who meet certain criteria.

Amount: $100–$6,060

Description: African-American Christian Ministry Scholarships are awarded to African-American students who are committed to a Christian ministry vocation. Scholarship may be renewed for up to eight semesters.

Amount: Up to one-half tuition

Description: College offers awards to athletes in baseball, basketball, cross-country, golf, tennis, swimming, soccer, softball, and volleyball.

Amount: $400–$9,130

Deadline: March 1

Central Connecticut State University
New Britain, CT

Type: Grants/Scholarships

Description: University offers Connecticut State and University Grants, also Honors Scholarships, and Central Connecticut State University Foundation Scholarships.

Amount: State Grants—$1,500
               University Grants—$200–$10,000
               Scholarships—Varies

Deadline: February 15

Chadron State College
Chadron, NE

Type: Grants/Scholarships

Description: College participates in federal and state aid programs and offers numerous institutional scholarships and grants, many of which have residency or academic criteria. Programs include Board of Trustees Scholarships, which provide scholarships for students graduating from Nebraska high schools.

Amount: Full tuition, renewable

Description: Numerous scholarships are available from the Elizabeth and Bertha Braddock Memorial Scholarship program. Students are selected on the basis of academics, activities, and character.

Amount: $500–$1,000

Description: The college also offers a number of departmental scholarships and awards in various major fields of interest.

Amount: Various

Description: African-American students may qualify for BIA Grants.

Amount: $600–$3,000

Description: A number of tuition remission waivers and grants are awarded to men and women participating in college athletics. Information may be obtained by contacting the Director of Athletics. In addition, the college offers a number of individual athletic scholarships for students who meet certain athletic and/or academic criteria.

Amount: $100–$2,000

Type: Tuition waivers

Description: First-time freshmen may qualify for Dean's Scholarships awarded in the form of waivers.

Amount: One half of the in-state tuition for one year

Description: Presidential Scholarships are available to first-time freshmen with demonstrated talent, high academics, and leadership abilities.

Amount: A waiver of the in-state portion of tuition

Deadline: Various

Claremont McKenna College
Claremont, CA

Type: Grants/Scholarships

Description: College offers more than 400 need-based grants to students each year.

Amount: $500–$19,731

Description: African-American students may qualify for the Black Alumnae Merit Award (BAMA) based on academic achievement and other criteria.

Amount: $3,500

Deadline: February 1

Clarion University of Pennsylvania
Clarion, PA

Type: Grants/Scholarships

Description: College offers over 1,000 scholarship and grant awards to students, some with restrictions. Includes academic, athletic, and need-based award programs.

Amount: Various

Description: Clarence & Janet Lesser Scholarships make awards to 25 to 30 high school students who have exhibited a high interest and achievement particularly in the areas of art, music and intercollegiate athletics. Awards are paid each semester as a tuition credit. Contact the financial aid office for information.

Amount: $200–$500

Description: The Clarion University Alumni Association Scholarships provide ten tuition credit awards annually to students who have completed at least 16 credits at Clarion. Applications are available in September, and awards are made during October. Recipients are selected by a committee of the Alumni Association. Contact Mr. Ron Wilshire, Director of University Relations, for information and applications.

Amount: $300

Description: The Mary/Martha Colegrove Educational Foundation Scholarships award two women from McKean County attending Clarion University. The award is renewable if the student remains in attendance and maintains a GPA of 3.0. Contact the Dean of Enrollment Management and Academic Records or McKean County High Schools guidance counselors for more information.

Amount: $3,500

Description: The Clarion University Foundation makes available 32 departmental scholarships to sophomore- and junior-level students in the form of tuition credits. Application is made during the spring semester to individual department committees.

Amount: $500

Description: Foundation Honors Scholarships are awarded to academically talented students at Clarion University who participate in the

Honors Program. These annual scholarships are awarded on the basis of academic achievement and are renewable for four years, provided students maintain the academic standards required. Contact the director of the Honors Program for more information.

Amount: $650

Description: State Board of Governors Scholarship awards are made each semester to minority students. Candidates must possess a minimum 3.0 GPA. These tuition-based scholarships may vary in amount, depending on the student's need. Applications may be obtained in the Admissions Office.

Amount: Various

Description: College offers the Ernest W. Johnson Memorial Baseball Scholarship, which provides an award to a member of the Clarion University baseball team who is a resident of Pennsylvania.

Amount: $700

Description: Fran Shope Scholarships are awarded to junior or senior women who have made outstanding contributions to the school's athletics.

Amount: $300

Description: George W. Williams Memorial Wrestling Scholarships and W. S. Tippin Scholarships for men and women are available to athletes who compete on intercollegiate teams at Clarion. Contact the athletic department for information.

Amount: Various, average $2,000

Deadline: January 1

Description: Walter L. Hart Scholarships are awarded annually to incoming freshmen, with special consideration given to students who rank in the top 10 percent of their graduating class, with SAT scores in excess of 1000. Interested students are encouraged to submit a letter of application along with three letters of recommendation to the Dean of Enrollment Management and Academic Records.

Amount: $2,000

Deadline: Before March 30

Description: Four Presidential Scholarships are made annually to incoming freshmen and transfer students. Special emphasis is placed on outstanding academic achievement, demonstrated leadership, and involvement in extracurricular activities. The scholarships are paid as a tuition credit each semester. Completed applications, essay, and three letters of recommendation must be submitted to the Dean of Enrollment Management and Academic Records.

Amount:　　　$1,000

Deadline:　　　Before March 30

Description:　　Several Dana S. Still Scholarships are awarded annually to incoming students based on financial need. An application must be submitted for this one-year award. Contact the Dean of Enrollment Management and Academic Records.

Amount:　　　$200

Deadline:　　　March 30

Clemson University
Clemson, SC

Type:　　　　　Grants/Scholarships

Description:　　College participates in federal and state aid programs as well as institutional grants and scholarships, including: Clemson Alumni, Faculty and Staff Scholarships, IPTAY Scholarships, Alumni Presidential Scholarships.

Amount:　　　Various

Description:　　General university scholarships are awarded to students who meet academic and other criteria.

Amount:　　　$250–$6,000

Description:　　The Robert C. Edwards Scholarships are available to eligible African-Americans and other minority students.

Amount:　　　Various

Description:　　African-Americans and other minority students may receive university scholarships.

Amount:　　　$2,000–$4,000

Description:　　Athletic awards are available in basketball, cross-country, swimming and diving, track and field, golf, soccer, football, and volleyball.

Amount:　　　$100–full tuition

Deadline:　　　April 1

Colorado School of Mines
Golden, CO

Type: Scholarships

Description: College offers nearly $400,000 in Colorado State Grants and Scholarships and over $3 million in Colorado School of Mines institutional grant and scholarship awards.

Amount: Various

Deadline: March 15

Concordia College
Moorhead, MN

Type: Grants/Scholarships

Description: College offers 45–50 Faculty Scholarship awards annually.

Amount: $4,750

Description: 30 Music Scholarships and two annual Theatre and Forensics Scholarships.

Amount: $1,750, renewable

Description: The college offers need-based Concordia Grants and Scholarships and other aid programs with amounts depending on individual financial need.

Amount: Various

Deadline: May 1

Cornell College
Mount Vernon, IA

Type: Grants

Description: Cornell Grants and Iowa Tuition Grants are available to eligible students.

Amount: $500–$9,500

Deadline: March 1

Description: A number of academic and departmental scholarships are available to eligible students, including the William Fletcher King Awards, Presidential Awards, Honor Scholarships, Distinguished Honor Scholarships, and awards in the physical and natural sciences.

Amount: $4,000–$7,000

Deadline: March 1

Cornell University
Ithaca, NY

Type: Grants/Scholarships

Description: All Cornell grants are need-based. University meets all financial
               aid need. In addition to federal and state grants and scholar-
               ships, Cornell awards financial aid through numerous endow-
               ments and gifts in restricted as well as unrestricted institutional
               grants, such as the Cornell National Scholars Awards, College
               Deans Awards, Cornell Traditional Awards. Over 4,000 institu-
               tional awards are made each year.

Amount: $100–$23,000

Description: No grants are awarded solely based on a student's racial/ethnic
               background; however, some restricted institutional scholar-
               ships and non-Cornell grants such as the Empire State Minor-
               ity Honors Awards are awarded only to minority students who
               demonstrate financial need.

Amount: Various

Deadline: February 15

Denison University
Granville, OH

Type: Grants/Scholarships

Description: Merit scholarships include Denison Scholarship in the Hu-
               manities, which is awarded based on outstanding academic
               performance/potential in the humanities major.

Amount: Three-quarters tuition

Description: Faculty Scholarships for Achievements are awarded to the
               Valedictorian or Salutatorian from an Ohio high school. Up to
               35 are awarded each year.

Amount: Full tuition

Description: Heritage Scholarships are awarded to students who have out-
               standing academic performance or potential. Up to 200 are
               awarded annually.

Amount: Half tuition

Description: National Merit Founders Scholarships are awarded and com-
               bined with National Merit stipends to students with outstand-
               ing performance on the College Board PSAT/NMSQT.

Amount: Half tuition

Description: National Achievement Scholarships awarded to students for outstanding test performance.

Amount: Half tuition

Description: Wells Scholarships in Science awarded for outstanding academic performance/potential by students who plan to major in science or math.

Amount: Three-quarters tuition

Description: Scholarships based on special talents or circumstances include: Battelle Memorial Institute Foundation Scholarship, which provides awards to students with demonstrated potential for superior academic work and outstanding leadership qualities.

Amount: Half tuition

Description: Park National Bank Scholarships awarded for superior academic performance/potential.

Amount: $2,000

Description: Flora Dodson Skipp Scholarships awarded to students who demonstrate special talent in music.

Amount: $1,000

Description: Tyree Scholarships awarded for outstanding academic performance/potential.

Amount: Half tuition

Description: Fisher & Meredith Scholarships and Bob & Nancy Good Scholarships are awarded to students with strong academic performance.

Amount: $1,500–$6,000

Description: Scholarships based on merit and financial need include: I Know I Can Scholarships, Honda Scholarships, Thomas Ewart Scholarships, Elizabeth Platt Clements Scholarships, Frederick P. & Mary T. Beaver Scholarships, John W. Beattie Scholarships, and Bricker Family Scholarships are awarded for outstanding academic performance/potential.

Amount: $500–$2,000

Description: Marimac Scholarships are awarded to students who demonstrate promise in a performing or visual art.

Amount: $500–$2,000

Description: Estelle King Van Beuren Scholarships are awarded to students who demonstrate special talent in music.

Amount: $1,000–$2,000

Description: Elizabeth Trembley Swisher Scholarships are awarded for superior academic/personal contributions.

Amount: $500–$2,000

Description: Alpha Phi Scholarships awarded for outstanding academic performance/potential.

Amount: $7,000

Description: Other aid includes Denison Grants based on financial need.

Amount: Up to $15,950

Description: Ohio Instructional Grants and Ohio Student Choice Grants for Ohio residents.

Amount: $588–$3,463

Description: Faculty Scholarships for Achievement.

Amount: $2,000–full tuition

Description: African-American students may qualify for the Black Achievers Scholarship, which is awarded to participants of the YMCA Black Achievers program for strong academic performance.

Amount: Half tuition

Description: I Know I Can Scholarships are available to graduates of a Columbus, Ohio, public high school.

Amount: $1,500

Deadline: April 1

Duke University
Durham, NC

Type: Grants/Scholarships

Description: University meets 100 percent of demonstrated financial need with grants, loan, and work-study financial aid packages.

Amount: Various

Description: Reggie Howard Scholarships are awarded to African-Americans and other minority students who meet certain criteria.

Amount: $6,000; seven awarded annually

Deadline: February 1

D'Youville College
Buffalo, NY

Type: Grants/Scholarships

Description: College offers a number of need-based and non-need-based awards, including Presidential Scholarships.

Amount: $3,250

Description: College offers 12 Division awards annually.

Amount: $500–$2,500

Description: Ten Residential scholarships are awarded each year.

Amount: Room waiver ($1,810)

Deadline: April 15

East Carolina University
Greenville, NC

Type: Grants/Scholarships

Description: University provides a number of need-based and non-need-based aid opportunities for eligible students.

Amount: Various

Description: African-American students and other minority students may qualify for Minority Presence Grants for North Carolina residents.

Amount: $1,500 per year for four years

Description: The Chancellor's Minority Student Leadership program provides awards to eligible students.

Amount: $1,000

Deadline: April 15

Eastern New Mexico University
Portales, NM

Type: Grants/Scholarships

Description: College offers a number of general scholarships including Friends of Eastern Foundation Awards, Harrison Schmitt Scholarship Awards, VSO Scholarships, Dobbs-Burke Memorial Scholarships, ENMU Alumni Association Scholarships, ENMU Women Awards, Jay Price Memorial Scholarships, Morton Gragg Endowed Scholarships, Portales Rotary Club Freshmen Awards, and numerous other awards. Academic, residency, and other criteria may apply.

Amount: $50–$500

Deadline: March 1

Elizabethtown College
Elizabethtown, PA

Type: Grants/Scholarships

Description: Presidential Scholarships are offered to students who meet certain criteria.

Amount: $8,000

Description: More than 100 Provost Scholarships are awarded annually to students who meet certain academic and other criteria.

Amount: $3,000–$6,000

Description: Armstrong World Industries Scholarships offer scholarship awards to eligible students.

Amount: Up to $10,000

Description: Scholarships are also available through the Dial Corporation Scholarship, Faculty Minority Scholarship program, Ethnic Understanding Scholarship, Good's Furniture and Carpet Scholarship, Tyson Foods Scholarship, and United Parcel Service Scholarship.

Amount: Various

Deadline: April 1

Hampton University
Hampton, VA

Type: Grants/Scholarships

Description: Participates in federal and state financial aid programs and offers institutional grants and scholarships; strives to meet student financial need. Scholarship and other aid programs include: AT&T Bell Scholarships and Internship program, Given, Elizabeth and Harry Howe, Daniel W. and Louise Armstrong, Fostine Glenn Riddick, Chi Eta Phi, and the Brown and Williamson Scholarships for nursing students, as well as departmental, corporate, and private aid programs.

Amount: Various

Deadline: March 31

Harvard/Radcliffe
Cambridge, MA

Type: Grants/Scholarships

Description: All financial aid at Harvard/Radcliffe is awarded on the basis
                     of financial need with 45 percent of students receiving some
                     type of aid. Financial aid is not only for the neediest families.
                     Last year the average family income of a student receiving
                     scholarship aid was $54,000. Over 1,000 families with incomes
                     above $60,000 qualified for grants, as did over 180 families
                     with incomes over $100,000.

Amount: Various, average $11,000

Deadline: February 15

Kent State University
Kent, OH

Type: Grants/Scholarships

Description: Oscar Ritchie Scholarships are awarded to academically tal-
                     ented African-Americans and other minority students.

Amount: $1,500–full tuition, fees, room and board

Deadline: Spring of junior year in high school

Description: The Founders Scholars Program makes awards to incoming
                     freshmen each year. Scholarships are based on academic
                     record and competitive exam. Candidates are eligible by invita-
                     tion only.

Amount: Up to full tuition, fees, room and board

Deadline: December 1

Description: Minority Incentive Scholarships are offered to African-
                     Americans and other minority students based on academic
                     achievement. Awards are made to high school seniors who do
                     not participate in or were not awarded a scholarship from the
                     Oscar Ritchie Memorial Scholarship program. Students must
                     have a GPA of 2.75 to qualify.

Amount: $2,000–$3,500, renewable

Deadline: May 1

Description: Scholarships for Excellence are awarded to incoming fresh-
                     men, valedictorians of an Ohio high school; academics are also
                     considered.

Amount: $1,000

Deadline: Various

Description:	Honors Scholarships are offered to students based on academic achievement and ACT or SAT scores.
Amount:	$800–full tuition
Deadline:	Various
Description:	University Scholarships are awarded to Ohio residents based on academic record and SAT or ACT scores.
Amount:	$500
Deadline:	February 15
Description:	President's Grants are available to incoming freshmen, children of Kent alumni, and non-Ohio residents.
Amount:	$3,740
Deadline:	April 1
Description:	Ohio Instructional Grants are offered to residents with demonstrated financial need.
Amount:	$228–$1,392
Description:	The African-American Scholarships are awarded to undergraduate and graduate students. Students with high GPA's are given priority consideration.
Amount:	$250–$500 per year
Deadline:	April 1

King's College
Wilkes-Barre, PA

Type:	Grants/Scholarships
Description:	College offers academic, merit, and other grant awards to students, some with restrictions. Students who rank in the top 5 percent of their high school graduating class, have attained a score of 1200 or higher on the SAT, and who plan to attend full-time may compete for Presidential Scholarships. Recipients must maintain at least a 3.25 GPA at the College.
Amount:	Full tuition
Description:	Students who rank in the top 10 percent of their high school class and plan to attend full-time may compete for the Moreau Scholarship, named for the Very Reverend Basil Anthony Moreau, C.S.C., founder of the Holy Cross Fathers and Brothers. The award may be combined with federal and state grants not to exceed annual tuition.
Amount:	Various, minimum $3,000

Description: Students who are high academic achievers may be eligible for various Academic Scholarships. Recipients maintain at least a 3.00 GPA.

Amount: Various, minimum $1,500 per year for four years

Description: Merit Scholarships are awarded to students who have demonstrated the ability to maintain an above average academic record while being involved in extracurricular, leadership, and/or community service activities. Recipients must maintain at least a 2.5 GPA.

Amount: Various, minimum award $1,500

Description: Grants-in-Aid may be awarded to students who have financial need and who have exhausted all possibilities of receiving grant assistance from outside sources and who are active in campus activities. Recipients must maintain a 2.0 GPA. Holy Cross Father Scholarships are awarded to students who demonstrate extreme financial need. Recipients are selected by the Holy Cross Fathers.

Amount: Various

Deadline: March 1

Lafayette College
Easton, PA

Type: Grants/Scholarships

Description: Nearly 800 scholarship and grant awards are made annually. All financial aid is awarded on the basis of need.

Amount: Various

Deadline: February 15

Lander University
Greenwood, SC

Type: Grants/Scholarships

Description: College offers over 540 scholarship and grant awards to students, some with restrictions. Includes academic, athletic and need-based award programs, and 100 scholarship awards.

Amount: Various, up to full tuition

Description: An annual award is given to selected minority students ranked in the top 10 percent of their class. There is no minimum SAT score requirement. No limit on the number of students who may receive this award. Awards are made annually.

Amount: $2,000, renewable

Description: College offers more than 60 athletic scholarships, including 13 men's basketball, 11 women's basketball, ten men's tennis, four women's tennis, 11 men's soccer, and 15 men's and women's cross-country scholarship awards.

Amount: Men's—$500–$6,300
Women's—$500–$5,626

Deadline: January 1

Lebanon Valley College
Annville, PA

Type: Grants/Scholarships

Description: College offers a number of need-based as well as non-need-based scholarship and grant awards to students, some with restrictions.

Amount: Various

Description: Academic scholarships are available through the Presidential Scholarship Program. Awards include the Vickroy Scholarship, open to high school seniors who rank in the top 10 percent of their class.

Amount: One-half tuition

Description: Leadership Awards are offered to high school seniors who rank in the top 20 percent of their class.

Amount: One-third tuition

Description: Achievement Awards are offered to high school seniors who rank in the top 30 percent of their class. All scholarships are renewable for four years.

Amount: One-fourth tuition

Deadline: Before April 1 (for the fall semester)

Lewis and Clark College
Portland, OR

Type: Grants/Scholarships

Description: College participates in state and federal aid programs and offers a number of grant and scholarship programs including Barbara Hirschi Neely Scholarships and Trustee Scholarships, as well as institutional grants and scholarships.

Amount: Various

Description: African-American students may qualify for Lewis and Clark Grants.

Amount:	$1,000–$5,000

Description: African-Americans and other minority students may qualify for Oregon Need Grants and Major Mission Awards.

Amount: $500–$3,180

Deadline: February 15

Linfield College
McMinnville, OR

Type: Grants/Scholarships

Description: Linfield College offers a variety of scholarships, grants, loans, and employment to assist students in financing their education. Financial aid awards are made on the basis of financial need and academics. Programs include Linfield College Competitive Scholarships, Linfield Scholarships, Presidential Passport to the World Awards.

Amount: Various

Description: Diversity Grants, Special Endowed Fund, and Yearly Restricted Scholarships are available to African-Americans and other minority students who meet certain criteria.

Amount: Various

Deadline: February 1

Menlo College
Atherton, CA

Type: Grants/Scholarships

Description: Presidential Scholarships, Leadership Scholarships, and Transfer Scholarships.

Amount: $1,000–$3,000

Description: Cal Grants are available to residents and Menlo Aid is available to students with demonstrated need.

Amount: $5,250–$13,900

Deadline: March 2

Mississippi University for Women
Columbus, MS

Type: Grants/Scholarships

Description: More than $1.8 million is awarded annually in grants and scholarships, including federal and state programs.

Amount: $150–$2,250

Description: African-Americans and other minority students receive over 300 awards in grant and scholarship programs each year.

Amount: $150–$6,592

Deadline: June 1

Mississippi Valley State University
Itta Bena, MS

Type: Grants/Scholarships

Description: More than 100 academic scholarships awarded annually, based on merit and other criteria.

Amount: $200–$6,845

Description: More than 3,000 awards of federal and state grant programs made each year to students.

Amount: $100–$2,300

Deadline: April 1

Moorhead State University
Moorhead, MN

Type: Grants/Scholarships

Description: The university offers over 2,400 scholarship and grant awards to students, some with restrictions. More than 1,800 Minnesota State Grants are awarded annually.

Amount: Up to $3,318

Description: Over 450 Moorhead State University Scholarships are awarded to eligible students.

Amount: $500–$2,000

Description: Students may also qualify for the Honors Apprentice program, which requires that students participate eight hours weekly in apprenticeship training.

Amount: Tuition and fees for 48 credit hours

Description: More than 300 additional scholarship awards are made to students annually.

Amount: Various

Description: African-American students may qualify for General Minority Scholarships.

Amount: $500–$2,400

Description:	African-Americans and other minority students may qualify for Sanders Scholarships.
Amount:	$1,500 annually
Deadline:	March 1

Morgan State University
Baltimore, MD

Type:	Grants/Scholarships
Description:	Morgan participates in federal and state grant and scholarship programs and offers a number of private and institutional aid programs, including Curriculum-Based Honors Scholarships, Incentive Grants, and departmental awards.
Amount:	Various
Description:	Maryland residents may qualify for General State Scholarships.
Amount:	$200–$2,500
Description:	Senatorial Scholarships and House of Delegates Scholarships
Amount:	$400–$2,000—Senatorial Awards Minimum $200—Delegate Awards
Description:	Distinguished Scholar Awards
Amount:	$3,000
Description:	Teacher Education Distinguished Scholar Awards
Amount:	$3,000
Description:	Maryland State Nursing Scholarships
Amount:	Up to $2,400
Description:	Sharon Christa McAuliffe Educational Awards
Amount:	Tuition, fees, room and board
Description:	Paul Douglas Teachers' Scholarships
Amount:	Up to $5,000
Description:	Child Care Provider Awards
Amount:	$500–$2,000
Deadline:	March 1

New York University
New York, NY

Type:	Grants/Scholarships

Description: All eligible incoming freshmen are automatically reviewed for New York University need-based and merit scholarships and grants, including Trustees Scholarships, Presidential Scholarships, Merit & Achievement Scholarships, and the Martin Luther King, Jr., Scholarship Program.

Amount: Various

Description: The University offers the Higher Education Opportunity Program and C-STEP Program, designed to provide academic and financial support to African-American students and other minorities.

Amount: Various

Deadline: February 15

Northeast Missouri State University
Kirksville, MO

Type: Grants/Scholarships

Description: More than 630 Higher Education–Bright Flight grants are awarded annually, including two to African-American students.

Amount: $2,000

Description: Ten Byrd Scholarships and 17 Missouri Grants are awarded annually to students who meet certain criteria.

Amount: $1,118–$1,500

Description: Nearly 650 teachers' scholarships, including Paul Douglas Teachers' Scholarships and Missouri Teachers' Scholarships, are awarded annually.

Amount: $2,000–$5,000

Description: More than 600 private scholarships are awarded each year to students who meet certain criteria.

Amount: $50–$7,694

Description: Over 2,500 NMSU scholarships are awarded annually to students who meet certain criteria.

Amount: $100–$7,416

Description: Seventy-eight Minority Scholarships, including nine President's Honorary grants and 30 various Northeast Awards.

Amount:	$459–$7,416—Northeast Awards
	$2,728–$7,516—President's Honorary Grants
Deadline:	April 1

Northwestern College
St. Paul, MN

Type:	Grants/Scholarships
Description:	College offers more than 2,000 grant and scholarship programs in addition to federal aid programs, including Northwestern Grants.
Amount:	$300–$4,200
Description:	Honor Scholarships available to students who meet certain academic and other criteria.
Amount:	$200–$1,500
Description:	State residents may qualify for Minnesota State Grants.
Amount:	$100–$5,889
Description:	Academic Tuition Benefits are available to students who meet certain criteria.
Amount:	$390–$2,000
Description:	The college offers non-need awards, including Presidential Scholarships, STEP Scholarships.
Amount:	Various
Description:	Students with interest and talent in music and the performing arts may qualify to receive Bronson String Scholarships and music performance grants.
Amount:	Various
Deadline:	April 1

Pitzer College
Claremont, CA

Type:	Grants/Scholarships
Description:	College offers a number of need-based grants and scholarships to students each year.
Amount:	$250–$18,616
Deadline:	February 1

Providence College
Providence, RI

Type: Grants/Scholarships

Description: In addition to federal and institutional scholarships and grants, several aid programs are available to African-American students.

Amount: Various

Description: The college awards 90 Martin Luther King Scholarships each year.

Amount: Full tuition

Description: Five William & Doris Davis Scholarships are awarded each year.

Amount: Half tuition

Description: Four Margaret Brent-Plona Scholarships are awarded to cover the cost of books.

Amount: $400

Description: Four Mary Benson Scholarships are awarded each year to African-American students.

Amount: $4,000

Description: One Dominic Cardi Scholarship is awarded to an African-American student each year.

Amount: $1,000

Description: The College awards 160 to 180 athletic scholarships annually to all students, including African-Americans.

Amount: $1,000–$20,000

Deadline: February 15

Purchase College of The State of New York
Purchase, NY

Type: Grants/Scholarships

Description: A quarter of a million dollars is given annually to students for scholarships with amounts varying depending on the program and its eligibility requirements. The Tuition Assistance Program (TAP) provides awards to New York residents.

Amount: Up to $2,600 per year

Description: The Economic Opportunity Program provides awards to students who are residents of New York State.

Amount: Up to $1,250 per year

Description: Residents may receive a grant through the SUNY Tuition Assistance program.

Amount: $200 per year

Type: Work aid

Description: Residents may also be eligible for assistance through the Aid for Part-Time Study program.

Amount: Various

Type: Scholarships

Description: African-American and other minority students may be eligible for scholarship awards through the State University of New York Minority Honors Scholarship.

Amount: Up to $1,250 per year

Description: The Pepsico Scholarship for Minorities provides an annual award to eligible minority students.

Amount: $1,000 per year

Deadline: February 15

Purdue University
West Lafayette, IN

Type: Scholarships

Description: Purdue offers over 4,000 Indiana State Grants to students each year. Academic and residency criteria may apply to some awards.

Amount: $200–$1,700

Description: Over 2,400 Purdue Scholarships are awarded to students who meet certain criteria.

Amount: $200–$2,000

Description: Purdue Fee Remission awards are offered to students based on certain criteria.

Amount: $200–$6,150

Description: African-American and other minority students may qualify for 50 Purdue Special Achievement awards.

Amount: $1,000–$5,000

Description: African-Americans and other minority students may qualify for one of 20 General Motors EEOC Scholarships.

Amount: $200–$2,000

Description:	Two EDS Incentive Alumni Scholarships are awarded to African-American and other minority students.
Amount:	$200–$2,000
Deadline:	March 1

Richard Stockton College of New Jersey
Pomona, NJ

Type:	Grants/Scholarships
Description:	More than 1,600 awards of federal grants made annually.
Amount:	$200–$2,300
Description:	Tuition Grants available to students who meet certain criteria. Over 1,500 awarded annually.
Amount:	$400–$2,176
Description:	Over 300 EOF Grants made to students.
Amount:	$400–$1,000
Description:	50 Bloustein District Scholars receive awards based on a variety of criteria, including residency.
Amount:	$1,000
Description:	Over 90 Garden State Scholarships awarded based on a variety of criteria.
Amount:	$500
Description:	Over 70 Stockton Presidential Scholarships and 28 Stockton Distinguished Scholarships awarded to students who meet certain criteria.
Amount:	Various
Description:	More than 100 Foundation Scholarships.
Amount:	$100–full tuition
Deadline:	March 1

Rosemont College
Rosemont, PA

Type:	Grants/Scholarships
Description:	The College offers a number of need-based and merit scholarship and grant programs, some with restrictions. More than 500 federal, state, institutional, and private scholarships and grants are available.
Amount:	$100–$10,700

Description: Up to ten scholarships are awarded annually to academically talented freshmen through the Rosemont Scholars Scholarship. Students must achieve a minimum of 1200 combined score on the SAT, have a B+ average, and graduate in the top 10 percent of their high school class.

Amount: $1,500–$10,700, up to full tuition

Description: Two Connelly Scholarships are awarded annually to graduates of the Philadelphia Archdiocesan High Schools. They are based on academic excellence and financial need. Candidates must be nominated by a teacher or counselor, rank in the top 20 percent of their class, and have strong SAT scores.

Amount: Full tuition

Description: The McShain Scholarship program awards two scholarships on the basis of academic merit and financial need. Candidates must be in the top two-fifths of their class and have a combined score of at least 1000 on the SAT.

Amount: Full tuition

Description: A number of Trustee Scholarships are awarded to residents of Bucks, Chester, Delaware, Montgomery, or Philadelphia counties. Candidates must rank in the top two-fifths of their class and have a combined score of at least 1000 on the SAT.

Amount: Half tuition

Description: The Alumnae Scholarship provides one new scholarship annually, based on academic merit and involvement in extracurricular activities.

Amount: $1,500

Description: One Presidential Scholarship is awarded annually, based competitively on academic excellence.

Amount: Full tuition

Description: Rosemont Academic Scholarships are offered to students based on academic merit and financial need. Recipients must rank in the top two-fifths of their class and have at least 500 on each section of the SAT.

Amount: Up to half tuition

Description: The Revere Scholarship provides scholarships to a student planning to major in art. Faculty members from the Arts Division select the recipient based on a portfolio review.

Amount: One full tuition (or two half tuition)

Description: A limited number of W. W. Smith Scholarships are awarded to candidates in good academic standing and financial need.

Amount: Various

Description: One Sherman Scholarship is awarded to a commuter student based on academic standing and financial need.

Amount: Various

Description: One full and two partial Rosemont Opportunity Grants are awarded annually to students who have overcome significant educational, economic, or historical disadvantages in pursuit of higher education.

Amount: Various

Description: Several Community and Junior College Scholarships are awarded to highly qualified graduates of surrounding area junior and community colleges.

Amount: Various

Deadline: March 1

St. John's College—New Mexico
Santa Fe, NM

Type: Grants/Scholarships

Description: College offers a number of state and institutional financial aid programs, including the New Mexico State Incentive Grant, to eligible students.

Amount: $2,000 per year

Description: The New Mexico Student Choice Grants are available to students who meet certain criteria.

Amount: Various, average award $4,200 per year

Description: The New Mexico Scholars and the New Mexico Scholars/ St. John's Match programs are available, based on a variety of criteria.

Amount: Various, average award $1,800 per year

Description: St. John's College Grants

Amount: $400–$16,000

Description: Endowed Grants

Amount: $400–$10,000 per year

Description: African-Americans and other minority students may qualify for awards through the Southwest Scholars Program.

Amount: $2,500 per year

Deadline: March 1

St. John's University
Jamaica, NY

Type: Grants/Scholarships

Description: Scholarships and grants are awarded on the basis of academic achievement. Presidential Scholarships are awarded to entering freshmen with a 95 percent average and a 1200 combined score on the SAT.

Amount: Full tuition, less Tuition Assistance Program award

Description: Scholastic Excellence Scholarships are awarded to entering freshmen with a 92 percent average and an 1100 combined score on the SAT.

Amount: One-half tuition per year

Description: St. Vincent de Paul Scholarships are awarded to entering freshmen not eligible for the Presidential or Scholastic Excellence Scholarships. Students must have an average of at least 85–89 percent with at least an 1100 combined score on the SAT.

Amount: One-quarter tuition

Description: University Transfer Scholarships are awarded to any accepted new transfer student with a transfer index of at least 3.25 based on a minimum of one year or 24 credits of college-level study.

Amount: One-quarter–one-half tuition

Description: Competitive Scholarships are available to high school seniors with an 85 percent average and who take a competitive examination on the campus of St. John's University. The exam is held in the fall. One hundred scholarships are awarded annually through this program.

Amount: $2,500

Deadline: Various

Description: Daniel J. Tracy Scholarships are available to children of New York City firefighters with an 80 percent high school grade point average who compete in an examination. The exam is held in the spring each year in high schools.

Amount: $2,500–full tuition

Deadline: May 1

Description: African-American Catholic students may be eligible for a scholarship, based on academic achievement and other criteria.

Amount: Full tuition

Deadline: April 1

St. Lawrence University
Canton, NY

Type: Grants/Scholarships

Description: University offers a number of need-based and non-need-based awards in addition to federal and state aid programs.

Amount: Various

Description: Over $250,000 is awarded in the University Scholars Awards program to students who meet certain criteria.

Amount: Various

Description: African-American students may qualify for St. Lawrence University Scholarships.

Amount: $500–$23,500

Deadline: February 15

St. Mary's College
St. Mary's City, MD

Type: Grants/Scholarships

Description: College offers institutional grants and scholarships to students based on academic and other criteria.

Amount: $500–$2,500

Description: College offers state grants and scholarships to Maryland residents.

Amount: $500–$2,100

Description: Academic awards include Matthias D'Sousa Awards, Margaret Brent/Leonard Calvert Awards, Ark and Dove Scholarships, Presidential Awards, Landers Awards, St. Mary's College Merit Awards.

Amount: Various

Description: Students interested in studying biology may qualify for the Izaak Walton Scholarship.

Amount: Various

Description:	African-American students may qualify for minority grants and scholarships.
Amount:	$500–$4,000
Deadline:	March 1

St. Paul's College
Lawrenceville, VA

Type:	Grants/Scholarships
Description:	College awards over 300 Virginia State Tuition Assistance Grants, over 70 College Scholarship Assistance Grants, five Presidential Scholarships, and ten Academic Scholarships.
Amount:	$200–$1,500
Description:	While St. Paul's enrollment is predominantly African-American, the College provides a number of annual awards specifically to African-Americans and other minority students, including the Nelson Mandela Scholarship, Martin Luther King Scholarship, 30 United Negro College Fund grants, five D.C. Incentive Grants, and two $750 Minority Presence Grants.
Amount:	$750–$5,000
Description:	College offers athletic scholarships, including eight men's and three women's basketball awards, women's tennis awards, three softball awards, two volleyball awards, and five track and field awards.
Amount:	$500–$9,371
Deadline:	April 15
Type:	Child Care/Academic Support
Description:	St. Paul's College Single Parent Support System provides assistance, academic support, child development and child care services to single parents who are students. This unique model program is designed to help single parent students overcome the financial, academic, and emotional obstacles that may impede their obtaining a college education. The College also offers Upward Bound, a program designed to increase the academic skills and levels of motivation in low-income and/or first-generation college students, and provide financial and other support.
Amount:	Various
Deadline:	Various

Scripps College
Claremont, CA

Type:	Grants/Scholarships
Description:	College offers a number of academic scholarships, including James E. Scripps Scholarships, Dorothy Drake Scholarships, and Dean's Awards.
Amount:	$7,500–$10,000
Description:	Students with demonstrated music talent and interest may qualify for Alice Shapiro Awards, or Jaqua Harden Awards.
Amount:	Various
Deadline:	February 1

Seattle University
Seattle, WA

Type:	Grants/Scholarships
Description:	Presidential Scholarships
Amount:	$7,200
Description:	Trustee Scholarships and Ignatian Scholarships
Amount:	$4,200–$5,400
Description:	Students may qualify for grants, including the Washington State Need Grant.
Amount:	$300–$2,625
Description:	The Seattle University Grants and Educational Opportunity Grants are awarded to students who meet certain criteria.
Amount:	$300–$8,000
Description:	The Regents' Scholarship and the Central Area Scholarship programs providing scholarships for 11 students from Seattle's central area are two of a number of scholarships the university has available for ethnic American students.
Amount:	$2,000
Description:	The Alliant Techsystems Engineering Scholarships are designed to encourage diversity in the field of engineering. The scholarship is renewable.
Amount:	$2,000
Description:	Boeing Company Corporate Scholarships are awarded to a minority entering their junior or senior year. The scholarship is not renewable.

Amount: $6,000

Description: Seafirst Bank Minority Scholarships award ten scholarships to full-time juniors who have established financial need and are majoring in the field of business. The scholarship is renewable if the student maintains a 3.33 GPA.

Amount: $1,000

Description: The Robert Truex Scholarships provide funds to minority students majoring in business. Scholarship is renewable.

Amount: Various

Description: The U.S. Bank Business Scholarships award ten scholarships annually to minority students in the Albers School of Business and Economics.

Amount: $3,000

Description: KING-5 Television Scholarships provide three annual awards to minorities who are juniors majoring in communications.

Amount: Various

Description: Athletic Need Grants and Athletic Talent Scholarships are available in various amounts. Athletic Room awards are also available to eligible student athletes in basketball, soccer, and tennis.

Amount: Various

Deadline: February 15

Sonoma State University
Rohnert Park, CA

Type: Grants/Scholarships

Description: California State residents who have demonstrated financial need may qualify for State University Grants, Educational Opportunity Grants, Cal Grant A and Cal Grant B.

Amount: $540–$2,820 each year

Description: The African-American Scholarship Program provides awards to students who meet certain academic and other criteria.

Amount: $1,000 each year

Description: The Claudia Hampton Award offers an annual award to African-American students and other minorities.

Amount: $3,000

Description: African-American students may also receive financial aid information and assistance through SSU Information and Outreach Programs provided by the Educational Opportunity Program, the Pre-College Program, Black Student Union and Financial Aid Office personnel.

Amount: Various

Deadline: March 2

Description: The SSU Scholarship Program provides approximately 150 scholarship awards to students who have demonstrated academic excellence. Students with financial need may be considered as well but some restrictions may apply such as residency, or major field of interest. Incoming freshmen as well as undergraduate students are eligible.

Amount: $250–$2,000 annually

Deadline: Students may apply in November of each year, and submit a completed application package by March 1 of the following year. Awards for the succeeding Fall and Spring semesters are announced in June.

Write: For information and an application contact: Sonoma State University, Scholarship Office, Rohnert Park, CA 94928; or call the Scholarship Coordinator at 707-664-2261.

Southern Illinois University at Carbondale
Carbondale, IL

Type: Grants/Scholarships

Description: College offers a number of grants and scholarships, including SIU Scholarships.

Amount: $500–$24,400 over four years

Description: University offers Army and Air Force ROTC grants and awards to students who are enrolled in these programs.

Amount: Up to full tuition and fees

Description: Students who meet certain criteria may qualify for a Illinois Veterans' Grant.

Amount: $1,365 per semester

Description: African-Americans and other minority students may qualify for Minority Participation Scholarships based on academic and other criteria.

Amount: Up to tuition, fees, room and board, books and supplies

Description: African-American and other minority students interested in pursuing undergraduate training in engineering may qualify for Minority Engineering Scholarships.

Amount: Up to tuition, fees, books, room and board

Deadline: February 1

Southern Nazarene University
Bethany, OK

Type: Grants/Scholarships

Description: Oklahoma Tuition Aid Grants provide awards to students who meet need, residency, and other criteria.

Amount: $1,000

Description: Nearly 200 Dean's Scholarships are awarded to students who meet academic and other criteria.

Amount: $800

Description: More than 100 Presidential Scholarships are awarded to students for academic achievement.

Amount: $1,600

Description: About 40 Honors Scholarships are available to students each year.

Amount: $3,420–$8,500

Description: More than 325 general scholarship awards are made to eligible students each year.

Amount: $100–$4,000

Description: Other awards include the Parman Foundation Scholarship, Church Matching Scholarship, District Matching Scholarship, 15 awards from the Oklahoma State Regents, and nearly 100 miscellaneous local church scholarships.

Amount: $66–$3,500

Description: African-American students may qualify for Ethnic Minority Scholarships.

Amount: $150

Deadline: April 15

Stanford University
Stanford, CA

Type: Grants/Scholarships

Description: College offers more than 400 need-based grants to students
                  each year.

Amount: $500–$19,731

Description: California residents may qualify for Cal Grant A and Cal Grant
                  B awards.

Amount: $600–$5,250

Description: African-American students may qualify for the Black Alum-
                  nae Merit Award (BAMA) based on academic achievement
                  and other criteria.

Amount: $3,500

Deadline: February 1

Stonehill College
North Easton, MA

Type: Grants/Scholarships

Description: Stonehill Scholarship awards are given to students who meet
                  certain criteria.

Amount: $1,500–$12,170 (full tuition)

Description: State Scholarships.

Amount: $300–$2,500

Description: Cultural Diversity Scholarships and State Street Scholars pro-
                  gram provide for students of color.

Amount: $2,000–$12,170 (full tuition) awards annually

Description: College offers basketball scholarships to talented athletes.

Amount: Up to $18,800, includes tuition, room and board, fees and
                  books

Deadline: February 15

Syracuse University
Syracuse, NY

Type: Grants/Scholarships

Description: University provides need-based scholarships and grants to eli-
                  gible students.

Amount: Various, average award $7,400

Description: New York State Tuition Assistance program awards are available to students who qualify.

Amount: Various, average award $2,500

Deadline: March 1

**Tarleton State University
Stephenville, TX**

Type: Grants/Scholarships

Description: College offers need- and non-need-based scholarships and grants, including State Student Incentive Grants, Texas Public Education Grants for resident and nonresident students, and University and private scholarships.

Amount: Various

Description: Over 50 scholarship awards totaling more than $30,000 provided to African-Americans and other minorities.

Amount: Various

Deadline: Various

**The Citadel
Charleston, SC**

Type: Grants/Scholarships

Description: College offers over 700 need- and non-need-based scholarships and grants, including 25 scholarships offered through the Citadel Scholars Program.

Amount: Various, up to full tuition

Description: 70 Citadel Development Foundation Grants are awarded to African-Americans and other minority students.

Amount: $1,000

Description: 77 one-year grants are awarded each year to African-Americans and other minorities.

Amount: $1,000

Description: 145 scholarships are awarded to eligible athletes in a variety of sports.

Amount: $500 to full tuition

Deadline: March 15

Trinity College
Hartford, CT

Type:	Grants/Scholarships
Description:	Trinity awards approximately $9 million of its own funds in scholarship aid to students. Nearly half of the student body receives need-based aid, including grant and scholarship awards.
Amount:	$1,000–$26,000
Deadline:	February 1

Tuskegee University
Tuskegee, AL

Type:	Scholarships
Description:	As a predominantly Black university, most aid programs benefit African-American students, who may qualify for one of six Louell World Peace Awards, 20 Distinguished Scholars and Presidential Citation Awards, and 125 general scholarships.
Amount:	Various
Deadline:	April 15

University of North Dakota
Grand Forks, ND

Type:	Grants/Scholarships
Description:	College offers over 2,600 scholarship and grant programs to students, some with restrictions. Includes academic, athletic, and need-based award programs.
Amount:	Various
Description:	African-Americans and other minority students may be eligible for the Cultural Diversity Tuition Waiver award.
Amount:	$900–$1,900
Description:	Athletic scholarships are offered to upperclass-level students (none awarded to freshmen) in men's baseball, football, ice hockey, wrestling, women's softball, swimming, volleyball, and men's and women's basketball, track.
Amount:	$150–$8,290
Deadline:	April 15

University of Pittsburgh
Pittsburgh, PA

Type:	Grants/Scholarships
Description:	PITT combined its admissions and financial aid office, and also takes a different approach to deciding who receives finan-

cial aid. The family's ability to pay is first determined by a government standardized formula. This is the EFC (Expected Family Contribution). Then the cost to attend PITT is computed, taking into account factors like tuition, fees, housing and marital status, state of residency, food and book costs. The Expected Family Contribution (EFC) is then subtracted from that number to establish a student's financial need, and that's the figure PITT uses to award aid. Students are usually awarded a combination of "gift" money (grants and scholarships), and "self-help" money such as work-study. Academic scholarships are also awarded to freshmen based on their high school credentials.

Amount: Various

Description: Chancellor's Scholarships
Amount: Tuition, room and board

Description: Engineering Honors Scholarships
Amount: $500–$9,000

Description: One Valedictorian Scholarship is awarded each year.
Amount: $500

Description: PITT awards Challenge Scholarships to entering African-American freshman students.
Amount: $1,000–$4,000
Deadline: March 1

University of Texas at Arlington
Arlington, TX

Type: Grants/Scholarships
Description: The University also designates 29 scholarships and grants for African-Americans.
Amount: $100–$4,000
Description: The college currently awards 45 athletic scholarships for various sports to African-American students.
Amount: Various
Deadline: Various

University of Virginia
Charlottesville, VA

Type: Grants/Scholarships
Description: UVA participates in federal and state grant and scholarship programs and offers institutional and private scholarships as

well. Over 20 percent of all students on campus receive some type of financial assistance.

Amount: Various

Description: University awards five Jerome Holland Scholarships to out-of-state African-American students. Stipend is renewable. Students are selected on academic achievement and their ability to demonstrate genuine interest in learning.

Amount: $10,000, renewable

Description: Fifty University Achievement Awards are granted annually to the top-rated first-year African-American students from the Commonwealth of Virginia. Award is renewable.

Amount: Full tuition and fees, renewable

Deadline: March 1

University of Wisconsin—Whitewater
Whitewater, WI

Type: Grants/Scholarships

Description: Wisconsin Higher Educational Grants are available to Wisconsin residents.

Amount: Up to $1,350

Description: Wisconsin Talent Incentive Program provides awards to Wisconsin resident students in extreme financial need who meet specific requirements.

Amount: Up to $1,800

Description: Nonresidential Tuition Remission Grants are available to out-of-state students who demonstrate financial need and high academic achievement.

Amount: Various

Description: African-Americans and other minority students may qualify for Advanced Opportunity Grants.

Amount: Various

Description: African-Americans may qualify to receive a Lawton Undergraduate Minority Retention Grant for Wisconsin residents.

Amount: $100–$2,100

Description: Funds may also be available to eligible students through Federal and State Vocational Rehabilitation Grant programs, Wisconsin National Guard Education Assistance Program, Veterans and U.S. Army Reserve Officer Training Corps.

Amount: Various

Deadline: April 15

Vanderbilt University
Nashville, TN

Type: Grants/Scholarships

Description: Nearly 2,000 need-based and 300 non-need-based scholarship
                 and grant funds totaling over $20 million are made available to
                 students annually. These aid programs include Harold S. Van-
                 derbilt Awards, James Stewart awards in engineering, George
                 Peabody scholarships in education, Engineering School Hon-
                 ors Awards, Dean's Select Scholarships in arts and sciences, the
                 Windrow Honor Scholarships, Memphis-Vanderbilt Scholar-
                 ships, Paul Harrawood Scholarships, National Merit Scholar-
                 ship awards, and numerous other awards.

Amount: Various

Description: Over 235 grants in scholarships are awarded to African-American
                 students, including National Achievement Scholarships.

Amount: $500–$19,550

Description: 194 grants and scholarships are awarded to eligible athletes in
                 a variety of sports.

Amount: $500–$22,472

Deadline: February 15

Virginia Polytechnic Institute & State University
Blacksburg, VA

Type: Grants/Scholarships

Description: Presidential Scholarships, the university's most prestigious
                 award. In addition to the scholarship award, recipients are as-
                 signed the university president as their faculty adviser. Four
                 awards are made each year.

Amount: Full tuition, room and board, fees, books for four years, and a
                 personal computer

Description: National Merit Scholarships are awarded to up to 75 students.
                 Candidates are National Merit finalists who have named Vir-
                 ginia Tech as their first-choice school.

Amount: $2,000 per year for four years and a personal computer

Description: National Achievement Scholarships are awarded to up to 20 re-
                 cipients each year.

Amount: $3,000 for four years and a personal computer

Description: Alumni Presidential and Distinguished University Scholars are awarded.

Amount: $3,000 per year for four years

Description: College Scholarships are awarded to 35 freshmen each year.

Amount: $1,000

Description: Grants and scholarships are available through the colleges of engineering, agriculture and life sciences, business, and the departments of art, mathematics, music and theatre arts.

Amount: Various

Description: Virginia residents may qualify for other aid programs, including College Scholarship Assistance for students with high levels of demonstrated financial need.

Amount: Up to $2,000

Description: Virginia Tech Grants are awarded to Virginia residents with demonstrated financial need.

Amount: Up to $2,000

Description: Virginia Scholars Program provides merit-based scholarships to Virginia residents.

Amount: $3,000 per year

Description: Athletic scholarships are awarded in a variety of sports based on the regulations of the Metro Conference and the NCAA.

Amount: Up to the cost of attendance

Description: National Achievement Scholarships are awarded to African-American finalists who name Virginia Tech as their first-choice school.

Amount: Various

Deadline: February 15

Washington State University
Pullman, WA

Type: Grants/Scholarships

Description: More than 1,600 state grants are awarded to students who meet criteria such as academic achievement and residency requirements.

Amount: Various, average $975

Description: Alumni Leadership Awards, Glen Terrell Presidential Scholarships, Provost Waivers, and departmental scholarships are available to students who meet certain criteria.

Amount: Various

Description: African-American students may qualify for one of nearly 80 Multicultural Scholarships awarded each year.

Amount: $1,500–$3,000

Description: Transfer students may qualify for one of 70 awards through the College of Business and Economics.

Amount: $1,000

Description: The William and Ruth Anderson Scholarship offers an award to African-Americans and other minority students.

Amount: $500

Description: U.S. Bank Multicultural Scholarship is awarded to African-Americans and other minority students who meet certain criteria.

Amount: $1,000–$4,000

Description: Refco Minority Scholarship is awarded to students who meet certain criteria.

Amount: Full tuition

Description: Students who wish to study pharmacy may qualify for scholarships through the Multicultural Scholarship program at the College of Pharmacy.

Amount: $1,000–one-half tuition

Description: Over 100 scholarships are awarded to women athletes and about 120 scholarships are awarded to men in a variety of sports.

Amount: $500–$12,000

Deadline: March 1

Type: Scholarship Service/Support Services

Description: University provides a free scholarship service to students.

Amount: College Knowledge for the Mind (CKM) multicultural program targets middle and high school students and their parents to encourage higher education among minority students.

Wayne State College
Wayne, NE

Type:	Grants/Scholarships
Description:	College offers need-based, non-need-based, academic and institutional grant and scholarship programs including over 1,600 need-based grants.
Amount:	$200–$2,300
Description:	College awards more than 400 academic scholarships annually.
Amount:	$40–$2,752
Description:	College provides students over 250 Annual and Endowed Foundation Scholarships.
Amount:	$60–$2,500
Description:	African-American students may qualify for Lawrence Travis Scholarships.
Amount:	$500
Description:	Multicultural Scholarships are also available to African-Americans and other minority students who meet certain criteria.
Amount:	$1,146–full tuition
Description:	Other funding is also available to African-Americans and other minority students based on various criteria including academics, residency, major field of interest.
Amount:	$390–$2,802
Deadline:	May 1

Wells College
Aurora, NY

Type:	Grants/Scholarships
Description:	College offers, among other programs, New York State (TAP) Grants.
Amount:	$100–$4,050
Description:	Entering students may be eligible to receive Wells Grants.
Amount:	$250–$14,500
Description:	African-American and other minority students may qualify for Thomas Funds, which provide annual awards to eligible students.
Amount:	$2,000–$5,000
Deadline:	February 15

Whitman College
Walla Walla, WA

Type: Grants/Scholarships

Description: College awards over $2,000,000 each year in Whitman Scholarships and $130,000 in Washington State Need Grants to eligible students.

Amount: Various

Description: Nearly all African-American students receive Diversity Scholarships, which provide financial assistance for 80 percent of student need.

Amount: Various

Deadline: February 15

William Paterson College of New Jersey
Wayne, NJ

Type: Grants/Scholarships

Description: College offers a number of private scholarships and awards, some with academic and other criteria including: Harry Leaky Scholarships, C. Kent Warren Scholarships, Academic Excellence Scholarships, WPC Distinguished Scholars program.

Amount: $500–$1,000

Description: College offers Academic Achievement Awards and Thad Jones Memorial Scholarships, based on academic and other criteria.

Amount: Various

Description: Enid Hoffman Scholarships are awarded, based on a variety of criteria.

Amount: $2,000

Description: Students with demonstrated music ability may qualify for a Music Department Talent Scholarship.

Amount: Full tuition (in-state)

Description: Students with music talent may also qualify for Music Department Awards.

Amount: $300–$500

Description: African-Americans and other minority students may qualify for one of 30 WPC Trustee Scholarships awarded each year.

Amount: Tuition and fees

Description: African-Americans and other minority students may qualify for Paul P. Vourco Minority Student Scholarships or WPC Scholarships for African-American and Hispanic Students.

Amount: $500–$1,000

Deadline: April 1

Winthrop University
Rock Hill, SC

Type: Grants/Scholarships

Description: Trustee's Scholarships are awarded to students with a minimum SAT of 1300 (ACT of 31), and who rank in the top 10 percent of their high school class. Awards renewable for eight semesters.

Amount: Full tuition, room and board, renewable

Description: The Founder's Scholarship is awarded to students with a minimum SAT of 1300 (ACT 31), and who rank in the top 10 percent of their high school class. Awards renewable for eight semesters.

Amount: Full tuition and room, renewable

Description: Winthrop Scholars Award provides scholarships to South Carolina residents who are: top ranked in a South Carolina high school with a minimum SAT of 1100 (ACT of 26); the top African-American and other minority graduates with a minimum SAT of 950 (ACT of 23); Palmetto Fellows; South Carolina National Merit Semifinalists with a minimum SAT of 1100 (ACT 26) who rank in the top 25 percent of their high school class; or South Carolina National Achievement Semifinalists with a minimum SAT of 950 (ACT 23) who rank in the top 25 percent of their high school class. Other applicants are considered on the basis of their academic record, SAT/ACT scores, and extracurricular activities.

Amount: Full tuition

Description: S.C. Governor's School of Science and Mathematics Scholarships are awarded to graduates of the Governor's School who have a minimum SAT of 1100 (ACT of 26). Renewable for eight semesters.

Amount: Full tuition, renewable

Description: International Baccalaureate Scholarship candidates must have an International Baccalaureate Diploma, minimum SAT of 1100 (ACT 26), and admission to Winthrop University. Renewable for eight semesters of undergraduate study.

Amount: Full tuition, renewable

Description: President's Scholar Award recipients are selected on the basis
                 of their academic accomplishments and the ability to bring
                 a variety of experiences, backgrounds, and cultures to the
                 Winthrop community. Renewable for eight semesters.

Amount: Half tuition, renewable

Description: Alumni Honor Awards made to South Carolina residents with
                 a minimum SAT of 1000 (ACT 24) who rank in the top 25 per-
                 cent of their high school class.

Amount: Half tuition

Description: Out-of-State Scholars Awards available to out-of-state stu-
                 dents with a minimum SAT of 1000 (ACT 24) who rank in
                 the top 25 percent of their high school class. Renewable for
                 eight semesters.

Amount: Out-of-state fees, renewable

Description: Teacher Cadet Scholarships available to Teacher Cadet Pro-
                 gram participants who demonstrate commitment to teaching,
                 leadership, and high academic achievement.

Amount: $1,000

Description: One-time freshman award of Werts Scholarship available to
                 Teacher Cadet Program participants.

Amount: $500

Description: One-time freshman award of Dean's Merit Scholarship avail-
                 able to students with artistic ability and academic achievement.

Amount: Up to $1,000

Description: One-time freshman award of Art/Visual General Scholarship
                 available upon portfolio review. Renewable for up to eight
                 semesters.

Amount: Up to $1,200, renewable

Description: Dance General Scholarship available upon a successful audi-
                 tion. Renewable for up to eight semesters.

Amount: $500, renewable

Description: Interior Design General Scholarship is available upon portfo-
                 lio approval. Renewable for up to eight semesters.

Amount: Up to $1,200, renewable

Description: Music Scholarship available upon a successful audition. Renewable for up to eight semesters.

Amount: Up to $1,200, renewable

Description: Theatre Firstnighter Scholarship available upon a successful audition. Renewable for up to eight semesters.

Amount: Up to $1,000, renewable

Description: President's Scholar Award available based on academic achievement and student ability to bring a variety of experiences, backgrounds, and cultures to the Winthrop community.

Amount: Half-tuition

Deadline: May 1

Xavier University
New Orleans, LA

Type: Grants/Scholarships

Description: Every student who applies to Xavier is automatically considered for an Xavier University Scholarship, based on academic achievement or talent in art, music, and athletics.

Amount: Various

Description: Honor Scholarships, Presidential Scholarships, and Trustee Scholarships are awarded to students based on academic and other criteria.

Amount: Various

Description: Students with demonstrated talent in the visual and performing arts may qualify for the Mother McAuly Scholarships, National Scholastic Art Scholarships or Performing Arts Grants.

Amount: Various

Description: Students in ROUSSEVE Scholars Program may qualify for grants.

Amount: Various

Description: Students majoring in biology, chemistry, physics/engineering, pharmacy, mathematics, or computer science may receive scholarships through several programs, including E. E. Just Scholars, M.A.R.C. Biomedical Fellows, M.B.R.S. Research Apprentices, O.N.R. Future Scientists, and the RCMS Program.

Description: As a member of the United Negro College Fund, Xavier may nominate students for UNCF Scholarships. Students must have a GPA of 3.0 or higher to qualify.

Amount: Various

Description:	Louise Drexel Morrell Scholarships are offered to "worthy" young African-American men who have financial need.
Amount:	Various
Description:	The Sisters of the Blessed Sacrament Teachers' Education Grants are awarded annually to incoming freshmen majoring in Education.
Amount:	$2,500, renewable for four years
Description:	Paul Douglas Teachers' Scholarships are awarded to students interested in careers in teaching.
Amount:	Various
Description:	General Motors Scholarships are awarded to minorities and women according to academic ability. Preference is given to dependents of General Motors employees.
Amount:	Various
Description:	Xavier University also participates in the National Merit/ Achievement Scholarship Program.
Amount:	Various
Deadline:	Various

Yale University
New Haven, CT

Type:	Grants/Scholarships
Description:	Yale awards scholarships and grants on the basis of need and academic achievement.
Amount:	Various
Deadline:	February 1

Minority/Race-Specific

Adrian College
Adrian, MI

Type:	Grants/Scholarships
Description:	Leadership Scholarships are available to any student who demonstrates leadership in the area of diversity, multiculturalism, and civil rights.
Amount:	75 percent tuition paid or $1,000 annually, renewable
Deadline:	March 15

Allegheny College
Meadville, PA

Type:	Grants/Scholarships
Description:	The Allegheny Minority Scholarship for Research Careers in Science is awarded to African-Americans and other minorities who are interested in science or math and have high academic achievement in these areas. Selected students receive an award each academic year, regardless of the student's financial circumstances. Students who receive this award may also be eligible to receive Allegheny's Presidential Scholarship of up to $7,500 each year or the Dean's Achievement Award of up to $5,000 per year.
Amount:	$5,000
Deadline:	February 15

Antioch College
Yellow Springs, OH

Type:	Grants/Scholarships
Description:	Alfred Hampton Memorial Scholarships are available to first-year African-Americans and other minority students with strong academics.
Amount:	Up to $5,000
Description:	E. Y. "Yip" Harburg Scholarships for African-American Men are available to male African-American students who show evidence of social concern and have graduated from high school with at least a C average.
Amount:	$1,500
Description:	Upward Bound Scholarships are available to students who have participated in an Upward Bound–type program.
Amount:	Up to $3,000
Description:	Paula Carlson Scholarships are available to first-year female students.
Amount:	$2,000
Description:	Foreign Exchange Student Scholarships are open to first-year students who have spent time living and/or working abroad in an American Field Service or other foreign student exchange program.
Amount:	Up to $3,000
Description:	International Student Scholarships are available to first-year foreign students with excellent academics.

Amount:	Up to $3,000
Deadline:	February 15

Appalachian State University
Boone, NC

Type:	Grants/Scholarships
Description:	53 North Carolina Minority Presence Grants are awarded to eligible African-Americans and other minority students.
Amount:	$100–$1,500
Description:	34 African-American Scholarships are awarded to eligible students each year.
Amount:	$100–$1,000
Description:	The College of Business awards three African-American Scholarships each year.
Amount:	$100–$1,000
Deadline:	January 1

Ashland University
Ashland, OH

Type:	Grants/Scholarships
Description:	The University offers financial support to African-American students and other minorities through several programs, including the Society Scholarship National City Bank Scholarship and the Hearst Scholarship program.
Amount:	$500–$3,375
Deadline:	Various

Auburn University
Auburn University, AL

Type:	Grants and Scholarships
Description:	Auburn awards Presidential Opportunity Scholarships to superior minority freshmen each year.
Amount:	Resident tuition, 25 awarded
Description:	Students may also qualify for Charles Barkley Scholarships.
Amount:	$1,750
Description:	Students who meet certain criteria may qualify to receive a W. S. Ball Endowed Scholarship.
Amount:	$1,500

Description: Auburn also offers scholarships to National Achievement Scholarship Program finalists who list Auburn as their first-choice school.

Amount: Various

Description: Naval NROTC and Air Force AFROTC programs on campus also offer financial assistance to minority students with superior ACT/SAT scores who are accepted and enrolled in Auburn University.

Amount: Various

Description: African-American and other minority students interested in studying engineering may qualify for Sonat Minority Engineering Scholarships.

Amount: $2,000

Deadline: April 15

Austin Peay State University
Clarksville, TN

Type: Grants/Scholarships

Description: The Martin Luther King Scholarship

Amount: $2,000

Description: MAAPS Multicultural Scholarship awards

Amount: $500–$2,000

Description: The Delta Sigma Theta makes four annual awards to African-American students.

Amount: $200–$500

Description: The Alpha Kappa Alpha makes six annual awards to African-American students.

Amount: $500–$1,200

Deadline: April 1

Bates College
Lewiston, ME

Type: Grants/Scholarships

Description: Bates appoints several African-American students each year to be Mays Scholars. The program is named in honor of Dr. Benjamin E. Mays, a 1920 alumnus of Bates who later served as President of Morehouse College for more than twenty years.

Mays Scholars are selected on the basis of scholarship, leadership, and character.

Amount: Various

Description: The Admissions and Financial Aid Offices at Bates work together to ensure that eligible African-Americans and other multicultural students receive financial aid packages which will meet their needs.

Amount: Various

Deadline: February 11

Benedictine College
Atchison, KS

Type: Grants

Description: Through the Ethnic Minority Award program, Benedictine matches dollar for dollar the higher of any Federal Pell Grant or Kansas Tuition Grant money that the student is awarded.

Amount: Varies

Deadline: March 1

Bethany College
Bethany, WV

Type: Grants/Scholarships

Description: African-American students may qualify for Multicultural Awards.

Amount: $1,000–$3,000

Deadline: March 15

Boston College
Chestnut Hill, MA

Type: Financial Assistance/Scholarships

Description: African-Americans, Hispanics, Asians, and Native Americans (AHANA) may receive academic assistance, personal counseling, employment, and scholarship information through the services of the Office of AHANA Student Programs. For more information contact: The Office of AHANA Student Programs, c/o Thea Bowman Center, 72 College Road, Chestnut Hill, MA 02167; 617-552-3358.

Amount: Various

Deadline: February 1

Bowdoin College
Brunswick, ME

Type: Loan

Description: Russwurm Scholars, named for journalist and publisher John Brown Russwurm, an alumnus of Bowdoin, provides loans to selected African-American students.

Amount: $500

Deadline: March 1

Bowie State University
Bowie, MD

Type: Grants/Scholarships

Description: African-Americans and other minority students may be eligible for one of more than 45 High Ability Scholarships. Awards based on academic achievement and other criteria.

Amount: Tuition–tuition and fees

Description: African-Americans and other minority students may be eligible for one of more than 45 private scholarships offered by the University, some with academic and other criteria.

Amount: $250–$2,000

Deadline: April 1

California State Polytechnic University
Pomona, CA

Type: Scholarships

Description: The IREM Foundation Minority Scholarship Program awards two scholarships to eligible African-Americans and other minority students who are real estate, business, finance, and marketing majors with an emphasis on real estate.

Amount: $1,000

Deadline: March 15

Write: Financial Aid Office, *or*
                 IREM Foundation Coordinator
                 Institute of Real Estate Management Foundation
                 P. O. Box 109025
                 Chicago, IL 60610-9025
                 312-329-6008

Description: Twenty scholarships are available to eligible first- or second-year African-American graduate students in business administration or management programs through the Coca-Cola Company. Apply to your college financial aid office.

Amount:	$3,000
Deadline:	March 27
Description:	The CSU Scholarship Program for African-American Students and the Cal Poly Black Faculty & Staff Association Academic Incentive Awards provide scholarship and grant awards to African-American students each year.
Amount:	Grants—$100–$550 Scholarships—$1,000
Deadline:	January 1

Campbellsville College
Campbellsville, KY

Type:	Grants/Scholarships
Description:	African-American Christian Ministry Scholarships are awarded to African-American students who are committed to a Christian ministry vocation. Scholarship may be renewed for up to eight semesters.
Amount:	Up to one-half tuition
Deadline:	March 1

Centenary College of Louisiana
Shreveport, LA

Type:	Grants/Scholarships
Description:	The college awards three Endowment Scholarships to African-American students.
Amount:	$300–$500
Deadline:	March 15

Central Connecticut State University
New Britain, CT

Type:	Scholarships
Description:	African-Americans and other minority students may be eligible for Stanley Works Scholarships and the D & L Scholarship Program.
Amount:	Varies
Deadline:	February 15

Chadron State College
Chadron, NE

Type: Grants/Scholarships

Description: African-American students may qualify for BIA Grants.

Amount: $600–$3,000

Deadline: Various

Chapman University
Orange, CA

Type: Scholarships

Description: Thurgood Marshall Awards are available to minority students in the top 10 percent of their high school graduating class.

Amount: 50 percent of tuition

Deadline: March 2

Claremont McKenna College
Claremont, CA

Type: Scholarships

Description: African-American students may qualify for the Black Alumnae Merit Award (BAMA), based on academic achievement and other criteria.

Amount: $3,500

Deadline: February 1

Clarion University of Pennsylvania
Clarion, PA

Type: Grants/Scholarships

Description: State Board of Governors Scholarship awards are made each semester to minority students. Candidates must possess a minimum 3.0 GPA. This tuition-based scholarship may vary in amount, depending on the student's need. Applications may be obtained in the Admissions Office.

Amount: Various

Deadline: January 1

Clemson University
Clemson, SC

Type: Grants/Scholarships

Description: The Robert C. Edwards Scholarship is available to eligible African-American and minority students.

Amount: Various

Description: African-Americans and other minority students may receive university scholarships.

Amount: $2,000–$4,000

Deadline: April 1

Colorado School of Mines
Golden, CO

Type: Scholarships

Description: The African-American Achievement Scholarship program makes awards annually to eligible students.

Amount: $4,100–$18,000 a year

Deadline: March 15

Columbia College
Columbia, MO

Type: Grants/Scholarships

Description: A limited number of matching grant awards are made to state residents through the NAACP Matching Fund program.

Amount: Up to $750

Deadline: March 15

Concordia College
Moorhead, MN

Type: Grants/Scholarships

Description: While the college has no race-based scholarship or aid programs, it does meet all financial need. For students of color, the amount of gift aid may be increased while the amount of loan is decreased to reduce financial burden after graduation. The college has also paid for such expenses as transportation for a student to visit the college to experience the campus first-hand, thereby making an informed decision about attending the school.

Amount: Various

Deadline: May 1

Cornell University
Ithaca, NY

Type: Grants/Scholarships

Description: No grants are awarded based solely on a student's racial/ethnic background; however, some restricted institutional scholarships and non-Cornell grants, such as the Empire State Minority Honors Awards, are awarded only to minority students who demonstrate financial need.

Amount: Various

Deadline: February 15

Denison University
Granville, OH

Type: Grants/Scholarships

Description: African-American students may qualify for the Black Achievers Scholarship which is awarded to participants of the YMCA Black Achievers program for strong academic performance.

Amount: Half tuition

Description: I Know I Can Scholarships are available to graduates of a Columbus, Ohio, public high school.

Amount: $1,500

Deadline: April 1

Duke University
Durham, NC

Type: Scholarships

Description: Reggie Howard Scholarships are awarded to African-Americans and other minority students who meet certain criteria.

Amount: $6,000, seven awarded annually

Deadline: February 1

East Carolina University
Greenville, NC

Type: Grants/Scholarships

Description: African-American students and other minority students may qualify for Minority Presence Grants for North Carolina residents.

Amount: $1,500 per year for four years

Description: The Chancellor's Minority Student Leadership program provides awards to eligible students.

Amount: $1,000

Deadline: April 15

Eckerd College
St. Petersburg, FL

Type: Scholarships

Description: African-American students may qualify for full tuition awards
                    through the Special Honors Scholarships for National Achieve-
                    ment Scholar Finalists and Semifinalists. Also, Eckerd College
                    awards up to $100,000 per year in scholarship assistance to grad-
                    uates of the ALPHA Leadership Program for African-American
                    high school juniors in Pinellas County, Florida.

Amount: Various

Deadline: March 1

Elizabethtown College
Elizabethtown, PA

Type: Scholarships

Description: African-American students may qualify for a number of
                    grant and scholarship programs, including Build the Bridge
                    Scholarships.

Amount: Full tuition

Deadline: April 1

Florida Institute of Technology
Melbourne, FL

Type: Scholarships

Description: Scholarship opportunities available to minority students in-
                    clude: Presidential Scholarships, Faculty Scholarships, Articula-
                    tion Scholarships, Merit Scholarships, National Merit Academic
                    Scholarships, National Achievement Scholarships, Robert C.
                    Byrd Honors Scholarships, Chappie James Most Promising
                    Teacher Scholarships, and Paul Douglas Scholarships.

Amount: $1,500–$7,500

Deadline: March 1

Georgetown University
Washington, D.C.

Type: Scholarships

Description: Georgetown University maintains a number of supportive aca-
                    demic and financial programs for African-Americans and
                    other students of color through the Center for Minority Stu-
                    dent Affairs.

Amount: Various

Write: Center for Minority Student Affairs
                        Georgetown University
                        P. O. Box 2266, Hoya Station
                        B-17 Copley Hall
                        Washington, D.C. 20057-1003
                        202-687-4054

Georgian Court College
Lakewood, NJ

Type: Grants/Scholarships

Description: The Delores Parron Scholarship is available to an entering
                        freshman undergraduate minority woman student in the top
                        10 percent of her high school graduating class who has a com-
                        bined SAT score of 1000. The scholarship is renewable annu-
                        ally, provided the recipient maintains a 3.0 cumulative grade
                        point average.

Amount: Full tuition

Deadline: October 1

Hamline University
St. Paul, MN

Type: Grants/Scholarships

Description: Minority Education Project (MEP) awards to students who re-
                        side in St. Paul, Minnesota, based on need.

Amount: Up to $5,000

Deadline: March 15

Hood College
Frederick, MD

Type: Scholarships

Description: African-American students with academic potential/achieve-
                        ment may qualify for Opportunity Awards. These awards are
                        academically competitive and not need-based.

Amount: One-half tuition

Description: Three one-year scholarships are awarded to underrepresented
                        minorities each year.

Amount: $5,000

Deadline: March 1

Kent State University
Kent, OH

Type:	Grants/Scholarships
Description:	Oscar Ritchie Scholarships are awarded to academically talented African-Americans and other minority students.
Amount:	$1,500—full tuition, fees, room and board
Deadline:	Spring of junior year in high school
Description:	Minority Incentive Scholarships are offered to African-Americans and other minority students based on academic achievement. Awards are made to high school seniors who did not participate in or were not awarded a scholarship from the Oscar Ritchie Memorial Scholarship program. Students must have a GPA of 2.75 to qualify.
Amount:	$2,000–$3,500, renewable
Deadline:	May 1
Description:	The African-American Scholarship is awarded to undergraduate and graduate students. Students with high GPA's are given priority consideration.
Amount:	$250–$500 per year
Deadline:	April 1

Kenyon College
Gambier, OH

Type:	Scholarships
Description:	The Kenyon African-American/Latino Scholarship is awarded to approximately ten academically outstanding African-American and Latino students who are also involved in school and community activities and who have achieved at honors level at their secondary school.
Amount:	$9,500–$19,000
Deadline:	February 15

Lander University
Greenwood, SC

Type:	Grants/Scholarships
Description:	An annual award given to selected minority students ranked in the top ten percent of their class. There is no SAT score minimum requirement. No limit on the number of students who may receive this award. Awards are made annually.
Amount:	$2,000, renewable
Deadline:	January 1

Lewis and Clark College
Portland, OR

Type: Grants/Scholarships

Description: African-American students may qualify for Lewis and Clark Grants.

Amount: $1,000–$5,000

Description: African-Americans and other minority students may qualify for Oregon Need Grants and Major Mission Awards.

Amount: $500–$3,180

Deadline: February 15

Linfield College
McMinnville, OR

Type: Grants/Scholarships

Description: Diversity Grants, Special Endowed Fund and Yearly Restricted Scholarships are available to African-Americans and other minority students who meet certain criteria.

Amount: Various

Deadline: February 1

Loras College
Dubuque, IA

Type: Grants

Description: Diversity Grants are available to African-Americans and other minorities who enroll as full-time students.

Amount: Various

Deadline: April 15

Loyola College in Maryland
Baltimore, MD

Type: Grants/Scholarships

Description: African-American students may qualify for Claver Scholarships. Applicants are considered based on academic potential and evidence of community service and involvement.

Amount: $3,000 to full tuition per year for four years

Description: Claver Grants are available to African-American undergraduates with exceptional financial need.

Amount: Award amount varies, depending on need

Deadline: March 1

Mary Baldwin College
Staunton, VA

Type: Grants/Scholarships

Description: African-Americans and other minority students may qualify
                 for Minority Scholarships.

Amount: $2,000

Deadline: January 1

Menlo College
Atherton, CA

Type: Grants/Scholarships

Description: Awards for African-Americans include: Agnes Jones Jackson
                 Scholarship, Alpha Kappa Alpha Educational Advancement
                 Scholarship, Bay Area Urban League Grant, Earl Warren Le-
                 gal Training Program, Music Assistance Fund, National Con-
                 ference of Black Political Scientists, Organization of Black
                 Airline Pilots Aviation Scholarship, American Association of
                 Advertising Agencies, American Bar Foundation, American
                 College of Healthcare Executives, American Fund for Dental
                 Health, American Institute of Certified Public Accountants,
                 American Institute of Architects, American Planning Asso-
                 ciation, American Society for Microbiology, AT&T Bell Labo-
                 ratories, California Library Association, Council on Legal
                 Education Opportunity, Golden State Minority Foundation,
                 James B. Black College Scholarship Program, Kodak Minority
                 Academic Awards, Marine Biological Laboratory, National Ac-
                 tion Council for Minorities in Engineering, University of Cali-
                 fornia Davis Summer Undergraduate Research Program in
                 Science & Engineering, California Association of Student Fi-
                 nancial Aid Administrators Ethnic Diversity Scholarships.

Amount: Various

Deadline: March 2

Type: Scholarships

Description: Students who are from racially ethnic backgrounds that are
                 underrepresented in the field of engineering may qualify for
                 awards from the National Action Council for Minorities in En-
                 gineering. Applicants must have a 2.5 grade point average and
                 have financial need.

Amount: $500–$3,000

Deadline: March 2

Moorhead State University
Moorhead, MN

Type: Grants/Scholarships

Description: African-American students may qualify for General Minority Scholarships.

Amount: $500–$2,400

Description: African-Americans and other minority students may qualify for a Sanders Scholarship.

Amount: $1,500 annually

Deadline: March 1

Murray State University
Murray, KY

Type: Grants/Scholarships

Description: Marvin D. Mills scholarship program awards to African-American freshmen or full-time transfer students who are residents of Kentucky, have a composite score of 21 on the ACT and rank in the top 25 percent of their class (if transferring, have completed 12 semester hours with a GPA of 2.75), and have exhibited leadership abilities in school, church, job, or other related organizations. Applicants must submit a 200-word essay on a current event or public topic of choice, as well as a recent official transcript.

Amount: Full tuition

Description: The John Fetterman Minority Journalism Scholarship is awarded annually to one minority student in the department of journalism with a grade point average of 2.5.

Amount: Various

Description: The J. J. Roberts Upward Bound Scholarship awards a small stipend of at least $50 a year to an Upward Bound graduate who has earned at least a 2.8 GPA in high school and maintained a minimum of 2.5 on at least 24 credit hours per year.

Amount: Various, average award $50

Description: The Paducah Sun Minority Scholarships are awarded to full-time minority students who are preparing for a career in the field of newspaper journalism. Applicants must have a GPA of 2.75. Recipients will also receive a summer internship with the *Paducah Sun* newspaper.

Amount: Various

Deadline: April 1

New York University
New York, NY

Type: Grants/Scholarships

Description: The University offers the Higher Education Opportunity Program and C-STEP Program, designed to provide academic and financial support to African-American students and other minorities.

Amount: Various

Deadline: February 15

Northeast Missouri State University
Kirksville, MO

Type: Grants/Scholarships

Description: More than 630 Higher Education–Bright Flight grants are awarded annually including to two African-American students.

Amount: $2,000

Description: 78 Minority Scholarships, including nine President's Honorary grants and 30 various Northeast Awards.

Amount: $459–$7,416—Northeast Awards
                 $2,728–$7,516—President's Honorary Grants

Deadline: April 1

Pittsburg State University
Pittsburg, KS

Type: Scholarships

Description: African-American and female students majoring in engineering technology may qualify for a Female/Minority Engineering Technology or Plastics Technology Scholarship, sponsored by Phillips Petroleum.

Amount: Various

Deadline: March 1

Type: Scholarships

Description: Ethnic Minority Scholarship provides financial assistance to needy African-Americans and other minorities who have strong academics with a grade point average of 3.0, and ACT score of 21 or SAT score of 816, and/or meet a number of other requirements.

Amount: Various

Deadline: March 1

Potsdam College of the State University of New York
Potsdam, NY

Type: Grants/Scholarships

Description: College offers approximately 49 New York State TAP Grants to African-American students each year.

Amount: $100–$2,650

Description: Four New York State SUSTA awards are made to African-American students.

Amount: $50–$200

Description: The college also offers special financial aid opportunities to African-Americans and other minority students through the New York State Educational Opportunity Program (EOP). Thirty grants are awarded each year to African-American students through this program.

Amount: $200–$1,800

Deadline: March 1

Providence College
Providence, RI

Type: Grants/Scholarships

Description: In addition to federal and institutional scholarships and grants, several aid programs are available to African-American students.

Amount: Various

Description: The college awards 90 Martin Luther King Scholarships each year.

Amount: Full tuition

Description: Four Mary Benson Scholarships are awarded each year to African-American students.

Amount: $4,000

Description: One Dominic Cardi Scholarship is awarded to an African-American student each year.

Amount: $1,000

Deadline: February 15

Purchase College of The State of New York
Purchase, NY

Type: Grants/Scholarships

Description: African-Americans and other minority students may be eligible
                 for scholarship awards through the State University of New
                 York Minority Honors Scholarship.

Amount: Up to $1,250 per year

Description: The Pepsico Scholarship for Minorities provides an annual
                 award to eligible minority students.

Amount: $1,000 per year

Deadline: February 15

Purdue University
West Lafayette, IN

Type: Scholarships

Description: African-Americans and other minority students may qualify for
                 Purdue Special Achievement awards.

Amount: $1,000–$5,000; 50 awarded

Description: African-Americans and other minority students may qualify
                 for one of 20 General Motors EEOC Scholarships.

Amount: $200–$2,000

Description: EDS Incentive Alumni Scholarships are awarded to African-
                 Americans and other minority students.

Amount: $200–$2,000; two awarded

Deadline: March 1

St. John Fisher College
Rochester, NY

Type: Grants/Scholarships

Description: African-Americans and other minority students may be eligible
                 to receive one of 20 Cultural Diversity awards made each year.

Amount: Half to full tuition

Description: African-Americans and other minority students may be eligible
                 to receive an Urban League Scholarship.

Amount: Half to full tuition

Deadline: March 1

St. John's College—New Mexico
Santa Fe, NM

Type: Grants/Scholarships

Description: African-Americans and other minority students may qualify for awards through the Southwest Scholars Program.

Amount: $2,500 per year

Deadline: March 1

St. John's University
Jamaica, NY

Type: Grants/Scholarships

Description: African-American Catholic students may be eligible for scholarships, based on academic achievement and other criteria.

Amount: Full tuition

Deadline: April 1

St. Lawrence University
Canton, NY

Type: Grants/Scholarships

Description: African-American students may qualify for St. Lawrence University Scholarships.

Amount: $500–$23,500

Deadline: February 15

St. Mary's College
St. Mary's City, MD

Type: Grants/Scholarships

Description: African-American students may qualify for minority grants and scholarships.

Amount: $500–$4,000

Deadline: March 1

St. Paul's College
Lawrenceville, VA

Type: Grants/Scholarships

Description: While St. Paul's enrollment is predominantly African-American, the College provides a number of annual awards specifically to African-Americans and other minority students, including the Nelson Mandela Scholarship, Martin Luther King Scholarship, 30 United Negro College Fund grants, five D.C. Incentive Grants, and two $750 Minority Presence Grants.

Amount:	$750–$5,000
Deadline:	April 15

Sarah Lawrence College
Bronxville, NY

Type:	Grants/Scholarships
Description:	Scholarship and grant opportunities for minority students include Sarah Lawrence Gifts, Supplemental Grants, State Grant programs, and various other public and private grant awards.
Amount:	Various
Deadline:	February 1

Seattle University
Seattle, WA

Type:	Grants/Scholarships
Description:	The Regents' Scholarship and the Central Area Scholarship programs providing scholarships for 11 students from Seattle's central area are two of a number of scholarships the University has available for ethnic American students.
Amount:	$2,000
Description:	The Alliant Techsystems Engineering Scholarship is designed to encourage diversity in the field of engineering. The scholarship is renewable.
Amount:	$2,000
Description:	Boeing Company Corporate Scholarship is awarded to a minority entering his or her junior or senior year. The scholarship is not renewable.
Amount:	$6,000
Description:	Seafirst Bank Minority Scholarship awards ten scholarships to full-time juniors who have established financial need and are majoring in the field of business. The scholarship is renewable if the student maintains a 3.33 GPA.
Amount:	$1,000
Description:	The Robert Truex Scholarship provides funds to minority students majoring in business. Scholarship is renewable.
Amount:	Various
Description:	The U.S. Bank Business Scholarship awards ten scholarships annually to minority students in the Albers School of Business and Economics.

Amount: $3,000

Description: KING-5 Television Scholarships provide three annual awards
                 to minorities who are juniors majoring in communications.

Amount: Various

Deadline: February 15

Sonoma State University
Rohnert Park, CA

Type: Grants/Scholarships

Description: The African-American Scholarship Program provides awards
                 to students who meet certain academic and other criteria.

Amount: $1,000 each year

Description: The Claudia Hampton Award is offered annually to African-
                 American students and other minorities.

Amount: $3,000

Description: African-American students may also receive financial aid infor-
                 mation and assistance through SSU Information and Outreach
                 Programs provided by the Educational Opportunity Program,
                 the Pre-College Program, Black Student Union, and Financial
                 Aid Office personnel.

Amount: Various

Deadline: March 2

Southern Illinois University at Carbondale
Carbondale, IL

Type: Grants/Scholarships

Description: African-Americans and other minority students may qualify for
                 Minority Participation Scholarships, based on academic and
                 other criteria.

Amount: Up to tuition, fees, room and board, books and supplies

Description: African-Americans and other minority students interested in
                 pursuing undergraduate training in engineering may qualify
                 for Minority Engineering Scholarships.

Amount: Up to tuition, fees, books, room and board

Deadline: February 1

Southern Methodist University
Dallas, TX

Type: Grants/Scholarships

Description: The University provides a number of full-tuition Diversity Scholarships and Diversity Awards to students who have demonstrated leadership potential and exceptional academic achievement. Diversity awards are also available to minority students in the middle range of scholastic ability who show a promising academic future. Awards have specific requirements and restrictions, depending on the scholarship program.

Amount: $3,000 per year for four years up to full tuition

Description: The University is also a program sponsor of the National Achievement Scholarships for African-American Scholars. Any Achievement Finalist who indicates Southern Methodist University as a first college choice and who satisfies all admission requirements will be considered for a scholarship award.

Amount: Minimum of half tuition

Deadline: February 1

Southern Nazarene University
Bethany, OK

Type: Scholarships

Description: African-American students may qualify for Ethnic Minority Scholarships.

Amount: $150

Deadline: April 15

Southwest Missouri State University
Springfield, MO

Type: Grants/Scholarships

Description: African-Americans and other minority students may be eligible for Minority Leadership Scholarships, which provide for entering students who graduate in the upper one half of their class and demonstrate leadership in the minority community.

Amount: In-state tuition and fees, renewable

Deadline: March 31

Southwestern University
Georgetown, TX

Type: Scholarships

Description: The Presidential Scholarship program awards two entering African-American and two entering Hispanic students with scholarships that are renewable for four years. Recipients must rank in the top 10 percent of their high school graduating class and score 1100 on the SAT or 25 on the ACT.

Amount: Full tuition

Deadline: March 15

Stanford University
Stanford, CA

Type: Grants/Scholarships

Description: University Scholarships and merit-based scholarships and grants are available to African-Americans and other minority students who meet certain academic and other criteria.

Amount: Various

Description: African-American students may qualify for the Black Alumnae Merit Award (BAMA), based on academic achievement and other criteria.

Amount: $3,500

Deadline: February 1

State University College at Oneonta
Oneonta, NY

Type: Grants/Scholarships

Description: African-Americans and other minority students may qualify for Oneonta Minority Honors Scholarships. Students must demonstrate superior academic achievement represented by a B average or better.

Amount: Up to $1,000 per year, renewable

Description: Minority students may also qualify for a Scott-Jenkins Fund Scholarship. Eligible students must be "needy and worthy" and maintain at least a C or better academic record. Students must apply annually to receive the awards.

Amount: Various

Deadline: April 15

Stonehill College
North Easton, MA

Type: Grants/Scholarships

Description: Cultural Diversity Scholarships and State Street Scholars program provide for students of color.

Amount:	$2,000 to $12,170 (full tuition) awards annually
Deadline:	February 15

Tarleton State University
Stephenville, TX

Type:	Grants/Scholarships
Description:	Over 50 scholarship awards totaling more than $30,000 are provided to African-Americans and other minorities.
Amount:	Various
Deadline:	Various

Thomas More College
Crestview Hills, KY

Type:	Grants/Scholarships
Description:	African-Americans and other minority students may be eligible for Minority Grants. Recipients must reapply each year.
Amount:	$2,500 per year
Deadline:	March 1

Towson State University
Towson, MD

Type:	Grants/Scholarships
Description:	African-American students may qualify for Minority Awards for Academic Excellence, which are available to U.S. minority citizens based on academic achievement and leadership potential.
Amount:	$1,000–full tuition and fees
Deadline:	March 15

Trenton State College
Trenton, NJ

Type:	Grants/Scholarships
Description:	African-American students may qualify for Presidential Scholar awards.
Amount:	$3,000
Description:	African-Americans and other students may qualify for Trenton State College Scholar awards.
Amount:	$1,500
Deadline:	May 1

United States International University
San Diego, CA

Type:	Scholarships
Description:	African-American students and other minority students may qualify for Reynolds Minority Scholarships.
Amount:	Up to 50 percent of tuition
Deadline:	January 1

University of Alabama at Birmingham
Birmingham, AL

Type:	Scholarships
Description:	African-American students may qualify for Coca-Cola Fellows Scholarships.
Amount:	$3,500 per year for four years
Description:	UAB Minority Presidential Scholarships
Amount:	$3,500
Description:	Dottie Monro Minority Presidential Scholarships
Amount:	$2,500
Description:	Alliance Minority Participation Scholarships
Amount:	$3,330 per year for four years plus $2,000 in internship awards
Description:	A. G. Gaston Scholarships
Amount:	$625
Description:	Camille Armstrong Scholarships
Amount:	$500
Description:	G.E. Scholarships
Amount:	$2,500 per year for four years
Description:	Amoco Foundation Scholarships
Amount:	$3,500 per year for four years
Description:	3M Scholarships
Amount:	$3,500 per year for four years
Description:	Time Warner/Southern Progress Scholarships
Amount:	$3,500 per year for four years
Deadline:	May 1

University of Florida
Gainesville, FL

Type:	Scholarships
Description:	Honors Minority Undergraduate Transfer Scholarships for African-American Students are awarded to entering transfer students with at least a 3.0 grade point average.
Amount:	$1,500
Description:	Honors Minority Scholarships for African-American Beginning Freshmen are awarded for one year only to students with at least a 3.0 high school grade point average.
Amount:	$2,000
Description:	Presidential Minority Scholarships for African-American Beginning Freshmen are awarded to students with at least a 3.0 high school grade point average and a score of 1000 or above on the SAT or 24 or above on the ACT.
Amount:	$2,000
Description:	Howard and Susan Kaskel Minority Scholarships are awarded to minority students from South Florida, with priority given to African-American students who are designated finalists in the National Merit Scholarship program.
Deadline:	January 1

University of Idaho
Moscow, ID

Type:	Scholarships
Description:	African-American students who are residents and/or graduates of an Idaho high school may qualify for State of Idaho Minority and At Risk Scholarships. Students must be of a racial minority, demonstrate substantial financial need, be disabled as defined in 29 U.S. codes, section 794, be a first-generation college student, or be a migrant farm worker/dependent of a migrant farm worker.
Amount:	Various
Description:	Full-time minority students may apply for the Minority Student Scholarship award.
Amount:	$500
Description:	The Loise L. Slade Scholarship, Charles Decker Scholarship, and the Ruth & Royal B. Irving Scholarship offer small awards to qualified students.
Amount:	$200–$500
Deadline:	February 15

University of Illinois at Urbana-Champaign
Champaign, IL

Type:	Scholarships
Description:	Minority students interested in pursuing a teaching career may also receive funds through the Minority Teachers Scholarship program. Applicants must be Illinois residents.
Amount:	Up to $5,000
Description:	Presidents Award program provides awards to African-Americans and other minority students.
Amount:	Up to $3,000
Description:	University participates in the National Action Council for Minorities in Engineering, which provides scholarship awards to eligible students.
Amount:	$250–$1,000
Deadline:	March 15

University of Miami
Coral Gables, FL

Type:	Scholarships
Description:	University of Miami Grants are awarded to African-Americans and other minority students who meet certain criteria.
Amount:	Various
Description:	The John F. Kennedy/Martin Luther King Scholarship makes awards based on demonstrated financial need and academic promise.
Amount:	$1,900
Description:	The Golden Drum/Ronald A. Hammond Scholarship provides awards to exceptionally well-qualified African-American high school seniors.
Amount:	Full-tuition scholarship
Deadline:	March 1

University of Missouri—Columbia
Columbia, MO

Type:	Grants/Scholarships
Description:	30 Brooks Grants are awarded to minorities each year.
Amount:	$7,000–$12,625

Description: The African-American Achievement Award provides financial assistance to eligible students.

Amount: $3,000–$9,000

Deadline: March 1

University of Missouri—St. Louis
St. Louis, MO

Type: Grants/Scholarships

Description: Minority students receive more than $320,000 in scholarship and grant awards including 35 awards from the Margaret Bush Wilson Scholarship, five awards from the Marian Oldham Scholarship, three Monsanto Scholarship awards, and three Mark Twain Scholarships, 15 awards from the Interco Scholarship, four Monxmode Scholarship awards, and 64 awards from the Center for Academic Development.

Amount: $1,500–$6,800

Deadline: April 1

University of Northern Colorado
Greeley, CO

Type: Grants/Scholarships

Description: African-Americans and other minority students may qualify for Colorado Diversity Grants.

Amount: $800

Description: President's Honor Cultural Diversity Scholarships

Amount: $1,500

Description: Presidential Cultural Diversity Transfer Scholarships

Amount: $500

Description: Local scholarships, including the UNC—Boettcher Minority Scholarship.

Amount: $2,500

Deadline: March 1

University of North Dakota
Grand Forks, ND

Type: Grants/Scholarships

Description: African-Americans and other minority students may be eligible for Cultural Diversity Tuition Waiver awards.

Amount: $900–$1,900

Deadline: April 15

University of Pittsburgh
Pittsburgh, PA

Type: Grants/Scholarships

Description: PITT awards Challenge Scholarships to entering African-American freshman students.

Amount: $1,000–$4,000

Deadline: March 1

University of San Diego
San Diego, CA

Type: Scholarships

Description: Duchesne Scholarships are offered through the School of Education to ethnic minority students interested in becoming elementary and secondary teachers.

Amount: Up to $3,000

Description: Cal Grants are offered through the State of California to residents who have demonstrated academic achievement and financial need.

Amount: $1,410–$6,660

Description: Cultural Diversity Grants are offered to students with demonstrated financial need whose experience, background, and culture will add diversity to the University environment.

Amount: Up to $2,000 per year

Deadline: February 20

University of Southern Indiana
Evansville, IN

Type: Scholarships

Description: The Herschel Moore Memorial Scholarship is available to an enrolled single African-American woman (preference given to a single parent) who has demonstrated outstanding academic achievement and financial need.

Amount: $1,500, renewable for up to three years

Description: The Rolland M. Eckels Scholarship Award provides an award annually to an outstanding African-American high school senior graduating from Vanderburgh, Gibson, Posey, or Warrick counties in Indiana.

Amount: $500

Description: The John Edgar George Memorial Scholarship provides an award annually to an outstanding African-American high school senior with a minimum GPA of 2.5 (preference is given to North High School [Indiana] graduates).

Amount: Up to $2,000

University of Texas at Arlington
Arlington, TX

Type: Grants/Scholarships

Description: The University designates 29 scholarships and grants for African-Americans.

Amount: $100–$4,000

Description: The college currently awards 45 athletic scholarships for various sports to African-American students.

Amount: Various

Deadline: Various

University of Virginia
Charlottesville, VA

Type: Grants/Scholarships

Description: University awards five Jerome Holland Scholarships to out-of-state African-American students. Stipend is renewable. Students are selected on academic achievement and their ability to demonstrate genuine interest in learning.

Amount: $10,000, renewable

Description: Fifty University Achievement Awards are granted annually to the top-rated first-year African-American students from the Commonwealth of Virginia. Award is renewable.

Amount: Full tuition and fees, renewable

Description: The School of Engineering and Applied Science offers annual renewable scholarships based on academic excellence and leadership to qualified African-American students both from Virginia and outside the state.

Amount: Various

Deadline: March 1

Description: The School of Engineering and Applied Science offers annual renewable scholarships based on academic excellence and leadership to qualified African-American students both from Virginia and outside the state.

Amount: Various

Description: The Jefferson Scholars Program is a competitive program sponsored by the UVA Alumni Association, which awards scholarships to entering first-year students with academic excellence, initiative, creativity, and leadership.

Amount: Full tuition for four years, renewable

Deadline: March 1

University of Wisconsin—Whitewater
Whitewater, WI

Type: Grants/Scholarships

Description: African-Americans and other minority students may qualify for Advanced Opportunity Grants.

Amount: Various

Description: African-Americans may qualify to receive Lawton Undergraduate Minority Retention Grants for Wisconsin residents.

Amount: $100–$2,100

Deadline: April 15

Vanderbilt University
Nashville, TN

Type: Grants/Scholarships

Description: Over 235 grants in scholarships are awarded to African-American students, including National Achievement Scholarships.

Amount: $500–$19,550

Deadline: February 15

Virginia Polytechnic Institute & State University
Blacksburg, VA

Type: Grants/Scholarships

Description: National Achievement Scholarships are awarded to African-American finalists who name Virginia Tech as their first-choice school.

Amount: Various

Deadline: February 15

Washington State University
Pullman, WA

Type: Grants/Scholarships

Description: African-American students may qualify for one of nearly 80
               Multicultural Scholarships awarded each year.

Amount: $1,500–$3,000

Description: The William and Ruth Anderson Scholarship offers an award
               to African-Americans and other minority students.

Amount: $500

Description: U.S. Bank Multicultural Scholarships awarded to African-
               Americans and other minority students who meet certain
               criteria.

Amount: $1,000–$4,000

Description: Refco Minority Scholarships awarded to students who meet
               certain criteria.

Amount: Full tuition

Description: Students who wish to study pharmacy may qualify for scholar-
               ships through the Multicultural Scholarship program at the
               College of Pharmacy.

Amount: $1,000 awards to up to one-half tuition

Deadline: March 1

Wayne State College
Wayne, NE

Type: Grants/Scholarship

Description: African-American students may qualify for Lawrence Travis
               Scholarships.

Amount: $500

Description: Multicultural Scholarships are also available to African-
               Americans and other minority students who meet certain
               criteria.

Amount: $1,146–full tuition

Description: Other funding is also available to African-Americans and
               other minority students, based on various criteria including
               academics, residency, major field of interest.

Amount: $390–$2,802

Deadline: May 1

Wells College
Aurora, NY

Type: Grants/Scholarships

Description: College offers, among other programs, New York State (TAP) Grants.

Amount: $100–$4,050

Description: Entering students may be eligible to receive Wells Grants.

Amount: $250–$14,500

Description: African-Americans and other minority students may qualify for Thomas Funds, which provide annual awards to eligible students.

Amount: $2,000–$5,000

Deadline: February 15

Description: The Minority Teacher Scholarship is awarded to African-American and/or Hispanic students who are enrolled in programs leading to Indiana Teacher certification, who plan to teach full-time in Indiana following graduation.

Amount: $1,000 per academic year

Deadline: March 1

Western Illinois University
Macomb, IL

Type: Grants/Scholarships

Description: State programs for African-Americans and other minorities include: Women & Minorities in Educational Administration awards and Minority Teacher Incentive Grants.

Amount: $1,620–$4,178

Deadline: March 1

Whitman College
Walla Walla, WA

Type: Grants/Scholarships

Description: Nearly all African-American students receive Diversity Scholarships, which provide financial assistance for 80 percent of student need.

Amount: Various

Deadline: February 15

William Paterson College of New Jersey
Wayne, NJ

Type:	Grants/Scholarships
Description:	African-Americans and other minority students may qualify for one of 30 WPC Trustee Scholarships awarded each year.
Amount:	Tuition and fees
Description:	African-Americans and other minority students may qualify for Paul P. Vourco Minority Student Scholarships or WPC Scholarships for African-American and Hispanic Students.
Amount:	$500–$1,000
Deadline:	April 1

Winthrop University
Rock Hill, SC

Type:	Grants/Scholarships
Description:	Winthrop Scholars Awards provide scholarships to South Carolina residents who are: top ranked in a South Carolina high school with a minimum SAT of 1100 (ACT of 26), the top African-American and other minority graduates with a minimum SAT of 950 (ACT of 23), Palmetto Fellows, South Carolina National Merit Semifinalists with a minimum SAT of 1100 (ACT 26) who rank in the top 25 percent of their high school class, or South Carolina National Achievement Semifinalists with a minimum SAT of 950 (ACT 23) who rank in the top 25 percent of their high school class. Other applicants are considered on the basis of their academic records, SAT/ACT scores, and extracurricular activities.
Amount:	Full tuition
Description:	President's Scholar Award available, based on academic achievement and student ability to bring a variety of experiences, backgrounds, and cultures to the Winthrop community.
Amount:	Half tuition
Deadline:	May 1

Xavier University
New Orleans, LA

Type:	Grants/Scholarships
Description:	As a member of the United Negro College Fund, Xavier may nominate students for UNCF Scholarships. Students must have a GPA of 3.0 or higher to qualify.
Amount:	Various

Description: Louise Drexel Morrell Scholarships are offered to "worthy" young African-American men who have financial need.

Amount: Various

Description: General Motors Scholarships are awarded to minorities and women according to academic ability. Preference is given to dependents of General Motors employees.

Amount: Various

Deadline: Various

Other

Agnes Scott College
Decatur, GA

Type: Tuition Payment Plan

Description: Agnes Scott College Ten-Month Payment Plan divides college costs into interest-free monthly payments. Extended Repayment Plans offered through the Richard C. Knight Agency are available to parents who wish to spread the cost of college over a long period of time—up to ten years.

Amount: Payment installments based on current cost of tuition

Deadline: Various

Austin Peay State University
Clarskville, TN

Type: Grants/Scholarships

Description: Educational Opportunity Center offers financial aid counseling and assistance in obtaining needed aid at no charge.

Amount: Various

Deadline: Various

Description: The Delta Sigma Theta provides four annual awards to African-American students.

Amount: $200–$500

Description: The Alpha Kappa Alpha makes six annual awards to African-American students.

Amount: $500–$1,200

Deadline: April 1

Other   247

Boston College
Chestnut Hill, MA

Type: Financial Assistance/Scholarships

Description: African-Americans, Hispanics, Asians, and Native Americans
                   (AHANA) may receive academic assistance, personal counsel-
                   ing, employment, and scholarship information through the
                   services of the Office of AHANA Student Programs. For more
                   information contact: The Office of AHANA Student Programs,
                   c/o Thea Bowman Center, 72 College Road, Chestnut Hill,
                   MA 02167; 617-552-3358.

Amount: Various

Deadline: February 1

California State Polytechnic University
Pomona, CA

Type: Grants/Scholarships

Description: The University has compiled a Scholarship Resource Guide for
                   students, which provides information on scholarships that Cal-
                   Poly offers. The guide is available at no charge.

Amount: Varies

Deadline: Varies

Cornell University
Ithaca, NY

Type: Financial assistance/support services

Description: The University participates in programs such as the New York
                   Higher Education Program and Education Opportunity Pro-
                   gram, providing a network of services to African-Americans
                   and other minorities with financial aid assistance, tutoring,
                   and a prefreshman summer program which assists admitted
                   students. In addition, minority students receive assistance
                   through the Committee on Special Education Projects
                   (COSEP).

Amount: Various

Deadline: Various

Eckerd College
St. Petersburg, FL

Type: Scholarship Search Service

Description: College provides student access to the CASHE database of
                   scholarship and grant information at no charge.

Amount: Various

Georgetown University
Washington, D.C.

Type: Scholarships

Description: The Office of Student Financial Services maintains a library of information about grant, scholarship, fellowship, and other educational financing opportunities and publishes a bimonthly scholarship opportunities newsletter which is available to students. The University also offers a free scholarship search/database service to enrolled students, which matches them with aid for which they may qualify.

                   In addition, the University maintains a number of supportive academic and financial programs for African-Americans and other students of color through the Center for Minority Student Affairs.

Amount: Various

Type: Tuition Payment Plan

Description: The University offers a tuition installment payment plan.

Amount: Various

Write: For more information, contact: The Georgetown University Office of Student Accounts at 202-687-4092.

Hamline University
St. Paul, MN

Type: Grants/Scholarships

Description: The Page Foundation offers awards to eligible students. Recipients are selected by committee.

Amount: Up to $1,000 per year

Deadline: March 15

King's College
Wilkes-Barre, PA

Type: Loans/Tuition Payment Plans

Description: The Insured Tuition Payment Plan is a savings plan offered by the college which allows students and parents to make monthly payments into an FDIC-insured bank account to pay for educational costs. Interest is earned at current Money Market rates.

Amount: Various

Description: A parent may reserve education funds to cover four years of college costs through the Extended Repayment Plan.

Amount: Various

Description: The King's College Deferred Payment Plan allows students and parents to spread all or a portion of educational costs over an eight-month period.

Amount: Various

Deadline: Various

Description: TERI—The Educational Resources Institute—provides innovative financing, information services, loan programs, and tuition plans for students and parents. For more information, contact 1-800-255-TERI.

Description: ABLE—A Better Loan for Education—allows creditworthy applicants to repay one year of educational costs over 15 years. The interest rate is variable and adjusted quarterly, based on the prime rate.

Amount: Various

Write: For more information, contact:
                 Knight Tuition Payment Plans
                 855 Boylston Street
                 Boston, MA 02116
                 1-800-225-6783

Description: The College offers a number of deferred tuition payment plans, including Academic Management Services (AMS), a low-cost, flexible system for paying educational expenses through regularly scheduled payments.

Amount: Various

Write: For further information, contact:
                 Academic Management Services
                 50 Vision Blvd.
                 East Providence, Rhode Island 02914
                 1-800-635-0120

Northeast Missouri State University
Kirksville, MO

Type: Grants/Scholarships

Description: Over 50 Vocational Rehabilitation grants are awarded to students who meet certain criteria.

Amount: $656–$4,736

Deadline: April 1

Rosemont College
Rosemont, PA

Type: Grants/Scholarships

Description: One full and two partial Rosemont Opportunity Grants are
                 awarded annually to students who have overcome significant
                 educational, economic, or historical disadvantages in pursuit
                 of higher education.

Amount: Various

Description: Several Community and Junior College Scholarships are
                 awarded to highly qualified graduates of surrounding area ju-
                 nior and community colleges.

Amount: Various

Deadline: March 1

St. Paul's College
Lawrenceville, VA

Type: Child Care/Academic Support

Description: St. Paul's College Single Parent Support System provides assis-
                 tance, academic support, child development, and child care
                 services to single parents who are students. This unique model
                 program is designed to help single parent students overcome
                 the financial, academic, and emotional obstacles that may im-
                 pede their obtaining a college education. The College also of-
                 fers Upward Bound, a program designed to increase the
                 academic skills and levels of motivation in low-income and/or
                 first-generation college students, and provide financial and
                 other support.

Amount: Various

Deadline: Various

Southwest Missouri State University
Springfield, MO

Type: Work aid

Description: SMSU offers the largest Cooperative Education program in Mis-
                 souri, through which students are allowed to earn an income
                 through career-related employment while attending college.

Amount: Various

Type: Grants/Scholarships

Description: Numerous academic, departmental and nondepartmental
                 scholarships and grants are available to incoming and upper-
                 class students. University produces an 80-page handbook, *Schol-*

arships and Financial Aid, which describes in detail scholarship and other aid programs available at Southwest Missouri State University, and includes a freshman scholarship application.

Amount: Various

Description: Vocational Rehabilitation provides financial and other assistance to students with physical or emotional limitations.

Amount: Various

Deadline: March 31

Syracuse University
Syracuse, NY

Type: Minority assistance programs

Description: In addition to financial aid opportunities, Syracuse University special outreach efforts to African-Americans and other minority students include: the New York State Higher Education Opportunity Program, Student Support Services Program, Syracuse University Summer Bridge Program, and Syracuse Challenge Program.

Amount: Various

Deadline: Various

Thomas More College
Crestview Hills, KY

Type: Grants/Scholarships

Description: College sponsors the Academic Management Services Plan (AMS), which allows you to spread college costs over a period of months without paying any interest charges. The plan may be used to supplement all other forms of financial aid. Applications may be obtained from the Bursar's Office, Admissions, or Financial Aid Office.

A college-developed software program and database is available to students at no charge to locate additional sources of financial aid.

Amount: Various

Deadline: Various

University of Florida
Gainesville, FL

Type: Scholarships/Tuition Reductions

Description: The University publishes a booklet, *Financial Aid for Minority Students,* which will be helpful in learning about and applying for the many funding opportunities available at this institution.

Amount: Various

Deadline: April 15

Description: Out-of-State Tuition Reductions are awarded to approximately fifty top entering freshmen who are non-Florida residents.

Amount: This award reduces fees by $2,500

Deadline: April 15

University of Northern Colorado
Greeley, CO

Type: Scholarships

Description: The START Scholarship Search Service is available to students for a fee of $20.

Amount: Various

Description: The UNC Scholarships handbook provides detailed information on aid programs available at the University.

Amount: Various

Deadline: Various

University of San Diego
San Diego, CA

Type: Scholarships

Description: USD Copley Library offers students access to the scholarship search service, College Fund Finder, at no charge, and publishes a free *Guide to Outside Resources of Financial Aid.* In addition, the USD financial aid staff offers several workshops at high schools and community colleges on financial aid, including "How to Apply for Financial Aid, How to Apply for Outside Scholarships, and How to Cover Your College Costs."

Amount: Various

Deadline: Various

University of Southern Indiana
Evansville, IN

Type: Scholarships

Description: The University provides the Financial Aid Finders Software to students at no charge. In addition, African-American students may take advantage of mentoring and counseling services through the University Multi-Cultural Center.

Amount: Various

Deadline: Various

University of Wisconsin—Whitewater
Whitewater, WI

Type: Grants/Scholarships

Description: Funds may also be available to eligible students through Federal and State Vocational Rehabilitation Grant programs, Wisconsin National Guard Education Assistance Programs, Veterans and U.S. Army Reserve Officer Training Corps.

Amount: Various

Deadline: April 15

Washington State University
Pullman, WA

Type: Scholarship Service/Support Services

Description: University provides a free scholarship service to students.

                 College Knowledge for the Mind (CKM) mutlicultural program targets middle and high school students and their parents, to encourage higher education among minority students.

Wayne State College
Wayne, NE

Type: Grants/Scholarships

Description: Other funding is also available to African-Americans and other minority students, based on various criteria including academics, residency, major field of interest.

Amount: Various

Deadline: Various

Wells College
Aurora, NY

Type: Installment payment plans/waivers

Description: College offers tuition plans and full or partial waivers for employees or children of employees. The Wells Program sponsors one-day workshops on college admissions and financial aid for area minority students.

Amount: Various

Deadline: Various

Winthrop University
Rock Hill, SC

Type: Grants/Scholarships

Description: International Baccalaureate Scholarship candidates must have an International Baccalaureate Diploma, minimum SAT of

1100 (ACT 26), and admission to Winthrop University. Renewable for eight semesters of undergraduate study.

Amount:	Full tuition, renewable

Description: President's Scholar Award recipients are selected on basis of their academic accomplishments and ability to bring a variety of experiences, backgrounds, and cultures to the Winthrop community. Renewable for eight semesters.

Amount: Half tuition, renewable

Description: Out-of-State Scholars Award available to out-of-state students with a minimum SAT of 1000 (ACT 24) who rank in the top 25 percent of their high school class. Renewable for eight semesters.

Amount: Out-of-state fees, renewable

Deadline: May 1

Veterans/Military

Austin Peay State University
Clarksville, TN

Type: Grants/Scholarships

Description: The Center for Creative Arts awards scholarships in disciplines including art, music, speech, communication & theatre, creative writing; various athletic, department, private and military scholarships and grants.

Amount: Various

Deadline: April 1

Florida A&M University
Tallahassee, FL

Type: Grants/Scholarships

Description: Students who are dependent children of veterans in the State of Florida may qualify for grant and scholarship awards under the Dependent Children of Deceased War Veterans program.

Amount: Various

Deadline: Various

Type: Scholarships

Description: The President's Special Military Scholarship for High Achieving Students is intended for those active duty military personnel who have demonstrated high academic potential. Available through the Army ROTC program.

Amount:	Free tuition, academic expenses, room and board, and $100 per month stipend
Deadline:	April 1

Howard University
Washington, D.C.

Type:	Scholarships
Description:	La Verne Noyes Scholarships are available to students who are direct descendants of veterans of World War I, who have demonstrated need.
Amount:	Up to full tuition
Deadline:	April 1

Southern Illinois University at Carbondale
Carbondale, IL

Type:	Grants/Scholarships
Description:	University offers Army and Air Force ROTC grants and awards to students who are enrolled in these programs.
Amount:	Up to full tuition and fees
Description:	Students who meet certain criteria may qualify for an Illinois Veterans' Grant.
Amount:	$1,365 per semester
Deadline:	February 1

United States Air Force Academy
USAF Academy, CO

Type:	Scholarships
Description:	The United States Air Force Academy provides financial assistance to students who qualify for entry into the Academy. Entering freshmen are required to provide a $2,000 student deposit to defray the cost of uniforms and a personal computer.
Amount:	Four-year scholarship, including free room and board, medical care, and a monthly salary of $543.90
Deadline:	January 31

University of Illinois at Urbana-Champaign
Champaign, IL

Type:	Scholarships
Description:	Child of Veteran awards and Illinois Veterans Grants provided to eligible students.

Amount: Full tuition

Deadline: March 15

University of Wisconsin—Whitewater
Whitewater, WI

Type: Grants/Scholarships

Description: Funds may also be available to eligible students through Federal and State Vocational Rehabilitation Grant programs, Wisconsin National Guard Education Assistance Program, and Veterans and U.S. Army Reserve Officer Training Corps.

Amount: Various

Deadline: April 15

Western Illinois University
Macomb, IL

Type: Grants/Scholarships

Description: National Guard Scholarships

Amount: $1,489

Description: Scholarships for Dependents of POW/MIAs

Amount: $1,554

Deadline: March 1

SECTION V: PRIVATE SCHOLARSHIPS BY FIELD

Agriculture—Animal Science

Alabama Cattlemen's Foundation
Montgomery, AL

Type: Scholarships

Description: Awards scholarships to students majoring in Animal Science at Auburn University.

Amount: $1,500

Write: Dr. Billy Powell
                 P.O. Box 2499
                 Montgomery, AL 36102

Dexter Hobbs Scholarship
Montgomery, AL

Type: Scholarships

Description: Awards one scholarship to a student majoring in Animal Science at Auburn University.

Amount: $1,500

Deadline: April 15

Write: Dr. Billy Powell
                 P.O. Box 2499
                 Montgomery, AL 36102

Agriculture—Forestry

Alabama Farmers Federation
Montgomery, AL

Type: Scholarships

Description: Awards to full-time students at Colleges of Agriculture, School of Forestry to major in Agriculture Education or Agricultural Engineering. Must be a U.S. citizen, and have good moral character, excellent academics.

Deadline: March 15

Write: Cheryl Mitchell, Executive Secretary
              P.O. Box 11000
              Montgomery, AL 36191-0001
              205-288-3900

Biological Sciences

Association of Official Analytical Chemists, International
Arlington, VA

Type: Scholarships

Description: Harvey W. Wiley Scholarships are awarded to undergraduate
              students at the junior level majoring in chemistry, micro-
              biology, and related sciences. Students with majors in dental,
              nursing, medicine, or related fields may also apply. One-year
              award must be applied to fourth year of undergraduate work.

Amount: $1,000

Deadline: Various

Write: Association of Official Analytical
              Chemists International
              2200 Wilson Blvd., Suite 400
              Arlington, VA 22201-3301

Clare Boothe Luce Scholarships in Science and Engineering
New York, NY

Type: Scholarships

Description: Offers scholarships to encourage women to enter the engineer-
              ing and science fields. Awards are made to students majoring in
              biology, chemistry, computer science, engineering, mathemat-
              ics, and physics. Scholarship awards are made through individ-
              ual colleges and universities. Participating schools include:
              Boston University, Colby College, Creighton University, Ford-
              ham University, Georgetown University, Marymount University,
              Mount Holyoke College, Mundelein College, St. John's Univer-
              sity, Santa Clara University, Seton Hall University, Trinity Col-
              lege, University of Notre Dame, Villanova Preparatory School.

Amount: Various

Deadline: Various

Write: College or university financial aid office *or*
              Clare Boothe Luce Scholarships in Science
              and Engineering
              c/o Henry Luce Foundation, Inc.
              111 W. 50th Street
              New York, NY 10020

Business—Accounting

Alcoa Foundation
Pittsburgh, PA

Type: Scholarships

Description: Alcoa Foundation supports minority scholarships in a number
                        of fields at several schools, including several Historically Black
                        Colleges and Universities. Awards are made to students pursu-
                        ing courses in accounting, business information, business man-
                        agement, chemical engineering, computer-based management
                        information systems, electrical engineering, management, mar-
                        keting, mathematics, mechanical engineering, nursing.

                        Schools attended by scholarship winners include: Central State
                        University, Florida A & M University, Georgia Institute of Tech-
                        nology, Hampton University, Howard University, Illinois Insti-
                        tute of Technology, Indiana University, Knoxville College,
                        Livingston College, Pennsylvania State University, Prairie View
                        A & M University, University of Idaho, Virginia Polytechnic In-
                        stitute, Washington State University, Wingate College.

Amount: Various

Write: Alcoa Foundation
                       Alcoa Building
                       Pittsburgh, PA 15219
                       412-553-4696

American Society of Women Accountants
Chicago, IL

Type: Scholarships

Description: The Society awards scholarships to women majoring in the
                        field of accounting. The scholarship is designed to increase
                        opportunities for women in the field. Scholarships are offered
                        at the chapter and national levels. There are currently more
                        than 130 chapters located throughout the United States.

Amount: Various

Write: Miriam Green, Executive Director
                       American Society of Women Accountants
                       35 E. Wacker Drive
                       Suite 2250
                       Chicago, IL 60601
                       312-726-9030

American Society of Women Accountants
Montgomery, AL

Type:	Scholarships
Description:	Awards one scholarship to a student majoring in Accounting at Auburn University at Montgomery.
Amount:	One quarter's tuition
Deadline:	February 15
Write:	AUM Office of Financial Aid 7300 University Drive Montgomery, AL 36117 205-244-3623

Scholarships for Minority Accounting Students
The American Institute of Certified Public Accountants (AICPA)
New York, NY

Type:	Scholarships
Description:	Scholarships are awarded to full-time undergraduate and graduate students at accredited institutions. Students must be declared accounting majors and have satisfactorily completed at least 30 semester hours or 45 quarter hours, or equivalent college work, including six hours in accounting, to be eligible. Applicants must complete a Financial Aid Form (FAF) and submit it to the College Scholarship Service to be considered (even if they have already completed a FAFSA). All applications must include an official transcript. Payments are made for the academic year following application and are sent directly to the school of attendance. The scholarship may be renewed annually, but students must reapply each year.
Amount:	Up to $5,000; renewable annually
Deadline:	July 1
Write:	Gregory Johnson, CPA Manager, Minority Initiatives 212-596-6270

National Association of Black Accountants, Inc.
Washington, D.C.

Type:	Scholarships
Description:	Awards scholarships to college undergraduates who have a 3.5 grade point average and have completed 18 credit hours in accounting. Applicants must also be members of the Association's student chapter or affiliated with one of the professional chapters.

Applications may be obtained from the national office and should be returned with a 500-word autobiographical sketch, a 500-word essay, two letters of recommendation, and three references.

Students interested in chapter scholarships may contact the nearest chapter office.

Amount: Various

Write: National Association of Black Accountants, Inc.
            300 "I" Street, N.E., Suite 107
            Washington, D.C. 20002
            202-543-6656

Business—Actuarial Science

Actuarial Scholarships for Minority Students
Society of Actuaries/Casualty Actuarial Society
Itasca, IL

Type: Scholarships

Description: The Society awards scholarships to African-Americans and other minority students who are interested in pursuing actuarial careers. Awards are made on the basis of merit and financial need. Applicants should have taken Exam 100 of the Actuarial Examinations, the SAT or ACT Assessment, and must be admitted to a college or university offering either a program in Actuarial Science or courses which will serve to prepare the student for an actuarial career.

Amount: Various, award determined by a committee of members of the Society

Write: Contact the chairman of the Mathematics (Actuarial Science) Department, the placement office or guidance office at your college or university or:

                Society of Actuaries/Casualty Actuarial Society
                500 Park Boulevard
                Itasca, IL 60143
                312-706-3500

Business—Business Administration

Armco Insurance Group
Middletown, OH

Type: Scholarships

Description: African-Americans and other minority students interested in
                 pursuing undergraduate study in Business with emphasis on
                 insurance may qualify for the ARMCO Minorities in Insur-
                 ance and Risk Management Scholarship. Candidates must at-
                 tend high schools in communities in which an Armco facility
                 is located and be seniors who rank in the upper one half
                 of their class. Scholarship recipients must attend one of the
                 following colleges or universities: University of Cincinnati,
                 Cincinnati, OH; College of Insurance, New York, NY; Drake
                 University, Des Moines, IA; Howard University, Washington,
                 D.C.; University of Iowa, Iowa City, IA; University of North
                 Texas, Denton, TX; Ohio State University, Columbus, OH;
                 Oregon State University, Corvallis, OR; Southern Methodist
                 University, Dallas, TX; University of Wisconsin, Madison, WI.

Amount: $2,000, renewable

Deadline: November 1

Write: Armco Insurance Group
                 703 Curtis Street
                 Middletown, OH 45043

Duracell/National Urban League Scholarship
National Urban League, Inc.
New York, NY

Type: Scholarships

Description: Scholarships available to students attending a four-year school
                 and in the top 25 percent of the class while pursuing a major
                 in engineering, sales, marketing, manufacturing operations,
                 finance, or business administration.

Amount: Five $10,000 and five $1,000 awards available

Deadline: April 15

Write: National Urban League, Inc.
                 500 E. 62nd Street, 11th Floor
                 New York, NY 10021
                 212-310-9000

Fukunaga Scholarship Foundation
Honolulu, HI

Type: Scholarships

Description: Scholarships are awarded to high school students who are interested in pursuing undergraduate study in business administration. Awards are made on the basis of academic achievement, recommendations, and financial need.

Amount: $6,000–$8,000

Deadline: March 15

Write: Fukunaga Scholarship Foundation
                 900 Fort Street Mall, Suite 500
                 P.O. Box 2788
                 Honolulu, HI 96803

General Electric Foundation Minority Student Scholarships
General Electric Foundation
Fairfield, CT

Type: Scholarships

Description: Scholarships available to assist African-Americans and other minority students majoring in engineering and business. Awards are made to universities and organizations directly, which select the individuals to receive scholarship awards.

Amount: $1,000,000 in funds available for awards

Write: College financial aid office

Deadline: Various

Golden State Minority Foundation
Los Angeles, CA

Type: Scholarships

Description: Scholarships awarded to full-time undergraduate students enrolled as juniors or above in an accredited four-year college or university (60 units of college credit required). Students must have a major field of interest in Business Administration, Economics, Life Insurance, or related field, have a minimum 3.0 to 4.0 overall GPA or be students in good standing at an accredited four-year college or university with no GPA scale, be a U.S. citizen or Permanent Legal Resident, be a qualified minority (African-American, Latino, Native American, or other represented ethnic minority), be employed no more than 28 hours per week, and attend school or be a resident of California, Detroit, Michigan, or Houston, Texas.

Amount: Various

Deadline: Northern California and Houston, Texas: *August 1–October 1*
                 Detroit, Michigan: *December 1–February 1*
                 Southern California: *February 1–April 1*

Write: Golden State Minority Foundation
                        1999 West Adams Boulevard
                        Los Angeles, CA 90016
                        1-800-666-4763

James S. Kemper Foundation
Long Grove, IL

Type: Scholarships

Description: Offers approximately 15 scholarships each year to college freshmen majoring in business administration or insurance. Awards are made by individual colleges and universities.

Amount: $1,000–$3,500

Deadline: Various

Write: College or university financial aid office, *or*
                        James S. Kemper Foundation
                        Kemper Insurance Company
                        One Kemper Drive
                        Long Grove, IL 60049

National Association of Plumbing-Heating-Cooling Contractors
Falls Church, VA

Type: Scholarships

Description: Awards scholarships to high school seniors and college freshmen who are enrolled in undergraduate programs in business administration. Candidates must be sponsored by a member of the Association in good standing.

Amount: $2,500

Deadline: March 1

Write: National Association of Plumbing-Heating-
                        Cooling Contractors
                        P.O. Box 6808
                        Falls Church, VA 22040-1148
                        1-800-533-7694

National Electronic Distributor Association Education Foundation
Chicago, IL

Type: Scholarships

Description: Awards scholarships to undergraduate students majoring in business administration and related fields including industrial distribution, marketing, or retailing. To obtain an application, send a 52-cent stamped, self-addressed, 9″×12″ envelope to NEDA.

Amount: $1,000, renewable

Deadline: May

Write: National Electronic Distributor Association
                   Education Foundation
                   35 E. Wacker Drive, Suite 1100
                   Chicago, IL 60601

National Urban League
New York, NY

Type: Scholarships

Description: The National Urban League, working in concert with 113 affili-
                   ate organizations in 34 states and the District of Columbia, pro-
                   vides programs of direct service to people nationwide including
                   scholarships for full-time students pursuing a Bachelor's De-
                   gree at accredited institutions of higher learning. Candidates
                   must be classified as a junior, or third-year student, at the time
                   the scholarship award commences, and must also rank within
                   the top 25 percent of their class. Candidates must also major in
                   courses leading to a professional career in engineering, sales,
                   marketing, manufacturing operations, finance, or business
                   administration, to qualify. This scholarship is offered in con-
                   junction with Kraft, Inc. Candidates may apply to any Na-
                   tional Urban League affiliate, or write to the national office.

Amount: Various, ten awards to minority students

Deadline: April 15; education officials at the National Urban League
                   will interview each semifinalist

Write: Director of Education
                   National Urban League
                   500 E. 62nd Street
                   New York, NY 10021

Pepsi-Cola's Summer Internship Program
Pepsi-Cola Company
Somers, NY

Type: Internships/Scholarships

Description: Students who have completed their sophomore year in col-
                   lege are eligible to be part of this program to provide African-
                   Americans and other minority college students hands-on
                   business experience, and to give Pepsi-Cola expanded access to
                   a qualified pool of potential employees. Recipients have the op-
                   tion of working in four areas within the corporation—sales,
                   manufacturing, finance, and personnel/employee relations. Ap-
                   plicants should be enrolled in a four-year college or university.

                   Interested students may arrange to speak to the Pepsi-Cola
                   recruiters through their school's college placement office or
                   send a letter with their résumé to the National College Re-
                   cruiting Manager at Pepsi-Cola.

Amount:	Promising interns may receive $2,000 scholarships
Write:	National College Recruiting Manager
Pepsi-Cola's Summer Internship Program
Pepsi-Cola Company
Somers, NY 10589
914-767-7434

Thomas A. Watson Scholarship
Lincoln National Life Insurance Corporation
Fort Wayne, IN

Type:	Scholarships
Description:	Scholarships are awarded to African-Americans and other minorities who are graduates of Allen County High School and are pursuing a four-year degree in a business-related field. Awards are made by a scholarship committee. Recipients are also offered an opportunity to gain company and corporate exposure by accepting meaningful and challenging summer work assignments.
	The scholarship is designed to promote career mobility through higher education to African-Americans and other minority students who reside in the Fort Wayne, IN, community.
Amount:	Various
Write:	Thomas A. Watson Scholarship
Lincoln National Life Insurance Corporation
Human Resources Division/Affirmative Action
1300 S. Clinton Street
Fort Wayne, IN 46801
219-427-2000

Business—Hospitality Administration

The Club Managers Association of America
Bethesda, MD

Type:	Scholarships
Description:	The Club Managers Association provides scholarships to students who have expressed an interest in the club-management profession. Scholarships are awarded on the basis of merit to students attending accredited four-year colleges and universities. Candidates must show evidence of employment interest in the club-management profession and must have completed their freshman year in college and have maintained a grade point average of at least 2.0.

The application process includes submission of a 500-word essay on career objectives.

Amount: Various

Write: The Club Managers Association of America
               7615 Winterberry Place
               Bethesda, MD 20817
               301-229-3600

Business—Information Management

Alcoa Foundation
Pittsburgh, PA

Type: Scholarships

Description: Alcoa Foundation supports minority scholarships in a number of fields at several schools, including several Historically Black Colleges and Universities. Awards are made to students pursuing courses in accounting, business information, business management, chemical engineering, computer-based management information systems, electrical engineering, management, marketing, mathematics, mechanical engineering, nursing.

               Schools attended by scholarship winners include: Central State University, Florida A & M University, Georgia Institute of Technology, Hampton University, Howard University, Illinois Institute of Technology, Indiana University, Knoxville College, Livingston College, Pennsylvania State University, Prairie View A & M University, University of Idaho, Virginia Polytechnic Institute, Washington State University, Wingate College.

Amount: Various

Write: Alcoa Foundation
               Alcoa Building
               Pittsburgh, PA 15219
               412-553-4696

Business—Management

Alcoa Foundation
Pittsburgh, PA

Type: Scholarships

Description: Alcoa Foundation supports minority scholarships in a number of fields at several schools, including several historically Black colleges and universities. Awards are made to students pursuing courses in accounting, business information, business management, chemical engineering, computer-based management information systems, electrical engineering, management, marketing, mathematics, mechanical engineering, nursing.

Schools attended by scholarship winners include: Central State University, Florida A & M University, Georgia Institute of Technology, Hampton University, Howard University, Illinois Institute of Technology, Indiana University, Knoxville College, Livingston College, Pennsylvania State University, Prairie View A & M University, University of Idaho, Virginia Polytechnic Institute, Washington State University, Wingate College.

Amount:	Various
Write:	Alcoa Foundation Alcoa Building Pittsburgh, PA 15219 412-553-4696

Business—Marketing/Sales

Alcoa Foundation
Pittsburgh, PA

Type:	Scholarships
Description:	Alcoa Foundation supports minority scholarships in a number of fields at several schools, including several historically Black colleges and universities. Awards are made to students pursuing courses in accounting, business information, business management, chemical engineering, computer-based management information systems, electrical engineering, management, marketing, mathematics, mechanical engineering, nursing.

Schools attended by scholarship winners include: Central State University, Florida A & M University, Georgia Institute of Technology, Hampton University, Howard University, Illinois Institute of Technology, Indiana University, Knoxville College, Livingston College, Pennsylvania State University, Prairie View A&M University, University of Idaho, Virginia Polytechnic Institute, Washington State University, Wingate College.

Amount:	Various
Write:	Alcoa Foundation Alcoa Building Pittsburgh, PA 15219 412-553-4696

Asbury Park Press Scholarships for Minority Students
Neptune, NJ

Type:	Scholarships
Description:	Offered to one graduating high school student from Monmouth County, New Jersey, and one from Ocean County, New Jersey, who will enter college seeking a career in the field of communications including reporting, broadcasting, marketing, and advertising. Scholarship offered to African-Americans and other minority students. Renewable for a total of four years with continued satisfactory work.
Amount:	$1,500
Write:	Editorial Department Asbury Park Press 3601 Highway 66 P.O. Box 1550 Neptune, NJ 07754

J. Victor Herd Memorial Scholarship
Center for Insurance Education
Howard University
Washington, D.C.

Type:	Scholarships
Description:	Two-year scholarships are awarded to cover tuition, room, board, and expenses for students attending Howard University during their junior and senior years of study. Applicants must have a concentration in insurance studies and must also have demonstrated superior academic ability and leadership potential.
	The scholarships were named for the late J. Victor Herd, who served as chairman of Continental Insurance and who was instrumental in establishing the Center for Insurance Education at Howard University.
Amount:	Full tuition and expenses for two years at Howard University
Write:	Center for Insurance Education Howard University 2600 6th Street, N.W. Washington, D.C. 20059 202-636-5118

Business—Real Estate

American Institute of Real Estate Appraisers
Chicago, IL

Type: Scholarships

Description: Organization awards approximately 20 scholarships annually
                 through the Institute's Research and Educational Trust Fund.
                 Awards are made on the basis of academic achievement and
                 are intended to help finance the costs of college work, lead-
                 ing to a degree in real estate appraisal, land economics, real
                 estate, or allied fields.

Amount: $2,000 and $3,0000 awards made annually

Deadline: March 15

Write: Education Department
                 American Institute of Real Estate Appraisers
                 430 N. Michigan Avenue
                 Chicago, IL 60611-4088
                 312-329-8559

Business—Transportation Management

General Motors Institute
GMI Engineering Management Institute
Flint, MI

Type: Cooperative Education

Description: The GMI Engineering and Management Institute is an ac-
                 credited college offering degree programs in electrical engi-
                 neering, industrial engineering, mechanical engineering,
                 manufacturing systems engineering, and management sys-
                 tems. Enrolled students alternate between periods of study
                 on campus and related work experience in more than 250
                 sponsoring companies. Freshmen admitted to the program
                 must be selected by a corporate sponsor.

Amount: Selected students are paid wages averaging $1,200 per month
                 during the 24 weeks of work experience for freshmen. Stu-
                 dents may also receive some fringe benefits in terms of insur-
                 ance, seniority accrual, or vacation. Wages normally increase
                 as the student progresses. Students can expect to earn an ap-
                 proximate annual wage of $10,000 over the five-year period.

Deadline: Applications, which may be obtained from GMI, high school
                 guidance counselors, and GMI corporate sponsors, must be
                 submitted in the fall.

Write: GMI Engineering and Management Institute
1700 W. Third Avenue
Flint, MI 48502
1-800-521-7436

Communications— Advertising/Public Relations

Asbury Park Press Scholarships for Minority Students
Neptune, NJ

Type: Scholarships

Description: Offered to one graduating high school student from Monmouth County, New Jersey, and one from Ocean County, New Jersey, who will enter college seeking careers in the field of communications, including reporting, broadcasting, marketing, and advertising. Scholarship offered to African-Americans and other minority students. Renewable for a total of four years with continued satisfactory work.

Amount: $1,500

Write: Editorial Department
Asbury Park Press
3601 Highway 66
P.O. Box 1550
Neptune, NJ 07754

Black Communicators Scholarship
Dallas-Fort Worth Association of
Dallas, TX

Type: Scholarships

Description: Several scholarships are awarded to high school seniors and college students who are pursuing careers in print, broadcasting, photojournalism, graphic arts, or public relations.

Amount: Minimum $1,500

Deadline: March 1

Write: Rochelle Riley
President DPF/ABC
c/o Dallas Morning News
Communication Center
P.O. Box 227455
Dallas, TX 75222

Gannett Foundation Scholarships
Gannett Foundation
Rochester, NY

Type: Scholarships

Description: The Foundation administers three scholarships for students interested in studying journalism. Scholarships are awarded on a competitive basis to students with outstanding scholastic and extracurricular records. Journalism scholarships for entering freshmen and undergraduates are awarded to students interested in pursuing careers in news, editorial, broadcasting, and advertising.

Amount: Various

Write: Priscilla C. Kennedy
                Scholarship Administrator
                Gannett Foundation
                Lincoln Tower
                Rochester, NY 14604
                716-262-3315

Minority Advertising Internships
American Association of Advertising Agencies
New York, NY

Type: Internships

Description: African-Americans and other minority students obtain realistic job experience in an advertising agency which will help prepare them for entry-level professional positions in advertising. The ten-week program takes place June–August at agencies in Chicago, Detroit, Los Angeles, San Francisco, and New York. Applicants must be racial minorities and be in an undergraduate- or graduate-level program, having completed at least their junior year by the summer for which they are applying. Students are not required to have a specific major field of interest to apply. Candidates must submit an application form, undergraduate school transcript, letters of recommendation from a professor and a previous employer, and supporting material like sample writing or artwork.

Amount: Undergraduates receive a salary of $250 per week, with a higher salary to graduate students. Housing and transportation allowances are also available.

Deadline: January 15

Write: Minority Advertising Intern Program
                American Association of Advertising Agencies
                666 Third Avenue
                New York, NY 10017

The Poynter Fund
Times Publishing Company
St. Petersburg, FL

Type: Scholarships

Description: The Fund provides scholarships to undergraduate and gradu-
                   ate students interested in careers in communications and
                   journalism. Scholarships are awarded on the basis of merit and
                   career interest in the areas of newswriting, editing, and admin-
                   istration. They are also granted to those wanting to study busi-
                   ness, administration and marketing, including sales, art layout,
                   promotion and research, and for the technological aspects of
                   journalism, including mechanical production.

                   Grantees will be asked to sign a statement of understanding
                   that they intend to work in one of the above career fields for
                   at least three years following completion of their education.

Amount: Various

Deadline: July 1

Write: The Poynter Fund
                   Personnel Department
                   Times Publishing Company
                   P.O. Box 1121
                   St. Petersburg, FL 33731
                   813-893-8556

Communications—Journalism/ Radio and Television Broadcasting

Academy of Television Arts & Sciences
Burbank, CA

Type: Paid Internships

Description: The Academy sponsors an internship program designed to
                   give college students in-depth exposure to professional facili-
                   ties, techniques, and practices in 23 areas of the television in-
                   dustry. Sponsors for each category are working professionals
                   who agree to take one intern for the summer session, and serve
                   as mentor, supervising the intern's work.

                   Interns work 40-hour weeks and are paid a stipend and $300
                   travel allowance if they reside outside Los Angeles County.

                   Each intern signs a contract with the Academy which defines
                   the terms of the internship agreement.

Amount: $1,600 stipend for an eight-week internship, plus a $300
                   travel allowance

Write: Academy of Television Arts & Sciences
                Student Internship Program
                3500 W. Olive Avenue, #700
                Burbank, CA 951505
                815-953-7575

Asbury Park Press Scholarships for Minority Students
Neptune, NJ

Type: Scholarships

Description: Offered to one graduating high school student from Mon-
                mouth County, New Jersey, and one from Ocean County,
                New Jersey, who will enter college seeking careers in the
                field of communications, including reporting, broadcasting,
                marketing, and advertising. Scholarships offered to African-
                Americans and other minority students. Renewable for a total
                of four years with continued satisfactory work.

Amount: $1,500

Write: Editorial Department
                Asbury Park Press
                3601 Highway 66
                P.O. Box 1550
                Neptune, NJ 07754

Aviation-Space Writers' Association
Columbus, OH

Type: Cash awards

Description: Offers awards to students who are interested in pursuing ca-
                reers in communications with special interest in aviation/
                space writing or photojournalism. Candidates must submit
                writing samples which have been published during the year
                prior to the award year.

Amount: $100–$500; 21 awards offered each year

Deadline: February 14

Write: Aviation-Space Writers' Association
                AWA Writing Awards
                17 South High Street #1200
                Columbus, OH 43215

Black Communicators Scholarship
Dallas-Fort Worth Association of
Dallas, TX

Type: Scholarships

Description: Several scholarships awarded to high school seniors and col-
                lege students who are pursuing careers in print, broadcast-
                ing, photojournalism, graphic arts, or public relations.

Amount: Minimum $1,500

Deadline: March 1

Write: Rochelle Riley
                   President DPF/ABC
                   c/o Dallas Morning News
                   Communication Center
                   P.O. Box 227455
                   Dallas, TX 75222

Chicago Association of Black Journalists Scholarship
Chicago, IL

Type: Scholarships

Description: Scholarships are open to any African-American or other mi-
                   nority full-time junior, senior, or graduate student who is
                   majoring in print or broadcast journalism at an accredited
                   college or university in the Chicago metropolitan area.

Amount: $1,000

Deadline: March 31

Write: Chicago Association of Black Journalists
                   P.O. Box 11425
                   Chicago, IL 60611

Chip Quinn Scholars Program
c/o Howard University
Washington, D.C.

Type: Scholarships/Internships

Description: Chip Quinn Scholars are matched with appropriate paid
                   summer internships at cooperating newspapers and matched
                   with mentor editors. Winners receive travel stipends and,
                   upon successful completion of the internship, scholarship
                   awards. Students who are juniors may be nominated for this
                   program if they are enrolled in a journalism program that is a
                   member of the Association of Black College Journalism and
                   Mass Communications Program.

Amount: $1,000 scholarships and paid summer internships

Write: Dr. Lawrence Kaggwa
                   Department of Journalism
                   School of Communications
                   Howard University
                   Washington, D.C. 20059
                   202-806-7855

Concerned Media Professionals Scholarship
Tucson, AZ

Type: Scholarships

Description: A number of scholarships are awarded to African-Americans and other minority college students majoring in print or broadcast journalism. Applicants must be Arizona residents attending an Arizona college or university.

Amount: $500–$1,000

Deadline: March 31

Write: Concerned Media Professionals
                Scholarship Committee
                P.O. Box 44034
                Tucson, AZ 85733

Cox Newspapers
Minority Journalism Scholarship
Atlanta, GA

Type: Scholarships

Description: Full scholarships, including tuition, room, board and books, are available to graduating high school seniors from racial minorities in the public schools of Atlanta, Georgia, who are in need of financial assistance. Applicants must have at least a B average and an interest in journalism. Recipients will attend Georgia State University or one of the colleges in the Atlanta University Center and have a major or minor in journalism.

Amount: All educational expenses

Deadline: April 30

Write: Mrs. Alexis Scott Reeves
                Cox Newspapers
                P.O. Box 4689
                Atlanta, GA 30302

Detroit Free Press Minority Journalism Scholarship
Detroit Free Press
Detroit, MI

Type: Scholarships

Description: Scholarships are available to African-Americans and other minority students who plan to become writers, editors, or photojournalists and have a 3.0 grade point average. Scholarships are given to encourage outstanding minorities to enter the field of journalism. Awards are based on grades, a written essay detailing why the student wants to become a journalist, and recommendations from the high school. Application must also be accompanied by SAT/ACT scores. Finalists have an in-person interview.

Amount:	Competitive selection, with two first-place winners receiving $1,000 awards and one second-place winner a $750 award. First-place winners automatically compete for $20,000 scholarships offered by Knight-Ridder, Inc.
Deadline:	January 6
Write:	Louise Reid Ritchie Detroit Free Press 321 W. Lafayette Blvd. Detroit, MI 48226 800-678-6400

Dow Jones Minority Scholarship Competition for College Sophomores
The Dow Jones Newspaper Fund
Princeton, NJ

Type:	Scholarships
Description:	The Reporting Scholarship Competition offers minority college sophomores who have completed a reporting internship at a newspaper an opportunity to compete for one of five $1,000 scholarships. Students must find their own internships and complete them during the sophomore year or summer before the junior year. Members of minority groups who will have worked as a reporting intern at a daily or weekly newspaper will be eligible for the award.
Amount:	$1,000
Write:	The Dow Jones Newspaper Fund P.O. Box 300 Princeton, NJ 08543-0300 609-452-2820
Deadline:	Various

Florida Society of Newspaper Editors
Journalism Scholarship
Tallahassee, FL

Type:	Scholarships
Description:	Eight scholarships are awarded to Florida minority high school graduates who plan to attend a Florida public community college. Applicants must have a 3.0 high school grade point average and be interested in pursuing a journalism career. Scholarships are renewable for up to two years. Students should contact the financial aid office or journalism department at their community college for an application and additional information.
Amount:	$1,200 per year ($600 per semester)
Write:	Contact the financial aid office or journalism department at a Florida public community college.
Deadline:	Various

Foundation Scholarships for Minority Freshmen
American Society of Newspaper Editors
Washington, D.C.

Type: Scholarships

Description: Sixty scholarships are awarded to college-bound African-Americans and other minority students. Students must submit a formal application form, two letters of recommendation, and write an essay stating their career interests and journalism-related activities while they were seniors in high school. Applicants must have a 2.5 grade point average in their high school courses and sign a statement of intent to pursue a career in journalism.

Amount: $750

Deadline: First week in November

Write: Minority Affairs Director
                ASNE
                P.O. Box 17004
                Washington, D.C. 20041
                703-648-1146

Frank E. Johnson Scholarship
The Arizona Daily Star
Tucson, AZ

Type: Scholarships

Description: Scholarship awarded to an African-American or other minority student at Pima Community College. Award based on scholarship, financial need, and interest in journalism. Apply to the Department of Media Communications at Pima Community College.

Amount: $500

Write: Department of Media Communications
                Pima Community College
                2202 W. Anklam Road
                Tucson, AZ 85709

Gannett Foundation Scholarships
Gannett Foundation
Rochester, NY

Type: Scholarships

Description: The Foundation administers three scholarships to students interested in studying journalism. Scholarships are awarded on a competitive basis to students with outstanding scholastic and extracurricular records. Journalism scholarships for entering freshmen and undergraduates are awarded to students interested in pursuing careers in news, editorial, broadcasting, and advertising.

Amount:	Various
Write:	Priscilla C. Kennedy
	Scholarship Administrator
	Gannett Foundation
	Lincoln Tower
	Rochester, NY 14604
	716-262-3315

Garth Reeves Jr. Memorial Scholarship
Miami, FL

Type:	Scholarships
Description:	One or more scholarships offered by the Greater Miami Chapter, Society of Professional Journalists to undergraduate and graduate-level African-American and other minority students majoring in journalism. Preference is given to students from South Florida or students attending college in South Florida.
Amount:	Amount determined by financial need; minimum award $500
Deadline:	March 1
Write:	Mike Haggerty
	Miami Herald
	One Herald Plaza
	Miami, FL 33132

Hearst Foundation Minority Scholarship
Northwestern University
Evanston, IL

Type:	Scholarships
Description:	Scholarship offered by The Medill School of Journalism at Northwestern University is awarded to an African-American graduate editorial student every fall quarter. Recipient will have graduated from a historically Black college or university, and demonstrate superior writing and journalistic potential. All admitted African-American editorial students are eligible for the scholarship; no additional application materials are required.
Amount:	$24,000
Write:	The Medill School of Journalism
	Northwestern University
	Evanston, IL 60208

Institute for Education in Journalism/Afro-American Affairs
New York University
New York, NY

Type: Summer Internships

Description: Selected students are placed for ten weeks in an entry-level position as full-time writers with news publications in the New York and New Jersey area. Preference given to full-time juniors or seniors who intend to go on to graduate school. Program open to African-Americans and other minority students. Applicants are required to submit an application including reasons for wanting to pursue a career in journalism and an autobiographical essay, college transcript, résumé, samples of work, and two recommendations.

Amount: Minimum stipend is $200 per week

Deadline: Mid-December

Write: New York University
                    Institute of Afro-American Affairs
                    289 Mercer Street, Suite 601
                    New York, NY 10003
                    212-998-2130

Ken Inouye Scholarship
Los Angeles Professional Chapter
Society of Professional Journalists
Torrance, CA

Type: Scholarships

Description: Scholarship awarded to an African-American or other minority junior, senior, or graduate student attending a Los Angeles County college or university, or Los Angeles County resident attending a school elsewhere. Applicants must intend to pursue a journalism career with an emphasis in news work. Scholarship awarded on basis of accomplishments, potential, and need.

Amount: $1,000

Write: Ms. Janet Rae-Dupree
                    c/o Los Angeles Times
                    South Bay Bureau
                    23133 Hawthorn Blvd. #20
                    Torrance, CA 90505

Knight-Ridder Scholarship Program for Minorities
Miami, FL

Type: Scholarships

Description: Awards scholarship to graduating high school seniors who attend high school in an area served by Knight-Ridder. The scholarship is renewable for up to four years based on a student's academic performance and includes a summer internship at a Knight-Ridder newspaper. Interested high school students should contact their school counselor or journalism teacher during the first semester of their senior year for application information.

Amount: $5,000

Write: Contact your high school counselor or journalism teacher for more information.

KNTV Minority Scholarship
KNTV Television
San Jose, CA

Type: Scholarships

Description: Scholarships available to African-Americans and other minority students who are residents of Santa Clara, Santa Cruz, Monterey, or San Benito counties of California. Students must be accepted for admission to an accredited California four-year college or university and major in television production, journalism, or a related field (marketing, public relations, advertising, graphics, or engineering with interest in television). Undergraduate applicants must have one full year of undergraduate work remaining and carry a minimum of 12 semester units during each semester. Scholarships are awarded with preference to students with financial need who demonstrate an interest and potential in the field of television production and television journalism.

Amount: Two $750 scholarships awarded

Deadline: April

Write: KNTV Minority Scholarship Application
                 KNTV Television
                 645 Park Avenue
                 San Jose, CA 95110

Leonard M. Perryman Communications Scholarship
for Ethnic Minority Students
New York, NY

Type: Scholarships

Description: Scholarships available to African-Americans and other minority undergraduate students who are juniors or seniors and have the intention of pursuing a career in religious communications. Candidates must attend an accredited institution of higher education in the United States. Students may pursue careers in various areas of communications including audiovisual, electronic, and print journalism. This scholarship is offered in recognition of Leonard M. Perryman, a journalist for the United Methodist Church for nearly 30 years.

Amount:	$2,500
Deadline:	February 15
Write:	Scholarship Committee
	United Methodist Communications
	475 Riverside Drive, Suite 1901
	New York, NY 10115

National Association of Black Journalists Scholarship
Washington, D.C.

Type:	Scholarships
Description:	Scholarships available to undergraduate and graduate students. Applicants must have completed at least one full semester of college to be eligible.
Amount:	$2,500
Deadline:	Late Fall
Write:	Scholarship Coordinator
	NABJ
	P.O. Box 17212
	Washington, D.C. 20041

National Association of Media Women, Inc., Scholarship
Atlanta, GA

Type:	Scholarships
Description:	Scholarships offered by the Atlanta chapter of the National Association of Media Women, Inc., to an undergraduate minority female student majoring in mass communications. Applicants must attend a college or university in Georgia.
Amount:	Minimum award $500
Deadline:	March 15
Write:	Alexis Scott Reeves
	National Association of Media Women, Inc.
	P.O. Box 4689
	Atlanta, GA 30302

National Newspaper Publishers Association Grants
Washington, D.C.

Type:	Grants
Description:	Provides information and helps administer grants to minority college students pursuing journalism careers.
Amount:	Ten grants awarded annually, valued at $2,000 each

Write: Chairman
                  NNPA Scholarship Committee
                  948 National Press Building
                  Washington, D.C. 20045

Newsday Scholarship in Communications for Minorities
Melville, NY

Type: Scholarships

Description: Up to two scholarships awarded to minority students graduat-
                  ing from high school in Nassau or Suffolk County who plan
                  to attend a four-year college in the United States. The schol-
                  arships are to be applied toward the cost of tuition for the fall
                  following graduation. High school students must contact
                  their guidance counselors for applications and details.

Amount: $5,000

Deadline: March 31

Write: Mr. Reginald Tuggle
                  Community Affairs Director
                  Newsday
                  235 Pinelawn Road
                  Melville, NY 11747-4250
                  516-454-2183

New York Association of Black Journalists
Stephen H. Gayle Memorial Scholarship
New York, NY

Type: Scholarships

Description: Scholarships available to African-American college students
                  or graduating high school seniors planning careers in jour-
                  nalism. Candidates must write an autobiographical essay re-
                  lated to why they want to enter the field of journalism.

Amount: Minimum award $1,500

Deadline: October 19

Write: NYABJ
                  P.O. Box 2446
                  Rockefeller Center
                  New York, NY 10185

Sacramento Bee Minority Media Scholarships
Sacramento, CA

Type: Scholarships

Description: Twelve scholarships awarded to minority students living in
                  the Sacramento circulation area. Applicants may be entering
                  freshmen or currently enrolled students and may attend any

college but have an interest in pursuing a career in mass media. Applicants should have a 3.0 grade point average.

Amount: $1,000

Deadline: March 15

Write: Monica Bagood
               Community Relations Department
               Sacramento Bee
               P.O. Box 15779
               Sacramento, CA 95852

Syracuse Newspapers Journalism Scholarship
The Herald-Journal
Syracuse, NY

Type: Scholarships

Description: Full scholarships to study print journalism at Syracuse University are available to minority students who attend Syracuse high schools. Students must attend a special journalism course taught by the Syracuse Newspapers staff prior to enrolling in Syracuse University as a journalism major. A committee of professional journalists and college professors will select the student based on potential and interest in making newspaper journalism her or his career.

Amount: Four-year grant valued at approximately $80,000

Write: Mr. Timothy Bunn, Executive Editor
               The Herald-Journal
               P.O. Box 4915
               Syracuse, NY 13221

The Poynter Fund
Times Publishing Company
St. Petersburg, FL

Type: Scholarships

Description: The Fund provides scholarships to undergraduate and graduate students interested in careers in communications and journalism. Scholarships are awarded on the basis of merit and career interest in the areas of newswriting, editing, and administration. They are also granted for those wanting to study business, administration and marketing, including sales, art layout, promotion and research, and for the technological aspects of journalism, including mechanical production.

               Grantees will be asked to sign a statement of understanding that they intend to work in one of the above career fields for at least three years following completion of their education.

Amount: Various

Deadline: July 1

Write: The Poynter Fund
                   Personnel Department
                   Times Publishing Company
                   P.O. Box 1121
                   St. Petersburg, FL 33731
                   813-893-8556

Communications—Library Science

American Library Association (ALA)
Chicago, IL

Type: Scholarships

Description: The LITA/OCLC Minority Scholarship is awarded to mem-
                   bers of a principal minority group (African-American, Ameri-
                   can Indian or Alaskan Native, Asian or Pacific Islander, or
                   Hispanic). Scholarships are awarded on the basis of academic
                   excellence, leadership potential, and evidence of commit-
                   ment to a career in library education, with an emphasis on li-
                   brary automation and information technology, with prior
                   activity and experience in those fields. Recipients must enter
                   or be enrolled in an ALA-accredited master's degree pro-
                   gram of library education or library automation. Applicants
                   must be U.S. or Canadian citizens.

Amount: $2,500

Deadline: April 1

Write: Library and Information Technology Association
                   American Library Association
                   50 E. Huron Street
                   Chicago, IL 60611
                   312-280-4270

Louise Giles Minority Scholarship
American Library Association (ALA)
Chicago, IL

Type: Scholarships

Description: The Louise Giles Minority Scholarship is awarded to mem-
                   bers of a principal minority group (African-American, Ameri-
                   can Indian or Alaskan Native, Asian or Pacific Islander, or
                   Hispanic). Applicants cannot have completed more than 12
                   semester hours (or its equivalent) towards a master's degree
                   in library science prior to June 1. Scholarships are awarded
                   on the basis of academic excellence, leadership, and evi-
                   dence of commitment to a career in librarianship. Individu-

als need not have been accepted into a library education program at the time of application, but winners must enter an ALA-accredited master's degree program. Applicants must be U.S. or Canadian citizens.

Amount: Two $3,000 scholarships awarded annually

Deadline: Postmarked no later than January 14

Write: Staff Liaison
             ALA Scholarship Juries
             50 E. Huron Street
             Chicago, IL 60611
             312-280-4277 or 280-4281/4282

Communications—Speech

A. G. Bell Association for the Deaf
Washington, D.C.

Type: Scholarships

Description: Forty annual scholarships are available to auditory-oral college students who are severely or profoundly impaired who are attending regular colleges and universities.

Amount: $250–$1,000

Deadline: April 15

Write: Scholarship Coordinator
              A. G. Bell Association for the Deaf
              3417 Volta Place, N.W.
              Washington, D.C. 20007
              202-337-5220

Communications— Telecommunications

Radio Technical Commission for Aeronautics
Washington, D.C.

Type: Award competition

Description: Awards made on the basis of an essay or thesis paper that has been completed within the last three years. Candidates may be undergraduate or graduate level students studying aviation electronics, aviation, or telecommunications.

Amount: $1,500

Deadline: June 30

Write: Radio Technical Commission for Aeronautics
                  William Jackson Award
                  1717 H Street, N.W.
                  Washington, D.C. 20006

Computer Science and Mathematics

Alcoa Foundation
Pittsburgh, PA

Type: Scholarships

Description: Alcoa Foundation supports minority scholarships in a number
                  of fields at several schools, including several historically Black
                  colleges and universities. Awards are made to students pursuing
                  courses in accounting, business information, business manage-
                  ment, chemical engineering, computer-based management
                  information systems, electrical engineering, management, mar-
                  keting, mathematics, mechanical engineering, nursing.

                  Schools attended by scholarship winners include: Central State
                  University, Florida A & M University, Georgia Institute of Tech-
                  nology, Hampton University, Howard University, Illinois Insti-
                  tute of Technology, Indiana University, Knoxville College,
                  Livingston College, Pennsylvania State University, Prairie View
                  A & M University, University of Idaho, Virginia Polytechnic In-
                  stitute, Washington State University, Wingate College.

Amount: Various

Write: Alcoa Foundation
                  Alcoa Building
                  Pittsburgh, PA 15219
                  412-553-4696

Scholarships & Summer Programs
AT&T Research & Development
Holmdel, NJ

Type: Scholarships and Summer Employment Programs

Description: AT&T offers several scholarship and employment programs
                  to minority students interested in pursuing careers in engi-
                  neering, computer science, and research.

                  The **Engineering Scholarship Program (ESP)** is designed to
                  encourage selected outstanding minorities and women to
                  pursue undergraduate degrees in Computer Science or se-
                  lected Engineering disciplines. ESP provides full tuition, a
                  book allowance, fees, room and board, a challenging summer
                  job each year at AT&T, and an appropriate mentor. Applicants

must be high school seniors who are applying as full-time students to colleges with strong curricula. Fifteen candidates are selected each year. **Application deadline date is January 15. Students interested in applying should call 908-949-4301.**

Dual Degree Scholarship Program (DDSP) is designed to encourage talented minorities to enter the Engineering field. The DDSP is sponsored through a coordinated effort with The Atlanta University Center in Atlanta, Georgia. Through this collaboration, Dual Degree scholars earn a BA degree in Math or Physics from Spelman, Morehouse, Clark, or Morris Brown colleges in three years and then go on to earn a BS degree in Engineering or Computer Science. The second degree may be earned from Georgia Institute of Technology, University of Alabama, or Boston University over a two-year period. The DDSP provides full tuition, books, fees, room and board, a challenging summer job each year at AT&T, and an appropriate mentor. Three candidates are selected to participate in the program. **Application deadline date is June 10. Outstanding minority students interested in this program should call 908-949-4301.**

The Summer Research Program for Minorities and Women (SRP) provides outstanding minorities and women an opportunity to work for a summer within the research environment of AT&T Bell Laboratories. The program is open to students who have completed 3 years of education in selected engineering disciplines. The program also provides an AT&T Bell Laboratories scientist as a mentor. 60–100 candidates are accepted each year in the program. **Application deadline is December 1. For more information, call 908-949-3728.**

The University Relations Summer Program (UR) provides summer employment for outstanding BS, MS, and Ph.D candidates who are within two years of graduation and pursuing studies in selected engineering disciplines. The purpose of the program is to provide work experience for talented students on a well-defined project in an R&D (Research and Development) environment. An AT&T Member of Technical Staff is assigned to each student as a mentor. To be eligible, candidates must be available for Career Employment within two years of Summer Employment. 200–300 candidates are selected for the program each year. **Application deadline date is February 15. For additional information, call 908-949-5592.**

Amount: (See individual programs)

Deadline: (See individual programs)

Write: For a brochure on the program write:
            AT&T
            101 Crawfords Corner Road
            Holmdel, NJ 07733-3030

Clare Boothe Luce Scholarships in Science and Engineering
New York, NY

Type: Scholarships

Description: Offers scholarships to encourage women to enter the engineering and science field. Awards are made to students majoring in biology, chemistry, computer science, engineering, mathematics, and physics. Scholarship awards are made through individual colleges and universities. Participating schools include: Boston University, Colby College, Creighton University, Fordham University, Georgetown University, Marymount University, Mount Holyoke College, Mundelein College, St. John's University, Santa Clara University, Seton Hall University, Trinity College, University of Notre Dame, Villanova Preparatory School.

Amount: Various

Deadline: Various

Write: College or university financial aid office, *or*
                     Clare Boothe Luce Scholarships in Science
                     and Engineering
                     c/o Henry Luce Foundation, Inc.
                     111 W. 50th Street
                     New York, NY 10020

NAACP Willems Scholarship
National Association for the Advancement of Colored People (NAACP)
Baltimore, MD

Type: Scholarships

Description: Scholarships available to undergraduate and graduate students who are majoring in engineering, chemistry, physics, or computer and mathematical sciences, and have a grade point average of at least 3.0 or a B average. Applicants must be members of the NAACP.

Amount: Undergraduate maximum award is $8,000, paid in annual installments of $2,000

Deadline: April 30

Write: NAACP Willems Scholarship
                     NAACP
                     4805 Mt. Hope Drive
                     Baltimore, MD 21215-3297
                     410-358-8900

National Scholarship Trust Fund (NSTF)
Pittsburgh, PA

Type: Scholarships

Description: The National Scholarship Trust Fund of the Education Council
                     of the Graphic Arts Industry, Inc., offers graphics art scholar-
                     ships to students who are interested in careers in graphic
                     communications, engineering science, management, design,
                     manufacturing, or other areas leading to a career in the
                     printing and publishing industries.

                     Applicants must be graduating high school seniors or college
                     freshmen, sophomores or juniors enrolled in a two-year or
                     four-year college and attending on a full-time basis.

                     Applications and additional information are available by con-
                     tacting the national office of NSTF.

Amount: More than 50 four-year scholarships are available in amounts
                     ranging from $300–$1,000 per academic year, in most cases,
                     for each of four years

Write: National Scholarship Trust Fund
                     4615 Forbes Avenue
                     Pittsburgh, PA 15213
                     412-621-6941

Creative/Visual/Performing Arts

Thurgood Marshall Scholarship Fund
Washington, D.C.

Type: Scholarships

Description: The Thurgood Marshall Scholarship Fund, a cooperative ef-
                     fort of the Miller Brewing Company and the Office for the
                     Advancement of Black Colleges, provides merit scholarships
                     to the nation's 36 historically Black public colleges and uni-
                     versities. The Fund complements the efforts of the United
                     Negro College Fund, which raises millions of dollars annually
                     to support Black colleges. Thurgood Marshall Scholars demon-
                     strate exemplary achievement in academic studies or excep-
                     tional talent in the creative and performing arts.

                     Member institutions include:
                     Alabama A&M University, AL
                     Alabama State University, AL
                     Albany State College, GA
                     Alcorn State University, MS
                     Bowie State University, MD
                     Central State University, OH
                     Cheyney University of Pennsylvania, PA

Coppin State College, MD
Delaware State College, DE
Elizabeth City State University, NC
Fayetteville State University, NC
Florida A&M University, FL
Fort Valley State College, GA
Grambling State University, LA
Jackson State University, MS
Kentucky State University, KY
Lincoln University, MO
Mississippi Valley State University, MS
Morgan State University, MD
Norfolk State University, VA
North Carolina A&T State University, NC
North Carolina Central University, NC
Prairie View A&M University, TX
Savannah State College, GA
Southern University System, LA
Tennessee State University, TN
Texas Southern University, TX
Tuskegee University, AL
University of Arkansas at Pine Bluff, AR
University of Maryland Eastern Shore, MD
Virginia State University, VA
Winston-Salem State University, NC
University of the Virgin Islands

Amount: Merit scholarships of $16,000 per institution cover tuition, fees, room and board for a four-year period

Write: Thurgood Marshall Scholarship Fund
                One Dupont Circle, Suite 710
                Washington, D.C. 20036
                202-778-0818

Creative/Visual/Performing Arts— Architecture/Landscape Architecture

American Institute of Architects
Washington, D.C.

Type: Scholarships

Description: Scholarships are awarded to African-Americans, other minorities, and other disadvantaged groups who may not otherwise be able to pursue undergraduate studies in architecture. Candidates must be nominated by an individual architect or an architectural firm, guidance counselor, teacher, dean, director of community or civic organization, or administrator of an accredited architecture school.

Amount: $500–$2,500. Approximately 20 awards made annually

Deadline: Nominations by December 1; applications by first week in January

Write: American Institute of Architects
                 1735 New York Avenue, N.W.
                 Washington, D.C. 20006
                 202-626-7300

American Society of Naval Engineers, Inc.
Alexandria, VA

Type: Scholarships

Description: Offers scholarships to encourage students to enter the field of naval engineering, including programs in naval architecture, marine, mechanical, civil, electrical and electronic engineering, and the physical sciences. Scholarship awards apply to the students' final one or two years of undergraduate education.

Amount: $2,000

Deadline: February 15

Write: American Society of Naval Engineers, Inc.
                 1452 Duke Street
                 Alexandria, VA 22314

Association for Women in Architecture
Los Angeles, CA

Type: Scholarships

Description: Scholarships awarded to encourage women to enter the field of architecture. Candidates must be California residents or attending a California school. Awards are made for students in their second year of study.

Amount: $500–$2,000; 10 awards made annually

Deadline: Various

Write: Association for Women in Architecture
                 2550 Beverly Blvd.
                 Los Angeles, CA 90057

Landscape Architecture Foundation
Washington, D.C.

Type: Scholarships/Internships

Description: Scholarships and internships are awarded to students interested in pursuing careers in landscape architecture. The Associates Minority Scholarship is available to African-Americans and other minority students in the final two years of undergraduate study. Candidates must submit an essay (500 words maximum) and two letters of recommendation to qualify.

Amount: $1,000

Deadline: May 1

Description: The Raymond E. Page Scholarship is awarded to an undergraduate or graduate student based on financial need. Candidates must submit a two-page description of how the money will be used and submit a letter of reference from a professor or employer.

Amount: $500

Deadline: May 4

Write: Landscape Architecture Foundation
                 4401 Connecticut Avenue, N.W., #500
                 Washington, D.C. 20008

Creative/Visual/Performing Arts— Drama/Theatre

Arts Council of Montgomery
Montgomery, AL

Type: Scholarships

Description: Awards 25 to 30 summer study scholarships to artistically talented junior high students in the Montgomery area. Auditions are required.

Amount: $200

Deadline: Various

Write: Program Coordinator
                 1018 Madison Ave.
                 Montgomery, AL 36104
                 205-241-2787

Lorraine Hansberry Playwriting Award
John F. Kennedy Center for the Performing Arts
Washington, D.C.

Type: Scholarships/Playwright Award

Description: Award recognizes student authors of plays on the African-American experience in America. Candidates must be full-time or part-time students enrolled in undergraduate or graduate schools. Eligible plays must be regular entries in the Playwriting Award Program of the American College Theatre Festival.

Amount:	First place award of $2,500 and an all-expense-paid fellowship to attend Shenandoah Valley Playwrights Retreat. Second place award $1,000
Deadline:	November
Write:	American College Theatre Festival John F. Kennedy Center for the Performing Arts Washington, D.C. 20566 202-254-3437

Creative/Visual/Performing Arts— Film/Photography

Black American Film Makers Grants Program
Black American Cinema Society
Los Angeles, CA

Type:	Grants
Description:	Awards recognize outstanding African-American film and video makers in annual competition. Award is presented annually.
Amount:	First prize $1,000, second prize $750, third prize $500
Deadline:	Varies year to year
Write:	Black American Cinema Society c/o Western States Black Research Center 3617 Montclair Los Angeles, CA 90018 213-737-3292

Creative/Visual/Performing Arts— Graphic/Visual Arts

Black Communicators Scholarship
Dallas-Fort Worth Association of
Dallas, TX

Type:	Scholarships
Description:	Several scholarships awarded to high school seniors and college students who are pursuing careers in print, broadcast, photojournalism, graphic arts, or public relations.
Amount:	Minimum $1,500
Deadline:	March 1

Write: Rochelle Riley
President DPF/ABC
c/o Dallas Morning News
Communication Center
P.O. Box 227455
Dallas, TX 75222

National Scholarship Trust Fund (NSTF)
Pittsburgh, PA

Type: Scholarships

Description: The National Scholarship Trust Fund of the Education Council of the Graphic Arts Industry, Inc., offers graphics art scholarships to students who are interested in careers in graphic communications, engineering science, management, design, manufacturing or other areas leading to careers in the printing and publishing industries.

Applicants must be graduating high school seniors or college freshmen, sophomores or juniors enrolled in a two-year or four-year college and attending on a full-time basis.

Applications and additional information are available by contacting the national office of NSTF.

Amount: More than 50 four-year scholarships are available in amounts ranging from $300–$1,000 per academic year, in most cases, for each of four years

Write: National Scholarship Trust Fund
4615 Forbes Avenue
Pittsburgh, PA 15213
412-621-6941

Deadline: Various

National Scholarship Trust Fund of the Graphic Arts, Inc.
Pittsburgh, PA

Type: Scholarships

Description: Awards scholarships annually to undergraduate students with an interest in printing management, printing technology and graphic arts education. Recipients must maintain a B average to renew the scholarship.

Amount: $500–$1,000. Approximately 150 awarded each year; renewable

Deadline: March 1

Write: National Scholarship Trust Fund of the
Graphic Arts, Inc.
4615 Forbes Avenue
Pittsburgh, PA 15213-3796

The Poynter Fund
Times Publishing Company
St. Petersburg, FL

Type:	Scholarships
Description:	The Fund provides scholarships to undergraduate and graduate students interested in careers in communications and journalism. Scholarships are awarded on the basis of merit and career interest in the areas of newswriting, editing, and administration. They are also granted for those wanting to study business, administration and marketing, including sales, art layout, promotion and research, and for the technological aspects of journalism, including mechanical production.
	Grantees will be asked to sign a statement of understanding that they intend to work in one of the above career fields for at least three years following completion of their education.
Amount:	Various
Deadline:	July 1
Write:	The Poynter Fund Personnel Department Times Publishing Company P.O. Box 1121 St. Petersburg, FL 33731 813-893-8556

Creative/Visual/Performing Arts— Music

Music Assistance Fund Scholarship
American Symphony Orchestral League
Washington, D.C.

Type:	Scholarships
Description:	The Music Assistance Fund encourages and supports gifted student musicians and young professionals of African-American heritage who wish to pursue careers in this country's symphony orchestras. Created by the New York Philharmonic in 1965, the Music Assistance Fund Scholarships are granted on the basis of an audition and financial need. Eligibility is limited to U.S. citizens of African descent (African-American, Afro-Caribbean, or similar heritage).
Amount:	$2,500
Deadline:	March 1

Write: American Symphony Orchestral League
                  777 Fourteenth Street, N.W., Suite 500
                  Washington, D.C. 20005
                  202-628-0099

Education

Civitan International Foundation
Birmingham, AL

Type: Scholarships

Description: The Foundation offers one-year scholarships to undergradu-
                  ate- or graduate-level students in accredited colleges or uni-
                  versities. The Shropshire Memorial Scholarship is a one-year
                  scholarship grant for students working to complete the final
                  year of undergraduate or master's level work. The award may
                  only be used for tuition and approved purposes which are sat-
                  isfactory to the applicants and the school.

                  Awards for the Shropshire Scholarship are based on acade-
                  mics, professional objectives, and financial need. Applicants
                  are required to be planning a career in the field of higher edu-
                  cation, special education, health care services, or the teaching
                  of social studies.

Amount: $500–$1,000

Description: CIF/Junior Civitan Scholarship for high school students en-
                  tering college. The award is given to outstanding Junior Civi-
                  tans who have demonstrated financial need. Applicants must
                  have held membership in a Junior Civitan Club for at least
                  two years and be planning to attend a two-year or four-year
                  college or university.

Amount: $1,000; eight nonrenewable awards annually

Deadline: March 1

Write: Civitan International Foundation
                  P.O. Box 2102
                  Birmingham, AL 35201
                  205-591-8910

Indiana Minority Teacher and Special Education Scholarships
Indiana State Student Assistance Commission
Indianapolis, IN

Type: Scholarships

Description: Scholarships are available to African-Americans and other mi-
                  nority students who are residents of the State of Indiana and
                  interested in teaching. Students must be admitted to eligible

institutions as full-time students or already in attendance at such institutions, and also meet academic requirements. Each college is responsible for making the awards which are based on academics and financial need.

Amount: $1,000 annually

Deadline: Obtain application and details from college or university financial aid office, high school guidance counselor office, or State Student Assistance Commission.

Write: Indiana State Student Assistance Commission
              964 N. Pennsylvania Street
              Indianapolis, IN 46204
              317-232-2350

United Federation of Teachers (UFT) Scholarship Fund
New York, NY

Type: Scholarships

Description: Scholarships available to undergraduate and graduate students who are graduates of a New York City high school. The Fund awards 300 four-year scholarships each year and offers Master's Degree scholarships as well.

              Applications for undergraduate scholarships are available each fall from the UFT Chapter Leaders in all New York City public high schools.

Amount: Undergraduate award is $1,000 per year; graduate-level award is $1,500 over two semesters to former undergraduate scholarship winners.

Write: United Federation of Teachers (UFT)
              Scholarship Fund
              260 Park Avenue South
              New York, NY 10010
              212-777-7500

Education—Earth Science Education

American Geological Institute (AGI)
Alexandria, VA

Type: Scholarships

Description: The American Geological Institute sponsors scholarships for geoscience majors (geology, geophysics, hydrology, meteorology, physical oceanography, planetary geology, and earth-science education) to African-Americans and members of other ethnic minority groups that are underrepresented in the geosciences, in an effort to increase their numbers in the field. Scholarship recipients must be U.S. citizens. Applicants must be enrolled full-time in a college or university with a major in the geosciences. Successful candidates are bright, energetic, hardworking individuals with a strong academic background. Selections are based on academic excellence and financial need.

Candidates must submit completed applications including a financial profile and an essay, official academic transcripts (high school and college), standardized test scores (i.e. SAT, ACT), and three letters of recommendation. This award is renewable if performance is satisfactory (based on GPA and three letters of recommendation from current faculty).

Amount: Scholarship awards up to $10,000 a year. Award is renewable; recipients must reapply

Deadline: All application materials must be received by AGI no later than February 1.

Write: Director, AGI Minority Geoscience Scholarships
                 American Geological Institute
                 4220 King Street
                 Alexandria, VA 22302-1507
                 703-379-2480

Education—Elementary/Secondary Education

Paul Douglas Teaching Scholarship Program
U.S. Department of Education
Washington, D.C.

Type: Scholarships

Description: The Paul Douglas Teaching Scholarship Program is a national scholarship program administered by the U.S. Department of Education in each of the 50 states. The program offers scholarships for prospective teachers who qualify under standards set by each state. High school students who plan to teach at the preschool, elementary, junior or senior high school level are eligible to apply. Applicants must be enrolled in a state-appointed teaching program.

                 Recipients are generally required to teach two years for each year of scholarship assistance they receive. This obligation may be reduced under certain circumstances.

Amount: $5,000; renewable

Write: Contact the education department of your state
                 or contact:
                 Paul Douglas Teaching Scholarship Program
                 U.S. Department of Education
                 Seventh & D Streets, S.W.
                 Washington, D.C. 20202-5447
                 202-732-4507

Education—Health Education

March of Dimes Award
National Black Nurses' Assn., Inc.
Boston, MA

Type: Scholarship/Essay Competition

Description: Scholarship essay contest for nursing students who are mem-
                 bers of National Black Nurses' Association. They may be en-
                 rolled in LPN/LVN programs, associate degree programs,
                 diploma programs, or baccalaureate programs. Award recog-
                 nizes the best essay written by a Black nursing student on
                 "Prevention of Teenage Pregnancy and Decrease in Infant
                 Mortality Rates." Essays are judged on the basis of the state-
                 ment of the problem, proposal for dealing with the problem,
                 creativity and innovation of the approach, grammar, style,
                 clarity, and format. The contest is cosponsored by the March
                 of Dimes Birth Defects Foundation.

                 Awards are presented at the association's national institute
                 and conference.

Amount: $1,000

Deadline: May of each year

Write: National Black Nurses' Association, Inc.
                 P.O. Box 18358
                 Boston, MA 02118
                 617-266-9703

Engineering

Alcoa Foundation
Pittsburgh, PA

Type: Scholarships

Description: Alcoa Foundation supports minority scholarships in a number
                 of fields at several schools, including several historically Black
                 colleges and universities. Awards are made to students pursu-
                 ing courses in accounting, business information, business man-

agement, chemical engineering, computer-based management information systems, electrical engineering, management, marketing, mathematics, mechanical engineering, nursing.

Schools attended by scholarship winners include: Central State University, Florida A&M University, Georgia Institute of Technology, Hampton University, Howard University, Illinois Institute of Technology, Indiana University, Knoxville College, Livingston College, Pennsylvania State University, Prairie View A&M University, University of Idaho, Virginia Polytechnic Institute, Washington State University, Wingate College.

Amount:	Various
Write:	Alcoa Foundation Alcoa Building Pittsburgh, PA 15219 412-553-4696

American Society of Naval Engineers, Inc.
Alexandria, VA

Type:	Scholarships
Description:	Offers scholarships to encourage students to enter the field of naval engineering, including programs in naval architecture, marine, mechanical, civil, electrical and electronic engineering, and the physical sciences. Scholarship awards apply to the students' final one or two years of undergraduate education.
Amount:	$2,000
Deadline:	February 15
Write:	American Society of Naval Engineers, Inc. 1452 Duke Street Alexandria, VA 22314

Scholarships & Summer Programs
AT&T Research & Development
Holmdel, NJ

Type:	Scholarships and Summer Employment Programs
Description:	AT&T offers several scholarship and employment programs to minority students interested in pursuing careers in engineering, computer science, and research.

The **Engineering Scholarship Program (ESP)** is designed to encourage selected outstanding minorities and women to pursue an undergraduate degree in Computer Science or selected Engineering disciplines. ESP provides full tuition, a book allowance, fees, room and board, a challenging summer job each year at AT&T, and an appropriate mentor. Applicants must be high school seniors who are applying as full-time students to colleges with strong curricula. Fifteen candidates are selected each year. **Application deadline date is January 15. Students interested in applying should call 908-949-4301.**

Dual Degree Scholarship Program (DDSP) is designed to encourage talented minorities to enter the Engineering field. The DDSP is sponsored through a coordinated effort with The Atlanta University Center in Atlanta, Georgia. Through this collaboration, Dual Degree scholars earn a BA degree in Math or Physics from Spelman, Morehouse, Clark, or Morris Brown colleges in 3 years and then go on to earn a BS degree in Engineering or Computer Science. The second degree may be earned from Georgia Institute of Technology, University of Alabama, or Boston University over a two-year period. The DDSP provides full tuition, books, fees, room and board, a challenging summer job each year at AT&T, and an appropriate mentor. Three candidates are selected to participate in the program. **Application deadline date is June 10. Outstanding minority students interested in this program should call 908-949-4301.**

The Summer Research Program For Minorities and Women (SRP) provides outstanding minorities and women an opportunity to work for a summer within the research environment of AT&T Bell Laboratories. The program is open to students who have completed three years of education in selected engineering disciplines. The program also provides an AT&T Bell Laboratories scientist as a mentor. 60–100 candidates are accepted each year in the program. **Application deadline date is December 1. For more information, call 908-949-3728.**

The University Relations Summer Program (UR) provides summer employment for outstanding BS, MS, and Ph.D candidates who are within two years of graduation and pursuing studies in selected engineering disciplines. The purpose of the program is to provide work experience for talented students on a well-defined project in an R&D (Research and Development) environment. An AT&T Member of Technical Staff is assigned to each student as a mentor. To be eligible, candidates must be available for Career Employment within two years of Summer Employment. 200–300 candidates are selected for the program each year. **Application deadline date is February 15. For additional information, call 908-949-5592.**

Amount: (See individual programs)

Deadline: (See individual programs)

Write: For a brochure on the program write:
AT&T
101 Crawfords Corner Road
Holmdel, NJ 07733-3030

Clare Boothe Luce Scholarships in Science and Engineering
New York, NY

Type:	Scholarships
Description:	Offers scholarships to encourage women to enter the engineering and science fields. Awards are made to students majoring in biology, chemistry, computer science, engineering, mathematics, and physics. Scholarship awards are made through individual colleges and universities. Participating schools include: Boston University, Colby College, Creighton University, Fordham University, Georgetown University, Marymount University, Mount Holyoke College, Mundelein College, St. John's University, Santa Clara University, Seton Hall University, Trinity College, University of Notre Dame, Villanova Preparatory School.
Amount:	Various
Deadline:	Various
Write:	College or university financial aid office, *or* Clare Boothe Luce Scholarships in Science and Engineering c/o Henry Luce Foundation, Inc. 111 W. 50th Street New York, NY 10020

Construction Education Foundation
Washington, D.C.

Type:	Scholarships
Description:	Offers scholarships to undergraduate students who are enrolled in an accredited four-year program and have completed their first year of study. Candidates must intend to pursue a career in the construction industry. Applications are available in October. Other criteria such as membership in the local chapter of the organization may apply.
Amount:	$500–$2,000
Deadline:	December 15
Write:	Construction Education Foundation 729 15th Street, N.W. Washington, D.C. 20005

Duracell/National Urban League Scholarship
National Urban League, Inc.
New York, NY

Type:	Scholarships
Description:	Scholarships available to students attending a four-year school and in the top 25 percent of the class while pursuing a major

in engineering, sales, marketing, manufacturing operations, finance, or business administration.

Amount: Five $10,000 and five $1,000 awards available

Deadline: April 15

Write: National Urban League, Inc.
                 500 E. 62nd Street, 11th Floor
                 New York, NY 10021
                 212-310-9000

General Motors Institute
GMI Engineering and Management Institute
Flint, MI

Type: Cooperative Education

Description: The GMI Engineering and Management Institute is an ac-
                 credited college offering degree programs in electrical engi-
                 neering, industrial engineering, mechanical engineering,
                 manufacturing systems engineering, and management sys-
                 tems. Enrolled students alternate between periods of study
                 on campus and related work experience in more than 250
                 sponsoring companies. Freshmen admitted to the program
                 must be selected by a corporate sponsor.

Amount: Selected students are paid wages averaging $1,200 per month
                 during the 24 weeks of work experience for freshmen. Stu-
                 dents may also receive some fringe benefits in terms of insur-
                 ance, seniority accrual, or vacation. Wages normally increase
                 as the student progresses. Students can expect to earn an ap-
                 proximate annual wage of $10,000 over the five-year period.

Deadline: Students submit applications in the fall, which may be ob-
                 tained from GMI, high school guidance counselors, and GMI
                 corporate sponsors

Write: GMI Engineering and Management Institute
                 1700 W. Third Avenue
                 Flint, MI 48502
                 1-800-521-7436

NAACP Willems Scholarship
National Association for the Advancement of Colored People (NAACP)
Baltimore, MD

Type: Scholarships

Description: Scholarships available to undergraduate and graduate stu-
                 dents who are majoring in engineering, chemistry, physics, or
                 computer and mathematical sciences, and have a grade point
                 average of at least 3.0 or a B average. Applicants must be
                 members of the NAACP.

Amount:	Undergraduate maximum award is $8,000, paid in annual installments of $2,000
Deadline:	April 30
Write:	NAACP Willems Scholarship NAACP 4805 Mt. Hope Drive Baltimore, MD 21215-3297 410-358-8900

National Action Council For Minorities in Engineering
New York, NY

Type:	Scholarships
Description:	The National Action Council for Minorities in Engineering, Inc., is a nonprofit coalition of corporations, universities, local programs, and others committed to increasing the number of minority engineers. The major portion of NACME's budget is directed to minority students through incentive grant scholarships, which are administered by selected engineering colleges.
Amount:	Various
Deadline:	Various
Write:	National Action Council for Minorities in Engineering, Inc. 3 West 35th Street New York, NY 10001

National Scholarship Trust Fund (NSTF)
Pittsburgh, PA

Type:	Scholarships
Description:	The National Scholarship Trust Fund of the Education Council of the Graphic Arts Industry, Inc., offers graphics art scholarships to students who are interested in careers in graphic communications, engineering science, management, design, manufacturing, or other areas leading to careers in the printing and publishing industries. Applicants must be graduating high school seniors or college freshmen, sophomores, or juniors enrolled in a two-year or four-year college and attending on a full-time basis. Applications and additional information are available by contacting the national office of NSTF.
Amount:	More than 50 four-year scholarships are available in amounts ranging from $300–$1,000 per academic year, in most cases, for each of four years

Write: National Scholarship Trust Fund
     4615 Forbes Avenue
     Pittsburgh, PA 15213
     412-621-6941

National Society of Professional Engineers Scholarships
Education Foundation
Washington, D.C.

Type: Scholarships

Description: Scholarships are offered to over 150 students pursuing careers in the field of engineering; a number of awards are designated to African-Americans and other minority students. Requirements include SAT scores of 600 in the math category and 500 in the verbal category. Students are also required to be U.S. citizens or permanent residents and rank in the top 25 percent of their high school standings.

Amount: $1,000

Deadline: September 1

Write: National Society of Professional Engineers
     2029 K Street, N.W.
     Washington, D.C. 20006

National Urban League
New York, NY

Type: Scholarships

Description: The National Urban League, working in concert with 113 affiliate organizations in 34 states and the District of Columbia, provides programs of direct service to people nationwide, including scholarships for full-time students pursuing a Bachelor's Degree at accredited institutions of higher learning. Candidates must be classified as juniors, or third-year, students at the time the scholarship award commences, and must also rank within the top 25 percent of their class. Candidates must also major in courses leading to professional careers in engineering, sales, marketing, manufacturing operations, finance, or business administration to qualify. This scholarship is offered in conjunction with Kraft, Inc. Candidates may apply to any National Urban League affiliate or write to the national office.

Amount: Various; ten awards to minority students

Deadline: April 15; education officials at the National Urban League will interview each semifinalist

Write: Director of Education
     National Urban League
     500 E. 62nd Street
     New York, NY 10021

Spence Reese Scholarship
San Diego, CA

Type: Scholarships

Description: Scholarships are awarded to high school seniors who are in-
                   terested in studying law, political science, engineering, or
                   medicine. The award is made to a male student and prefer-
                   ence is given to students living within 250 miles of San Diego.
                   Interested students should send a self-addressed, stamped en-
                   velope to receive an application. A $10 processing fee is re-
                   quired with the completed application.

Amount: $2,000; renewable for up to $8,000

Deadline: May 15

Write: Spence Reese Scholarship
                   c/o Boys and Girls Clubs of San Diego
                   3760 Fourth Avenue, Suite 1
                   San Diego, CA 92103

Engineering—Aeronautical Engineering

Radio Technical Commission for Aeronautics
Washington, D.C.

Type: Award competition

Description: Awards made on the basis of an essay or thesis paper that has
                   been completed within the last three years. Candidates may
                   be undergraduate- or graduate-level students studying avia-
                   tion electronics, aviation, or telecommunications.

Amount: $1,500

Deadline: June 30

Write: Radio Technical Commission for Aeronautics
                   William Jackson Award
                   1717 H Street, N.W.
                   Washington, D.C. 20006

Engineering—Agricultural Engineering

Alabama Farmers Federation
Montgomery, AL

Type: Scholarships

Description: Awards to full-time students at Colleges of Agriculture, School of Forestry to major in Agriculture Education or Agricultural Engineering. Must be a U.S. citizen, and have good moral character, excellent academics.

Amount: Up to $1,750

Deadline: March 15

Write: Cheryl Mitchell, Executive Secretary
                 P.O. Box 11000
                 Montgomery, AL 36191-0001
                 205-288-3900

Engineering—Civil and Construction Engineering

AGC (Associated General Contractors)
Education and Research Foundation
Washington, D.C.

Type: Scholarships

Description: Scholarships available to college freshmen, sophomores, and juniors enrolled, or planning to enroll, in a four- or five-year degree program in construction and/or civil engineering. The renewable award is in the amount of $1,500 per year for each year of undergraduate education, up to a maximum of $6,000. **High School seniors are *not* eligible.** Scholarships are offered through the following special awards programs: Henry Boh Memorial Scholarships, the Build America Scholarships, G.E. Byrne Memorial Scholarships, Billy R. Carter Memorial Scholarships, Ival R. Cianchette Scholarships, Ralph E. Dailey Scholarships, Robert B. & Celine Fay Scholarships, Pete & Wanda Gilvin Scholarships, Richard & Elizabeth Hall Scholarships, Ben M. Hogan Scholarships, James D. McClary Scholarships, Robert B. McEachern Memorial Scholarships, Stanley F. Pepper Scholarships, James D. Pitcock Scholarships, Pizzagalli Construction Company Scholarships. **(Only one application is needed to compete for all of the above scholarships.)**

Amount: $1,500 per year for a maximum of $6,000

Deadline: Applications for competition are available September 1 of
                  each year. Only complete packages containing original appli-
                  cations, transcripts, 3 adult evaluations, and a completed and
                  stamped "Notification of Receipt" card are to be submitted
                  for this competition. INCOMPLETE PACKAGES WILL NOT
                  BE CONSIDERED! **Applications must be postmarked by No-
                  vember 15.**

Write: Director of Programs
                  AGC Education and Research Foundation
                  1957 E Street, N.W.
                  Washington, D.C. 20006
                  202-393-2040

Associated General Contractors Education & Research Foundation Washington, D.C.

Type: Scholarships

Description: Awards 60–70 scholarships to college freshmen, sophomores,
                  or juniors in bachelor's degree programs in Construction or
                  Civil Engineering.

Amount: $1,500 per year, renewable

Deadline: November 15

Write: Dennis Langley, Director of Programs
                  AGC Education & Research Foundation
                  1957 E Street, N.W.
                  Washington, D.C. 20006
                  202-393-2040

American Society of Civil Engineers New York, NY

Type: Scholarships

Description: Awards to members of an ASCE Student Chapter and National
                  Student members in good standing.

Amount: Various

Deadline: February 15

Write: ASCE Student Services Dept.
                  345 E. 47th Street
                  New York, NY 10017-2398

Engineering—Metallurgical

American Society for Metals Foundation
Metals Park, OH

Type:	Scholarships
Description:	Offers scholarships to undergraduate students at the sophomore level who are studying metallurgy. Candidates must be citizens of the United States of America, Canada, or Mexico.
Amount:	$500–$2,000; 37 scholarships awarded
Deadline:	June 15
Write:	American Society for Metals Foundation Scholarship Selection Committee Metals Park, OH 44073

Engineering—Nuclear Engineering

American Nuclear Society
La Grange Park, IL

Type:	Scholarships
Description:	To advance science and engineering related to the study of atomic energy, the Society and its member organizations award numerous scholarships and grants including the Nuclear Engineering Education for the Disadvantaged program.
Amount:	Various
Deadline:	Various
Description:	Other Society members and opportunities include: Engineering Scholarships for Women Society of Women Engineers 345 East 47th Street New York, NY 10017 212-705-7855
	Research Grants in Nuclear Medicine Society of Nuclear Medicine 136 Madison Avenue New York, NY 10016 212-889-0717
Amount:	Various
Write:	The American Nuclear Society 555 N. Kensington Avenue Le Grange Park, IL 60525 312-352-6611

Nuclear Energy Training Program
Historically Black Colleges and Universities
Oak Ridge, TN

Type: Scholarships

Description: The Nuclear Energy Training Program, in cooperation with seven Historically Black Colleges and Universities, provides scholarships for African-Americans and other minority students at participating HBCU's. The program is made possible by the U.S. Department of Energy.

                For more information about the program, contact the participating institutions directly—Atlanta University, Lincoln University, Howard University, North Carolina A&M State University, South Carolina State College, Tennessee State University, and Virginia State University. You may also contact the U.S. Department of Energy.

Amount: The awards consist of full tuition and fees, plus a $6,000 annual stipend

Deadline: Various

Write: Nuclear Energy Training Program
                Oak Ridge Associated Universities
                University Programs
                P.O. Box 117
                Oak Ridge, TN 37831
                615-576-3428

Health

Association of Official Analytical Chemists, International
Arlington, VA

Type: Scholarships

Description: Harvey W. Wiley Scholarships are awarded to undergraduate students at the junior level majoring in chemistry, microbiology, and related sciences. Students with majors in dental, nursing, medicine, or related fields may also apply. One-year award must be applied to fourth year of undergraduate work.

Amount: $1,000

Deadline: Various

Write: Association of Official Analytical
                Chemists International
                2200 Wilson Blvd., Suite 400
                Arlington, VA 22201-3301

Civitan International Foundation
Birmingham, AL

Type:	Scholarships
Description:	The Foundation offers one-year scholarships to undergraduate- or graduate-level students in accredited colleges or universities. The Shropshire Memorial Scholarship is a one-year scholarship grant for students working to complete the final year of undergraduate or master's level work. The award may only be used for tuition and approved purposes that are satisfactory to the applicants and the school.
	Awards for the Shropshire Scholarship are based on academics, professional objectives, and financial need. Applicants are required to be planning a career in the field of higher education, special education, health care services, or the teaching of social studies.
Amount:	$500–$1,000
Description:	CIF/Junior Civitan Scholarship for high school students entering college. The award is given to outstanding Junior Civitans who have demonstrated financial need. Applicants must have held membership in a Junior Civitan Club for at least two years and be planning to attend a two-year or four-year college or university.
Amount:	$1,000; eight nonrenewable awards annually
Deadline:	March 1
Write:	Civitan International Foundation P.O. Box 2102 Birmingham, AL 35201 205-591-8910

Spence Reese Scholarship
San Diego, CA

Type:	Scholarships
Description:	Scholarships are awarded to high school seniors who are interested in studying law, political science, engineering, or medicine. The award is made to a male student and preference is given to students living within 250 miles of San Diego. Interested students should send a self-addressed, stamped envelope to receive an application. A $10 processing fee is required with the completed application.
Amount:	$2,000; renewable for up to $8,000
Deadline:	May 15

Write: Spence Reese Scholarship
c/o Boys and Girls Clubs of San Diego
3760 Fourth Avenue, Suite 1
San Diego, CA 92103

Health—Dental Hygiene

American Dental Assistants Association
Chicago, IL

Type: Scholarships

Description: Students interested in pursuing careers as dental assistants may qualify for Southard Trust Scholarships. These awards must be repaid if students fail to complete their course of study. Awards are also available to students interested in pursuing careers as teachers in this field.

Amount: $100–$2,500

Deadline: Various

Write: American Dental Assistants Association
919 N. Michigan Avenue, Suite 3400
Chicago, IL 60611

ADHA Minority Scholarship Program
The American Dental Hygienists' Association Institute
Chicago, IL

Type: Scholarships

Description: Scholarships available to African-Americans and other minorities underrepresented in the dental hygiene field. Male applicants are not required to be members of minority groups. Applicants must have completed a minimum of one year in a dental hygiene curriculum and have a grade point average of 3.0 for the time enrolled in a dental hygiene curriculum. Applicants must be full-time students during the academic year for which they are applying, and have demonstrated financial need of at least $1,500.

Amount: Various

Deadline: May 1

Write: Request: Scholarship Application Packet
American Dental Hygienists' Assn. Institute
Institute of Oral Health
Minority Scholarship Program
444 N. Michigan Avenue, Suite 3400
Chicago, IL 60611

Health—Medical Technology

American Medical Technologists' Scholarship Program
Park Ridge, IL

Type: Scholarships

Description: Offers scholarships to high school graduates interested in pursuing careers in medical technology or medical assisting. Recipients must be enrolled in an accredited school and have demonstrated financial need. Consideration is given to academic achievement, involvement in extracurricular activities, personal goals, and references, in making award.

Amount: Various

Deadline: April 1

Write: American Medical Technologists' Scholarship
                710 Higgins Road
                Park Ridge, IL 60068

Health—Nursing/Public Health

Alcoa Foundation
Pittsburgh, PA

Type: Scholarships

Description: Alcoa Foundation supports minority scholarships in a number of fields at several schools, including several Historically Black Colleges and Universities. Awards are made to students pursuing courses in accounting, business information, business management, chemical engineering, computer-based management information systems, electrical engineering, management, marketing, mathematics, mechanical engineering, nursing.

                Schools attended by scholarship winners include: Central State University, Florida A&M University, Georgia Institute of Technology, Hampton University, Howard University, Illinois Institute of Technology, Indiana University, Knoxville College, Livingston College, Pennsylvania State University, Prairie View A&M University, University of Idaho, Virginia Polytechnic Institute, Washington State University, Wingate College.

Amount: Various

Write: Alcoa Foundation
                Alcoa Building
                Pittsburgh, PA 15219
                412-553-4696

Baptist Health Care Foundation
Montgomery, AL

Type: Scholarships

Description: Auxiliary/Nursing awards are provided to students based on academic performance, commitment to excellence, and genuine need.

Amount: $1,000

Deadline: July 15

Description: Allied health awards are based on academic performance, commitment to excellence, and genuine need.

Amount: $1,000

Deadline: July 15

Description: Howard S. Durden & Arthur M. Mead Scholarship awarded to students enrolled in Auburn University at Montgomery (AUM) in the Nursing or Pre-nursing curriculum; academics considered.

Amount: Based on cost of tuition at AUM

Deadline: Various

Write: Barbara Norman
                Baptist Health Care Foundation
                P.O. Box 11010
                Montgomery, AL 36111

Department of Veterans Affairs
Washington, D.C.

Type: Scholarships

Description: Offers scholarships to students who are accepted or enrolled in a nursing, occupational therapy, or physical therapy undergraduate or graduate program at an accredited college or university. Recipients must agree to serve a prescribed period of time in a Veterans Administration medical facility.

Amount: Various

Deadline: Various

Write: Department of Veterans Affairs
                Health Professionals Education Assistance
                Programs (143B)
                810 Vermont Avenue, NW
                Washington, D.C. 20420

Iowa College Student Aid Commission
Des Moines, IA

Type: Grants

Description: Residents may be eligible to receive grants to attend a private college or university located in Iowa. Open to students interested in majoring in business or nursing.

Amount: Up to $2,650

Deadline: April 1

Write: Iowa College Student Aid Commission
               914 Grand Avenue, Suite 201
               Des Moines, IA 50309-2824

Lonzie L. Jones, Jr., National Sickle Cell Scholarship Program
National Association for Sickle Cell Disease, Inc.
Los Angeles, CA

Type: Scholarship/Essay Competition

Description: Annual scholarship essay contest for high school students. Award recognizes the most outstanding high school student essay on sickle cell disease. Contest open to all high school students. They enter local contests, which are held in conjunction with National Sickle Cell Month. Local winners are considered in a national judging.

Amount: First-place winner receives $2,500; runners-up receive $1,000–$1,500 to cover college costs. Three awards are made annually.

Deadline: Essays are usually due in September.

Write: National Association for Sickle Cell Disease, Inc.
               4221 Wilshire Boulevard, Suite 360
               Los Angeles, CA 90010-3503
               213-936-7205

March of Dimes Award
National Black Nurses' Assn., Inc.
Boston, MA

Type: Scholarship/Essay Competition

Description: Scholarship essay contest for nursing students who are members of National Black Nurses' Association. They may be enrolled in LPN/LVN programs, associate degree programs, diploma programs, or baccalaureate programs. Award recognizes the best essay written by a Black nursing student on "Prevention of Teenage Pregnancy and Decrease in Infant Mortality Rates." Essays are judged on the basis of the statement of the problem, proposal for dealing with the problem, creativity and innovation of the approach, grammar, style, clarity, and format. The contest is cosponsored by the March of Dimes Birth Defects Foundation.

Awards are presented at the association's national institute and conference.

Amount: $1,000

Deadline: May

Write: National Black Nurses' Association, Inc.
            P.O. Box 18358
            Boston, MA 02118
            617-266-9703

Health—Occupational/Physical Therapy

American Occupational Therapy Association, Inc.
Rockville, MD

Type: Scholarships

Description: Offers scholarships to undergraduates enrolled in the field of occupational therapy. Awards made on the basis of financial need and academic achievement. Applications for scholarship program available in September.

Amount: Various

Deadline: December 15

Write: American Occupational Therapy Association, Inc.
             1383 Piccard Drive, Suite 300
             Rockville, MD 20850

Department of Veterans Affairs
Washington, D.C.

Type: Scholarships

Description: Offers scholarships to students who are accepted or enrolled in a nursing, occupational therapy, or physical therapy undergraduate or graduate program at an accredited college or university. Recipients must agree to serve a prescribed period of time in a Veterans Administration medical facility.

Amount: Various

Deadline: Various

Write: Department of Veterans Affairs
             Health Professionals Education Assistance
             Programs (143B)
             810 Vermont Avenue, NW
             Washington, D.C. 20420

Language/Literature/Humanities—English/Writing

Detroit Free Press Minority Journalism Scholarship
Detroit Free Press
Detroit, MI

Type:	Scholarships
Description:	Scholarships available to African-Americans and other minority students who plan to become writers, editors, or photojournalists, and have a 3.0 grade point average. Scholarships are given to encourage outstanding minorities to enter the field of journalism. Awards are based on grades, a written essay detailing why the student wants to become a journalist, and recommendations from high school. Applications must also be accompanied by SAT/ACT scores. Finalists have in-person interview.
Amount:	Competitive selection, with two first-place winners receiving $1,000 awards, and second-place winner, $750 award. First-place winners automatically compete for $20,000 scholarships offered by Knight-Ridder, Inc.
Deadline:	January 6
Write:	Louise Reid Ritchie Detroit Free Press 321 W. Lafayette Blvd. Detroit, MI 48226 800-678-6400

Lorraine Hansberry Playwriting Award
John F. Kennedy Center for the Performing Arts
Washington, D.C.

Type:	Scholarships/Playwright Awards
Description:	Award recognizes student authors of plays on the African-American experience in America. Candidates must be full-time or part-time students enrolled in undergraduate or graduate schools. Eligible plays must be regular entries in the Playwriting Award Program of the American College Theatre Festival.
Amount:	First-place award is $2,500 and an all-expense-paid fellowship to attend Shenandoah Valley Playwrights Retreat. Second-place award is $1,000.
Deadline:	November 1
Write:	American College Theatre Festival John F. Kennedy Center for the Performing Arts Washington, D.C. 20566 202-254-3437

Physical Sciences

American Society of Naval Engineers, Inc.
Alexandria, VA

Type:	Scholarships
Description:	Offers scholarships to encourage students to enter the field of naval engineering, including programs in naval architecture, marine, mechanical, civil, electrical and electronic engineering, and the physical sciences. Scholarship awards apply to the students' final one or two years of undergraduate education.
Amount:	$2,000
Deadline:	February 15
Write:	American Society of Naval Engineers, Inc. 1452 Duke Street Alexandria, VA 22314

Clare Boothe Luce Scholarships in Science and Engineering
New York, NY

Type:	Scholarships
Description:	Offers scholarships to encourage women to enter the engineering and science fields. Awards are made to students majoring in biology, chemistry, computer science, engineering, mathematics, and physics. Scholarship awards are made through individual colleges and universities. Participating schools include: Boston University, Colby College, Creighton University, Fordham University, Georgetown University, Marymount University, Mount Holyoke College, Mundelein College, St. John's University, Santa Clara University, Seton Hall University, Trinity College, University of Notre Dame, Villanova Preparatory School.
Amount:	Various
Deadline:	Various
Write:	College or university financial aid office, *or* Clare Boothe Luce Scholarships in Science and Engineering c/o Henry Luce Foundation, Inc. 111 W. 50th Street New York, NY 10020

Physical Sciences—Chemistry

Association of Official Analytical Chemists International
Arlington, VA

Type:	Scholarships
Description:	Harvey W. Wiley Scholarships are awarded to undergraduate students at the junior level majoring in chemistry, micro-biology, and related sciences. Students with majors in dental, nursing, medicine, or related fields may also apply. One-year award must be applied to fourth year of undergraduate work.
Amount:	$1,000
Deadline:	Various
Write:	Association of Official Analytical Chemists International 2200 Wilson Blvd., Suite 400 Arlington, VA 22201-3301

Physical Sciences—Geological Sciences (see also Education, Minority/Race-Specific)

American Geological Institute (AGI)
Alexandria, VA

Type:	Scholarships
Description:	The American Geological Institute sponsors scholarships for geoscience majors (geology, geophysics, hydrology, meteorology, physical oceanography, planetary geology, and earth-science education) to African-Americans and members of other ethnic minority groups that are underrepresented in the geosciences, in an effort to increase their numbers in the field. Scholarship recipients must be U.S. citizens. Applicants must be enrolled full-time in a college or university with a major in the geosciences. Successful candidates are bright, energetic, hardworking individuals with a strong academic background. Selections are based on academic excellence and financial need.
	Candidates must submit completed applications including a financial profile and an essay, official academic transcripts (high school and college), standardized test scores (i.e. SAT, ACT), and three letters of recommendation. This award is renewable if performance is satisfactory (based on GPA and three letters of recommendation from current faculty).

Amount: Scholarship awards up to $10,000 a year. Award is renewable; recipients must reapply

Deadline: All application materials must be received by AGI no later than February 1

Write: Director, AGI Minority Geoscience Scholarships
                     American Geological Institute
                     4220 King Street
                     Alexandria, VA 22302-1507
                     703-379-2480

Physical Sciences—Meteorology

American Meteorological Society
Boston, MA

Type: Scholarships

Description: Howard T. Orville and Howard H. Hanks, Jr., scholarships are awarded to students interested in pursuing studies in the field of meteorology. In addition, two AMS minority scholarships are available to African-Americans and other minority students.

Amount: $700–$3,000

Deadline: Various

Write: American Meteorological Society
                     45 Beacon Street
                     Boston, MA 02108-3693

Physical Sciences—Physics

APS Minorities Scholarship Program
American Physical Society
College Park, MD

Type: Scholarships

Description: The American Physical Society Corporate-Sponsored Scholarship program is targeted to undergraduate students who major in physics. The purpose of the program is to increase the level of underrepresented minority participation in the field of physics. Each scholarship is sponsored by a corporation and recipients will normally be designated as the sponsor of the "Scholarship for Minority Undergraduate Students in Physics" at the host college or university. A selection committee determines who will receive the APS Scholarship and will provide an accomplished physicist as a mentor for each scholarship recipient. The scholarship is open to any African-

American, Hispanic-American, or Native American U.S. Citizen who is majoring or plans to major in physics and who is a high school senior, college freshman, or sophomore.

Amount: Scholarship consists of $2,000 awarded to the student for tuition, room, or board and a $500 award to each college or university physics department that hosts one or more APS minority undergraduate scholars. The scholarship may be renewed one time, based on approval by the selection committee.

Deadline: February 14

Write: APS Minorities Scholarship Program
               The American Center for Physics
               1 Physics Ellipse
               College Park, MD 20740

Social Science—Law/Political Science

American Association of Law Libraries
Chicago, IL

Type: Scholarships

Description: Scholarships awarded to students interested in pursuing careers as Law Librarians.

Amount: Up to $3,500

Deadline: March 1

Write: Scholarship Committee
               American Association of Law Libraries
               53 W. Jackson Blvd., Suite 940
               Chicago, IL 60604
               312-939-4764

St. John's University
Jamaica, NY

Type: Scholarships

Description: Scholarships are awarded to students interested in pursuing a law degree through a joint program sponsored by the School of Law at St. John's University and the United Negro College Fund. Candidates must have completed three years of undergraduate study at a UNCF institution to apply, and at the end of the program will receive both a bachelor's degree from their UNCF school as well as a law degree from St. John's.

Amount: Tuition and books

Deadline: Various

Write: St. John's University
                 School of Law
                 8000 Utopia Parkway
                 Jamaica, NY 11439

Spence Reese Scholarship
San Diego, CA

Type: Scholarships

Description: Scholarships are awarded to high school seniors who are in-
                 terested in studying law, political science, engineering, or med-
                 icine. The award is made to a male student and preference is
                 given to students living within 250 miles of San Diego. Inter-
                 ested students should send a self-addressed, stamped envelope
                 to receive an application. A $10 processing fee is required with
                 the completed application.

Amount: $2,000; renewable for up to $8,000

Deadline: May 15

Write: Spence Reese Scholarship
                 c/o Boys and Girls Clubs of San Diego
                 3760 Fourth Avenue, Suite 1
                 San Diego, CA 92103

Social Science—Public Administration

Harry S. Truman Scholarship Foundation
Washington, D.C.

Type: Scholarships

Description: Awards scholarships to students on the basis of merit and out-
                 standing potential for leadership in public service. Candidates
                 must be college juniors in the next academic year and be en-
                 rolled or accepted for enrollment as full-time students at an
                 accredited institution of higher learning. The scholars must
                 pursue a baccalaureate degree program that will prepare
                 them for some aspect of government employment.

Amount: Various

Deadline: College or university presidents appoint a Truman Scholar-
                 ship Program faculty representative who conducts a campus-
                 wide competition during the fall semester to select one or
                 two scholarship nominees. **The foundation does not accept
                 direct applications from students.**

Write: Contact college or university or write:
                      Harry S. Truman Scholarship Foundation
                      712 Jackson Place, N.W.
                      Washington, D.C. 20006
                      202-395-4831

New York State Senate Student Programs
Albany, NY

Type: Internships/Grants

Description: Internships and grants available to undergraduate, graduate, and postgraduate students interested in public sector service careers. The positions are in the Senate in Albany, New York.

                      Applicants must be New York State residents who are full-time juniors or seniors at an accredited college or university in the state. Freshmen are ineligible and only exceptional sophomores will be considered.

Amount: Undergraduate assistants receive grants of $2,000

Deadline: Various

Write: New York State Senate Student Programs
                      State Capitol, Room 500A
                      Albany, NY 12247
                      518-455-2611

Social Science—Social Work

National Civil Community Corps
An AmeriCorps Program
Washington, D.C.

Type: Community Job Service/Financial Aid Program

Description: The National Civilian Community Corps (NCCC) is a residential national service program that provides young Americans the opportunity to work in urban and rural service projects that improve America's communities and help them earn a yearly allowance and an education award. The NCCC focuses on projects that protect and conserve natural resources, promote public safety, and help meet the educational and human needs of children, older persons, and others in the community. Many corps members are also trained to do disaster relief and recovery projects. Young adults between the ages of 18–24 who are willing to commit to an 11-month program of service are eligible. The eight-week summer program is open to 14–17-year-olds.

                      The NCCC is committed to offering opportunities to individuals of all races and ethnic backgrounds, incomes, education, and job skill levels. Corps members must be U.S. citizens or permanent residents of the U.S.

Amount:	All Corps members receive lodging, meals, and uniforms. **They also earn $8,000 for the 11 months they serve plus a $4,725 education award that can be applied to future tuition costs or repayment of student loans.** Corps may choose to take half the education award in cash.
Deadline:	April 15
Write:	National Civilian Community Corps Recruitment Division 1100 Vermont Avenue, N.W., 11th Floor Washington, D.C. 20525 1-800-94-ACORPS

Academic

Agnes Jones Jackson Scholarship
National Association for the Advancement of Colored People (NAACP)
Baltimore, MD

Type:	Scholarships
Description:	Scholarships are available to undergraduate and graduate students who are current regular members of the NAACP (at least one year), or fully-paid life members of the organization. Undergraduates must have a grade point average of at least 2.5 and graduate students at least a 3.0 or B average. Applicants must not have reached the age of 25 by April 30 of the year of application. Application forms are available from the NAACP in January.
Amount:	Undergraduate award is $1,500 and graduate award $2,500
Deadline:	April 30
Write:	Agnes Jones Jackson Scholarship NAACP 4805 Mt. Hope Drive Baltimore, MD 21215-3297 410-358-8900

Aid Association for Lutherans
Appleton, WI

Type:	Scholarships
Description:	Awards scholarships to Aid Association for Lutheran members. Awards renewable based on class rank, ACT or SAT scores.
Amount:	25—$2,000 awards; 50—$1,000 awards; 250—$500 awards and 500—$500 nonrenewable awards
Deadline:	November 30

Description: Lutheran Campus Scholarship Program awards scholarships based on financial need and individual achievement to members who plan to enroll at a Lutheran institution.

Amount: $200–$1,000

Deadline: Each Lutheran institution sets its own deadline—contact each directly for deadline

Write: Aid Association for Lutherans
                 4321 N. Ballard Rd.
                 Appleton, WI 54919-0001
                 (Request the AAL Scholarships Booklet)

Alabama Commission on Higher Education
Montgomery, AL

Type: Grants/Scholarships

Description: Students who are residents of the State of Alabama may qualify for Alabama Student Assistance Grants and Alabama Student Grants.

Amount: $300–$2,500 per year

Description: Paul Douglas Teachers' Scholarship Awards are available to students interested in teaching.

Amount: Up to $5,000

Description: Alabama Nursing Scholarships are available to residents interested in studying nursing.

Amount: Various

Description: Police Officers' and Firefighters' Survivors' Educational Assistance Programs are awarded to students who meet certain criteria.

Amount: Various

Deadline: Various

Write: Alabama Commission on Higher Education
                 3465 Norman Bridge Road
                 Montgomery, AL 36105-2310
                 334-242-1998

Alpha Kappa Alpha Sorority, Inc.
Chicago, IL

Type: Scholarships

Description: Alpha Kappa Alpha Sorority is an organization of 100,000 members in 750 chapters throughout the United States and abroad. The sorority selects 30 undergraduate women from throughout the nation each year to receive the sorority's Leadership Fellows Grant. Recipients undergo an intensive weeklong leadership development training and are then sent to work as interns for major agencies and corporations throughout the nation.

The organization also provides grants, through its educational advancement foundation, to various institutions of higher education.

Amount:	Various
Write:	Alpha Kappa Alpha Sorority, Inc.
	5656 So. Stony Island Avenue
	Chicago, IL 60637
	312-684-1282

AKA Sorority
ACCW Montgomery Deanery
Montgomery, AL

Type:	Scholarships
Description:	Awards one scholarship per year to an Alabama resident; renewable for four years.
Amount:	$1,000 per year ($500 per semester)
Deadline:	January
Write:	Sherrie A. Cook, AKA Sorority
	Beta Nu Omega Chapter
	2117 Woodmere Loop
	Montgomery, AL 36117

Bertina Maxwell Undergraduate Award
National Council for Black Studies
Bloomington, IN

Type:	Scholarships
Description:	Scholarship essay contest for undergraduate students. Award recognizes outstanding student scholarship among African-American students.
Amount:	$500, a plaque, and publication of the essay in a leading journal of Black Studies
Write:	Dr. Joseph J. Russell, Executive Director
	National Council for Black Studies
	Indiana University
	Memorial Hall East 129
	Bloomington, IN 47405
	812-335-6581

Catholic Interracial Council
New York, NY

Type:	Scholarships
Description:	Scholarship essay contest for graduating high school seniors. Two awards granted each year.
Amount:	$1,000
Deadline:	March 1
Write:	Mr. Herbert A. Johnson
	Executive Director
	Catholic Interracial Council
	899 Tenth Avenue, #635
	New York, NY 10019

Coca-Cola Scholars Foundation, Inc.
Atlanta, GA

Type: Scholarships

Description: The Coca-Cola Scholars Program is one of the largest and most comprehensive business-supported scholarship programs in the country. Each year high school seniors compete for 50 four-year $20,000 scholarships and 100 four-year $4,000 scholarships for study at any accredited U.S. college or university. The Scholars program was begun in 1986 and is supported by local Coca-Cola bottlers and the Coca-Cola Company. Applicants must be U.S. Citizens, U.S. Nationals, U.S. Permanent Residents, Temporary Residents (legalization program), Refugees, Asylees, Cuban-Haitian Entrants, or Humanitarian Parolees, and must be current full-time secondary school students who anticipate graduating during the academic year in which application is made. They must also be planning to pursue a degree at an accredited U.S. postsecondary institution. Selections are based on a number of factors, with special emphasis on each individual's character, personal merit, and background. Merit may be demonstrated in leadership in school, civic, and other extracurricular activities, through academic achievement, and motivation to serve and succeed in all endeavors. Selection is sensitive to the ethnic and economic backgrounds of applicants, and tries to reflect the demographic profiles of the eleven Selection Districts throughout the country, including Hawaii, Alaska, and internationally in schools on U.S. military bases.

The selection process is done in three phases, beginning each fall and culminating in the following spring with the announcement of award recipients. Your guidance counselor will be sent a schedule of key days and deadlines. Up to 2,000 semifinalists are selected in the first phase, and the final selection of 150 scholars is made among them. Award recipients will attend the National Competition in Atlanta, Georgia, which is convened by the Foundation at its expense in April.

Amount: 50 four-year $20,000 scholarships and 100 four-year $4,000 scholarships awarded annually

Deadline: To apply, students must obtain applications from school guidance counselors, and mail the completed forms to the designated address by October 31 of the year prior to award

Write: Contact your school guidance counselor or for a brochure on the program write:
Coca-Cola Scholars Foundation, Inc.
One Buckhead Plaza, Suite 1000
3060 Peachtree Road, N.W.
Atlanta, GA 30305
404-237-1300

Earl P. Andrews, Jr. Memorial Scholarship
Montgomery, AL

Type: Scholarships

Description: Awards scholarships to students who are residents of a public housing project and public school students in Alabama. Students must have a C+ high school grade point average to quality.

Amount: Room, board, and tuition (renewable)

Deadline: Spring

Write: S.T.E.P.
P.O. Box 241347
Montgomery, AL 36124-1347

Florida Society of Newspaper Editors
Journalism Scholarship
Tallahassee, FL

Type: Scholarships

Description: Eight scholarships are awarded to Florida minority high school graduates who plan to attend a Florida public community college. Applicants must have a 3.0 high school grade point average and be interested in pursuing a journalism career. Scholarships are renewable for up to two years. Students should contact the financial aid office or journalism department at their community college for an application and additional information.

Amount: $1,200 per year ($600 per semester)

Deadline: Various

Write: Contact financial aid office or journalism department at community college

Fukunaga Scholarship Foundation
Honolulu, HI

Type:	Scholarships
Description:	Scholarships are awarded to high school students who are interested in pursuing undergraduate study in business administration. Awards are made on the basis of academic achievement, recommendations, and financial need.
Amount:	$6,000–$8,000
Deadline:	March 15
Write:	Fukunaga Scholarship Foundation 900 Fort Street Mall, Suite 500 P.O. Box 2788 Honolulu, HI 96803

Grandmet/National Urban League Scholarship
New York, NY

Type:	Scholarships
Description:	Scholarships available to high school seniors or undergraduate students who are attending or plan to attend a four-year school. Fifteen scholarships are awarded each year.
Amount:	$1,000
Deadline:	April 26
Write:	National Urban League, Inc. 500 E. 62nd Street, 11th Floor New York, NY 10021 212-310-9000

Harry S. Truman Scholarship Foundation
Washington, D.C.

Type:	Scholarships
Description:	Awards scholarships to students on the basis of merit and outstanding potential for leadership in public service. Candidates must be college juniors in the next academic year and be enrolled or accepted for enrollment as full-time students at an accredited institution of higher learning. The scholars must pursue a baccalaureate degree program that will prepare them for some aspect of government employment.
Amount:	Various
Deadline:	College or university presidents appoint a Truman Scholarship Program faculty representative, who conducts a campus-wide competition during the fall semester to select one or two scholarship nominees. **The foundation does not accept direct applications from students.**

Write: Contact college or university or write:
                    Harry S. Truman Scholarship Foundation
                    712 Jackson Place, N.W.
                    Washington, D.C. 20006
                    202-395-4831

Jackie Robinson Foundation Scholarship Program
New York, NY

Type: Scholarships

Description: Scholarships are awarded to minority students who are high
                    school seniors, and have demonstrated high academic
                    achievement and financial need. Recipients also have leader-
                    ship potential and have been accepted to an accredited
                    four-year college or university. Scholarship applications are
                    available November 1.

Amount: Various

Deadline: March 30

Write: Jackie Robinson Foundation
                    Scholarship Program
                    80–90 Eighth Avenue
                    New York, NY 10011

Mary McLeod Bethune Scholarship Challenge Grant
Florida Department of Education
Tallahassee, FL

Type: Grants

Description: Available to Florida residents who are enrolled at Florida
                    Agricultural and Mechanical University, Bethune-Cookman
                    College, Edward Waters College, or Florida Memorial Col-
                    lege for a minimum of 12 credit hours per term. Student
                    must have a grade point average of 3.0 in high school and
                    meet Florida's general requirements to qualify for state aid
                    and meet other criteria. Students must also have demonstrated
                    financial need. Grant is renewable to students who maintain
                    required academic levels. Renewal awards take precedence
                    over new selections.

Amount: $3,000 per academic year; renewable for maximum of eight
                    semesters or 12 quarters

Deadline: Analysis form by April 15, grant application by April 30, renewal
                    applications by April 30

Write: Office of Student Financial Aid
                    Florida Department of Education
                    1344 Florida Education Center
                    Tallahassee, FL 32399-0400
                    904-487-0049

Maryland State Scholarship Board
Baltimore, MD

Type: Grants/scholarships

Description: Scholarships and grants awarded to Maryland residents, some based on financial need and/or academic merit. The Maryland State Scholarship Board was established by the state legislature and administers 16 different programs for general and special financial aid.

Amount: Various

Deadline: Complete Maryland Financial Aid Form (FAF) by March 1

Write: Maryland State Scholarship Board
                 2100 Guilford Avenue, Room 207
                 Baltimore, MD 21218-5888
                 410-333-6420

Missouri Student Grant Program
c/o Coordinating Board for Higher Education
Jefferson City, MO

Type: Grants

Description: Provides state grants to help students obtain a college education. Applicants must be Missouri residents, demonstrate financial need, and have satisfactory academic performance as students. Applications may be obtained at high schools or colleges, or from the Coordinating Board for Higher Education.

Amount: $100–$1,500

Deadline: April 30

Write: Missouri Student Grant Program
                 c/o Coordinating Board for Higher Education
                 101 Adams Street
                 Jefferson City, MO 65101
                 314-751-2361

NAACP-Roy Wilkins Scholarships
NAACP Youth and College Division
Baltimore, MD

Type: Scholarships

Description: Scholarships are available to needy African-American students in the 12th grade or in their first year of college. Candidates must submit an application form, transcript, recommendations, and essay. 15–20 scholarship awards are made annually. Applications are available after January 1 of every year. Students should send a letter in December with a self-addressed, stamped envelope, requesting an application package.

Amount:	Up to $1,000
Deadline:	May 1
Write:	NAACP Youth and College Division 4805 Mt. Hope Drive Baltimore, MD 21212-3297

NAACP Willems Scholarship
National Association for the Advancement of Colored People (NAACP)
Baltimore, MD

Type:	Scholarships
Description:	Scholarships available to undergraduate and graduate students who are majoring in engineering, chemistry, physics, or computer and mathematical sciences, and have a grade point average of at least 3.0 or a B average. Applicants must be members of the NAACP.
Amount:	Undergraduate maximum award is $8,000 paid in annual installments of $2,000
Deadline:	April 30
Write:	NAACP Willems Scholarship NAACP 4805 Mt. Hope Drive Baltimore, MD 21215-3297 410-358-8900

National Achievement Scholarship Program for Outstanding
Negro Students
Evanston, IL

Type:	Scholarships
Description:	700 Scholarships awarded to African-American high school students who have taken the Preliminary Scholastic Aptitude Test/National Merit Scholarship Qualifying Test. Candidates must be U.S. citizens. Test is administered through high school.
Amount:	$2,000 for one-time awards and $250–$8,000 annually for four-year scholarship awards
Deadline:	Various
Write:	Contact your high school counselor, *or* National Achievement Scholarship Program for Outstanding Negro Students One American Plaza 1560 Sherman Avenue Evanston, IL 60201

National Urban League
New York, NY

Type:	Scholarships
Description:	The National Urban League, working in concert with 113 affiliate organizations in 34 states and the District of Columbia, provides programs of direct service to people nationwide, including scholarships for full-time students pursuing a Bachelor's Degree at accredited institutions of higher learning. Candidates must be classified as juniors or third-year students at the time the scholarship award commences, and must also rank within the top 25 percent of their class. Candidates must also major in courses leading to professional careers in engineering, sales, marketing, manufacturing operations, finance, or business administration to qualify. This scholarship is offered in conjunction with Kraft, Inc. Candidates may apply to any National Urban League affiliate or write to the national office.
Amount:	Various; ten awards to minority students
Deadline:	April 15; education officials at the National Urban League will interview each semifinalist
Write:	Director of Education National Urban League 500 E. 62nd Street New York, NY 10021

Prince George's Chamber of Commerce Foundation, Inc.
Lanham, MD

Type:	Scholarships
Description:	Awards scholarships annually to residents of Prince George's County, Maryland. Preference is given to students who have demonstrated financial need.
Amount:	Various
Deadline:	May 15
Write:	Prince George's Chamber of Commerce Foundation, Inc. 4640 Forbes Boulevard, Suite 200 Lanham, MD 20706

The Foundation for Exceptional Children
Reston, VA

Type:	Scholarships
Description:	Scholarships are available for outstanding disabled and gifted students planning to continue their education and training beyond high school. The Foundation for Exceptional Children serves the needs of exceptional children and supports a

number of programs that seek to maximize the potential of exceptional children.

Amount:	Various
Deadline:	Various
Write:	The Foundation for Exceptional Children 1920 Association Drive Reston, VA 22091 703-620-3660

The Franam Scholarship Fund for Black Women
San Francisco State University
San Francisco, CA

Type:	Scholarships
Description:	The Franam Scholarship Fund recognizes the academic achievements and potential of Black women and assists them financially with the pursuit of their education. The scholarship is available to new and continuing students at San Francisco State University.
Amount:	Scholarship amount is up to $1,500; $750 each semester
Deadline:	May 2
Write:	Office of Student Financial Aid San Francisco State University Room 355, Administration Bldg. 1600 Holloway Avenue San Francisco, CA 94132 415-338-1581

The Fund for Theological Education, Inc.
New York, NY

Type:	Scholarships
Description:	Program provides scholarships to selected candidates for the Benjamin E. Mays Ministry Program for Black North Americans. Candidates must be nominated by either a minister, a church official, a member of a faculty or administration, or by a former FTE Scholar. The program seeks to strengthen Christian theological education in the United States and Canada by supporting Black North American women and men who demonstrate high promise for academic excellence and teaching effectiveness. A nominee must be a member of a Christian church, be a citizen of the United States or Canada, have completed one year of coursework in a Ph.D., Th.D., or Ed.D. degree program in fields of religious studies at an accredited university or seminary.
Amount:	Various

Deadline: Nominations must be received by the FTE by February 10. An application will be sent directly to nominees and the completed forms must be returned to the FTE by March 15.

Write: The Fund for Theological Education
                   475 Riverside Drive—Suite 832
                   New York, NY 10115-0008
                   212-870-2058

The Southern California Gas Company Scholarship
Los Angeles, CA

Type: Scholarships

Description: Scholarships are available to graduating high school seniors who plan to attend an accredited college, community college, or trade school. The scholarship is open to students from approximately 40 schools throughout southern California. Scholarship winners may also be offered one summer of paid employment with the Gas Company. Recipients must maintain a C average or better in high school and are usually from economically disadvantaged families.

                   Candidates are nominated by their teachers and principals from their schools.

Amount: Up to $1,000 a year; maximum total of $4,000

Deadline: Various

Write: Scholarship Coordinator
                   The Southern California Gas Company Scholarship
                   810 S. Flower Street
                   Los Angeles, CA 90017
                   213-689-3995

Thurgood Marshall Scholarship Fund
Washington, D.C.

Type: Scholarships

Description: The Thurgood Marshall Scholarship Fund, a cooperative effort of the Miller Brewing Company and the Office for the Advancement of Black Colleges, provides merit scholarships to the nation's 36 historically black public colleges and universities. The Fund complements the efforts of the United Negro College Fund, which raises millions of dollars annually to support Black colleges. Thurgood Marshall Scholars demonstrate exemplary achievement in academic studies, or exceptional talent in the creative and performing arts.

                   Member institutions include:
                   Alabama A&M University, AL
                   Alabama State University, AL
                   Albany State College, GA

Alcorn State University, MS
Bowie State University, MD
Central State University, OH
Cheyney University of Pennsylvania, PA
Coppin State College, MD
Delaware State College, DE
Elizabeth City State University, NC
Fayetteville State University, NC
Florida A&M University, FL
Fort Valley State College, GA
Grambling State University, LA
Jackson State University, MS
Kentucky State University, KY
Lincoln University, MO
Mississippi Valley State University, MS
Morgan State University, MD
Norfolk State University, VA
North Carolina A&M State University, NC
North Carolina Central University, NC
Prairie View A&M University, TX
Savannah State College, GA
Southern University System, LA
Tennessee State University, TN
Texas Southern University, TX
Tuskegee University, AL
University of Arkansas at Pine Bluff, AR
University of Maryland Eastern Shore, MD
Virginia State University, VA
Winston-Salem State University, NC
University of the Virgin Islands

Amount: Merit scholarships of $16,000 per institution cover tuition, fees, room, and board for a four-year period

Write: Thurgood Marshall Scholarship Fund
            One Dupont Circle, Suite 710
            Washington, D.C. 20036
            202-778-0818

United Federation of Teachers (UFT) Scholarship Fund
New York, NY

Type: Scholarships

Description: Scholarships are available to undergraduate and graduate students who are graduates of a New York City high school. The Fund awards 300 four-year scholarships each year and offers Master's Degree scholarships as well.

Applications for undergraduate scholarships are available each fall from the UFT Chapter Leaders in all New York City public high schools.

Amount:	Undergraduate award is $1,000 per year; graduate-level award is $1,500 over two semesters to former undergraduate scholarship winners
Deadline:	Various
Write:	United Federation of Teachers (UFT) Scholarship Fund 260 Park Avenue South New York, NY 10010 212-777-7500

Agnes Jones Jackson Scholarship
National Association for the Advancement of Colored People (NAACP)
Baltimore, MD

Type:	Scholarships
Description:	Scholarships are available to undergraduate and graduate students who are current regular members of the NAACP (at least one year), or fully-paid life members of the organization. Undergraduates must have a grade point average of at least 2.5 and graduate students at least a 3.0 or B average. Applicants must not have reached the age of 25 by April 30 of the year of application. Application forms are available from the NAACP in January.
Amount:	Undergraduate award is $1,500 and graduate award $2,500
Deadline:	April 30
Write:	Agnes Jones Jackson Scholarship NAACP 4805 Mt. Hope Drive Baltimore, MD 21215-3297 410-358-8900

Alpha Kappa Alpha Sorority, Inc.
Chicago, IL 60637

Type:	Scholarships
Description:	Alpha Kappa Alpha Sorority is an organization of 100,000 members in 750 chapters throughout the United States and abroad. The sorority selects 30 undergraduate women from throughout the nation each year to receive the sorority's Leadership Fellows Grant. Recipients undergo an intensive weeklong leadership development training and are then sent to work as interns for major agencies and corporations throughout the nation.
	The organization also provides grants, through its educational advancement foundation, to various institutions of higher education.

Amount:	Various
Deadline:	Various
Write:	Alpha Kappa Alpha Sorority, Inc. 5656 So. Stony Island Avenue Chicago, IL 60637 312-684-1282

American Library Association (ALA)
Chicago, IL

Type:	Scholarships
Description:	The LITA/OCLC Minority Scholarship is awarded to members of a principal minority group (African-American, American Indian or Alaskan Native, Asian or Pacific Islander, or Hispanic). Scholarships are awarded on the basis of academic excellence, leadership potential, and evidence of commitment to a career in library education, with an emphasis on library automation and information technology, with prior activity and experience in those fields. Recipients must enter or be enrolled in an ALA-accredited master's degree program of library education or library automation. Applicants must be U.S. or Canadian citizens.
Amount:	$2,500
Deadline:	April 1
Write:	Library and Information Technology Association American Library Association 50 E. Huron Street Chicago, IL 60611 312-280-4270

American Geological Institute (AGI)
Alexandria, VA

Type:	Scholarships
Description:	The American Geological Institute sponsors scholarships for geoscience majors (geology, geophysics, hydrology, meteorology, physical oceanography, planetary geology, and earth-science education) to African-Americans and members of other ethnic minority groups that are underrepresented in the geosciences, in an effort to increase their numbers in the field. Scholarship recipients must be U.S. citizens. Applicants must be enrolled full-time in a college or university with a major in the geosciences. Successful candidates are bright, energetic, hard-working individuals with a strong academic background. Selections are based on academic excellence and financial need.

Candidates must submit completed applications including a financial profile and an essay, official academic transcripts (high school and college), standardized test scores (i.e. SAT, ACT), and three letters of recommendation. This award is renewable if performance is satisfactory (based on GPA and three letters of recommendation from current faculty).

Amount: Scholarship awards up to $10,000 a year. Award is renewable; recipients must reapply

Deadline: All application materials must be received by AGI no later than February 1

Write: Director, AGI Minority Geoscience Scholarships
              American Geological Institute
              4220 King Street
              Alexandria, VA 22302-1507
              703-379-2480

American Meteorological Society
Boston, MA

Type: Scholarships

Description: Howard T. Orville and Howard H. Hanks, Jr., scholarships awarded to students interested in pursuing studies in the field of meteorology. In addition, two AMS minority scholarships are available to African-American and other minority students.

Amount: $700–$3,000

Deadline: Various

Write: American Meteorological Society
              45 Beacon Street
              Boston, MA 02108-3693

American Society of Women Accountants
Chicago, IL

Type: Scholarships

Description: The Society awards scholarships to women majoring in the field of accounting. The scholarships are designed to increase opportunities for women in the field. Scholarships are offered at the chapter and national levels. There are currently more than 130 chapters located throughout the United States.

Amount: Various

Write: American Society of Women Accountants
              35 E. Wacker Drive
              Suite 2250
              Chicago, IL 60601
              312-726-9030
              Miriam Green, Executive Director

APS Minorities Scholarship Program
American Physical Society
College Park, MD

Type:	Scholarships

Description: The American Physical Society Corporate-Sponsored Scholarship program is targeted to undergraduate students who major in physics. The purpose of the program is to increase the level of underrepresented minority participation in the field of physics. Each scholarship is sponsored by a corporation and recipients will normally be designated as the sponsors of the "Scholarship for Minority Undergraduate Students in Physics" at the host college or university. A selection committee determines who will receive the APS Scholarship and will provide an accomplished physicist as a mentor for each scholarship recipient. The scholarship is open to any African-American, Hispanic-American, or Native American U.S. citizen who is majoring or plans to major in physics and who is a high school senior or a college freshman or sophomore.

Amount: Scholarships consist of $2,000 awarded to the student for tuition, room, or board and a $500 award to each college or university physics department that hosts one or more APS minority undergraduate scholars. The scholarship may be renewed one time, based on approval by the selection committee.

Deadline: All application materials must be received by APS no later than February 14.

Write: APS Minorities Scholarship Program
The American Center for Physics
1 Physics Ellipse
College Park, MD 20740

Armco Insurance Group
Middletown, OH

Type: Scholarships

Description: African-American and other minority students interested in pursuing undergraduate study in Business with emphasis on insurance may qualify for the ARMCO Minorities in Insurance and Risk Management Scholarship. Candidates must attend high schools in communities in which an Armco facility is located and be seniors who rank in the upper half of their class. Scholarship recipients must attend one of the following colleges or universities: University of Cincinnati, Cincinnati, OH; College of Insurance, New York, NY; Drake University, Des Moines, IA; Howard University, Washington, D.C.; University of Iowa, Iowa City, IA; University of North Texas, Denton, TX; Ohio State University, Columbus, OH; Oregon State University, Corvallis, OR; Southern Methodist University, Dallas, TX; University of Wisconsin, Madison, WI.

Amount: $2,000, renewable

Deadline: November 1

Write: Armco Insurance Group
                  703 Curtis Street
                  Middletown, OH 45043

Asbury Park Press Scholarships for Minority Students
Neptune, NJ

Type: Scholarships

Description: Offered to one graduating high school student from Mon-
                  mouth County, New Jersey, and one from Ocean County,
                  New Jersey, who will enter college seeking a career in the
                  field of communications including reporting, broadcasting,
                  marketing, and advertising. Scholarship is offered to African-
                  American and other minority students. Renewable for a total
                  of four years with continued satisfactory work.

Amount: $1,500

Deadline: Various

Write: Editorial Department
                  Asbury Park Press
                  3601 Highway 66
                  P.O. Box 1550
                  Neptune, NJ 07754

Association for Women in Architecture
Los Angeles, CA

Type: Scholarships

Description: Scholarships are awarded to encourage women to enter the
                  field of architecture. Candidates must be California residents
                  or attending a California school. Awards are made for stu-
                  dents in their second year of study.

Amount: $500–$2,000; ten awards made annually

Deadline: Various

Write: Association for Women in Architecture
                  2550 Beverly Blvd.
                  Los Angeles, CA 90057

AT&T Research & Development
Scholarships & Summer Programs
Holmdel, NJ

Type: Scholarships and Summer Employment Programs

Description: AT&T offers several scholarship and employment programs
                  to minority students interested in pursuing careers in engi-
                  neering, computer science, and research.

The **Engineering Scholarship Program (ESP)** is designed to encourage selected outstanding minorities and women to pursue undergraduate degrees in Computer Science or selected Engineering disciplines. ESP provides full tuition, a book allowance, fees, room and board, a challenging summer job each year at AT&T, and an appropriate mentor. Applicants must be high school seniors who are applying as full-time students to colleges with strong curricula. Fifteen candidates are selected each year. **Application deadline date is January 15. Students interested in applying should call 908-949-4301.**

Dual Degree Scholarship Program (DDSP) is designed to encourage talented minorities to enter the Engineering field. The DDSP is sponsored through a coordinated effort with The Atlanta University Center in Atlanta, Georgia. Through this collaboration, Dual Degree scholars earn a BA degree in Math or Physics from Spelman, Morehouse, Clark, or Morris Brown colleges in three years and then go on to earn a BS degree in Engineering or Computer Science. The second degree may be earned from Georgia Institute of Technology, University of Alabama, or Boston University over a two-year period. The DDSP provides full tuition, books, fees, room and board, a challenging summer job each year at AT&T, and an appropriate mentor. Three candidates are selected to participate in the program. **Application deadline date is June 10. Outstanding minority students interested in this program should call 908-949-4301.**

The Summer Research Program For Minorities and Women (SRP) provides outstanding minorities and women an opportunity to work for a summer within the research environment of AT&T Bell Laboratories. The program is open to students who have completed three years of education in selected engineering disciplines. The program also provides an AT&T Bell Laboratories scientist as a mentor. 60–100 candidates are accepted each year in the program. **Application deadline date is December 1. For more information, call 908-949-3728.**

The University Relations Summer Program (UR) provides summer employment for outstanding BS, MS, and Ph.D candidates who are within two years of graduation and pursuing studies in selected engineering disciplines. The purpose of the program is to provide work experience for talented students on a well-defined project in an R&D (Research and Development) environment. An AT&T Member of Technical Staff is assigned to each student as a mentor. To be eligible, candidates must be available for Career Employment within two years of Summer Employment. 200–300 candidates are selected for the program each year. **Application deadline date is February 15. For additional information, call 908-949-5592.**

Amount:	(See individual programs)
Deadline:	(See individual programs)

Write: *For a brochure on the program write:*
                  AT&T
                  101 Crawfords Corner Road
                  Holmdel, NJ 07733-3030

Bertina Maxwell Undergraduate Awards
National Council for Black Studies
Bloomington, IN

Type: Scholarships

Description: Scholarship essay contest for undergraduate students. Award
                  recognizes outstanding student scholarship among African-
                  American students.

Amount: $500, a plaque, and publication of the essay in a leading jour-
                  nal of Black Studies

Deadline: Various

Write: Dr. Joseph J. Russell, Executive Director
                  National Council for Black Studies
                  Indiana University
                  Memorial Hall East 129
                  Bloomington, IN 47405
                  812-335-6581

Black American Film Makers Grants Program
Black American Cinema Society
Los Angeles, CA

Type: Grants

Description: Awards recognize outstanding African-American film and
                  video makers in annual competition. Award is presented
                  annually.

Amount: First prize $1,000; second prize $750; third prize $500

Deadline: Various

Write: Black American Cinema Society
                  c/o Western States Black Research Center
                  3617 Montclair
                  Los Angeles, CA 90018
                  213-737-3292

Black Communicators Scholarships
Dallas-Fort Worth Association of
Dallas, TX

Type: Scholarships

Description: Several scholarships are awarded to high school seniors and
                  college students who are pursuing careers in print, broadcast-
                  ing, photojournalism, graphic arts, or public relations.

Amount: Minimum $1,500

Deadline: March 1

Write: Rochelle Riley
                 President DPF/ABC
                 c/o Dallas Morning News
                 Communication Center
                 P.O. Box 227455
                 Dallas, TX 75222

Business and Professional Women's Foundation
Washington, D.C.

Type: Scholarships

Description: The Foundation offers scholarships for mature women seek-
                 ing the education necessary for entry into or advancement
                 within the workforce. Need-based scholarships are awarded
                 to women working towards financial security for themselves
                 and their families. Awards are made to women in various
                 high-growth fields. Application forms are available from the
                 Foundation.

Amount: Various

Deadline: Various

Write: Business and Professional
                 Women's Foundation
                 2012 Massachusetts Avenue, N.W.
                 Washington, D.C. 20036
                 202-293-1200

Carver Scholarship Program
Carver Federal Savings Bank
New York, NY

Type: Scholarships

Description: Bank provides scholarships for its depositors or members of
                 their families. Carver Bank is located in Central Harlem and
                 has branches in the five boroughs of New York City and on
                 Long Island. It is one of the most successful African-American
                 savings institutions in the United States.

Amount: Nearly $100,000 in scholarships for 77 students are awarded
                 annually

Deadline: Various

Write: Apply by mail or in person to:
                 Carver Federal Savings Bank
                 75 W. 125th Street
                 New York, NY 10027
                 212-876-4747

Chicago Association of Black Journalists Scholarships
Chicago, IL

Type: Scholarships

Description: Scholarships open to any African-American or other minority full-time junior, senior, or graduate student enrolled in an accredited college or university in the Chicago metropolitan area who is majoring in print or broadcast journalism.

Amount: $1,000

Deadline: March 31

Write: Chicago Association of Black Journalists
                 P.O. Box 11425
                 Chicago, IL 60611

Chip Quinn Scholars Program
c/o Howard University
Washington, D.C

Type: Scholarships/Internships

Description: Chip Quinn Scholars are matched with appropriate paid summer internships at cooperating newspapers and matched with a mentor editor. Winners receive a travel stipend and, upon successful completion of the internship, a scholarship award. Students who are juniors may be nominated for this program if they are enrolled in a journalism program that is a member of the Association of Black College Journalism and Mass Communications Program.

Amount: $1,000 scholarship and paid summer internship

Deadline: April 1

Write: Dr. Lawrence Kaggwa
                 Department of Journalism
                 School of Communications
                 Howard University
                 Washington, D.C. 20059
                 202-806-7855

Clare Boothe Luce Scholarships in Science and Engineering
New York, NY

Type: Scholarships

Description: Offers scholarships to encourage women to enter the engineering and science fields. Awards are made to students majoring in biology, chemistry, computer science, engineering, mathematics, and physics. Scholarship awards are made through individual colleges and universities. Participating schools include: Boston University, Colby College, Creighton University, Fordham University, Georgetown University, Marymount University,

Mount Holyoke College, Mundelein College, St. John's University, Santa Clara University, Seton Hall University, Trinity College, University of Notre Dame, Villanova Preparatory School.

Amount:	Various
Deadline:	Various
Write:	College or university financial aid office *or*
	Clare Boothe Luce Scholarships in Science
	and Engineering
	c/o Henry Luce Foundation, Inc.
	111 W. 50th Street
	New York, NY 10020

Coca-Cola Scholars Foundation, Inc.
Atlanta, GA

Type:	Scholarships
Description:	The Coca-Cola Scholars Program is one of the largest and most comprehensive business-supported scholarship programs in the country. Each year, high school seniors compete for 50 four-year $20,000 scholarships and 100 four-year $4,000 scholarships for study at any accredited U.S. college or university. The Scholars program was begun in 1986 and is supported by local Coca-Cola bottlers and the Coca-Cola Company. Applicants must be U.S. Citizens, U.S. Nationals, U.S. Permanent Residents, Temporary Residents (legalization program), Refugees, Asylees, Cuban-Haitian Entrants, or Humanitarian Parolees; and must be current full-time secondary school students who anticipate graduating during the academic year in which application is made. They must also be planning to pursue a degree at an accredited U.S. postsecondary institution. Selections are based on a number of factors, with special emphasis on each individual's character, personal merit, and background. Merit may be demonstrated in leadership in school, civic, and other extracurricular activities, through academic achievement and motivation to serve and succeed in all endeavors. Selection is sensitive to the ethnic and economic backgrounds of applicants, and try to reflect the demographic profiles of the eleven Selection Districts throughout the country, including Hawaii, Alaska, and internationally in schools on U.S. military bases.

The selection process is done in three phases, beginning each fall and culminating in the following spring with the announcement of award recipients. Your guidance counselor will be sent a schedule of key days and deadlines. Up to 2,000 semifinalists are selected in the first phase and the final selection of 150 scholars is made among them. Award recipients will attend the National Competition in Atlanta, Georgia, which is convened by the Foundation at its expense in April.

Amount:	50 four-year $20,000 scholarships and 100 four-year $4,000 scholarships awarded annually
Deadline:	To apply, students must obtain applications from school guidance counselors and mail the completed forms to the designated address by October 31 of the year prior to award
Write:	Contact your school guidance counselor *or*, For a brochure on the program write: Coca-Cola Scholars Foundation, Inc. One Buckhead Plaza, Suite 1000 3060 Peachtree Road, N.W. Atlanta, GA 30305 404-237-1300

Concerned Media Professionals Scholarships
Tucson, AZ

Type:	Scholarships
Description:	A number of scholarships are awarded to African-American and other minority college students majoring in print or broadcast journalism. Applicants must be Arizona residents attending an Arizona college or university.
Amount:	$500–$1,000
Deadline:	March 31
Write:	Concerned Media Professionals Scholarship Committee P.O. Box 44034 Tucson, AZ 85733

Cox Newspapers
Minority Journalism Scholarships
Atlanta, GA

Type:	Scholarships
Description:	Full scholarships, including tuition, room, board, and books, are available to graduating high school seniors from racial minorities in the public schools of Atlanta, Georgia, who are in need of financial assistance. Applicants must have at least a B average and an interest in journalism. Recipients will attend Georgia State University or one of the colleges in the Atlanta University Center, and have a major or minor in journalism.
Amount:	All educational expenses
Deadline:	April 30
Write:	Mrs. Alexis Scott Reeves Cox Newspapers P.O. Box 4689 Atlanta, GA 30302

Detroit Free Press Minority Journalism Scholarships
Detroit Free Press
Detroit, MI

Type:　　　　　Scholarships

Description:　　Scholarships available to African-Americans and other minority students who plan to become writers, editors, or photojournalists, and have a 3.0 grade point average. Scholarships are given to encourage outstanding minority students to enter the field of journalism. Awards are based on grades, a written essay detailing why the student wants to become a journalist, and recommendations from high school. Application must also be accompanied by SAT/ACT scores. Finalists have an in-person interview.

Amount:　　　 Competitive selection, with two first-place winners receiving $1,000 awards, and second-place winner, $750 award. First-place winners automatically compete for $20,000 scholarships offered by Knight-Ridder, Inc.

Deadline:　　　 January 6

Write:　　　　　Louise Reid Ritchie
　　　　　　　　Detroit Free Press
　　　　　　　　321 W. Lafayette Blvd.
　　　　　　　　Detroit, MI 48226
　　　　　　　　800-678-6400

Dow Jones Minority Scholarship Competition for College Sophomores
The Dow Jones Newspaper Fund
Princeton, NJ

Type:　　　　　Scholarships

Description:　　The Reporting Scholarship Competition offers minority college sophomores who have completed a reporting internship at a newspaper an opportunity to compete for one of five $1,000 scholarships. Students must find their own internships and complete them during the sophomore year or summer before the junior year. Members of minority groups who will have worked as reporting interns at a daily or weekly newspaper will be eligible for the award.

Amount:　　　 $1,000

Deadline:　　　 Various

Write:　　　　　The Dow Jones Newspaper Fund
　　　　　　　　P.O. Box 300
　　　　　　　　Princeton, NJ 08543-0300
　　　　　　　　609-452-2820

Florida Society of Newspaper Editors
Journalism Scholarships
Tallahassee, FL

Type: Scholarships

Description: Eight scholarships are awarded to Florida minority high school graduates who plan to attend a Florida public community college. Applicants must have a 3.0 high school grade point average and be interested in pursuing journalism careers. Scholarships are renewable for up to two years. Students should contact the financial aid office or journalism department at their community college for applications and additional information.

Amount: $1,200 per year ($600 per semester)

Deadline: Various

Write: Contact financial aid office or journalism department at community college

Foundation Scholarships for Minority Freshmen
American Society of Newspaper Editors
Washington, D.C.

Type: Scholarships

Description: 60 scholarships awarded to college-bound African-Americans and other minority students. Students must submit a formal application form, two letters of recommendation, and write an essay stating their career interests and journalism-related activities while they were seniors in high school. Applicants must have a 2.5 grade point average in their high school courses and sign a statement of intent to pursue a career in journalism.

Amount: $750

Deadline: First week in November

Write: Minority Affairs Director
                 ASNE
                 P.O. Box 17004
                 Washington, D.C. 20041
                 703-648-1146

Frank E. Johnson Scholarships
The Arizona Daily Star
Tucson, AZ

Type: Scholarships

Description: Scholarships are awarded to African-Americans or other minority students at Pima Community College. Awards are based on scholarship, financial need, and interest in journalism. Apply to the Department of Media Communications at Pima Community College.

Amount: $500

Deadline: Various

Write: Department of Media Communications
                 Pima Community College
                 2202 W. Anklam Road
                 Tucson, AZ 85709

Fukunaga Scholarship Foundation
Honolulu, HI

Type: Scholarships

Description: Scholarships are awarded to high school students who are inter-
                 ested in pursuing undergraduate study in business administra-
                 tion. Awards are made on the basis of academic achievement,
                 recommendations, and financial need.

Amount: $6,000–$8,000

Deadline: March 15

Write: Fukunaga Scholarship Foundation
                 900 Fort Street Mall, Suite 500
                 P.O. Box 2788
                 Honolulu, HI 96803

The Fund for Theological Education, Inc.
New York, NY

Type: Scholarships

Description: Program provides scholarships to selected candidates for the
                 Benjamin E. Mays Ministry Program for Black North Americans.
                 Candidates must be nominated by either a minister, a church of-
                 ficial, a member of a faculty or administration, or by a former
                 FTE Scholar. The program seeks to strengthen Christian theo-
                 logical education in the United States and Canada by support-
                 ing Black North American women and men who demonstrate
                 high promise for academic excellence and teaching effective-
                 ness. A nominee must be a member of a Christian church, be a
                 citizen of the United States or Canada, have completed one year
                 of coursework in a Ph.D., Th.D., or Ed.D. degree program in
                 fields of religious studies at an accredited university or seminary.

Amount: Various

Deadline: Nominations must be received by the FTE by February 10. An
                 application will be sent directly to nominees, and the com-
                 pleted forms must be returned to the FTE by March 15.

Write: The Fund for Theological Education
                 475 Riverside Drive, Suite 832
                 New York, NY 10115-0008
                 212-870-2058

Garth Reeves, Jr., Memorial Scholarships
Miami, FL

Type: Scholarships

Description: One or more scholarships offered by the Greater Miami Chapter, Society of Professional Journalists to undergraduate- and graduate-level African-Americans and other minority students majoring in journalism. Preference is given to students from South Florida, or students attending college in South Florida.

Amount: Amount determined by financial need; minimum award $500

Deadline: March 1

Write: Mike Haggerty
                Miami Herald
                One Herald Plaza
                Miami, FL 33132

General Electric Foundation Minority Student Scholarships
General Electric Foundation
Fairfield, CT

Type: Scholarships

Description: Scholarships available to assist African-Americans and other minority students majoring in engineering and business. Awards are made to universities and organizations directly, which select the individuals to receive scholarship awards.

Amount: $1,000,000 in funds available for awards

Deadline: Various

Write: College Financial Aid Office

Golden State Minority Foundation
Los Angeles, CA

Type: Scholarships

Description: Scholarships awarded to full-time undergraduate students enrolled as juniors or above in an accredited four-year college or university (60 units of college credit required). Students must have a major field of interest in Business Administration, Economics, Life Insurance or related field, have a minimum 3.0 to 4.0 overall GPA or be students in good standing at an accredited four-year college or university with no GPA scale, be U.S. citizens or permanent legal residents, be a qualified minority (African-American, Latino, Native American, or other represented ethnic minority), be employed no more than 28 hours per week, and attend school or be residents of California, Detroit, Michigan, or Houston, Texas.

Amount: Various

Deadline:	Northern California and Houston, Texas: August 1–October 1 Detroit, Michigan: December 1–February 1 Southern California: February 1–April 1
Write:	Golden State Minority Foundation 1999 West Adams Boulevard Los Angeles, CA 90016 1-800-666-4763

Hearst Foundation Minority Scholarships
Northwestern University
Evanston, IL

Type:	Scholarships
Description:	Scholarships offered by The Medill School of Journalism at Northwestern University are awarded to African-American graduate editorial students every fall quarter. Recipients will have graduated from a Historically Black College or University, and demonstrate superior writing and journalistic potential. All admitted African-American editorial students are eligible for the scholarship; no additional application materials are required.
Amount:	$24,000
Deadline:	Various
Write:	The Medill School of Journalism Northwestern University Evanston, IL 60208

Indiana Minority Teacher and Special Education Scholarships
Indiana State Student Assistance Commission
Indianapolis, IN

Type:	Scholarships
Description:	Scholarships available to African-Americans and other minority students who are residents of the State of Indiana and interested in teaching. Students must be admitted to eligible institutions as full-time students or already in attendance at such institutions, and also meet academic requirements. Each college is responsible for making the awards, which are based on academics and financial need.
Amount:	$1,000 annually
Deadline:	Obtain application and details from the college or university financial aid office, high school guidance counselor office, or State Student Assistance Commission
Write:	Indiana State Student Assistance Commission 964 N. Pennsylvania Street Indianapolis, IN 46204 317-232-2350

354   **Academic**

Jackie Robinson Foundation Scholarship Program
New York, NY

Type: Scholarships

Description: Scholarships are awarded to minority students who are high school seniors, and have demonstrated high academic achievement and financial need. Recipients also have leadership potential and have been accepted to an accredited four-year college or university. Scholarship applications are available November 1.

Amount: Various

Deadline: March 30

Write: Jackie Robinson Foundation
               Scholarship Program
               80–90 Eighth Avenue
               New York, NY 10011

Ken Inouye Scholarships
Los Angeles Professional Chapter
Society of Professional Journalists
Torrance, CA

Type: Scholarships

Description: Scholarships awarded to African-Americans or other minority juniors, seniors, or graduate students attending a Los Angeles County college or university, or Los Angeles County residents attending a school elsewhere. Applicants must intend to pursue a journalism career with an emphasis in news work. Scholarships awarded on basis of accomplishments, potential and need.

Amount: $1,000

Deadline: Various

Write: Ms. Janet Rae-Dupree
               c/o Los Angeles Times
               South Bay Bureau
               23133 Hawthorn Blvd. #20
               Torrance, CA 90505

Knight-Ridder Scholarship Program for Minorities
Miami, FL

Type: Scholarships

Description: Awards scholarships to graduating high school seniors who attend high school in an area served by Knight-Ridder. The scholarship is renewable for up to four years based on students' academic performance, and includes a summer internship at a Knight-Ridder newspaper. Interested high school students should contact their school counselor or journalism teacher during the first semester of their senior year for application information.

Amount:	$5,000
Deadline:	Various
Write:	Contact your high school counselor or journalism teacher for more information.

KNTV Minority Scholarships
KNTV Television
San Jose, CA

Type: Scholarships

Description: Scholarships are available to African-Americans and other minority students who are residents of Santa Clara, Santa Cruz, Monterey, or San Benito counties of California. Students must be accepted for admission to an accredited California four-year college or university and major in television production, journalism, or a related field (marketing, public relations, advertising, graphics, or engineering with interest in television). Undergraduate applicants must have one full year of undergraduate work remaining and carry a minimum of 12 semester units during each semester. Scholarships are awarded with preference to students with financial need who demonstrate an interest and potential in the field of television production and television journalism.

Amount: Two $750 scholarships

Deadline: April 1

Write: KNTV Minority Scholarship Application
KNTV Television
645 Park Avenue
San Jose, CA 95110

Ladies of Essence
Montgomery, AL

Type: Scholarships

Description: Awards scholarships to minority students who plan to attend four-year or two-year college, university, or technical college.

Amount: $500

Deadline: April 1

Write: Rosetta Ledyard
Ladies of Essence
3028 N. Rick Dr.
Montgomery, AL 36108

Landscape Architecture Foundation
Washington, D.C.

Type: Scholarships/Internships

Description: Scholarships and internships are awarded to students inter-
                 ested in pursuing a career in landscape architecture. The Asso-
                 ciates Minority Scholarship is available to African-Americans
                 and other minority students in the final two years of under-
                 graduate study. Candidates must submit an essay (500 words
                 maximum) and two letters of recommendation to qualify.

Amount: $1,000

Deadline: May 1

Description: The Raymond E. Page Scholarship is awarded to an under-
                 graduate or graduate student based on financial need. Candi-
                 dates must submit a two-page description of how the money
                 will be used, and submit a letter of reference from a professor
                 or employer.

Amount: $500

Deadline: May 4

Write: Landscape Architecture Foundation
                 4401 Connecticut Avenue, N.W., #500
                 Washington, D.C. 20008

Leonard M. Perryman Communications Scholarships
for Ethnic Minority Students
New York, NY

Type: Scholarships

Description: Scholarships are available to African-Americans and other mi-
                 nority undergraduate students who are juniors or seniors and
                 have the intention of pursuing a career in religious commu-
                 nications. Candidates must attend an accredited institution
                 of higher education in the United States. Students may pur-
                 sue careers in various areas of communications, including
                 audiovisual, electronic, and print journalism. These scholar-
                 ships are offered in recognition of Leonard M. Perryman, a
                 journalist for the United Methodist Church for nearly 30 years.

Amount: $2,500

Deadline: February 15

Write: Scholarship Committee
                 United Methodist Communications
                 475 Riverside Drive, Suite 1901
                 New York, NY 10115

Lonzie L. Jones, Jr., National Sickle Cell Scholarship Program
National Association for Sickle Cell Disease, Inc.
Los Angeles, CA

Type:	Scholarship/Essay Competition
Description:	Annual scholarship essay contest for high school students. Award recognizes the most outstanding high school student essay on sickle cell disease. Contest open to all high school students. Local contests are held in conjunction with National Sickle Cell Month. Local winners are considered in a national judging.
Amount:	First-place winner receives $2,500; runners-up receive $1,000–$1,500 to cover college costs. Three awards are made annually.
Deadline:	Essays are usually due in September
Write:	National Association for Sickle Cell Disease, Inc. 4221 Wilshire Boulevard, Suite 360 Los Angeles, CA 90010-3503 213-936-7205

Lorraine Hansberry Playwriting Awards
John F. Kennedy Center for the Performing Arts
Washington, D.C.

Type:	Scholarships/Playwright Awards
Description:	Awards recognize student authors of plays on the African-American experience in America. Candidates must be full-time or part-time students enrolled in undergraduate or graduate schools. Eligible plays must be regular entries in the Playwriting Award Program of the American College Theatre Festival.
Amount:	First-place award $2,500 and an all-expense paid fellowship to attend Shenandoah Valley Playwrights Retreat. Second place award $1,000
Deadline:	November
Write:	American College Theatre Festival John F. Kennedy Center for the Performing Arts Washington, D.C. 20566 202-254-3437

Louise Giles Minority Scholarships
American Library Association (ALA)
Chicago, IL

Type:	Scholarships
Description:	The Louise Giles Minority Scholarships are awarded to members of a principal minority group (African-American, American Indian or Alaskan Native, Asian or Pacific Islander, or Hispanic). Applicants cannot have completed more than 12 se-

mester hours (or its equivalent) towards a master's degree in library science prior to June 1. Scholarships are awarded on the basis of academic excellence, leadership, and evidence of commitment to a career in librarianship. Individuals need not have been accepted into a library education program at the time of application, but winners must enter an ALA-accredited master's degree program. Applicants must be U.S. or Canadian citizens.

Amount: Two $3,000 scholarships awarded annually

Deadline: Postmarked no later than January 14

Write: Staff Liaison
                 ALA Scholarship Juries
                 50 E. Huron Street
                 Chicago, IL 60611
                 312-280-4277 or 280-4281/4282

Music Assistance Fund Scholarship
American Symphony Orchestral League
Washington, D.C.

Type: Scholarships

Description: The Music Assistance Fund encourages and supports gifted student musicians and young professionals of African-American heritage who wish to pursue careers in this country's symphony orchestras. Created by the New York Philharmonic in 1965, the Music Assistance Fund Scholarships are granted on the basis of an audition and financial need. Eligibility is limited to U.S. citizens of African descent (African-American, Afro-Caribbean, or similar heritage).

Amount: $2,500

Deadline: March 1

Write: American Symphony Orchestral League
                 777 Fourteenth Street, N.W., Suite 500
                 Washington, D.C. 20005
                 202-628-0099

NAACP-Roy Wilkins Scholarships
NAACP Youth and College Division
Baltimore, MD

Type: Scholarships

Description: Scholarships are available to needy African-American students in the 12th grade or in their first year of college. Candidates must submit an application form, transcript, recommendations and essay. 15–20 scholarship awards are made annually. Applications are available after January 1 of every year. Students should send a letter in December with a self-addressed, stamped envelope requesting an application package.

Amount:	Up to $1,000

Deadline: May 1

Write: Request: Scholarship Application Packet
American Dental Hygienists' Assn. Institute
Minority Scholarship Program
444 N. Michigan Avenue, Suite 3400
Chicago, IL 60611

National Achievement Scholarship Program for Outstanding Negro Students
Evanston, IL

Type: Scholarships

Description: 700 Scholarships are awarded to African-American high school students who have taken the Preliminary Scholastic Aptitude Test/National Merit Scholarship Qualifying Test. Candidates must be U.S. citizens. Test is administered through high school.

Amount: $2,000 for one-time awards and $250–$8,000 annually for four-year scholarship awards

Deadline: Various

Write: Contact your high school counselor *or*:
National Achievement Scholarship Program
for Outstanding Negro Students
One American Plaza
1560 Sherman Avenue
Evanston, IL 60201

National Action Council for Minorities in Engineering
New York, NY

Type: Scholarships

Description: The National Action Council for Minorities in Engineering, Inc., is a nonprofit coalition of corporations, universities, local programs, and others committed to increasing the number of minority engineers. The major portion of NACME's budget is directed to minority students through incentive grant scholarships, which are administered by selected engineering colleges.

Amount: Various

Deadline: Various

Write: National Action Council for Minorities
in Engineering, Inc.
3 West 35th Street
New York, NY 10001

National Association of Black Accountants, Inc.
Washington, D.C.

Type: Scholarships

Description: Awards scholarships to college undergraduates who have a
                 3.5 grade point average and have completed 18 credit hours
                 in accounting. Applicants must also be members of the Asso-
                 ciation's student chapter or affiliated with one of the profes-
                 sional chapters.

                 Applications may be obtained from the national office and
                 should be returned with a 500-word autobiographical sketch,
                 a 500-word essay, two letters of recommendation, and three
                 references.

                 Students interested in chapter scholarships may contact the
                 nearest chapter office.

Amount: Various

Deadline: Various

Write: National Association of Black
                 Accountants, Inc.
                 300 "I" Street, N.E., Suite 107
                 Washington, D.C. 20002
                 202-543-6656

National Association of Black Journalists Scholarships
Washington, D.C.

Type: Scholarships

Description: Scholarships available to undergraduate and graduate students.
                 Applicants must have completed at least one full semester of
                 college to be eligible.

Amount: $2,500

Deadline: Late fall

Write: Scholarship Coordinator
                 NABJ
                 P.O. Box 17212
                 Washington, D.C. 20041

National Association of Media Women, Inc., Scholarships
Atlanta, GA

Type: Scholarships

Description: Scholarships are offered by the Atlanta chapter of the Na-
                 tional Association of Media Women, Inc., to undergraduate
                 minority female students majoring in mass communications.
                 Applicants must attend a college or university in Georgia.

Amount: Minimum award $500

Deadline: March 15

Write: Alexis Scott Reeves
               National Association of Media Women, Inc.
               P.O. Box 4689
               Atlanta, GA 30302

National Newspaper Publishers Association Grants
Washington, D.C.

Type: Grants

Description: Provides information and helps administer grants for minor-
               ity college students pursuing journalism careers.

Amount: Ten grants awarded annually, valued at $2,000 each

Deadline: Various

Write: Chairman
               NNPA Scholarship Committee
               948 National Press Building
               Washington, D.C. 20045

National Society of Professional Engineers Scholarships
Education Foundation
Washington, D.C.

Type: Scholarships

Description: Scholarships are offered to over 150 students pursuing a career
               in the field of engineering; a number of awards are designated
               to African-Americans and other minority students. Require-
               ments include SAT scores of 600 in the math category and 500
               in the verbal category. Students are also required to be U.S.
               citizens or permanent residents and rank in the top 25 percent
               of their high school standings.

Amount: $1,000

Deadline: September 1

Write: National Society of Professional Engineers
               2029 K Street, N.W.
               Washington, D.C. 20006

National Urban League
New York, NY

Type: Scholarships

Description: The National Urban League, working in concert with 113 affili-
               ate organizations in 34 states and the District of Columbia, pro-
               vides programs of direct service to people nationwide, including
               scholarships for full-time students pursuing a Bachelor's Degree

at accredited institutions of higher learning. Candidates must be classified as junior, or third-year, students at the time the scholarship award commences, and must also rank within the top 25 percent of their class. Candidates must also major in courses leading to a professional career in engineering, sales, marketing, manufacturing operations, finance, or business administration to qualify. This scholarship is offered in conjunction with Kraft, Inc. Candidates may apply to any National Urban League affiliate or write to the national office.

Amount: Various, ten awards to minority students

Deadline: April 15; education officials at the National Urban League will interview each semifinalist

Write: Director of Education
               National Urban League
               500 E. 62nd Street
               New York, NY 10021

Newsday Scholarships in Communications for Minorities
Melville, NY

Type: Scholarships

Description: Up to two scholarships are awarded to minority students graduating from high school in Nassau or Suffolk Counties who plan to attend a four-year college in the United States. The scholarships are to be applied toward the cost of tuition for the fall following graduation. High school students must contact their guidance counselors for applications and details.

Amount: $5,000

Deadline: March 31

Write: Mr. Reginald Tuggle
               Community Affairs Director
               Newsday
               235 Pinelawn Road
               Melville, NY 11747-4250
               516-454-2183

New York Association of Black Journalists
Stephen H. Gayle Memorial Scholarships
New York, NY

Type: Scholarships

Description: Scholarships are available to African-American college students or graduating high school seniors planning careers in journalism. Must write an autobiographical essay related to why one wants to enter the field of journalism.

Amount: Minimum award $1,500

Deadline: October 19

Write: NYABJ
                 P.O. Box 2446
                 Rockefeller Center
                 New York, NY 10185

Nuclear Energy Training Program
Historically Black Colleges and Universities
Oak Ridge, TN

Type: Scholarships

Description: The Nuclear Energy Training Program, in cooperation with
                 seven historically Black colleges and universities, provides
                 scholarships for African-Americans and other minority stu-
                 dents at participating HBCU's. The program is made possible
                 by the U.S. Department of Energy.

                 For more information about the program, contact the par-
                 ticipating institutions directly—Atlanta University, Lincoln
                 University, Howard University, North Carolina A&M State Uni-
                 versity, South Carolina State College, Tennessee State Univer-
                 sity, and Virginia State University. You may also contact the
                 U.S. Department of Energy.

Amount: The awards consist of full tuition and fees, plus a $6,000 an-
                 nual stipend

Deadline: Various

Write: Nuclear Energy Training Program
                 Oak Ridge Associated Universities
                 University Programs
                 P.O. Box 117
                 Oak Ridge, TN 37831
                 615-576-3428

Omega Psi Phi Fraternity, Inc.
Washington, D.C.

Type: Scholarships

Description: Omega Psi Phi Fraternity annually offers scholarships to
                 members and nonmembers, including:

                 The Founder's Memorial Scholarship, which commemorates
                 the founding of Omega Psi Phi Fraternity, Inc. Scholarships
                 are awarded to a fraternity brother in each district who has
                 attained sophomore or junior standing in undergraduate
                 school. The award is $300.

                 George E. Meares Scholarship was established in memory
                 of George E. Meares, who served as Grand Basileus of Omega
                 Psi Phi from 1964–67. Scholarships of $1,000 are awarded to

support graduate study in social work, the social sciences, and criminal justice.

Other scholarships are provided by local chapters of the fraternity in each district, or by the respective districts to high school seniors who are planning to enter postsecondary education. Contact the local affiliate for further information.

Amount: Various

Deadline: Various

Write: Local affiliate chapter *or*:
                Omega Psi Phi Fraternity, Inc.
                2714 Georgia Avenue
                Washington, D.C. 20001

Pepsi-Cola's Summer Internship Program
Pepsi-Cola Company
Somers, NY

Type: Internships/Scholarships

Description: Students who have completed their sophomore year in college are eligible to be part of this program to provide African-Americans and other minority college students hands-on business experience, and to give Pepsi-Cola expanded access to a qualified pool of potential employees. Recipients have the option of working in four areas within the corporation—sales, manufacturing, finance, and personnel/employee relations. Applicants should be enrolled in a four-year college or university.

Interested students may arrange to speak to the Pepsi-Cola recruiters through their school's College Placement Office or send a letter with their résumé to the National College Recruiting Manager at Pepsi-Cola.

Amount: Promising interns may receive $2,000 scholarships

Deadline: Various

Write: National College Recruiting Manager
                Pepsi-Cola's Summer Internship Program
                Pepsi-Cola Company
                Somers, NY 10589
                914-767-7434

Sacramento Bee Minority Media Scholarships
Sacramento, CA

Type: Scholarships

Description: Twelve scholarships are awarded to minority students living in the Sacramento circulation area. Applicants may be entering freshmen or currently enrolled students and may attend any college but have an interest in pursuing a career in mass media. Applicants should have a 3.0 grade point average.

Amount: $1,000

Deadline: March 15

Write: Monica Bagood
                Community Relations Department
                Sacramento Bee
                P.O. Box 15779
                Sacramento, CA 95852

Syracuse Newspapers Journalism Scholarships
The Herald-Journal
Syracuse, NY

Type: Scholarships

Description: Full scholarships to study print journalism at Syracuse University are available to minority students who attend Syracuse high schools. Students must attend a special journalism course taught by the Syracuse newspapers staff prior to enrolling in Syracuse University as journalism majors. A committee of professional journalists and college professors will select the students based on potential and interest in making newspaper journalism their career.

Amount: Four-year grant values at approximately $80,000

Deadline: Various

Write: Mr. Timothy Bunn, Executive Editor
                The Herald-Journal
                P.O. Box 4915
                Syracuse, NY 13221

The Foundation for Exceptional Children
Reston, VA

Type: Scholarships

Description: Scholarships are available to outstanding disabled and gifted students planning to continue their education and training beyond high school. The Foundation for Exceptional Children serves the needs of exceptional children and supports a number of programs that seek to maximize the potential of exceptional children.

Amount: Various

Deadline: Various

Write: The Foundation for Exceptional Children
                1920 Association Drive
                Reston, VA 22091
                703-620-3660

The Franan Scholarship Fund for Black Women
San Francisco State University
San Francisco, CA

Type: Scholarships

Description: The Franan Scholarship Fund recognizes the academic achieve-
                 ments and potential of Black women and assists them finan-
                 cially with the pursuit of their education. The scholarship is
                 available to new and continuing students at San Francisco
                 State University.

Amount: Scholarship amount is up to $1,500; $750 each semester

Deadline: May 2

Write: Office of Student Financial Aid
                 San Francisco State University
                 Room 355, Administration Bldg.
                 1600 Holloway Avenue
                 San Francisco, CA 94132
                 415-338-1581

Thomas A. Watson Scholarships
Lincoln National Life Insurance Corporation
Fort Wayne, IN

Type: Scholarships

Description: Scholarships are awarded to African-Americans and other mi-
                 norities who are graduates of Allen County High School and
                 are pursuing a four-year degree in a business-related field.
                 Awards are made by a scholarship committee. Recipients are
                 also offered an opportunity to gain company and corporate
                 exposure by providing meaningful and challenging summer
                 work assignments.

                 The scholarships are designed to promote career mobility
                 through higher education to African-Americans and other
                 minority students who reside in the Fort Wayne, Indiana,
                 community.

Amount: Various

Deadline: Various

Write: Thomas A. Watson Scholarship
                 Lincoln National Life Insurance Corporation
                 Human Resources Division/Affirmative Action
                 1300 S. Clinton Street
                 Fort Wayne, IN 46801
                 219-427-2000

Thurgood Marshall Scholarship Fund
Washington, D.C.

Type: Scholarships

Description: The Thurgood Marshall Scholarship Fund, a cooperative ef-
                 fort of the Miller Brewing Company and the Office for the Ad-
                 vancement of Black Colleges, provides merit scholarships to
                 the nation's 36 historically Black public colleges and universi-
                 ties. The Fund complements the efforts of the United Negro
                 College Fund, which raises millions of dollars annually to sup-
                 port Black colleges. Thurgood Marshall Scholars demonstrate
                 exemplary achievement in academic studies or exceptional
                 talent in the creative and performing arts.

                 Member institutions include:
                 Alabama A&M University, AL
                 Alabama State University, AL
                 Albany State College, GA
                 Alcorn State University, MS
                 Bowie State University, MD
                 Central State University, OH
                 Cheyney University of Pennsylvania, PA
                 Coppin State College, MD
                 Delaware State College, DE
                 Elizabeth City State University, NC
                 Fayetteville State University, NC
                 Florida A&M University, FL
                 Fort Valley State College, GA
                 Grambling State University, LA
                 Jackson State University, MS
                 Kentucky State University, KY
                 Lincoln University, MO
                 Mississippi Valley State University, MS
                 Morgan State University, MD
                 Norfolk State University, VA
                 North Carolina A&M State University, NC
                 North Carolina Central University, NC
                 Prairie View A&M University, TX
                 Savannah State College, GA
                 Southern University System, LA
                 Tennessee State University, TN
                 Texas Southern University, TX
                 Tuskegee University, AL
                 University of Arkansas at Pine Bluff, AR
                 University of Maryland Eastern Shore, MD
                 Virginia State University, VA
                 Winston-Salem State University, NC
                 University of the Virgin Islands

Amount: Merit scholarships of $16,000 per institution cover tuition,
                 fees, room and board for a four-year period

Deadline: Various

Write: Thurgood Marshall Scholarship Fund
              One Dupont Circle, Suite 710
              Washington, D.C. 20036
              202-778-0818

Other

A. G. Bell Association for the Deaf
Washington, D.C.

Type: Scholarships

Description: Forty scholarships are available annually to auditory-oral college students who are severely or profoundly impaired and who are attending regular colleges and universities.

Amount: $250–$1,000

Deadline: April 15

Write: Scholarship Coordinator
              A. G. Bell Association for the Deaf
              3417 Volta Place, N.W.
              Washington, D.C. 20007
              202-337-5220

American Meteorological Society
Boston, MA

Type: Scholarships

Description: Howard T. Orville and Howard H. Hanks, Jr., scholarships are awarded to students interested in pursuing studies in the field of meteorology. In addition, two AMS minority scholarships are available to African-Americans and other minority students.

Amount: $700–$3,000

Deadline: Various

Write: American Meteorological Society
              45 Beacon Street
              Boston, MA 02108-3693

American Society for Enology and Viticulture
Davis, CA

Type: Scholarships

Description: Scholarships are awarded to students interested in pursuing an undergraduate education in enology, viticulture, or a curriculum emphasizing the science of the wine and grape industry. Awards are made on the basis of recommendations from a Scholarship Committee. Candidates should be juniors and have a grade point average of at least 3.2.

Amount: Various

Deadline: March 1

Write: American Society of Enology and Viticulture
               P.O. Box 1855
               Davis, CA 95617

Carver Scholarship Program
Carver Federal Savings Bank
New York, NY

Type: Scholarships

Description: Bank provides scholarships for its depositors or members of their families. Carver Bank is located in Central Harlem and has branches in the five boroughs of New York City and on Long Island. It is one of the most successful African-American savings institutions in the United States.

Amount: Nearly $100,000 in scholarships for 77 students is awarded annually

Deadline: Various

Write: Apply by mail or in person to:
               Carver Federal Savings Bank
               75 W. 125th Street
               New York, NY 10027
               212-876-4747

Lonzie L. Jones, Jr., National Sickle Cell
Scholarship Program
National Association for Sickle Cell Disease, Inc.
Los Angeles, CA

Type: Scholarship/Essay Competition

Description: Annual scholarship essay contest for high school students. Award recognizes the most outstanding high school student essay on sickle cell disease. Contest open to all high school students. Local contests are held in conjunction with National Sickle Cell Month. Local winners are considered in a national judging.

Amount: First-place winner receives $2,500; runners-up receive $1,000–$1,500 to cover college costs. Three awards are made annually.

Deadline: Essays are usually due in September

Write: National Association for Sickle Cell Disease, Inc.
               4221 Wilshire Boulevard, Suite 360
               Los Angeles, CA 90010-3503
               213-936-7205

National Civil Community Corps
An AmeriCorps Program
Washington, D.C.

Type: Community Job Service/Financial Aid Program

Description: The National Civilian Community Corps (NCCC) is a residential national service program that provides young Americans the opportunity to work in urban and rural service projects that improve America's communities and help them earn a yearly allowance and an education award. The NCCC focuses on projects that protect and conserve natural resources, promote public safety, and help meet the educational and human needs of children, older persons, and others in the community. Many corps members are also trained to do disaster relief and recovery projects. Young adults between the ages of 18–24 who are willing to commit to an 11-month program of service are eligible. The 8-week summer program is open to 14–17-year-olds.

The NCCC is committed to offering opportunities to individuals of all races and ethnic backgrounds, incomes, education, and job skill levels. Corps members must be U.S. citizens or permanent residents of the U.S.

Amount: All Corps members receive lodging, meals, and uniforms. **They also earn $8,000 for the 11 months they serve plus a $4,725 education award that can be applied to future tuition costs or repayment of student loans.**

Corps may choose to take half the education award in cash.

Deadline: Various

Write: National Civilian Community Corps
                    Recruitment Division
                    1100 Vermont Avenue, N.W., 11th Floor
                    Washington, D.C. 20525
                    1-800-94-ACORPS

Radio Technical Commission for Aeronautics
Washington, D.C.

Type: Award competition

Description: Awards made on the basis of an essay or thesis paper which has been completed within the last three years. Candidates may be undergraduate- or graduate-level students studying aviation electronics, aviation, or telecommunications.

Amount: $1,500

Deadline: June 30

Write: Radio Technical Commission for Aeronautics
                    William Jackson Award
                    1717 H Street, N.W.
                    Washington, D.C. 20006

The Foundation for Exceptional Children
Reston, VA

Type:	Scholarships
Description:	Scholarships available to outstanding disabled and gifted students planning to continue their education and training beyond high school. The Foundation for Exceptional Children serves the needs of exceptional children and supports a number of programs that seek to maximize the potential of exceptional children.
Amount:	Various
Deadline:	Various
Write:	The Foundation for Exceptional Children 1920 Association Drive Reston, VA 22091 703-620-3660

Union/Club Affiliation

Agnes Jones Jackson Scholarships
National Association for the Advancement of Colored People (NAACP)
Baltimore, MD

Type:	Scholarships
Description:	Scholarships are available to undergraduate and graduate students who are current regular members of the NAACP (at least one year), or fully-paid life members of the organization. Undergraduates must have a grade point average of at least 2.5 and graduate students at least a 3.0 or B average. Applicants must not have reached the age of 25 by April 30 of the year of application. Application forms are available from the NAACP in January.
Amount:	Undergraduate award is $1,500 and graduate award $2,500
Deadline:	April 30
Write:	Agnes Jones Jackson Scholarship NAACP 4805 Mt. Hope Drive Baltimore, MD 21215-3297 410-358-8900

AKA Sorority
ACCW Montgomery Deanery
Montgomery, AL

Type:	Scholarships
Description:	Awards one scholarship per year to an Alabama resident, renewable for four years.

Amount: $1,000 per year ($500 per semester)

Deadline: January

Write: Sherrie A. Cook, AKA Sorority
                 Beta Nu Omega Chapter
                 117 Woodmere Loop
                 Montgomery, AL 36117

Alpha Kappa Alpha Sorority, Inc.
Chicago, IL

Type: Scholarships

Description: Alpha Kappa Alpha Sorority is an organization of 100,000 members in 750 chapters throughout the United States and abroad. The sorority selects 30 undergraduate women from throughout the nation each year to receive the sorority's Leadership Fellows Grant. Recipients undergo an intensive weeklong leadership development training and are then sent to work as interns for major agencies and corporations throughout the nation.

                 The organization also provides grants, through its educational advancement foundation, to various institutions of higher education.

Amount: Various

Deadline: Various

Write: Alpha Kappa Alpha Sorority, Inc.
                 5656 So. Stony Island Avenue
                 Chicago, IL 60637
                 312-684-1282

Business and Professional Women's Foundation
Washington, D.C.

Type: Scholarships

Description: The Foundation offers scholarships for mature women seeking the education necessary for entry into or advancement within the workforce. Need-based scholarships are awarded to women working towards financial security for themselves and their families. Awards are made to women in various high-growth fields. Application forms are available from the Foundation.

Amount: Various

Deadline: Various

Write: Business and Professional
                 Women's Foundation
                 2012 Massachusetts Avenue, N.W.
                 Washington, D.C. 20036
                 202-293-1200

Omega Psi Phi Fraternity, Inc.
Washington, D.C.

Type: Scholarships

Description: Omega Psi Phi Fraternity annually offers scholarships to members and nonmembers including:

The Founder's Memorial Scholarship, which commemorates the founding of Omega Psi Phi Fraternity, Inc. Scholarships are awarded to a fraternity brother in each district who has attained sophomore or junior standing in undergraduate school. The award is $300.

George E. Meares Scholarship was established in memory of George E. Meares, who served as Grand Basileus of Omega Psi Phi from 1964–67. Scholarships of $1,000 are awarded to support graduate study in social work, the social sciences, and criminal justice.

Other scholarships are provided by local chapters of the fraternity in each district, or by the respective districts to high school seniors who are planning to enter postsecondary education. Contact the local affiliate for further information.

Amount: Various

Deadline: Various

Write: Local affiliate chapter or:
                    Omega Psi Phi Fraternity, Inc.
                    2714 Georgia Avenue
                    Washington, D.C. 20001

Veterans/Military

Alabama Department of Veterans Affairs
Montgomery, AL

Type: Scholarships

Description: Tuition, instructional fees and books to dependents and survivors of certain veterans.

Amount: Various

Deadline: Various

Write: Veterans Service Officer
                    100 S. Lawrence Street
                    Montgomery, AL 36104
                    205-832-4950, ext. 392 or 393

FINANCIAL AID INFORMATION BY INSTITUTION

Adrian College
Adrian, MI

Four-Year Private College

Annual Financial Aid Budget: N/R

Undergraduate enrollment	1,215
African-American enrollment	6.3%
Average financial aid award	$11,747
Percentage African-American students receiving aid	97%
Tuition and fees	$10,020

Application Information: Complete and mail Free Application for Federal Student Aid (FAFSA) by March 15.

Write: Financial Aid Office
           Adrian College
           110 S. Madison Street
           Adrian, MI 49221
           1-800-877-2246

Agnes Scott College
Decatur, GA

Independent Liberal Arts College

Annual Financial Aid Budget: $3,365,571

Undergraduate enrollment	573
African-American enrollment	12.1%
Average financial aid award	$11,425
Percentage African-American students receiving aid	94%
Tuition and fees	$12,135

Application Information: Complete and mail Free Application for Federal Student Aid (FAFSA) and Financial Aid Form (FAF) between January 1 and March 5.

Write: Office of Financial Aid
           Agnes Scott College
           Decatur, GA 30030
           404-371-6395 or 1-800-868-8602

Alabama A&M University
Normal, AL

Public University

Undergraduate enrollment	3,533
African-American enrollment	91%
Average financial aid award	$2,400
Percentage African-American students receiving aid	76%
Tuition and fees..In-state	$1,600
....Out-of-state	$3,150

Application Information: Complete and mail Free Application for Federal Student Aid (FAFSA), Family Financial Statement (FFS), or Financial Aid Form (FAF) by June 1.

Write: Director of Student Financial Aid
                Alabama A&M University
                P.O. Box 907
                Normal, AL 35762-0907
                205-851-5000

Allegheny College
Meadville, PA

Private College

Annual Financial Aid Budget: $19,666,200

Undergraduate enrollment	1,751
African-American enrollment	2%
Average financial aid award	$15,269
Percentage African-American students receiving aid	87%
Tuition and fees	$15,750

Application Information: Complete and mail Free Application for Federal Student Aid (FAFSA), Financial Aid Form (FAF) by February 15.

Write: Financial Aid Office
                Allegheny College
                Meadville, PA 16335
                814-332-6755

Allentown College of Saint Francis de Sales
Center Valley, PA

Private Liberal Arts College/Affiliated with the Catholic Church

Undergraduate enrollment	900
African-American enrollment	less than 8%
Average financial aid award	N/R
Percentage of all students receiving financial aid	90%
Percentage of aid from college	65%
Tuition and fees	$8,590

Application Information: To receive aid one must be accepted to the college. Complete and return the Free Application for Federal Student Aid (FAFSA) as soon as possible after January 1. Students must list Allentown College's Code number: 003985. Students from Connecticut, Delaware, District of Columbia, Ohio, New Hampshire, Vermont, and West Virginia should also file a separate state grant application in their home state, since those states have grant programs that are reciprocal with Pennsylvania.

For the best chance of receiving a scholarship or grant, apply for financial aid by submitting the Allentown College Early Version Financial Aid Application. Deadline for scholarship consideration is February 15.

Write: Director of Financial Aid
Allentown College of Saint Francis de Sales
2755 Station Avenue
Center Valley, PA 18034-9568
1-800-228-5114 or 215-282-1100, ext. 1287

Antioch College
Yellow Springs, OH

Private College

Annual Financial Aid Budget: N/R

Undergraduate enrollment	650
African-American enrollment	9%
Average financial aid award	$13,800
Percentage African-American students receiving aid	80%
Tuition and fees	$19,532

Application Information: Complete and mail Free Application for Federal Student Aid (FAFSA) and Financial Aid Form (FAF) by February 15.

Write: Financial Aid Office
Antioch College
795 Livermore Street
Yellow Springs, OH 45387
513-767-6367

Appalachian State University
Boone, NC

Four-Year Public University

Annual Financial Aid Budget: N/R

Undergraduate enrollment		11,650
African-American enrollment		4%
Average financial aid award		$4,325
Percentage African-American students receiving aid		46%
Tuition and fees	In-state	$1,264
	Out-of-state	$6,936

Application Information: Complete and mail Free Application for Federal Student Aid (FAFSA) as soon as possible after January 1.

Write: Office of Financial Aid
                      Appalachian State University
                      Hagaman Hall
                      Boone, NC 28608
                      704-262-2190

Ashland University
Ashland, OH

Private University

Annual Financial Aid Budget: $7,000,000

Undergraduate enrollment	2,692
African-American enrollment	N/R
Average financial aid award	$8,500
Percentage African-American students receiving aid	N/R
Tuition and fees	$10,583

Application Information: Complete and mail Free Application for Federal Student Aid (FAFSA). University has a policy of "rolling" application dates. Contact the financial aid office directly for deadline.

Write: Financial Aid Office
                      Ashland University
                      310 Founders Hall
                      Ashland, OH 44805
                      419-289-5002

Auburn University
Auburn, AL

Public University

Undergraduate enrollment	18,349
African-American enrollment	5.8%
Average financial aid award	$5,015
Percentage African-American students receiving aid	N/R
Tuition and fees..In-state	$1,755
....Out-of-state	$5,265

Application Information: Complete and mail Free Application for Federal Student Aid (FAFSA) by April 15.

Write: Student Financial Aid Office
                      Auburn University
                      203 Martin Hall
                      Auburn, University, AL 36849
                      205-844-4723

Austin Peay State University
Clarksville, TN

Public University

Annual Financial Aid Budget: N/R

Undergraduate enrollment	N/R
African-American enrollment	20%
Average financial aid award (Students of color)	$4,036
Percentage African-American students receiving aid	16%
Tuition and fees..In-state	$1,726
....Out-of-state	$5,328

Application Information: Complete and mail Free Application for Federal Student Aid (FAFSA) before April 1.

Write: APSU Student Financial Aid Office
               Austin Peay State University
               P.O. Box 4546
               Clarksville, TN 37044
               615-648-7907

               Student Aid Information Center
               1-800-333-4636

               Tennessee Student Assistance Corporation
               1-800-342-1663 or 1-800-447-1523

Barber-Scotia College
Concord, NC

Private College

Annual Financial Aid Budget: N/A

Undergraduate enrollment	500
African-American enrollment	99%
Average financial aid award	$6,000
Percentage African-American students receiving aid	90%
Tuition and fees	$4,494

Application Information: Complete and mail Free Application for Federal Student Aid (FAFSA) by April 15.

Write: Director of Financial Aid
               Barber-Scotia College
               145 Cabarrus Avenue
               Concord, NC 28025
               704-786-5171 ext. 247

Bard College
Annandale, NY

Independent College

Annual Financial Aid Budget: $15,000,000

Undergraduate enrollment	1,020
African-American enrollment	10%
Average financial aid award	$16,200
Percentage African-American students receiving aid	68%
Tuition and fees	$19,154

Application Information: Complete and mail Free Application for Federal Student Aid (FAFSA) and Financial Aid Form (FAF) by March 15.

Write: Director of Financial Aid
                Bard College
                Annandale-on-Hudson, NY 12504
                914-758-7526

Bates College
Lewiston, ME

Private Liberal Arts College

Annual Financial Aid Budget: $12,730,731

Undergraduate enrollment	1,599
African-American enrollment	3%
Average financial aid award	$17,000
Percentage African-American students receiving aid	93%
Tuition and fees (comprehensive— includes room & board)	$22,850

Application Information: Complete and mail Free Application for Federal Student Aid (FAFSA), Financial Aid Form (FAF), and Bates Application for Financial Aid by February 11.

Write: Financial Aid Office
                Bates College
                23 Campus Avenue
                Lewiston, ME 04240
                207-786-6060

Bemidji State University
Bemidji, MN

Public University

Annual Financial Aid Budget: $17,000,000

Undergraduate enrollment	4,700
African-American enrollment	less than 1%
Average financial aid award	$3,300
Percentage African-American students receiving aid	100%
Tuition and fees...In-state	$2,413
....Out-of-state	$4,360

Application Information: Complete and mail Free Application for Federal Student Aid (FAFSA).

Write: Financial Aid Office
Bemidji State University
1500 Birchmont Drive, N.E.
Bemidji, MN 56601
218-755-2035

Benedictine College
Atchison, KS

Private Liberal Arts Catholic College

Annual Financial Aid Budget: N/R

Undergraduate enrollment	750
African-American enrollment	3%
Average financial aid award	$9,292
Percentage African-American students receiving aid	100%
Tuition and fees	$9,080

Application Information: Complete and mail Free Application for Federal Student Aid (FAFSA) or the Financial Aid Form (FAF) by April 1.

Write: Financial Aid Office
Benedictine College
1020 N. 2nd Street
Atchison, KS 66002
913-367-5340 ext. 2484

Berea College
Berea, KY

Private College

Annual Financial Aid Budget: $17,379,400

Undergraduate enrollment	1,591
African-American enrollment	9%
Average financial aid award	$11,300
Percentage African-American students receiving aid	100%
Tuition and fees	-0-

Application Information: Complete and mail Free Application for Federal Student Aid (FAFSA) as soon as possible after January 1; early May for continuing students.

Write: Office of Admissions
Berea College
CPO 2344
Berea, KY 40404
606-986-9341 ext. 5311

Bethany College
Bethany, WV

Private College

Annual Financial Aid Budget: $5,000,000

Undergraduate enrollment	750
African-American enrollment	8%
Average financial aid award	$9,670
Percentage African-American students receiving aid	100%
Tuition and fees	$12,647

Application Information: Complete and mail Free Application for Federal Student Aid (FAFSA) as soon as possible after January 1.

Write: Financial Aid Office
                Bethany College
                Bethany, WV 26032
                304-829-7611

Birmingham-Southern College
Birmingham, AL

Private College

Undergraduate enrollment	1,582
African-American enrollment	7%
Average financial aid award	$10,180
Percentage African-American students receiving aid	N/R
Tuition and fees	$15,034

Application Information: Complete and mail Free Application for Federal Student Aid (FAFSA) and state form by March 15.

Write: Director of Financial Aid
                Birmingham-Southern College
                900 Arkadelphia Road
                Birmingham, AL 35254
                205-226-4688

Boston College
Chestnut Hill, MA

Independent College

Annual Financial Aid Budget: $32,131,000

Undergraduate enrollment	8,807
African-American enrollment	3.4%
Average financial aid award	$21,380
Percentage African-American students receiving aid	93%
Tuition and fees	$15,002

Application Information: Complete and mail Free Application for Federal Student Aid (FAFSA), Financial Aid Form (FAF), and Boston College Financial Aid Application by February 1.

Write: Financial Aid Office
                 Boston College
                 140 Commonwealth Avenue
                 Chestnut Hill, MA 02167
                 617-552-3320

Bowdoin College
Brunswick, ME

Private College

Annual Financial Aid Budget: $10,000,000

Undergraduate enrollment	1,604
African-American enrollment	3%
Average financial aid award	$15,560
Percentage African-American students receiving aid	N/R
Tuition and fees	$17,035

Application Information: Complete and mail Free Application for Federal Student Aid (FAFSA), Financial Aid Form (FAF), and Bowdoin College financial aid form by March 1.

Write: Student Aid Office
                 Bowdoin College
                 Brunswick, ME 04011
                 207-725-3273

Bowie State University
Bowie, MD

Public University

Annual Financial Aid Budget: $7,800,000

Undergraduate enrollment	3,268
African-American enrollment	78%
Average financial aid award	$3,200
Percentage African-American students receiving aid	62%
Tuition and fees...In-state	$2,736
....Out-of-state	$5,128

Application Information: Complete and mail Free Application for Federal Student Aid (FAFSA), Financial Aid Form (FAF), and institutional form by April 1.

Write: Financial Aid Office
                 Bowie State University
                 Bowie, MD 20715-3318
                 301-464-6544

Bucknell University
Lewisburg, PA

Private University

Annual Financial Aid Budget: $12,000,000

Undergraduate enrollment	3,300
African-American enrollment	2.4%
Average financial aid award	$13,765
Percentage African-American students receiving aid	85%
Tuition and fees	$18,550

Application Information: Complete and mail Financial Aid Form (FAF) by February 1.

Write: Director of Financial Aid
                Bucknell University
                Lewisburg, PA 17837
                717-424-1331

California State Polytechnic University
Pomona, CA

Four-Year Public University

Undergraduate enrollment	15,205
African-American enrollment	3.7%
Average financial aid award	$5,000–$5,750
Percentage African-American students receiving aid	N/R
Tuition and fees..In-state	$1,384
....Out-of-state	$7,456

Application Information: Complete and mail Free Application for Federal Student Aid (FAFSA) and the Student Aid Application for California (SAAC) as soon as possible after January 1 and before deadline of March 2.

Write: *For information on all scholarship and grant programs available to students, contact:*

                Financial Aid Office
                Scholarship Technician or Administrator
                Cal Poly University
                3801 W. Temple Avenue
                Pomona, CA 91768-4008
                909-869-3700

Campbellsville College
Campbellsville, KY

Private College

Annual Financial Aid Budget: N/R

Undergraduate enrollment	1,163
African-American enrollment	8%
Average financial aid award	$4,950

Percentage African-American students receiving aid   N/R
Tuition and fees $5,400

Application Information: Complete and mail Free Application for Federal Student Aid (FAFSA) and Campbellsville College Financial Aid Application by March 1.

Write: Financial Aid Office
           Campbellsville College
           200 W. College Street
           Campbellsville, KY 42718
           502-789-5207

Centenary College of Louisiana
Shreveport, LA

Private College

Annual Financial Aid Budget: $5,200,000

Undergraduate enrollment   817
African-American enrollment   8%
Average financial aid award $6,439
Percentage African-American students receiving aid   92%
Tuition and fees $8,150

Application Information: Complete and mail Free Application for Federal Student Aid (FAFSA) by March 15.

Write: Financial Aid Office
           Centenary College of Louisiana
           P.O. Box 41188
           Shreveport, LA 71134-1188
           318-869-5137

Central Connecticut State University
New Britain, CT

Public University

Annual Financial Aid Budget: $5,000,000

Undergraduate enrollment   10,780
African-American enrollment   N/R
Average financial aid award $3,500
Percentage African-American students receiving aid   N/R
Tuition and fees..In-state $2,804
....Out-of-state $7,160

Application Information: Complete and mail Free Application for Federal Student Aid (FAFSA) by February 15.

Write: Financial Aid Office
           Central Connecticut State University
           1615 Stanley Street
           New Britain, CT 06050
           203-827-7330

Chadron State College
Chadron, NE

Public College

Annual Financial Aid Budget: $5,300,000

Undergraduate enrollment	2,513
African-American enrollment	1%
Average financial aid award	$2,522
Percentage African-American students receiving aid	95%
Tuition and fees..In-state	$1,575
....Out-of-state	$2,670

Application Information: Complete and mail Free Application for Federal Student Aid (FAFSA). No deadline date.

Write: Financial Aid Office
                Chadron State College
                1000 Main Street
                Chadron, NE 69337
                308-432-6230

Chapman University
Orange, CA

Private University

Annual Financial Aid Budget: $10,000,000 *(Plus Federal and State Funds)*

Undergraduate enrollment	1,770
African-American enrollment	5%
Average financial aid award	$16,500
Percentage African-American students receiving aid	N/R
Tuition and fees	$15,592

Application Information: Complete and mail Free Application for Federal Student Aid (FAFSA) and Financial Aid Form (FAF) by March 2.

Write: Financial Aid Office
                Chapman University
                333 N. Glassell
                Orange, CA 92666
                714-997-6741

Claremont McKenna College
Claremont, CA

Private College

Annual Financial Aid Budget: $4,887,000

Undergraduate enrollment	877
African-American enrollment	5%
Average financial aid award	$14,017
Percentage African-American students receiving aid	83%
Tuition and fees	$16,400

Application Information: Complete and mail Free Application for Federal Student Aid (FAFSA) and Financial Aid Form (FAF) by February 1.

Write: Financial Aid Office
                Claremont McKenna College
                890 Columbia Avenue
                Claremont, CA 91711
                909-621-8356

Clarion University of Pennsylvania
Clarion, PA

Four-Year Public University

Annual Financial Aid Budget: $24,226,244

Undergraduate enrollment	5,621
African-American enrollment	3%
Average financial aid award	$4,932
Percentage African-American students receiving aid	98%
Tuition and fees..In-state	$3,328
....Out-of-state	$6,830

Application Information: Complete and mail Free Application for Federal Student Aid (FAFSA) as soon as possible after January 1; May 1 for Pennsylvania residents.

Write: Office of Financial Aid
                Clarion University of Pennsylvania
                Wood Street
                Clarion, PA 16214
                814-226-2315

Clemson University
Clemson, SC

Public University

Annual Financial Aid Budget: N/R

Undergraduate enrollment	13,285
African-American enrollment	7%
Average financial aid award	$3,300
Percentage African-American students receiving aid	95%
Tuition and fees..In-state	$2,778
....Out-of-state	$7,394

Application Information: Complete and mail Free Application for Federal Student Aid (FAFSA) and institutional financial aid form by April 1.

Write: Student Financial Aid Office
                Clemson University
                G-01 Sikes Hall
                Clemson, SC 29634-5123
                803-656-2280

Colorado School of Mines
Golden, CO

Public College

Annual Financial Aid Budget: $3,300,000

Undergraduate enrollment	2,660
African-American enrollment	2%
Average financial aid award	$7,000
Percentage African-American students receiving aid	100%
Tuition fees..In-state	$4,288
....Out-of-state	$11,204

Application Information: Complete and mail Free Application for Federal Student Aid (FAFSA) by March 15.

Write: Financial Aid Office
                 Colorado School of Mines
                 1500 Illinois Street
                 Golden, CO 80401
                 303-273-3301

Columbia College
Columbia, MO

Private College—Independent Religious

Annual Financial Aid Budget: N/R

Undergraduate enrollment	814
African-American enrollment	11%
Average financial aid award	$5,000
Percentage African-American students receiving aid	14%
Tuition and fees (comprehensive— includes room & board)	$7,900

Application Information: Complete and mail Free Application for Federal Student Aid (FAFSA) by March 15.

Write: Financial Aid Office
                 Columbia College
                 1001 Rogers
                 Columbia, MO 65216
                 314-875-7362 / 1-800-231-2391

Concordia College
Moorhead, MN

Four-Year Private College, Religious Affiliation

Annual Financial Aid Budget: $7,334,431

Undergraduate enrollment	2,999
African-American enrollment	less than 1%
Average financial aid award	$8,469

Percentage African-American students receiving aid 100%
Tuition and fees $9,200

Application Information: Complete and mail Free Application for Federal Student Aid (FAFSA) as soon as possible after January 1.

Write: Financial Aid Office
      Concordia College
      901 S. 8th Street
      Moorhead, MN 56562
      218-299-3004

Cornell College
Mount Vernon, IA

Private College

Annual Financial Aid Budget: N/R

Undergraduate enrollment	1,145
African-American enrollment	3%
Average financial aid award	$13,000
Percentage African-American students receiving aid	N/R
Tuition and fees	$13,129

Application Information: Complete and mail Free Application for Federal Student Aid (FAFSA) by March 1.

Write: Financial Aid Office
      Cornell College
      600 First Street West
      Mount Vernon, IA 52314
      1-800-747-1112

Cornell University
Ithaca, NY

Independent University

Annual Financial Aid Budget: $11,300,000

Undergraduate enrollment	12,813
African-American enrollment	5%
Average financial aid award	$14,200
Percentage African-American students receiving aid	90%
Tuition and fees	$17,276

Application Information: Complete and mail Free Application for Federal Student Aid (FAFSA) by February 15.

Write: Office of Financial Aid/Student Employment
      Cornell University
      203 Day Hall
      Ithaca, NY 14853
      607-255-5145

Denison University
Granville, OH

Private University

Annual Financial Aid Budget: $9,500,000

Undergraduate enrollment	1,915
African-American enrollment	4%
Average financial aid award	$16,590
Percentage African-American students receiving aid	96%
Tuition and fees	$21,180

Application Information: Complete and mail Free Application for Federal Student Aid (FAFSA) and the Financial Aid Form (FAF) by April 1.

Write: Financial Aid Office
               Denison University
               216 S. Pearl Street
               Granville, OH 43203
               614-587-6270

Duke University
Durham, NC

Four-Year Private University

Annual Financial Aid Budget: N/R

Undergraduate enrollment	6,800
African-American enrollment	9%
Average financial aid award	N/R
Percentage African-American students receiving aid	N/R
Tuition and fees	$19,050

Application Information: Complete and mail Free Application for Federal Student Aid (FAFSA) and Financial Aid Form (FAF) by February 1.

Write: Director of Financial Aid
               Duke University
               2106 Campus Drive
               P.O. Box 90397
               Durham, NC 27708-0586
               919-684-6225

D'Youville College
Buffalo, NY

Private College

Annual Financial Aid Budget: $8,000,000

Undergraduate enrollment	1,900
African-American enrollment	9%
Average financial aid award	$6,400
Percentage African-American students receiving aid	N/R
Tuition and fees	$8,540

Application Information: Complete and mail Free Application for Federal Student Aid (FAFSA) and Financial Aid Form (FAF) by April 15.

Write: Director of Financial Aid
           D'Youville College
           320 Porter Avenue
           Buffalo, NY 14201-1084
           716-881-7691

East Carolina University
Greenville, NC

Public University

Annual Financial Aid Budget: $37,000,000

Undergraduate enrollment	14,770
African-American enrollment	9.3%
Average financial aid award	N/R
Percentage African-American students receiving aid	70%
Tuition and fees..In-state	$1,246
....Out-of-state	$6,918

Application Information: Complete and mail Free Application for Federal Student Aid (FAFSA) by April 15.

Write: Student Financial Aid Office
           East Carolina University
           Greenville, NC 27858
           919-757-6610

Eastern New Mexico University
Portales, NM

Public University

Annual Financial Aid Budget: N/R

Undergraduate enrollment	3,295
African-American enrollment	5%
Average financial aid award	N/R
Percentage African-American students receiving aid	N/R
Tuition and fees..In-state	$1,440
....Out-of-state	$5,280

Application Information: Complete and mail Financial Aid Form (FAF), Family Financial Statement (FFS), and state form (Free Application for Federal Student Aid [FAFSA] also acceptable), by March 1.

Write: Director of Admissions
           Eastern New Mexico University
           Station #5 ENMU
           Portales, NM 88130
           505-562-2178

Eckerd College
St. Petersburg, FL

Private College

Annual Financial Aid Budget: $7,200,000

Undergraduate enrollment	1,415
African-American enrollment	3%
Average financial aid award	$11,000
Percentage African-American students receiving aid	100%
Tuition and fees	$13,725

Application Information: Complete and mail Free Application for Federal Student Aid (FAFSA) March 1.

Write: Financial Aid Office
                Eckerd College
                P.O. Box 12560
                St. Petersburg, FL 33733
                1-800-456-9009 or 813-864-8331

Elizabethtown College
Elizabethtown, PA

Private College

Annual Financial Aid Budget: $7,000,000

Undergraduate enrollment	1,500
African-American enrollment	1.3%
Average financial aid award	$11,100
Percentage African-American students receiving aid	90%
Tuition and fees	$12,550

Application Information: Complete and mail Free Application for Federal Student Aid (FAFSA) and Elizabethtown College Financial Aid Application by April 1.

Write: Financial Aid Office
                Elizabethtown College
                One Alpha Drive
                Elizabethtown, PA 17022-2298
                717-361-1404

Emory University
Atlanta, GA

Independent University—Religious Affiliation

Annual Financial Aid Budget: N/R

Undergraduate enrollment	4,970
African-American enrollment	N/R
Average financial aid award	N/R
Percentage African-American students receiving aid	N/R
Tuition and fees	$16,820

Application Information: Complete and mail both the Free Application for Federal Student Aid (FAFSA) and Financial Aid Form (FAF) by February 15 to:

Write: Emory Financial Aid Office
                Emory University
                300 Jones Center
                Atlanta, GA 30322-1960
                404-727-6039 or 1-800-727-6036

Faulkner University
Montgomery, AL

Private University

Undergraduate enrollment	1,713
African-American enrollment	20%
Average financial aid award	$4,800
Percentage African-American students receiving aid	N/R
Tuition and fees	$8,300

Application Information: Complete and mail Free Application for Federal Student Aid (FAFSA), Family Financial Statement (FFS) or Financial Aid Form (FAF), institutional form, and state form by June 1.

Write: Director of Financial Aid
                Faulkner University
                Montgomery, AL 36109-3398
                205-272-5820 ext. 126

Florida A&M University
Tallahassee, FL

Public University

Undergraduate enrollment	7,500
African-American enrollment	98%
Average financial aid award	$2,800
Percentage African-American students receiving aid	74%
Tuition and fees...In-state	$1,749
....Out-of-state	$6,509

Application Information: Complete and mail Free Application for Federal Student Aid (FAFSA) by April 1.

Write: Office of Student Financial Aid
                Florida A&M University
                Tallahassee, FL 32307
                904-599-3796

Florida Institute of Technology
Melbourne, FL

Private College

Annual Financial Aid Budget: N/R

Undergraduate enrollment	2,098
African-American enrollment	4.7%
Average financial aid award	N/R
Percentage African-American students receiving aid	25%
Tuition and fees	$11,817

Application Information: Complete and mail Free Application for Federal Student Aid (FAFSA) March 1.

Write: Financial Aid Office
                Florida Institute of Technology
                150 W. University Blvd.
                Melbourne, FL 32901-6988
                407-768-8000, ext. 8070

Frostburg State University
Frostburg, MD

Public University

Annual Financial Aid Budget: N/R

Undergraduate enrollment	4,282
African-American enrollment	10%
Average financial aid award	$3,234
Percentage African-American students receiving aid	82%
Tuition and fees...In-state	$2,666
....Out-of-state	$5,294

Application Information: Complete and mail Free Application for Federal Student Aid (FAFSA), Financial Aid Form (FAF), and institutional form by April 1.

Write: Financial Aid Office
                Frostburg State University
                College Avenue
                Frostburg, MD 21532
                301-689-4301

Georgetown University
Washington, D.C.

Private University

Annual Financial Aid Budget: $50,125,804

Undergraduate enrollment	6,042
African-American enrollment	6.9%
Average financial aid award	$20,067
Percentage African-American students receiving aid	94.2%
Tuition and fees	$17,586

Application Information: Complete and mail Free Application for Federal Student Aid (FAFSA) and Financial Aid Form (FAF) by April 1.

Write: Office of Student Financial Services
                G-19 Healy Hall
                Georgetown University
                37th & O Streets, N.W.
                Washington, D.C. 20057-1051

George Washington University
Washington, D.C.

Private University

Annual Financial Aid Budget: $50,125,804

Undergraduate enrollment	5,900
African-American enrollment	9%
Average financial aid award	$13,687
Percentage African-American students receiving aid	N/R
Tuition and fees	$18,170

Application Information: Complete and mail Free Application for Federal Student Aid (FAFSA) and Financial Aid Form (FAF) by February 1.

Write: Director of Financial Assistance
                The George Washington University
                2121 I Street, NW, 3rd Floor
                Washington, D.C. 20052
                202-994-6620

Georgian Court College
Lakewood, NJ

Private Women's College (Religious Affiliation)

Annual Financial Aid Budget: $3,000,000

Undergraduate enrollment	1,880
African-American enrollment	4%
Average financial aid award	$5,000
Percentage African-American students receiving aid	N/R
Tuition and fees	$9,280

Application Information: Complete and mail Free Application for Federal Student Aid (FAFSA) and College Scholarship Service Financial Aid Form (FAF) by October 1.

Write: Financial Aid Director
                Georgian Court College
                Lakewood, NJ 08701
                908-364-2200

Hamline University
St. Paul, MN

Private University

Annual Financial Aid Budget: $14,000,000

Undergraduate enrollment	1,464
African-American enrollment	4%
Average financial aid award (Students of color)	$12,300
Percentage African-American students receiving aid	96%
Tuition and fees	$12,344

Application Information: Complete and mail Free Application for Federal Student Aid (FAFSA) by March 15.

Write: Financial Aid Office
                Hamline University
                1536 Hewitt Avenue
                St. Paul, MN 55104-1287
                612-641-2208

Hampton University
Hampton, VA

Private University

Annual Financial Aid Budget: N/R

Undergraduate enrollment	5,700
African-American enrollment	90%
Average financial aid award	N/R
Percentage African-American students receiving aid	64%
Tuition and fees	$7,006

Application Information: Complete and mail Financial Aid Form (FAF) by March 31.

Write: Financial Aid Office
                Hampton University
                Hampton, VA 23668
                804-727-5688

Harvard/Radcliffe
Cambridge, MA

Independent University

Annual Financial Aid Budget: $32,000,000

Undergraduate enrollment	6,620
African-American enrollment	N/R
Average financial aid award	$16,000
Percentage African-American students receiving aid	N/R
Tuition and fees	$24,880

Application Information: Complete and mail Free Application for Federal Student Aid (FAFSA) and institutional form by February 15.

Write: Office of Financial Aid
                Harvard/Radcliffe
                Byerly Hall, Third Floor
                8 Garden Street
                Cambridge, MA 02138
                617-495-1581

Henderson State University
Arkadelphia, AR

Public University

Undergraduate enrollment	3,445
African-American enrollment	14%
Average financial aid award	$2,215
Percentage African-American students receiving aid	N/R
Tuition and fees...In-state	$1,560
....Out-of-state	$3,120

Application Information: Complete and mail Free Application for Federal Student Aid (FAFSA), Family Financial Statement, and institutional form by March 15.

Write: Director of Financial Aid
                Henderson State University
                Box 7812
                Arkadelphia, AR 71999-0001
                501-246-5511, ext. 3264

Hood College
Frederick, MD

Private College

Annual Financial Aid Budget: $6,500,000

Undergraduate enrollment	1,100
African-American enrollment	29%
Average financial aid award	$11,000
Percentage African-American students receiving aid	85%
Tuition and fees	$13,258

Application Information: Complete and mail Free Application for Federal Student Aid (FAFSA) as soon as possible after March 1.

Write: Financial Aid Office
                Hood College
                401 Rosemont Avenue
                Frederick, MD 21701-8575
                301-696-3411

Howard University
Washington, D.C.

Private University

Undergraduate enrollment	12,299
African-American enrollment	66%
Average financial aid award	$6,000
Percentage African-American students receiving aid	80%
Tuition and fees	$6,981

Application Information: Complete and mail Financial Aid Form (FAF) by April 1.

Write: Office of Financial Aid and Student Employment
              Howard University
              2400 Sixth Street, N.W., Room 211
              Mordecai Wyatt Johnson Bldg.
              Washington, D.C. 20059
              202-806-2800

Huntingdon College
Montgomery, AL

Private College

Undergraduate enrollment	790
African-American enrollment	9%
Average financial aid award	$8,240
Percentage African-American students receiving aid	N/R
Tuition and fees	$11,400

Application Information: Complete and mail Free Application for Federal Student Aid (FAFSA), institutional form, Financial Aid Form (FAF), Family Financial Statement (FFS), and state form by May 1.

Write: Director of Student Financial Aid
              Huntingdon College
              1500 East Fairview Avenue
              Montgomery, AL 36106-2148
              205-265-0511 ext. 519

Jacksonville State University
Jacksonville, AL

Public University

Undergraduate enrollment	6,635
African-American enrollment	17%
Average financial aid award	N/R
Percentage African-American students receiving aid	N/R
Tuition and fees...In-state	$1,680
....Out-of-state	$2,520

Application Information: Complete and mail Free Application for Federal Student Aid (FAFSA), Financial Aid Form (FAF), and Family Financial Statement (FFS) by April 1.

Write: Director of Financial Aid
Jacksonville State University
Pelham Road
Jacksonville, AL 36265-9982
205-782-5006

Kent State University
Kent, OH

Public University

Annual Financial Aid Budget: $5,500,000

Undergraduate enrollment	22,000
African-American enrollment	6%
Average financial aid award	$4,800
Percentage African-American students receiving aid	95%
Tuition and fees..In-state	$3,740
....Out-of-state	$7,480

Application Information: Complete and mail Free Application For Federal Student Aid (FAFSA) by February 15.

Write: Financial Aid Office
Kent State University
P.O. Box 5190
Kent, OH 44242-0001
216-672-2972

Kenyon College
Gambier, OH

Private College

Annual Financial Aid Budget: $7,500,000

Undergraduate enrollment	1,450
African-American enrollment	5%
Average financial aid award	$15,000
Percentage African-American students receiving aid	75%
Tuition and fees	$17,060

Application Information: Complete and mail Free Application for Federal Student Aid (FAFSA) by February 15.

Write: Financial Aid Office
Kenyon College
Ransom Hall
Gambier, OH 43022
614-427-5782

King's College
Wilkes-Barre, PA

Four-Year Private College

Annual Financial Aid Budget: $4,300,000

Undergraduate enrollment	1,750
African-American enrollment	1%
Average financial aid award (Students of Color)	$4,200
Percentage African-American students receiving aid	100%
Tuition and fees	$9,770

Application Information: Complete and mail Free Application for Federal Student Aid (FAFSA), and if you are a Pennsylvania resident, the Pennsylvania Higher Education Assistance Agency (PHEAA) form, by March 1.

Write: King's College Financial Aid Office
6th Floor Administration Bldg.
133 N. River Street
Wilkes-Barre, PA 18711
717-826-5868

Lafayette College
Easton, PA

Private College

Annual Financial Aid Budget: $400,000 *(To African-Americans)*

Undergraduate enrollment	2,000
African-American enrollment	3.3%
Average financial aid award	$17,361
Percentage African-American students receiving aid	100%
Tuition and fees	$16,865

Application Information: Complete and mail Free Application for Federal Student Aid (FAFSA), Financial Aid Form (FAF), and institutional application by February 15.

Write: Financial Aid Office
Lafayette College
107 Markle Hall
Easton, PA 18042-1777
215-250-5055

Lander University
Greenwood, SC

Four-Year Public University

Annual Financial Aid Budget: $6,500,000

Undergraduate enrollment	2,423
African-American enrollment	465 (19%)
Average financial aid award	$3,700

Percentage African-American students receiving aid   65%
Tuition and fees...In-state $3,270
....Out-of-state $4,648

Application Information: Complete and mail Free Application for Federal Student Aid (FAFSA) as soon as possible after January 1.

Write: Financial Aid Office
                Lander University
                Greenwood, SC 29649
                803-229-8340

Lebanon Valley College
Annville, PA

Private Liberal Arts College

Annual Financial Aid Budget: $5,000,000

Undergraduate enrollment   960
African-American enrollment   1%
Average financial aid award $10,600
Percentage African-American students receiving aid   100%
Tuition and fees $12,875

Application Information: Complete and mail Free Application for Federal Student Aid (FAFSA) by March 1.

Write: Financial Aid Office
                Lebanon Valley College
                101 N. College Avenue
                Annville, PA 17003
                1-800-445-6181/717-867-6181

Lewis and Clark College
Portland, OR

Private College

Annual Financial Aid Budget: N/R

Undergraduate enrollment   1,767
African-American enrollment   2%
Average financial aid award $13,864
Percentage African-American students receiving aid   100%
Tuition and fees $14,265

Application Information: Complete and mail Free Application for Federal Student Aid (FAFSA) and Institutional Data Form (IDF) by February 15.

Write: Student Financial Aid Services
                Lewis and Clark College
                0615 S.W. Palatine Hill Road
                Portland, OR 97219
                503-768-7090

Linfield College
McMinnville, OR

Independent College—Religious Affiliation

Annual Financial Aid Budget: $12,700,000

Undergraduate enrollment	1,561
African-American enrollment	1%
Average financial aid award	$8,979
Percentage African-American students receiving aid	100%
Tuition and fees	$11,870

Application Information: Complete and mail Free Application for Federal Student Aid (FAFSA) and college aid form by February 1.

Write: Financial Aid Office
                Linfield College
                900 S. Baker Street
                McMinnville, OR 97128
                503-434-2225

Loras College
Dubuque, IA

Private College

Annual Financial Aid Budget: $4,689,000

Undergraduate enrollment	1,650
African-American enrollment	2%
Average financial aid award	$9,667
Percentage African-American students receiving aid	100%
Tuition and fees (comprehensive—includes room & board)	$9,978

Application Information: Complete and mail Free Application for Federal Student Aid (FAFSA), by April 15.

Write: Financial Aid Office
                Loras College
                1450 Alta Vista Street
                Dubuque, IA 52004-0178
                319-588-7166

Loyola College in Maryland
Baltimore, MD

Private College

Annual Financial Aid Budget: $16,000,000

Undergraduate enrollment	3,000
African-American enrollment	3.5%
Average financial aid award	$10,500
Percentage African-American students receiving aid	70%
Tuition and fees	$12,600

Application Information: Complete and mail Free Application for Federal Student Aid (FAFSA) and Financial Aid Form (FAF) by March 1.

Write: Financial Aid Office
Loyola College in Maryland
4501 N. Charles Street
Baltimore, MD 21210-2699
410-617-2576

Lynn University
Boca Raton, FL

Private University

Annual Financial Aid Budget: $6,500,000

Undergraduate enrollment	1,335
African-American enrollment	3%
Average financial aid award	$12,294
Percentage African-American students receiving aid	57%
Tuition and fees	$12,200

Application Information: Complete and mail Free Application for Federal Student Aid (FAFSA) by February 15.

Write: Financial Aid Office
Lynn University
3601 N. Military Trail
Boca Raton, FL 33431
407-994-0770/1-800-544-8035

Marietta College
Marietta, OH

Private Liberal Arts College

Annual Financial Aid Budget: N/R

Undergraduate enrollment	1,304
African-American enrollment	1%
Average financial aid award	$9,265
Percentage African-American students receiving aid	90%
Tuition and fees (comprehensive—includes room and board)	$12,370

Application Information: Complete and mail Financial Aid Form (FAF) by March 1.

Write: Financial Aid Office
Marietta College
Marietta, OH 45750-3031
1-800-331-7896

Mary Baldwin College
Staunton, VA

Private College—Religious Affiliation

Annual Financial Aid Budget: $4,000,000+

Undergraduate enrollment	1,000
African-American enrollment	6%
Average financial aid award	$11,000
Percentage African-American students receiving aid	90%
Tuition and fees	$10,654

Application Information: Complete and mail Free Application for Federal Student Aid (FAFSA) as soon as possible after January 1.

Write: Student Financial Aid Services
                Mary Baldwin College
                Staunton, VA 24401
                703-887-7022

Menlo College
Atherton, CA

Private College

Annual Financial Aid Budget: $1,659,785

Undergraduate enrollment	568
African-American enrollment	5%
Average financial aid award	$15,222
Percentage African-American students receiving aid	100%
Tuition and fees	$16,000

Application Information: Complete and mail Free Application for Federal Student Aid (FAFSA) or Financial Aid Form (FAF) and Institutional Application by March 2.

Write: Financial Aid Office
                Menlo College
                1000 El Camino Real
                Atherton, CA 94027
                415-688-3880

Minneapolis College of Art and Design
Minneapolis, MN

Private College

Annual Financial Aid Budget: $3,600,000

Undergraduate enrollment	550
African-American enrollment	1%
Average financial aid award	$6,500
Percentage African-American students receiving aid	100%
Tuition and fees	$11,090

Application Information: Complete and mail Free Application for Federal Student Aid (FAFSA) by April 1.

Write: Financial Aid Office
              Minneapolis College of Art and Design
              2501 Stevens Avenue South
              Minneapolis, MN 55404
              612-874-3782

Mississippi University for Women
Columbus, MS

Public University

Annual Financial Aid Budget: $8,034,000

Undergraduate enrollment	3,024
African-American enrollment	22.8%
Average financial aid award for African-American students	$3,160
Percentage African-American students receiving aid	95%
Tuition and fees..In-state	$2,239
....Out-of-state	$4,381

Application Information: Complete and mail Free Application for Federal Student Aid (FAFSA) by June 1.

Write: Financial Aid Office
              Mississippi University for Women
              Box W-1614
              Columbus, MS 39701
              601-329-7114

Mississippi Valley State University
Itta Bena, MS

Public University

Annual Financial Aid Budget: N/R

Undergraduate enrollment	2,243
African-American enrollment	99%
Average financial aid award for African-American students	$4,700–$7,000
Percentage African-American students receiving aid	95%
Tuition and fees..In-state	$2,164
....Out-of-state	$4,284

Application Information: Complete and mail Free Application for Federal Student Aid (FAFSA) by April 1.

Write: Financial Aid Office
              Mississippi Valley State University
              Box 1054, 1400 Highway 82 West
              Itta Bena, MS 38941
              601-254-3335

Morehouse College
Atlanta, GA

Independent Men's College

Annual Financial Aid Budget: N/R

Undergraduate enrollment	2,990
African-American enrollment	99%
Average financial aid award	$4,500
Percentage African-American students receiving aid	77%
Tuition and fees	$7,430

Application Information: Complete and mail Free Application for Federal Student Aid (FAFSA), Financial Aid Form (FAF), state and institutional forms by April 1.

Write: Financial Aid Office
                Morehouse College
                Atlanta, GA 30314
                404-215-2638/1-800-992-0642

Moorhead State University
Moorhead, MN

Public University

Annual Financial Aid Budget: N/R

Undergraduate enrollment		8,900
African-American enrollment		N/R
Average financial aid award		N/R
Percentage African-American students receiving aid		N/R
Tuition and fees..In-state		$2,299
....Out-of-state		$4,288

Application Information: Complete and mail Free Application for Federal Student Aid (FAFSA) and Moorhead State University Supplement by March 1.

Write: Financial Aid Office
                Moorhead State University
                1104 7th Avenue South
                Moorhead, MN 56563
                218-236-2251

Morgan State University
Baltimore, MD

Public University

Annual Financial Aid Budget: N/R

Undergraduate enrollment	5,100
African-American enrollment	96%
Average financial aid award	$2,000
Percentage African-American students receiving aid	90%

Tuition and fees...In-state $2,470
....Out-of-state $4,812

Application Information: Complete and mail Free Application for Federal Student Aid (FAFSA), Financial Aid Form (FAF), and institutional form by March 1.

Write: Financial Aid Office
                Morgan State University
                Baltimore, MD 21239

Murray State University
Murray, KY

Four-Year Public University

Annual Financial Aid Budget: $20,000,000

Undergraduate enrollment   6,923
African-American enrollment   N/R
Average financial aid award $4,400
Percentage African-American students receiving aid   75%
Tuition and fees...In-state $1,600
....Out-of-state $4,280

Application Information: Complete and mail Free Application for Federal Student Aid (FAFSA) and university financial aid application by April 1.

Write: Carmen Garland, Financial Aid Director
                Murray State University
                Scholarship Office
                P.O. Box 9, MSU
                Murray, KY 42071
                502-762-2546

New York University
New York, NY

Private University

Annual Financial Aid Budget: N/R

Undergraduate enrollment   15,225
African-American enrollment   9.4%
Average financial aid award   N/R
Percentage African-American students receiving aid   N/R
Tuition and fees $16,650

Application Information: Complete and mail Free Application for Federal Student Aid (FAFSA) by February 15 (for the Fall term), or December 1 (for the Spring term).

Write: Financial Aid Office
                25 W. 4th Street
                New York, NY
                212-998-4444

Northeast Missouri State University
Kirksville, MO

Public University

Annual Financial Aid Budget: $8,543,328

Undergraduate enrollment	5,906
African-American enrollment	3%
Average financial aid award for African-American students	$5,629
Percentage African-American students receiving aid	100%
Tuition and fees...In-state	$2,235
....Out-of-state	$3,939

Application Information: Complete and mail Free Application for Federal Student Aid (FAFSA) by April 1.

Write: Financial Aid Office
                Northeast Missouri State University
                103 McClain Hall
                Kirksville, MO 63501
                816-785-4130

Northwestern College
St. Paul, MN

Private College

Annual Financial Aid Budget: $10,500,000

Undergraduate enrollment	1,150
African-American enrollment	2%
Average financial aid award	$9,100
Percentage African-American students receiving aid	99%
Tuition and fees	$9,825

Application Information: Complete and mail Free Application for Federal Student Aid (FAFSA) and Financial Aid Form (FAF) by April 1.

Write: Financial Aid Office
                Northwestern College
                3003 Snelling Avenue North
                St. Paul, MN 55113-1598
                612-631-5212

Northwestern University
Evanston, IL

Private University

Annual Financial Aid Budget: $28,114,000

Undergraduate enrollment	7,450
African-American enrollment	6.4%
Average financial aid award	$13,150

Percentage African-American students receiving aid   92%
Tuition and fees $15,075

Application Information: Complete and mail Free Application for Federal Student Aid (FAFSA) and Financial Aid Form (FAF) by February 15.

Write: Office of Financial Aid
                Northwestern University
                1801 Hinman Avenue
                Evanston, IL 60208-1260
                708-491-7400

Northwest Nazarene College
Nampa, ID

Private College

Annual Financial Aid Budget: $7,000,000

Undergraduate enrollment   1,030
African-American enrollment   N/R
Average financial aid award $6,000
Percentage African-American students receiving aid   N/R
Tuition and fees $8,766

Application Information: Complete and mail Free Application for Federal Student Aid (FAFSA) by March 1.

Write: Financial Aid Office
                Northwest Nazarene College
                623 Holly Street
                Nampa, ID 83686
                208-467-8422

Nova University
Fort Lauderdale, FL

Private University

Annual Financial Aid Budget: $45,700,000

Undergraduate enrollment   3,189
African-American enrollment   N/R
Average financial aid award   N/R
Percentage African-American students receiving aid   N/R
Tuition and fees $8,230

Application Information: Complete and mail Free Application for Federal Student Aid (FAFSA) and the Nova University Application by April 1.

Write: Financial Aid Office
                Nova University
                3301 College Avenue
                Fort Lauderdale, FL 33314
                305-475-7411

Ohio Wesleyan University
Delaware, OH

Private University

Annual Financial Aid Budget: $7,500,000

Undergraduate enrollment	1,780
African-American enrollment	4%
Average financial aid award	$15,870
Percentage African-American students receiving aid	90%
Tuition and fees	$16,733

Application Information: Complete and mail Free Application for Federal Student Aid (FAFSA) and Financial Aid Form (FAF) by March 1.

Write: Director of Financial Aid
                Ohio Wesleyan University
                61 S. Sandusky Street
                Delaware, OH 43015
                614-368-3050

Oklahoma City University
Oklahoma City, OK

Private University

Annual Financial Aid Budget: $14,000,000

Undergraduate enrollment	2,010
African-American enrollment	6%
Average financial aid award	$6,347
Percentage African-American students receiving aid	94%
Tuition and fees	$5,700

Application Information: Complete and mail Free Application for Federal Student Aid (FAFSA). No deadline.

Write: Office of Financial Aid
                Oklahoma City University
                2501 N. Blackwelder
                Oklahoma City, OK 73106
                405-521-5211

Pittsburg State University
Pittsburg, KS

Public University

Annual Financial Aid Budget: $14,200,000

Undergraduate enrollment	5,382
African-American enrollment	2.2%
Average financial aid award	$3,250
Percentage African-American students receiving aid	N/R
Tuition and fees..In-state	$1,564
....Out-of-state	$4,444

Application Information: Complete and mail Free Application for Federal Student Aid (FAFSA) by March 1.

Write: Financial Aid Office
                   Pittsburg State University
                   1701 S. Broadway
                   Pittsburg, KS 66762
                   316-235-4240

Pitzer College
Claremont, CA

Private College

Annual Financial Aid Budget: N/R

Undergraduate enrollment	750
African-American enrollment	6%
Average financial aid award	$19,292
Percentage African-American students receiving aid	N/R
Tuition and fees	$18,198

Application Information: Complete and mail Free Application for Federal Student Aid (FAFSA) and Financial Aid Form (FAF) by February 1.

Write: Financial Aid Office
                   Pitzer College
                   1050 North Mills Avenue
                   Claremont, CA 91711
                   909-621-8208

Potsdam College of the State University of New York
Potsdam, NY

Public University

Annual Financial Aid Budget: $13,000,000

Undergraduate enrollment	3,832
African-American enrollment	2%
Average financial aid award	$5,500
Percentage of African-Americans receiving aid	82%
Tuition and fees..In-state	$2,890
....Out-of-state	$6,790

Application Information: To receive aid one must be accepted to the college. Complete and return the Free Application for Federal Student Aid (FAFSA) and the New York State TAP application for federal campus-based aid by March 1.

Write: Director of Financial Aid
                   Potsdam College of the State University
                   of New York (SUNY)
                   Pierrepont Avenue
                   Potsdam, NY 13676
                   315-267-2162

Providence College
Providence, RI

Four-Year Private College

Annual Financial Aid Budget: $12,000,000

Undergraduate enrollment	3,600
African-American enrollment	2%
Average financial aid award	N/R
Percentage African-American students receiving aid	85%
Tuition and fees	$12,700

Application Information: Complete and mail Free Application for Federal Student Aid (FAFSA) and the Financial Aid Form (FAF) by February 15.

Write: Herbert J. D'Arcy, Jr., Executive Director
                  Office of Financial Aid
                  Providence College
                  River & Eaton Street
                  Providence, RI 02918-0001
                  401-865-2286

Purchase College of the State of New York
Purchase, NY

Public College

Annual Financial Aid Budget: N/R

Undergraduate enrollment	2,560
African-American enrollment	N/R
Average financial aid award	$4,750
Percentage African-American students receiving aid	N/R
Tuition and fees...In-state	$2,911
....Out-of-state	$6,811

Application Information: Complete and mail Free Application for Federal Student Aid (FAFSA) and, for New York residents, the Tuition Assistance Program (TAP) form by February 15.

Write: Financial Aid Office
                  SUNY at Purchase
                  735 Anderson Hill Road
                  Purchase, NY 10577
                  914-251-6350

Purdue University
West Lafayette, IN

Four-Year Public University

Annual Financial Aid Budget: $103,000,000

Undergraduate enrollment	28,464
African-American enrollment	4%
Average financial aid award	$7,274

Percentage African-American students receiving aid   76%
Tuition and fees..In-state $2,696
....Out-of-State $8,848

Application Information: Complete and mail Free Application for Federal Student Aid (FAFSA) by March 1.

Write: Financial Aid Office
                     Purdue University
                     Schleman Hall, Room 305
                     West Lafayette, IN 47907
                     317-494-5050

Richard Stockton College of New Jersey
Pomona, NJ

Public College

Annual Financial Aid Budget: N/R

Undergraduate enrollment   5,782
African-American enrollment   8%
Average financial aid award $3,733
Percentage African-American students receiving aid   N/R
Tuition and fees..In-state $2,657
....Out-of-state $3,297

Application Information: Complete and mail Free Application for Federal Student Aid (FAFSA) by March 1.

Write: Financial Aid Office
                     Richard Stockton College of New Jersey
                     Pomona, NJ 08240
                     609-652-4201

Rosemont College
Rosemont, PA

Private Women's Liberal Arts College

Annual Financial Aid Budget: $1,094,000

Undergraduate enrollment   600
African-American enrollment   5%
Average financial aid award $9,000
Percentage African-American students receiving aid   90%
Tuition and fees $10,700

Application Information: Complete and mail Free Application for Federal Student Aid (FAFSA) by March 1.

Write: Financial Aid Office
                     Rosemont College
                     1400 Montgomery Avenue
                     Rosemont, PA 19010-1699
                     610-527-0200

St. John Fisher College
Rochester, NY

Private Liberal Arts College

Annual Financial Aid Budget: $17,000,000

Undergraduate enrollment	1,685
African-American enrollment	8%
Average financial aid award	$11,300
Percentage African-American students receiving aid	100%
Tuition and fees	$9,470

Application Information: Complete and mail Free Application for Federal Student Aid (FAFSA). College has rolling deadline date; priority deadline is March 1.

Write: Office of Financial Aid
                St. John Fisher College
                3690 East Avenue
                Rochester, NY 14618
                716-385-8042

St. John's College
Annapolis, MD

Private College

Annual Financial Aid Budget: $2,700,000

Undergraduate enrollment	400
African-American enrollment	2%
Average financial aid award	$13,200
Percentage African-American students receiving aid	90%
Tuition and fees	$15,400

Application Information: Complete and mail Free Application for Federal Student Aid (FAFSA), Financial Aid Form (FAF). No deadline date, recommend filing prior to March 1.

Write: Financial Aid Office
                St. John's College
                P.O. Box 2800
                Annapolis, MD 21403
                410-626-2502

St. John's College—New Mexico
Santa Fe, NM

Private College

Annual Financial Aid Budget: $4,500,000

Undergraduate enrollment	415
African-American enrollment	1%
Average financial aid award	$15,075

Percentage African-American students receiving aid   100%
Tuition and fees $15,400

Application Information: Complete and mail Free Application for Federal Student Aid (FAFSA) and Financial Aid Form (FAF) by March 1.

Write: Financial Aid Office
St. John's College—New Mexico
1160 Camino Cruz Blanca
Santa Fe, NM 87501
505-984-6058

St. John's University
Jamaica, NY

Private University

Annual Financial Aid Budget: N/R

Undergraduate enrollment   17,800
African-American enrollment   11%
Average financial aid award $8,600
Percentage African-American students receiving aid   75%
Tuition and fees $9,180

Application Information: Complete and mail Free Application for Federal Student Aid (FAFSA) and Financial Aid Form (FAF) by April 1.

Write: Financial Aid and Student Recruitment Services
St. John's University
8000 Utopia Parkway
Jamaica, NY 11439
718-990-6744

St. Lawrence University
Canton, NY

Private University

Annual Financial Aid Budget: N/R

Undergraduate enrollment   1,900
African-American enrollment   2%
Average financial aid award $11,918
Percentage African-American students receiving aid   N/R
Tuition and fees $16,820

Application Information: Complete and mail Free Application for Federal Student Aid (FAFSA) and Financial Aid Form (FAF) by February 15.

Write: Office of Financial Aid
St. Lawrence University
Canton, NY 13617
315-379-5265

St. Mary's College
St. Mary's City, MD

Public College

Annual Financial Aid Budget: $3,900,000

Undergraduate enrollment	1,524
African-American enrollment	9%
Average financial aid award	$3,286
Percentage African-American students receiving aid	88%
Tuition and fees..In-state	$3,880
....Out-of-state	$5,980

Application Information: Complete and mail Free Application for Federal Student Aid (FAFSA) and Financial Aid Form (FAF) by March 1.

Write: Financial Aid Office
                St. Mary's College
                St. Mary's City, MD 20686
                301-862-0300

St. Paul's College
Lawrenceville, VA

Four-Year Private College

Annual Financial Aid Budget: $4,079,553

Undergraduate enrollment	639
African-American enrollment	99%
Average financial aid award	$5,100
Percentage African-American students receiving aid	97%
Tuition and fees	$4,636

Application Information: Complete and mail Free Application for Federal Student Aid (FAFSA) by April 15.

Write: Financial Aid Office
                St. Paul's College
                406 Windsor Avenue
                Lawrenceville, VA 23868
                804-848-4505

Samford University
Birmingham, AL

Private University

Undergraduate enrollment	3,359
African-American enrollment	6%
Average financial aid award	$9,386
Percentage African-American students receiving aid	N/R
Tuition and fees	$7,770

Application Information: Complete and mail Free Application for Federal Student Aid (FAFSA), Financial Aid Form (FAF), institutional form, and state form by March 1.

Write: Director of Financial Aid
                Samford University
                Birmingham, AL 35229-0002
                205-870-2905

San Diego State University
San Diego, CA

Public University

Annual Financial Aid Budget: $60,000,000

Undergraduate enrollment	27,000
African-American enrollment	N/R
Average financial aid award	$4,500
Percentage African-American students receiving aid	N/R
Tuition and fees...In-state	$1,500
....Out-of-state	$7,572

Application Information: Complete and mail Free Application for Federal Student Aid (FAFSA) by March 1.

Write: Student Financial Aid Office
                San Diego State University
                5300 Campanile Drive, SSA 7
                San Diego, CA 92182-0587
                619-594-6323

Sarah Lawrence College
Bronxville, NY

Private College

Annual Financial Aid Budget: $5,000,000

Undergraduate enrollment	1020
African-American enrollment	6%
Average financial aid award	$15,838
Percentage African-American students receiving aid	100%
Tuition and fees	$17,640

Application Information: Complete and mail Free Application for Federal Student Aid (FAFSA) by February 1.

Write: Financial Aid Office
                Sarah Lawrence College
                1 Mead Way
                Bronxville, NY 10708
                914-395-2570

Scripps College
Claremont, CA

Private College

Annual Financial Aid Budget: $3,387,140

Undergraduate enrollment	603
African-American enrollment	4%
Average financial aid award	$17,969
Percentage African-American students receiving aid	N/R
Tuition and fees	$16,550

Application Information: Complete and mail Free Application for Federal Student Aid (FAFSA) and Financial Aid Form (FAF) by February 1.

Write: Financial Aid Office
                Scripps College
                1030 Columbia Avenue
                Claremont, CA 91711
                909-621-8275

Seattle University
Seattle, WA

Private University

Annual Financial Aid Budget: $28,000,000

Undergraduate enrollment	2,787
African-American enrollment	4%
Average financial aid award (African-American Students)	$13,972
Percentage African-American students receiving aid	67%
Tuition and fees	$11,520

Application Information: Complete and mail Free Application for Federal Student Aid (FAFSA) as soon as possible after January 1.

Write: Financial Aid Office
                Seattle University
                Broadway and Madison
                Seattle, WA 98122-4460
                206-296-5840

Smith College
Northampton, MA

Private Women's Liberal Arts College

Annual Financial Aid Budget: $25,465,570

Undergraduate enrollment	2,554
African-American enrollment	3.7%
Average financial aid award	$16,485
Percentage African-American students receiving aid	87%
Tuition and fees	$16,985

Application Information: Complete and mail Free Application for Federal Student Aid (FAFSA) and Smith College financial aid form by November 15 for Fall Early Decision, by January 1 for Winter Early Decision, and by February 1 for Regular Decision.

Write: Financial Aid Office
Smith College
Northampton, MA 01063
413-585-2530

Sonoma State University
Rohnert Park, CA

Four-Year Public University

Annual Financial Aid Budget: $11,213,690

Undergraduate enrollment	5,333
African-American enrollment	4%
Average financial aid award	$4,400
Percentage African-American students receiving aid	90%
Tuition and fees..In-state	$1,474
....Out-of-state	$7,546

Application Information: Complete and mail Free Application for Federal Student Aid (FAFSA) as soon as possible after January 1. Your form must be received by March 2. *California residents are urged to apply for a Cal Grant from the Student Aid Commission by completing "Section I: State Information" on the FAFSA.*

Write: Financial Aid Office, Village 600
Sonoma State University
Rohnert Park, CA 94928
707-664-2389

Southern Illinois University at Carbondale
Carbondale, IL

Public University

Annual Financial Aid Budget: N/R

Undergraduate enrollment	18,712
African-American enrollment	12%
Average financial aid award	$3,500
Percentage African-American students receiving aid	N/R
Tuition and fees..In-state	$3,052
....Out-of-state	$7,552

Application Information: Complete and mail Free Application for Federal Student Aid (FAFSA) by April 1.

Write: Financial Aid Office
Southern Illinois University at Carbondale
Mail Code 4702, SIUC
Carbondale, IL 62901-4710
618-453-4334

Southern Methodist University
Dallas, TX

Private University

Annual Financial Aid Budget: $68,900,000

Undergraduate enrollment	5,279
African-American enrollment	5%
Average financial aid award for African-American students	$9,192
Percentage African-American students receiving aid	90%
Tuition and fees	$13,580

Application Information: Complete and mail Free Application for Federal Student Aid (FAFSA) by February 1.

Write: Financial Aid Office
                Southern Methodist University
                P.O. Box 296
                Dallas, TX 75275
                214-768-3417

Southern Nazarene University
Bethany, OK

Private University—Religious Affiliation

Annual Financial Aid Budget: N/R

Undergraduate enrollment	1,371
African-American enrollment	2%
Average financial aid award	$3,702
Percentage African-American students receiving aid	90%
Tuition and fees	$5,835

Application Information: Complete and mail Free Application for Federal Student Aid (FAFSA) by April 15.

Write: Financial Assistance Office
                Southern Nazarene University
                6729 N.W. 39th Expressway
                Bethany, OK 73008
                405-491-6310

Southwestern University
Georgetown, TX

Private Religious-Affiliated University

Annual Financial Aid Budget: $7,769,868

Undergraduate enrollment	1,220
African-American enrollment	3%
Average financial aid award	$10,673
Percentage African-American students receiving aid	67%
Tuition and fees	$11,000

Application Information: Complete and mail Free Application for Federal Student Aid (FAFSA) and Southwestern University financial aid application by March 15.

Write: Financial Aid Office
                Southwestern University
                University at Maple
                Georgetown, TX 78626
                512-863-1259

Southwest Missouri State University
Springfield, MO

Public University

Annual Financial Aid Budget: $4,000,000 *(scholarships only)*

Undergraduate enrollment	20,000
African-American enrollment	N/R
Average financial aid award (Students of color)	N/R
Percentage African-American students receiving aid	N/R
Tuition and fees...In-state	$2,360
....Out-of-state	$4,580

Application Information: Complete and mail Free Application for Federal Financial Aid (FAFSA) before March 31.

Write: Scholarship Coordinator
                Office of Student Financial Aid
                Southwest Missouri State University
                101 Carrington Hall
                Springfield, MO 65804-0095
                1-800-492-7900/417-836-5262

Spelman College
Atlanta, GA

Independent Women's College

Undergraduate enrollment	1,900
African-American enrollment	100%
Average financial aid award	$4,578
Percentage African-American students receiving aid	86%
Tuition and fees	$7,077

Application Information: Complete and mail Free Application for Federal Student Aid (FAFSA), Financial Aid Form (FAF), and state form by April 1.

Write: Financial Aid Office
                Spelman College
                Atlanta, GA 30314
                1-800-241-3421

Stanford University
Stanford, CA

Private University

Annual Financial Aid Budget: $49,000,000

Undergraduate enrollment	13,549
African-American enrollment	6%
Average financial aid award	$9,964
Percentage African-American students receiving aid	60%
Tuition and fees (comprehensive— includes room & board)	$16,536

Application Information: Complete and mail Financial Aid Form (FAF) by February 1.

Write: Financial Aid Office
                Room 214 Old Union
                Stanford University
                Stanford, CA 94305-3021
                415-723-3058

State University College at Oneonta
Oneonta, NY

Public University

Annual Financial Aid Budget: N/R

Undergraduate enrollment	5,008
African-American enrollment	8%
Average financial aid award	$3,400
Percentage African-American students receiving aid	90%
Tuition and fees...In-state	$2,896
....Out-of-state	$6,796

Application Information: Complete and mail Free Application for Federal Student Aid (FAFSA). No specific deadline date.

Write: Financial Aid Office
                State University College at Oneonta
                Netzer Administration Building 123
                Ravine Parkway
                Oneonta, NY 13820-4015
                607-436-2532

Stonehill College
North Easton, MA

Four-Year Private College

Annual Financial Aid Budget: $4,600,000

Undergraduate enrollment	1,990
African-American enrollment	1%

Average financial aid award (Students of color) $10,000
Percentage African-American students receiving aid   100%
Tuition and fees $10,820

Application Information: Complete and mail Free Application for Federal Student Aid (FAFSA) as soon as possible after January 1.

Write: Financial Aid Office
                Stonehill College
                320 Washington Street
                North Easton, MA 02333
                508-230-1347

Syracuse University
Syracuse, NY

Private Research University

Annual Financial Aid Budget: N/R

Undergraduate enrollment   10,259
African-American enrollment   9%
Average financial aid award $13,000
Percentage African-American students receiving aid   77%
Tuition and fees $13,811

Application Information: Complete and mail Free Application for Federal Student Aid (FAFSA) and Financial Aid Form (FAF) by March 1.

Write: Financial Aid Office
                Syracuse University
                Syracuse, NY 13244
                315-443-1513

Tarleton State University
Stephenville, TX

Public University

Annual Financial Aid Budget: N/R

Undergraduate enrollment   5,580
African-American enrollment   3%
Average financial aid award $2,165
Percentage African-American students receiving aid   N/R
Tuition and fees...In-state $1,104
....Out-of-state $4,416

Application Information: Complete and mail Free Application for Federal Student Aid (FAFSA) by June 1 (Summer), November 1 (Fall), April 15 (Spring).

Write: Financial Aid Office
                Tarleton State University
                Box T-489, Tarleton Station
                Stephenville, TX 76402
                817-968-9070

The Citadel
Charleston, SC

Four-Year Public Military College

Annual Financial Aid Budget: $9,000,000

Undergraduate enrollment	2,000
African-American enrollment	6%
Average financial aid award	$4,200
Percentage African-American students receiving aid	90%
Tuition and fees...In-state	$2,949
....Out-of-state	$6,659

Application Information: Complete and mail Free Application for Federal Student Aid (FAFSA) March 15.

Write: Financial Aid and Scholarship Office
                The Citadel
                MSC 171 Moultrie Street
                Charleston, SC 29409
                1-800-868-1842

Thomas More College
Crestview Hills, KY

Private College—Religious Affiliation

Annual Financial Aid Budget: $1,680,000

Undergraduate enrollment	1,258
African-American enrollment	4.4%
Average financial aid award (Students of color)	N/R
Percentage African-American students receiving aid	96%
Tuition and fees	$9,620

Application Information: Complete and mail Free Application for Federal Financial Aid (FAFSA) and Thomas More College Application for Scholarships and Financial Aid by March 1. Students must reapply annually to receive ALL financial aid.

Write: Financial Aid Office
                Thomas More College
                333 Thomas More Parkway
                Crestview Hills, KY 41017
                606-344-3319

Towson State University
Towson, MD

Public University

Annual Financial Aid Budget: $14,621,916

Undergraduate enrollment	12,831
African-American enrollment	8%
Average financial aid award	$3,870

Percentage African-American students receiving aid   60%
Tuition and fees..In-state $3,287
....Out-of-state $6,287

Application Information: Complete and mail Free Application for Federal Student Aid (FAFSA) by March 15.

Write: Financial Aid Office
                Towson State University
                Towson, MD 21204
                410-830-2061

Trenton State College
Trenton, NJ

Public College

Annual Financial Aid Budget: N/R

Undergraduate enrollment   6,069
African-American enrollment   8%
Average financial aid award $4,250
Percentage African-American students receiving aid   90%
Tuition and fees..In-state $3,761
....Out-of-state $5,363

Application Information: Complete and mail Free Application for Federal Student Aid (FAFSA) by May 1.

Write: Financial Aid Office
                Trenton State College
                Hillwood Lakes, CN 4700
                Trenton, NJ 08650-4700
                609-771-2211

Trinity College
Hartford, CT

Private College

Annual Financial Aid Budget: $12,000,000

Undergraduate enrollment   1,750
African-American enrollment   6%
Average financial aid award $17,000
Percentage African-American students receiving aid   85%
Tuition and fees $18,700

Application Information: Complete and mail Free Application for Federal Student Aid (FAFSA) and Financial Aid Form (FAF) by February 1.

Write: Financial Aid Office
                Trinity College
                300 Summit Street
                Hartford, CT 06106-3100
                203-297-2046

Troy State University
Troy, AL

Public University

Undergraduate enrollment	4,650
African-American enrollment	19%
Average financial aid award	N/R
Percentage African-American students receiving aid	N/R
Tuition and fees..In-state	$1,746
....Out-of-state	$2,933

Application Information: Complete and mail Financial Aid Form (FAF) and institutional form. No deadline. Priority deadline May 1.

Write: Director of Financial Aid
                Troy State University
                Adams Administration Building 141
                Troy, AL 36082
                205-670-3186

Tuskegee University
Tuskegee, AL

Private University

Undergraduate enrollment	6,475
African-American enrollment	89%
Average financial aid award	$9,100
Percentage African-American students receiving aid	90%
Tuition and fees	$10,228

Application Information: Complete and mail Free Application for Federal Student Aid (FAFSA), Financial Aid Form (FAF), institutional form, and Family Financial Statement by April 15.

Write: Director of Financial Aid
                Tuskegee University
                Tuskegee, AL 36088
                205-727-8201

United States Air Force Academy
USAF Academy, CO

Public Institution

Annual Financial Aid Budget: N/R

Undergraduate enrollment	4,236
African-American enrollment	N/R
Average financial aid award	N/R
Percentage African-American students receiving aid	N/R
Tuition and fees	$0

Application Information: Deadline for applying is January 31.

Write: Col. Robert Foerster, Director of Admissions
U.S. Air Force Academy
2304 Cadet Drive, Suite 200
USAF Academy, CO 80840-5625
719-472-3070

United States International University
San Diego, CA

Private University

Annual Financial Aid Budget: $9,000,000

Undergraduate enrollment	300
African-American enrollment	11.5%
Average financial aid award	$9,500
Percentage African-American students receiving aid	N/R
Tuition and fees	$10,350

Application Information: Complete and mail Free Application for Federal Student Aid (FAFSA) as soon as possible after January 1.

Write: Financial Aid Office
United States International University
10455 Pomerado Road
San Diego, CA 92131
619-693-4559

University of Alabama at Birmingham
Birmingham, AL

Public University

Undergraduate enrollment	11,658
African-American enrollment	21%
Average financial aid award	$5,200
Percentage African-American students receiving aid	80%
Tuition and fees..In-state	$2,238
....Out-of-state	$4,248

Application Information: Complete and mail Free Application for Federal Student Aid (FAFSA) and institutional form by May 1.

Write: UAB Financial Aid Office
University of Alabama at Birmingham
317 Hill University Center
Birmingham, AL 35294-1150
205-934-8223

University of Alabama
Tuscaloosa, AL

Public University

Undergraduate enrollment	15,370
African-American enrollment	10%
Average financial aid award	$3,640
Percentage African-American students receiving aid	N/R
Tuition and fees..In-state	$2,172
....Out-of-state	$5,424

Application Information: Complete and mail Free Application for Federal Student Aid (FAFSA), Family Financial Statement (FFS), and institutional form by March 1.

Write: Director of Student Financial Aid
                University of Alabama
                P.O. Box 870162
                Tuscaloosa, Al 35487-0162
                205-348-6758

University of Florida
Gainesville, FL

Public University

Annual Financial Aid Budget: $120,000,000

Undergraduate enrollment	27,756
African-American enrollment	5.5%
Average financial aid award	$4,700
Percentage African-American students receiving aid	N/R
Tuition and fees..In-state	$1,770
....Out-of-state	$6,889

Application Information: Complete and mail Free Application for Federal Student Aid (FAFSA) and University of Florida Financial Aid Application by April 15.

Write: Office of Student Financial Affairs
                University of Florida
                S-103 Criser Hall
                Gainesville, FL 32611-2058
                904-392-1275

University of Idaho
Moscow, ID

Public University

Annual Financial Aid Budget: $28,000,000

Undergraduate enrollment	7,465
African-American enrollment	1%
Average financial aid award	$4,200
Percentage African-American students receiving aid	80%

Tuition and fees...In-state $1,296
....Out-of-state $4,196

Application Information: Complete and mail Free Application for Federal Student Aid (FAFSA) and Financial Aid Form (FAF) by February 15.

Write: Student Financial Aid Services
                University of Idaho
                Moscow, ID 83844-4291
                208-885-6312

University of Illinois at Urbana-Champaign
Champaign, IL

Public University

Annual Financial Aid Budget: $72,208,096

Undergraduate enrollment   26,333
African-American enrollment   7%
Average financial aid award $3,532
Percentage African-American students receiving aid   76%
Tuition and fees...In-state $3,458
....Out-of-state $7,970

Application Information: Complete and mail Free Application for Federal Student Aid (FAFSA) by March 15.

Write: Student Financial Aid Office
                University of Illinois at Urbana-Champaign
                601 E. John Street
                Champaign, IL 61820
                217-333-0100

University of Maryland—College Park
College Park, MD

Public University

Annual Financial Aid Budget: N/R

Undergraduate enrollment   23,331
African-American enrollment   12%
Average financial aid award $4,793
Percentage African-American students receiving aid   94%
Tuition and fees...In-state $2,778
....Out-of-state $8,382

Application Information: Complete and mail Free Application for Federal Student Aid (FAFSA) by February 15.

Write: Office of Student Financial Aid
                University of Maryland, College Park
                0102 Lee Building
                College Park, MD 20742
                301-314-8279

University of Miami
Coral Gables, FL

Private University

Annual Financial Aid Budget: $140,000,000

Undergraduate enrollment	8,500
African-American enrollment	11%
Average financial aid award	$14,400
Percentage African-American students receiving aid	77%
Tuition and fees	$15,700

Application Information: Complete and mail Free Application for Federal Student Aid (FAFSA) and University of Miami Financial Aid Application by March 1.

Write: Financial Aid Office
                University of Miami
                1204 Dickinson Drive
                Coral Gables, FL 33146
                305-284-5212

University of Missouri—Columbia
Columbia, MO

Public University

Annual Financial Aid Budget: N/R

Undergraduate enrollment	16,365
African-American enrollment	3.9%
Average financial aid award for African-American students	$5,660
Percentage African-American students receiving aid	88%
Tuition and fees...In-state	$2,812
....Out-of-state	$7,672

Application Information: Complete and mail Free Application for Federal Student Aid (FAFSA) by March 1.

Write: Financial Aid Office
                University of Missouri—Columbia
                130 Jesse Hall
                Columbia, MO 65211
                314-882-7506

University of Missouri—St. Louis
St. Louis, MO

Four-Year Public University

Annual Financial Aid Budget: $23,000,000

Undergraduate enrollment	12,662
African-American enrollment	12.5%
Average financial aid award	$3,540
Percentage African-American students receiving aid	43%

Tuition and fees...In-state $2,740

....Out-of-state $7,600

Application Information: Complete and mail Free Application for Federal Student Aid (FAFSA) by April 1.

Write: Financial Aid Office
                  University of Missouri—St. Louis
                  8001 Natural Bridge Road
                  St. Louis, MO 63121
                  314-553-5526

University of Northern Colorado
Greeley, CO

Public University

Annual Financial Aid Budget: $30,136,441

Undergraduate enrollment	8,786
African-American enrollment	2%
Average financial aid award	$4,141
Percentage African-American students receiving aid	83%
Tuition and fees...In-state	$2,027
....Out-of-state	$6,888

Application Information: Complete and mail Free Application for Federal Student Aid (FAFSA) by March 1.

Write: Student Financial Resources
                  University of Northern Colorado
                  Carter Hall, Room 1005
                  Greeley, CO 80639
                  303-351-2502

University of North Dakota
Grand Forks, ND

Public University

Annual Financial Aid Budget: N/R

Undergraduate enrollment	10,520
African-American enrollment	.6% (less than 1%)
Average financial aid award	$5,766
Percentage African-American students receiving aid	N/R
Tuition and fees...In-state	$7,950
....Out-of-state	$11,250

Application Information: Complete and mail Free Application for Federal Student Aid (FAFSA) by April 15.

Write: Financial Aid Office
                  University of North Dakota
                  Box 8371
                  Grand Forks, ND 58202
                  701-777-3121

University of Pittsburgh
Pittsburgh, PA

Public University

Annual Financial Aid Budget: N/R

Undergraduate enrollment	27,973
African-American enrollment	6%
Average financial aid award	$4,200
Percentage African-American students receiving aid	70%
Tuition and fees..In-state	$4,922
....Out-of-state	$10,066

Application Information: Complete and mail Financial Aid Form (FAF) by March 1.

Write: Office of Admissions and Financial Aid
                Bruce Hall, Second Floor
                University of Pittsburgh
                Pittsburgh, PA 15260
                412-624-PITT

University of San Diego
San Diego, CA

Private University

Annual Financial Aid Budget: $23,623,527 *(Undergraduate Budget)*

Undergraduate enrollment	3,915
African-American enrollment	2.4%
Average financial aid award	$12,500
Percentage African-American students receiving aid	91%
Tuition and fees	$12,240

Application Information: Complete and mail Free Application for Federal Student Aid (FAFSA) and Financial Aid Form (FAF) by February 20.

Write: Office of Financial Aid
                University of San Diego
                5998 Alcala Park
                San Diego, CA 92110-2492
                619-260-4514

University of Southern Indiana
Evansville, IN

Four-Year Public University

Annual Financial Aid Budget: N/R

Undergraduate enrollment	7,200
African-American enrollment	3.2%
Average financial aid award	$2,501
Percentage African-American students receiving aid	98%

Tuition and fees...In-state $2,062
....Out-of-state $4,922

Application Information: Complete and mail Free Application for Federal Student Aid (FAFSA) by March 1.

Write: Financial Aid Office
                University of Southern Indiana
                8600 University Blvd.
                Evansville, IN 47712
                812-464-1767

University of Texas at Arlington
Arlington, TX

Public University

Annual Financial Aid Budget: N/R

Undergraduate enrollment	22,500
African-American enrollment	N/R
Average financial aid award for African-Americans	$4,000
Tuition and fees...In-state	$1,236
....Out-of-state	$5,376

Application Information: To receive aid one must be accepted to the college. Complete and return the Free Application for Federal Student Aid (FAFSA) and the university financial aid application by June 1.

Write: Judy Schneider, Director of Financial Aid
                University of Texas at Arlington
                P.O. Box 19199
                Arlington, TX 76019
                817-273-3561

University of Virginia
Charlottesville, VA

Public University

Annual Financial Aid Budget: $9,200,000

Undergraduate enrollment	11,000
African-American enrollment	12%
Average financial aid award	N/R
Percentage African-American students receiving aid	75%
Tuition and fees...In-state	$3,890
....Out-of-state	$10,826

Application Information: Complete and mail the Financial Aid Form (FAF) by March 1.

Write: Office of Financial Aid
                Miller Hall
                University of Virginia
                Charlottesville, VA 22903
                804-924-3725

University of Wisconsin—Whitewater
Whitewater, WI

Public University

Annual Financial Aid Budget: N/R

Undergraduate enrollment	10,000
African-American enrollment	6%
Average financial aid award	$4,000
Percentage African-American students receiving aid	70%
Tuition and fees...In-state	$2,300
....Out-of-state	$7,100

Application Information: Complete and mail Free Application for Federal Student Aid (FAFSA) before April 15.

Write: Financial Aid Office
                University of Wisconsin—Whitewater
                800 W. Main Street
                Whitewater, WI 53190
                414-472-1130

Vanderbilt University
Nashville, TN

Private/Independent University

Annual Financial Aid Budget: $38,668,180

Undergraduate enrollment	5,579
African-American enrollment	4.4%
Average financial aid award	$14,630
Percentage African-American students receiving aid	100%
Tuition and fees	$16,274

Application Information: Complete and mail Free Application for Federal Student Aid (FAFSA), Financial Aid Form (FAF), and the Vanderbilt University Financial Aid Application by February 15.

Write: Office of Student Financial Aid
                Vanderbilt University
                2309 West End Avenue
                Nashville, TN 37203
                615-322-3591

Virginia Polytechnic Institute & State University
Blacksburg, VA

Public University

Annual Financial Aid Budget: $25,000,000

Undergraduate enrollment	19,308
African-American enrollment	5%
Average financial aid award	$5,447
Percentage African-American students receiving aid	90%

Tuition and fees..In-state $3,538
....Out-of-state $8,986

Application Information: Complete and mail the Financial Aid Form (FAF) by February 15.

Write: Office of Scholarships and Financial Aid
222 Burruss Hall
Virginia Tech
Blacksburg, VA 24061-0222
703-231-5179

Washington State University
Pullman, WA

Public University

Annual Financial Aid Budget: $49,944,274

Undergraduate enrollment	15,789
African-American enrollment	2%
Average financial aid award	$2,587
Percentage African-American students receiving aid	63%
Tuition and fees..In-state	$2,254
....Out-of-state	$6,345

Application Information: Complete and mail Financial Aid Form (FAF) by March 1.

Write: Financial Aid Office
Washington State University
342 French Administration
Pullman, WA 99164-1036
509-335-9711

Wayne State College
Wayne, NE

Public College

Annual Financial Aid Budget: $9,500,000

Undergraduate enrollment	3,179
African-American enrollment	2%
Average financial aid award	$3,627
Percentage African-American students receiving aid	83%
Tuition and fees..In-state	$1,599
....Out-of-state	$2,594

Application Information: Complete and mail Free Application for Federal Student Aid (FAFSA) by May 1.

Write: Financial Aid Office
Wayne State College
200 E. 10th Street
Wayne, NE 68787
402-375-7230

Wells College
Aurora, NY

Private College

Annual Financial Aid Budget: N/R

Undergraduate enrollment	400
African-American enrollment	5%
Average financial aid award	$15,350
Percentage African-American students receiving aid	95%
Tuition and fees	$13,800

Application Information: Complete and mail Free Application for Federal Student Aid (FAFSA), and College Scholarship Service (CSS) or Financial Aid Form (FAF) by February 15.

Write: Financial Aid Office
              Wells College
              Rte 90
              Aurora, NY 13026
              315-364-3289

Western Illinois University
Macomb, IL

Public University

Annual Financial Aid Budget: N/R

Undergraduate enrollment	10,802
African-American enrollment	8.1%
Average financial aid award	$1,658
Percentage African-American students receiving aid	92%
Tuition and fees..In-state	$2,454
....Out-of-state	$6,150

Application Information: Complete and mail Free Application for Federal Student Aid (FAFSA) by March 1.

Write: Financial Aid Office
              Western Illinois University
              900 West Adams
              Macomb, IL 61455
              309-298-2446

Whitman College
Walla Walla, WA

Private College

Annual Financial Aid Budget: $11,178,680

Undergraduate enrollment	1,200
African-American enrollment	2%
Average financial aid award	$13,802
Percentage African-American students receiving aid	100%
Tuition and fees	$14,360

Application Information: Complete and mail Free Application for Federal Student Aid (FAFSA) and Financial Aid Form (FAF) by February 15.

Write: Financial Aid Office
                Whitman College
                345 Boyer
                Walla Walla, WA 99362
                509-527-5178

William Paterson College of New Jersey
Wayne, NJ

Public College

Annual Financial Aid Budget: $14,000,000

Undergraduate enrollment	8,236
African-American enrollment	8%
Average financial aid award	$3,000
Percentage African-American students receiving aid	90%
Tuition and fees..In-state	$2,928
....Out-of-state	$3,856

Application Information: Complete and mail Free Application for Federal Student Aid (FAFSA) by April 1.

Write: Financial Aid Director
                William Paterson College of New Jersey
                300 Pompton Road
                Wayne, NJ 07470-8420
                201-595-2929

Winthrop University
Rock Hill, SC

Public University

Annual Financial Aid Budget: $11,000,000

Undergraduate enrollment	4,065
African-American enrollment	20%
Average financial aid award	N/R
Percentage African-American students receiving aid	63%
Tuition and fees..In-state	$3,112
....Out-of-state	$5,512

Application Information: Complete and mail Free Application for Federal Student Aid (FAFSA) and Winthrop University Institutional Application for Financial Assistance as soon as possible after January 1, and by May 1.

Write: Financial Resource Center
                Winthrop University
                Oakland Avenue
                Rock Hill, SC 29733
                803-323-2189

Xavier University
New Orleans, LA

Private University

Annual Financial Aid Budget: $22,003,349

Undergraduate enrollment	2,475
African-American enrollment	97%
Average financial aid award	$5,671
Percentage African-American students receiving aid	92%
Tuition and fees	$10,970

Application Information: Complete and mail Free Application for Federal Student Aid (FAFSA) (no deadline); priority consideration February 15.

Write: Financial Aid Office
                Xavier University
                7325 Palmetto Street
                New Orleans, LA 70125
                504-483-3517

Yale University
New Haven, CT

Private University

Annual Financial Aid Budget: $25,000,000

Undergraduate enrollment	5,236
African-American enrollment	9%
Average financial aid award	$16,000
Percentage African-American students receiving aid	64%
Tuition and fees	$18,630

Application Information: Complete and mail Free Application for Federal Student Aid (FAFSA), Financial Aid Form (FAF), and institutional form by February 1 (early action deadline November 1).

Write: Financial Aid Office
                Yale University
                2170 Yale Station
                143 Elm Street
                New Haven, CT 06520
                203-432-0360

APPENDIX A
COLLEGE ROTC PROGRAMS

Alabama
Alabama A&M University, Normal•
Alabama State University, Montgomery•
Auburn University
Auburn University, Montgomery
Birmingham-Southern College
Huntingdon College, Montgomery
Jacksonville State University
Judson College
Miles College, Birmingham•
Mobile College, Mobile
Samford University, Birmingham
Spring Hill College, Mobile
Talladega College•
Troy State University
Troy State University, Montgomery
Tuskegee University•
University of Alabama, Birmingham
University of Alabama, Huntsville
University of Alabama, Tuscaloosa
University of Montevallo
University of North Alabama, Florence
University of South Alabama, Mobile

Alaska
University of Alaska, Fairbanks

Arizona
Arizona State University, Tempe
Devry Institute of Technology, Phoenix
Embry-Riddle Aeronautical University, Prescott
Grand Canyon College, Phoenix
Northern Arizona University, Flagstaff
University of Arizona, Tucson,

Arkansas
Arkansas State University, Jonesboro
Arkansas Tech University, Russellville
Henderson State University, Arkadelphia
Hendrix College, Conway
John Brown University, Siloam Springs
Ouachita Baptist University, Arkadelphia

Southern Arkansas University, Magnolia
University of Arkansas, Conway
University of Arkansas, Fayetteville
University of Arkansas, Little Rock
University of Arkansas, Monticello
University of Arkansas, Pine Bluff•

California
Biola University, La Mirada
California Baptist College, Riverside
California Institute of Technology, Pasadena
California Lutheran University, Thousand Oaks
California Maritime Academy, Vallejo
California State Polytech University, Pomona
California State Polytech University, San Luis
    Obispo
California State University, Chico
California State University, Dominguez
    Hills/Carson
California State University, Fresno
California State University, Fullerton
California State University, Hayward
California State University, Long Beach
California State University, Los Angeles
California State University, Northridge
California State University, Sacramento
California State University, San Bernardino
Chapman College, Orange
Christian Heritage College, El Cajon
Claremont McKenna College, Claremont
Dominican College of San Rafael
Golden Gate University, San Francisco
Harvey Mudd College, Claremont
Holy Names College, Oakland
Loyola Marymount University, Los Angeles
Menlo College, Menlo Park
Mills College, Oakland
Mount St. Mary's College, Los Angeles
National University, San Diego
Northrop University, Inglewood
Occidental College, Los Angeles

•Predominantly or historically Black college

Pepperdine University, Malibu
Pitzer College, Claremont
Point Loma College, San Diego
Pomona College, Claremont
Saint Mary College of California, Moraga
San Diego State University
San Francisco State University
San Jose State University
Santa Clara University
Scripps College, Claremont
Sonoma State University, Rohnert Park
Stanford University
United States International University, San
    Diego
University of California, Berkeley
University of California, Davis
University of California, Irvine
University of California, La Jolla
University of California, Los Angeles
University of California, Riverside
University of California, San Diego
University of California, Santa Barbara
University of La Verne
University of Redlands
University of San Diego
University of San Francisco
University of Southern California, Los Angeles
University of the Pacific, Stockton
Westmont College, Santa Barbara
Whittier College

Colorado

Colorado School of Mines, Golden
Colorado State University, Fort Collins
Colorado Technical College, Colorado
    Springs
Mesa College, Grand Junction
Metropolitan State College, Denver
Regis College, Denver
University of Colorado, Boulder
University of Colorado, Colorado Springs
University of Colorado, Denver
University of Denver
University of Northern Colorado, Greeley
University of Southern Colorado, Pueblo

Connecticut

Central Connecticut State University, New
    Britain

Eastern Connecticut State University,
    Willimantic
Post College, Waterbury
Quinnipiac College, Hamden
Sacred Heart University, Bridgeport
Saint Joseph College, West Hartford
Southern Connecticut State University, New
    Haven
Trinity College, Hartford
University of Bridgeport
University of Connecticut, Storrs
University of Hartford, West Hartford
University of New Haven, West Haven
Wesleyan University, Middletown
Western Connecticut State University,
    Danbury
Yale University, New Haven

Delaware

Delaware State College, Dover•
University of Delaware, Newark
Wilmington College, New Castle

District of Columbia

American University
Catholic University of America
Georgetown University
George Washington University
Howard University•
Trinity College
University of the District of Columbia•

Florida

Barry University, Miami Shores
Bethune-Cookman College, Daytona Beach•
Embry-Riddle Aeronautical University,
    Daytona Beach
Florida A&M University, Tallahassee•
Florida Atlantic University, Boca Raton
Florida Institute of Technology, Melbourne
Florida International University, Miami
Florida Memorial College, Miami•
Florida Southern College, Lakeland
Florida State University, Tallahassee
Jacksonville University
Orlando College
Saint Leo College, Saint Leo
St. Thomas University, Miami
Southeastern College of the Assemblies of
    God, Lakeland

•Predominantly or historically Black college

Stetson University, Deland
University of Central Florida, Orlando
University of Florida, Gainesville
University of Miami, Coral Gables
University of North Florida, Jacksonville
University of South Florida, St. Petersburg
University of South Florida, Sarasota
University of South Florida, Tampa
University of West Florida, Pensacola
Webber College, Babson Park

Georgia

Agnes Scott College, Decatur
Albany State College•
Armstrong State College, Savannah
Augusta State College
Berry College, Mount Berry
Clark College, Atlanta•
Columbus College
Covenant College, Lookout Mountain
Fort Valley State College•
Georgia College, Milledgeville
Georgia Institute of Technology, Atlanta
Georgia Southern College, Statesboro
Georgia Southwestern College, Americus
Georgia State University, Atlanta
Kennesaw College, Marietta
Mercer University, Macon
Morehouse College, Atlanta•
North Georgia College, Dahlonega
Oglethorpe University, Atlanta
Savannah State College•
Southern Technical Institute, Marietta
Spelman College, Atlanta•
University of Georgia, Athens
Valdosta State College

Hawaii

Brigham Young University—Hawaii, Laie,
    Oahu
Charminade University of Honolulu
Hawaii Loa College, Kaneohe
Hawaii Pacific College, Honolulu
University of Hawaii at Manoa, Honolulu

Idaho

Boise State University
Idaho State University, Pocatello
University of Idaho, Moscow

Illinois

Bradley University, Peoria
Chicago State University•
Eastern Illinois University, Charleston
Elmhurst College
Illinois Institute of Technology, Chicago
Illinois State University, Normal
Knox College, Galesburg
Lewis University, Romeoville
Loyola University of Chicago, Chicago
McKendree College, Lebanon
North Central College, Naperville
Northeastern Illinois University, Chicago
Northern Illinois University, DeKalb
North Park College, Chicago
Northwestern University, Evanston
Parks College of St. Louis University,
    Cahokia
Saint Xavier College, Chicago
Southern Illinois University, Carbondale
Southern Illinois University, Edwardsville
University of Chicago
University of Illinois, Chicago
University of Illinois, Urbana-Champaign
Western Illinois University, Macomb
Wheaton College

Indiana

Ball State University, Muncie
Bethel College, Mishawaka
Butler University, Indianapolis
DePauw University, Greencastle
Indiana State University, Terre Haute
Indiana University, Bloomington
Indiana University-Purdue University,
    Indianapolis
Indiana University, South Bend
Indiana University Southeast, New Albany
Marian College, Indianapolis
Purdue University, West Lafayette
Rose-Hulman Institute of Technology, Terre
    Haute
Saint Mary's College, Notre Dame
University of Notre Dame

Iowa

Drake University, Des Moines
Iowa State University, Ames
University of Dubuque

•Predominantly or historically Black college

University of Iowa, Iowa City
University of Northern Iowa, Cedar Rapids

Kansas

Emporia State University
Fort Hays State University, Hays
Kansas State University, Manhattan
Mid-America Nazarene College, Olathe
Pittsburg State University
University of Kansas, Lawrence
Washburn University of Topeka
Wichita State University

Kentucky

Bellarmine College, Louisville
Cumberland College, Williamsburg
Eastern Kentucky University, Richmond
Georgetown College
Kentucky State University, Frankfort•
Morehead State University, Morehead
Murray State University, Murray
Northern Kentucky University, Highland
    Heights
Spalding University, Louisville
Thomas More College, Crestview Hills
Transylvania University, Lexington
University of Kentucky, Lexington
University of Louisville
Western Kentucky University, Bowling Green

Louisiana

Centenary College of Louisiana, Shreveport
Dillard University, New Orleans•
Grambling State University•
Louisiana State University and A&M College,
    Baton Rouge•
Louisiana State University, Shreveport
Louisiana Tech University, Ruston
Loyola University, New Orleans
McNeese State University, Lake Charles
Nicholls State University, Thibodaux
Northeast Louisiana University, Monroe
Northwestern State University of Louisiana,
    Natchitoches
Our Lady of Holy Cross College, New Orleans
Southeastern Louisiana University, Hammond
Southern University and A&M College, Baton
    Rouge•
Southern University in New Orleans•
Tulane University, New Orleans

University of New Orleans
University of Southwestern Louisiana,
    Lafayette
Xavier University of Louisiana, New Orleans•

Maine

Husson College, Bangor
Maine Maritime Academy, Castine
University of Maine, Orono
University of Southern Maine, Gorham

Maryland

Bowie State College•
Frostburg State College
John Hopkins University, Baltimore
Loyola College, Baltimore
Morgan State University, Baltimore•
Mount Saint Mary's College, Emitsburg
Salisbury State College
Towson State University, Baltimore
University of Maryland, College Park
Washington College, Chestertown
Western Maryland College, Westminister

Massachusetts

American International College, Springfield
Amherst College
Anna Maria College, Paxton
Assumption College, Worcester
Bentley College, Waltham
Boston University
Central New England College, Worcester
Clark University, Worcester
College of the Holy Cross, Worcester
Fitchburg State College
Gordon College, Wenham
Harvard and Radcliffe Colleges, Cambridge
Massachusetts Institute of Technology,
    Cambridge
Mount Holyoke College, South Hadley
Northeastern University, Boston
Salem State College, Salem
Smith College, Northampton
Springfield College
Stonehill College, North Easton
Suffolk University, Boston
Tufts University, Medford
University of Lowell
University of Massachusetts, Amherst
Wellesley College

•Predominantly or historically Black college

Western New England College, Springfield
Westfield State College
Worcester Polytechnic Institute
Worcester State College

Michigan
Central Michigan University, Mount Pleasant
Concordia College, Ann Arbor
Eastern Michigan University, Ypsilanti
Lawrence Institute of Technology, Southfield
Michigan State University, East Lansing
Northern Michigan University, Marquette
University of Detroit
University of Michigan, Ann Arbor
University of Michigan, Dearborn
Wayne State University, Detroit
Western Michigan University, Kalamazoo

Minnesota
Augsburg College, Minneapolis
Bemidji State University
Bethel College, St. Paul
College of St. Catherine, St. Paul
College of St. Scholastica, Duluth
College of St. Thomas, St. Paul
Concordia College, Moorhead
Concordia College, St. Paul
Hamline University, St. Paul
Macalester College, St. Paul
Mankato State University
Moorhead State University
Northwestern College, Roseville
Saint John's University, Collegeville
University of Minnesota, Duluth
University of Minnesota/Twin Cities,
    Minneapolis
Winona State University

Mississippi
Alcorn State University, Lorman•
Delta State University, Cleveland
Jackson State University•
Mississippi State University, Mississippi State
Mississippi University for Women, Columbus
Mississippi Valley State University, Itta Bena•
University of Mississippi, University
University of Southern Mississippi,
    Hattiesburg
William Carey College, Hattiesburg

Missouri
Central Missouri State University,
    Warrensburg
Columbia College
Harris-Stowe State College, St. Louis•
Lincoln University, Jefferson City•
Missouri Southern State College, Joplin
Missouri Western State College, St. Joseph
Northeast Missouri State University,
    Kirksville
St. Louis University
Southeast Missouri State University, Cape
    Girardeau
Southwest Missouri State University,
    Springfield
Stephens College, Columbia
University of Missouri, Columbia
University of Missouri, Rolla
University of Missouri, St. Louis
Westminster College, Fulton
William Woods College, Fulton

Montana
Eastern Montana College, Billings
Montana State University, Bozeman
University of Montana, Missoula

Nebraska
Bellevue College
College of Saint Mary, Omaha
Concordia Teachers College, Seward
Creighton University, Omaha
Kearney State College
Nebraska Wesleyan University, Lincoln
University of Nebraska, Omaha

Nevada
University of Nevada, Las Vegas
University of Nevada, Reno

New Hampshire
Colby-Sawyer College, New London
Daniel Webster College, Nashua
Dartmouth College, Hanover
Keene State College
New England College, Henniker
New Hampshire College, Manchester
Notre Dame College, Manchester
Plymouth State College
Rivier College, Nashua

•Predominantly or historically Black college

St. Anselm's College, Manchester
University of New Hampshire, Durham

New Jersey

Fairleigh Dickinson University/Teaneck-
  Hackensack, Teaneck
Jersey City State College
Kean College of New Jersey, Union
Monmouth College, West Long Branch
Montclair State College, Upper Montclair
New Jersey Institute of Technology, Newark
Princeton University
Rider College, Lawrenceville
Rutgers University/Camden College, Camden
Rutgers University, New Brunswick
Saint Peter's College, Jersey City
Seton Hall University, South Orange
Stevens Institute of Technology, Hoboken
Trenton State College
Upsala College, East Orange
William Paterson College of New Jersey,
  Wayne

New Mexico

Eastern New Mexico State University, Portales
New Mexico Highlands University, Las Vegas
New Mexico Institute of Mining and
  Technology, Socorro
New Mexico State University, Las Cruces
University of New Mexico, Albuquerque

New York

Adelphi University, Garden City
Albany College of Pharmacy of Union
  University, Albany
Alfred University
CUNY/John Jay College of Criminal Justice,
  New York
Clarkson University, Potsdam
College of Mount Saint Vincent, Riverdale
College of Saint Rose, Albany
Columbia University, New York
Cornell University, Ithaca
Dowling College, Oakdale
Fordham University, Bronx
Hobart College, Geneva
Hofstra University, Hempstead
Ithaca College, New Rochelle
Keuka College, Keuka Park
Le Moyne College, Syracuse

Long Island University/Brooklyn Center,
  Brooklyn
Long Island University/C. W. Post Campus,
  Greenvale
Manhattan College, Riverdale
Mercy College, Dobbs Ferry
Molloy College, Rockville Centre
Nazareth College of Rochester, Rochester
New School for Social Research, New York
New York Institute of Technology, Old
  Westbury
Niagara University, Niagara University
Pace University, New York
Polytechnic University/Pleasantville-Briarcliff,
  Pleasantville
Rensselaer Polytechnic Institute, Troy
Roberts Wesleyan College, Rochester
Rochester Institute of Technology
Russell Sage College, Troy
St. Bonaventure University
St. Francis College, Brooklyn
St. John Fisher College, Rochester
St. John's University, Jamaica
St. Joseph's College/Suffolk, Patchogue
St. Lawrence University, Canton
Siena College, Loudonville
Skidmore College, Saratoga Springs
State University of New York, Albany
State University of New York, Stony Brook
SUNY College, Brockport
SUNY College, Cortland
SUNY College, Fredonia
SUNY College, Geneseo
SUNY College, Old Westbury
SUNY College, Oswego
SUNY College, Potsdam
SUNY Maritime College, Bronx
Syracuse University, Syracuse
Union College, Schenectady
University of Rochester
Utica College of Syracuse University, Utica
Wagner College, Staten Island
Wells College, Aurora

North Carolina

Appalachian State University, Boone
Barber-Scotia College, Concord•
Belmont Abbey College, Belmont
Bennett College, Greensboro•

•Predominantly or historically Black college

Campbell University, Buies Creek
Davidson College
Duke University, Durham
East Carolina University, Greenville
Elon College
Fayetteville State University•
Greensboro College
Guilford College, Greensboro
High Point College
Johnson C. Smith University, Charlotte•
Meredith College, Raleigh
North Carolina A&M State University,
    Greensboro•
North Carolina Central University, Durham•
North Carolina State University, Raleigh
Pembroke State University
Queens College, Charlotte
Sacred Heart College, Belmont
Saint Augustine's College, Raleigh•
Shaw University, Raleigh•
University of North Carolina, Chapel Hill
University of North Carolina, Charlotte
University of North Carolina, Greensboro
University of North Carolina, Wilmington
Wake Forest University, Winston-Salem
Western Carolina University, Cullowhee
Wingate College
Winthrop College, Rock Hill

North Dakota
North Dakota State University, Fargo
University of North Dakota, Grand Forks

Ohio
Antioch College, Yellow Springs
Ashland College
Baldwin-Wallace College, Berea
Bowling Green State University
Capital University, Columbus
Case Western Reserve University, Cleveland
Cedarville College
Central State University, Wilberforce•
College of Mount St. Joseph, Mt. St. Joseph
Defiance College
Findlay College
Franklin University, Columbus
Heidelberg College, Tiffin
John Carroll University, University Heights
Kent State University

Miami University, Oxford
Mount Union College, Alliance
Ohio Dominican College, Columbus
Ohio Northern University, Ada
Ohio State University, Columbus
Ohio State University, Lima
Ohio State University, Mansfield
Ohio State University, Marion
Ohio State University, Newark
Ohio University, Athens
Ohio University, Belmont
Ohio University, Chillicothe
Ohio Wesleyan University, Delaware
Otterbein College, Westerville
Rio Grande College
University of Akron
University of Cincinnati
University of Dayton
University of Toledo
Urbana University
Wilberforce University•
Wilmington College
Wittenberg University, Springfield
Wright State University, Dayton
Xavier University, Cincinnati
Youngstown State University

Oklahoma
Cameron University, Lawton
Central State University, Edmond
East Central University, Ada
Northeastern Oklahoma State University,
    Tahlequah
Northwestern Oklahoma State University, Alva
Oklahoma Christian College, Oklahoma City
Oklahoma City University
Oklahoma State University, Stillwater
Southwestern Oklahoma State University,
    Weatherford
University of Oklahoma, Norman
University of Tulsa

Oregon
Concordia College, Portland
Eastern Oregon State College, La Grande
Oregon Institute of Technology, Klamath Falls
Oregon State University, Corvallis
Portland State University
University of Oregon, Eugene

•Predominantly or historically Black college

University of Portland
Warner Pacific College, Portland
Western Oregon State College, Monmouth
Willamette University, Salem

Pennsylvania
Allentown College of St. Francis de Sales,
    Center Valley
Bloomburg University
Bryn Mawr College, Bryn Mawr
Bucknell University, Lewisburg
California University of Pennsylvania,
    California
Carlow College, Pittsburgh
Carnegie-Mellon University, Pittsburgh
Cedar Crest College, Allentown
Chatham College, Pittsburgh
Cheyney University•
Clarion University
College Misericordia, Dallas
Dickinson College, Carlisle
Drexel University, Philadelphia
Duquesne University, Pittsburgh
Eastern College, St. Davids
East Stroudsburg University
Gannon University, Erie
Gettysburg College
Grove City College
Haverford College
Indiana University of Pennsylvania,
    Indiana
King's College, Wilkes-Barre
Kutztown State College, Kutztown
Lafayette College, Easton
LaRoche College, Pittsburgh
La Salle University, Philadelphia
Lehigh University, Bethlehem
Lincoln University, Lincoln University•
Lock Haven University, Lock Haven
Mansfield University
Marywood College, Scranton
Millersville University
Moravian College, Bethlehem
Muhlenberg College, Allentown
Pennsylvania State University, University Park
Point Park College, Pittsburgh
Robert Morris College, Corapolis
Saint Joseph's University, Philadelphia
Saint Vincent College, Latrobe

Shippensburg University
Slippery Rock University
Swarthmore College, Swarthmore
Temple University, Philadelphia
University of Pennsylvania, Philadelphia
University of Pittsburgh
University of Scranton
Villanova University
Washington and Jefferson College
West Chester University
Widener University, Chester
Wilkes College, Wilkes-Barre

Rhode Island
Bryant College, Smithfield
Providence College
Rhode Island College, Providence
University of Rhode Island, Kingston

South Carolina
Benedict College, Columbia•
Central Wesleyan College, Central
The Citadel, Charleston
Clemson University, Clemson
Erskine College, Due West
Francis Marion College, Florence
Furman University, Greenville
Presbyterian College, Clinton
South Carolina State College,
    Orangeburg•
University of South Carolina, Columbia
Wofford College, Spartanburg

South Dakota
Black Hills State University, Spearfish
Northern State College, Aberdeen
South Dakota School of Mines & Technology,
    Rapid City
South Dakota State University, Brookings
University of South Dakota, Vermillion

Tennessee
Austin Peay State University, Clarksville
Belmont College, Nashville
Christian Brothers College, Memphis
David Lipscomb College, Nashville
East Tennessee State University, Johnson
    City
Knoxville College•
LeMoyne-Owen College, Memphis•

•Predominantly or historically Black college

Memphis State University
Middle Tennessee State University,
   Murfreesboro
Rhodes College, Memphis
Tennessee State University, Nashville•
Tennessee Technological University,
   Cookeville
Trevecca Nazarene College
University of Tennessee, Chattanooga
University of Tennessee, Knoxville
University of Tennessee, Martin
Vanderbilt University, Nashville

Texas
Angelo State University, San Angelo
Baylor University, Waco
Bishop College, Dallas
Concordia Lutheran College
East Texas State University, Commerce
Hardin-Simmons University, Abilene
Houston Baptist University
Lamar University, Beaumont
Lubbock Christian College
Midwestern State University, Wichita Falls
Pan American University, Edinburg
Paul Quinn College, Waco•
Prairie View A&M University, Prairie View•
Rice University, Houston
St. Edward's University, Austin
St. Mary's University of San Antonio
Sam Houston State University
Southern Methodist University, Dallas
Southwest Texas State University, San Marcos
Stephen F. Austin State University,
   Nacogdoches
Tartleton State University
Texas A&M University, Kingsville
Texas Christian University, Ft. Worth
Texas College, Tyler•
Texas Lutheran College, Seguin
Texas Southern University, Houston•
Texas Tech University, Lubbock
Texas Wesleyan College, Ft. Worth
Texas Women's University, Denton
Trinity University, San Antonio
University of Dallas, Irving
University of Houston
University of Mary Hardin-Baylor, Belton
University of St. Thomas, Houston

University of Texas, Arlington
University of Texas, Austin
University of Texas, El Paso
University of Texas, San Antonio
West Texas A&M University, Canyon

Utah
Brigham Young University, Provo
University of Utah, Salt Lake City
Utah State University, Logan
Weber State College, Ogden
Westminster College, Salt Lake City

Vermont
Bennington College
Lyndon State College
Norwich University, Northfield
Saint Michael's College, Winooski
Trinity College, Burlington
University of Vermont, Burlington

Virginia
Christopher Newport College, Newport
   News
College of William & Mary, Williamsburg
George Mason University, Fairfax
Hampton University•
James Madison University, Harrisonburg
Longwood College
Norfolk State University•
Old Dominion University, Norfolk
University of Richmond
University of Virginia, Charlottesville
Virginia Military Institute, Lexington
Virginia Polytechnic Institute and State
   University, Blacksburg
Virginia State University, Petersburg•
Washington & Lee University, Lexington

Washington
Central Washington University, Ellensburg
Eastern Washington University, Cheney
Gonzaga University, Spokane
Pacific Lutheran University, Tacoma
St. Martin's College, Olympia
Seattle Pacific University
Seattle University
University of Puget Sound, Tacoma
University of Washington, Seattle
Washington State University

•Predominantly or historically Black college

West Virginia

Fairmont State College
Marshall University, Huntington
Shepherd College, Shepherdstown
West Virginia University, Morgantown

Wisconsin

Marquette University
Ripon College
St. Norbert College, De Pere

University of Wisconsin, La Crosse
University of Wisconsin, Madison
University of Wisconsin, Milwaukee
University of Wisconsin, Oshkosh
University of Wisconsin, Platteville
University of Wisconsin, Stevens Point
University of Wisconsin, Whitewater

Wyoming

University of Wyoming, Laramie

APPENDIX B

STATE DEPARTMENTS AND COMMISSIONS OF HIGHER EDUCATION

=:=

Alabama Department of Education
Administrative and Financial Services Division
Gordon Persons Bldg.
50 N. Ripley
Montgomery, AL 36130

Alaska Commission on Postsecondary Education
Student Financial Aid Division
Box 110505
Juneau, Alaska 99811
907-465-2962

Arizona Educational Loan Program
United Student Aid Funds, Inc.
Western Regional Center, Suite 400
25 S. Arizona Place
Chandler, AZ 85225
602-814-9988

Arkansas Department of Higher Education
114 E. Capitol
Little Rock, AR 72201
501-324-9300

California Student Aid Commission
P.O. Box 94285
Sacramento, CA 94245
916-445-0880

Colorado Diversity Grant Program
Colorado Commission on Higher Education
1300 Broadway, Second Floor
Denver, CO 80203
303-866-2723

Connecticut Department of Higher Education
51 Woodland St.
Hartford, CT 06105
203-566-2618

Delaware Postsecondary Scholarship Fund
Delaware Postsecondary Education Commission
Carvel State Office Building
820 N. French Street
Wilmington, DE 19801
302-571-3240

Higher Education Loan Program of
    Washington, D.C.
Suite 1050, 1030 15th St., N.W.
Washington, D.C. 20005

Office of Student Financial Assistance
Florida Department of Education
1344 Florida Education Center
Tallahassee, FL 32399-0400
904-487-0049

Georgia Student Finance Commission
Suite 200, 2082 E. Exchange Place
Tucker, GA 30084

Hawaii Education Loan Program
Suite 962, 1314 S. King Street
Honolulu, HI 96814

Student Loan Fund of Idaho
P.O. Box 730
Fruitland, ID 83619
1-800-528-9447

Illinois Student Assistance Commission
1755 Lake Cook Rd
Deerfield, IL 60015
708-948-8550

State Student Assistance Commission of Indiana
964 N. Pennsylvania Street, 1st Floor
Indianapolis, IN 46204
317-232-2350

Iowa College Student Aid Commission
201 Jewett Bldg.
914 Grand Avenue
Des Moines, IA 50309

Kansas State Scholarship and Tuition Grant
    Programs
Student Assistance Section
Suite 609, Capitol Tower
400 W. 8th Street
Topeka, KS 66603

Kentucky Higher Education Assistance
Authority
1050 U.S. 127 South, Suite 102
Frankfort, KY 40601
502-564-5279

Office of Student Financial Assistance
P.O. Box 91202
Baton Rouge, LA 70821-9202
1-800-259-LOAN

Finance Authority of Maine
Maine Education Assistance Division
Vickery-Hill Bldg.
State House Station 119
Augusta, ME 04333

Maryland State Scholarship Board
2100 Guilford Avenue, Room 207
Baltimore, MD 21218-5888
410-333-6420

Scholarship Office
Massachusetts Board of Regents of Higher
Education
330 Stuart St.
Boston, MA 02116

Student Financial Assistance
Michigan Department of Education
P.O. Box 30008
Lansing, MI 48909

Minnesota Higher Education Coordinating
Board
Capitol Square Bldg., Suite 400
550 Cedar St.
St. Paul, MN 55101
612-296-3974 or 1-800-657-3866

Student Financial Aid
Board of Trustees of State Institutions of
Higher Learning
3825 Ridgewood Rd.
Jackson, MS 39211-6453
601-982-6570 or 1-800-327-2980

Missouri Student Grant Program
c/o Coordinating Board for Higher
Education
101 Adams Street
Jefferson, MO 65101
314-751-2361

Office of the Commissioner of Higher
Education
Montana University System
35 S. Last Chance Gulch
Helena, MT 59620

Nevada Educational Loan Program
United Student Aid Funds, Inc.
8085 Knue Rd.
P.O. Box 50825
Indianapolis, IN 46250
1-800-824-7044

New Hampshire Postsecondary Education
Commission
Two Industrial Park Drive
Concord, NH 03301

New Jersey Department of Higher Education
Office of Student Assistance
4 Quakerbridge Plaza, C.N. 540
Trenton, NJ 08625
609-586-5092 or 1-800-792-8670

New Mexico Educational Assistance
Foundation
3900 Osuna Avenue, N.E., Box 27020
Albuquerque, NM 87109
505-345-3371

New York State Higher Education Services
Corporation
Student Information
Albany, NY 12255
1-800-642-6234

North Carolina State Education Assistance
Authority
Box 2688
Chapel Hill, NC 27515
919-549-8614

Ohio Board of Regents
Student Assistance Office
30 E. Broad Street
Columbus, OH 43266-0417
614-466-7420

Oklahoma State Regents for Higher
Education
500 Education Building
State Capitol Complex
Oklahoma City, OK 73105-4503
405-521-2444

Pennsylvania Higher Education Assistance
Agency
660 Boas Street
Harrisburg, PA 17102
717-257-2750

Rhode Island Higher Education Assistance
Authority
560 Jefferson Boulevard
Warwick, RI 02886
401-277-2050/TDD 401-277-6195

South Carolina Tuition Grants Commission
Keenan Bldg., 1st Floor
P.O. Box 12159
Columbia, SC 29211
803-734-1200

State of South Dakota
Department of Education and Cultural Affairs
700 Governors Drive
Pierre, SD 57501
605-773-3678

Tennessee Student Assistance Corporation
404 James Robertson Parkway
Suite 1950, Parkway Towers
Nashville, TN 37219
615-714-1346

Texas Higher Education Coordinating Board
P.O. Box 12788
Capitol Station
Austin, TX 78711
512-483-6340

Utah Higher Education Assistance Authority
355 W. South Temple, #3
Triad Center, Suite 550
Salt Lake City, UT 84180-1205

Vermont Student Assistance Corporation
Champlain Mill, Box 2000
Winooski, VT 05404-2601
802-655-9602 or 1-800-642-3177

Commonwealth of Virginia
State Education Assistance Authority
6 N. Sixth Street, Suite 300
Richmond, VA 23219
804-786-2035

State Council of Higher Education for
Virginia
James Monroe Building
101 N. Fourteenth Street
Richmond, VA 23219
804-225-2141

Higher Educational Coordinating Board
917 Lakeridge Way
Mail Stop 6V-11
Olympia, WA 98504
206-753-3571

West Virginia Board of Regents
Higher Education Grant Programs
Box 4007
Charleston, WV 25364
304-347-1266

State of Wisconsin Higher Education Aids
Board
25 W. Main Street
Madison, WI 53707
414-227-4942

Higher Education Assistance Foundation
1912 Capitol Avenue, Suite 320
Cheyenne, WY 82001
307-635-3529

APPENDIX C

AFRICAN-AMERICAN FRATERNAL AND PROFESSIONAL ORGANIZATIONS

A Better Chance
419 Boylston Street
Boston, MA 02116
617-421-0950

Alpha Kappa Alpha Sorority
5656 S. Stony Island Avenue
Chicago, IL 60637
312-684-1282

Alpha Phi Alpha Fraternity
4432 Martin Luther King Drive
Chicago, IL 60653
312-373-1819

Alpha Pi Chi Sorority
P.O. Box 255
Kensington, MD 20895

American Academy of Medical Directors•
One Urban Centre, Suite 648
Tampa, FL 33609
813-287-2000

American Association of Blacks in Energy
801 Pennsylvania Avenue, S.E., Suite 250
Washington, D.C. 20003
202-547-9378

American Baptist Black Caucus•
c/o St. John Missionary Baptist Church
34 W. Pleasant Street
Springfield, OH 45506
513-323-4401

American Black Chiropractors Association•
1918 E. Grand Boulevard
St. Louis, MO 63107
314-531-0615

Association of Black Sociologists
University of Missouri
5100 Rockhill Road, SSB 215
Kansas City, MO 64110
409-845-4944

Auxiliary to the National Medical Association•
1012 10th Street, N.W.
Washington, D.C. 20001
202-371-1674

Black American Cinema Society•
c/o Western States Black Research Center
3617 Montclair
Los Angeles, CA 90018
213-737-3292

Black Data Processing Associations•
P.O. Box 7466
Philadelphia, PA 19101
1-800-727-BDPA

Black Entertainment and Sports Lawyers
   Association
111 Broadway, 7th Floor
New York, NY 10006
212-587-0300

Black Tennis and Sports Foundation•
1893 Amsterdam Avenue
New York, NY 10032
212-926-5991

Black Women's Educational Alliance•
6625 Greene Street
Philadelphia, PA 19119

Blacks in Law Enforcement•
256 East McLemore Avenue
Memphis, TN 38106
901-774-1118

Catholic Interracial Council of New York•
899 10th Avenue
New York, NY 10019
212-237-8255

Chi Eta Phi Sorority•
3029 13th Street, N.W.
Washington, D.C. 20009
202-232-3858

•Awards Scholarships and Grants

Co-ette Club•
2020 W. Chicago Boulevard
Detroit, MI 48206
313-867-0880

Conference of Prince Hall Grand Masters
4311 Portland Avenue, South
Minneapolis, MN 55407
612-825-2474

Council on Career Development for
	Minorities•
1341 W. Mockingbird Lane, Suite 412-E
Dallas, TX 75247
214-631-3677

Council on Legal Education Opportunity
1800 "M" Street, N.W., Suite 290
Washington, D.C. 20036
202-785-4840

Delta Sigma Theta Sorority•
1707 New Hampshire Ave., N.W.
Washington, D.C. 20009
202-483-5460

Episcopal Commission for Black Ministries•
c/o Episcopal Church
815 2nd Avenue
New York, NY 10017
212-867-8400

Eta Phi Beta Sorority•
c/o Elizabeth Anderson
1724 Mohawk Boulevard
Tulsa, OK 74110
918-425-7717

Florence Ballard Fan Club•
P.O. Box 36A02
Los Angeles, CA 90036
213-658-5260

INROADS (Internship Opportunities)•
1221 Locust Street, Suite 800
St. Louis, MO 63103
314-241-7488

Iota Phi Lambda Sorority•
503 Patterson Street
Tuskegee, AL 36088
205-727-5201

Jack and Jill of America Foundation•
P.O. Drawer 3689
Chattanooga, TN 37404
615-622-4476

Kappa Alpha Psi Fraternity
2320 N. Broad Street
Philadelphia, PA 19132
215-228-7184

NAACP
4805 Mt. Hope Drive
Baltimore, MD 21212-3297

NAACP Legal Defense and Educational Fund•
99 Hudson Street, 16th Floor
New York, NY 10013
212-219-1900

National Action Council for Minorities in
	Engineering•
3 West 35th Street
New York, NY 10001

National Association for Sickle Cell Disease, Inc.•
4221 Wilshire Boulevard, Suite 360
Los Angeles, CA 90010-3503
213-936-7205

National Association of Black Accountants•
900 2nd Street, N.E., Suite 205
Washington, D.C. 20002
202-682-0222

National Association of Black Geologists and
	Geophysicists•
P.O. Box 720157
Houston, TX 77272

National Association of Black Hospitality
	Professionals•
P.O. Box 5443
Plainfield, NJ 07060
201-354-5117

National Association of Black Journalists•
P.O. Box 17212
Washington, D.C. 20041
703-648-1270

National Association of Black Women
	Attorneys•
3711 Macomb Street, N.W., 2nd Floor
Washington, D.C. 20016
202-966-9693

•Awards Scholarships and Grants

National Association of Negro Business and
    Professional Women's Clubs•
1806 New Hampshire Avenue, N.W.
Washington, D.C. 20009
202-483-4206

National Association of Negro Musicians•
P.O. Box S-011
237 E. 115th Street
Chicago, IL 60628
312-779-1325

National Association of University Women•
1553 Pine Forest Drive
Tallahassee, FL 32301
904-878-4660

National Association of Urban Bankers•
122 C Street, N.W., Suite 580
Washington, D.C. 20001
202-783-4743

National Bankers Association•
122 C Street, N.W., Suite 580
Washington, D.C. 20001
202-783-3200

National Bar Association•
Women Lawyers Division
1211 Connecticut Avenue, N.W., Suite 702
Washington, D.C. 20036
202-291-1979

National Black Law Student Association•
1225 11th Street, N.W.
Washington, D.C. 20001
202-583-1281

National Black MBA Association•
180 N. Michigan Avenue, Suite 1820
Chicago, IL 60601
312-236-2622

National Black Nurses Association, Inc.•
P.O. Box 1823
Washington, D.C. 20013
202-393-6870

National Black Police Association•
1919 Pennsylvania Avenue, N.W., Suite 300
Washington, D.C. 20006
202-457-0563

National Coalition of Black Meeting Planners•
50 F Street, N.W., Suite 1040
Washington, D.C. 20001
202-628-3952

National Coalition of 100 Black Women
50 Rockefeller Plaza, Concourse Level, Room 46
New York, NY 10020
212-974-6140

National Consortium for Graduate Degrees
    for Minorities in Science and
    Engineering•
P.O. Box 537
Notre Dame, IN 46556
219-287-1097

National Council for Black Studies•
Indiana University
Memorial Hall East 129
Bloomington, IN 47405
812-335-6581

National Council for Culture and Art
1600 Broadway, Suite 611C
New York, NY 10019
212-757-7933

National Dental Association
5506 Connecticut Avenue, N.W., Suite 24
Washington, D.C. 20015
202-244-7555

National Organization of Black Law
    Enforcement Executives•
908 Pennsylvania Avenue, S.E.
Washington, D.C. 20003
202-546-8811

National Organization of Minority Architects
120 Ralph McGill Blvd., Suite 815
Atlanta, GA 30308
404-876-3055

National Podiatric Medical Association
1638 E. 87th Street
Chicago, IL 60617
312-374-1616

National Scholarship Service and
    Fund for Negro Students (NSSFNS)•
965 Martin Luther King Jr. Drive, N.W.
Atlanta, GA 30314
404-577-3990

•Awards Scholarships and Grants

National Society of Black Engineers
344 Commerce Street
Alexandria, VA 22314
703-549-2207

National Society of Certified Public
    Accountants•
1313 E. Sibley Blvd., Suite 210
Dolton, IL 60419
312-849-0098

National Sorority of Phi Delta Kappa•
8233 S. Martin Luther King Drive
Chicago, IL 60619
312-783-7379

National Urban League
500 E. 62nd Street
New York, NY 10021
212-310-9000

Omega Psi Phi Fraternity, Inc.•
2714 Georgia Avenue, N.W.
Washington, D.C. 20001
202-667-7158

Organization of Black Airline Pilots•
P.O. Box 86, La Guardia Airport
New York, NY 11371
212-568-8145

Phi Beta Sigma Fraternity•
145 Kennedy Street, N.W.
Washington, D.C. 20011
202-726-5424

United Negro College Fund•
500 E. 62nd Street
New York, NY 10021
212-326-1118

Zeta Phi Beta Sorority•
1734 New Hampshire Avenue, N.W.
Washington, D.C. 20009
202-387-3103

•Awards Scholarships and Grants

INDEX OF ATHLETIC AWARDS
BY SPORT

≡≡≡≡≡≡≡≡≡≡≡≡≡≡≡≡≡≡≡≡≡≡≡≡≡≡≡≡≡≡≡≡≡≡≡≡≡≡≡

Baseball

	Men's	Women's
Benedictine College, KS	✓	
Bowie State University, MD	✓	
California State Polytechnic —Pomona, CA	✓	
Campbellsville College, KY	✓	
Centenary College, LA	✓	
Central Connecticut State University, CT	✓	
The Citadel, SC	✓	
Clarion University, PA	✓	
Colorado School of Mines, CO	✓	
Duke University, NC	✓	
East Carolina University, NC	✓	
Florida Institute of Technology, FL	✓	
Mississippi Valley State University, MS	✓	
Moorhead State University, MN	✓	
Northeast Missouri State University, MO	✓	
Northwestern College, MN	✓	
Northwestern University, IL	✓	
Oklahoma City University, OK	✓	
Pittsburg State University, KS	✓	
Providence College, RI	✓	
Purdue University, West Lafayette, IN	✓	

	Men's	Women's
St. Paul's College, VA	✓	
Southern Illinois University— Carbondale, IL		✓
Southwest Missouri State University, MO		✓
Towson State University, MD	✓	
Troy State University, AL	✓	
University of Florida, FL	✓	
University of Illinois at Urbana, IL		✓
University of Missouri— Columbia, MO		✓
University of Missouri— St. Louis, MO		✓
University of Northern Colorado, CO		✓
University of North Dakota, ND		✓
University of Pittsburgh, PA	✓	
University of Southern Indiana, IN		✓
University of Texas —Arlington, TX		✓
University of Virginia, VA		✓
Virginia Polytechnic, VA		✓
Wayne State College, NE		✓
Western Illinois University, IL		✓
Winthrop University, SC		✓
Xavier University, LA		✓

Basketball

	Men's	Women's
Alabama A&M University, AL	✓	✓
Appalachian State University, NC	✓	✓
Ashland University, OH	✓	✓
Auburn University, AL	✓	✓
Auburn University at Montgomery, AL	✓	✓
Austin Peay State University, TN	✓	✓

	Men's	Women's
Barber-Scotia College, NC	✓	✓
Bemidji State University, MN	✓	✓
Benedictine College, KS	✓	✓
Birmingham-Southern College, AL	✓	
Boston College, MA	✓	✓
Bowie State University, MD	✓	✓
California State Polytechnic Univ.—Pomona, CA	✓	✓

Basketball

	Men's	Women's		Men's	Women's
Campbellsville College, KS	✓	✓	Oklahoma City		
Centenary College, LA	✓		University, OK	✓	✓
Central Connecticut State			Ouachita Baptist		
University, CT	✓	✓	University, AR	✓	✓
Chadron State College, NE	✓	✓	Pittsburg State University, KS	✓	✓
The Citadel, SC	✓		Providence College, RI	✓	✓
Clarion University, PA	✓	✓	Purdue University, IN	✓	✓
Clemson University, SC	✓	✓	St. Paul's College, VA	✓	✓
Colorado School of			Samford University, AL	✓	
Mines, CO	✓	✓	San Diego State		
Columbia College, MO	✓		University, CA	✓	✓
Duke University, NC	✓	✓	Seattle University, WA	✓	✓
D'Youville College, NY	✓	✓	Southern Illinois University—		
East Carolina University, NC	✓	✓	Carbondale, IL	✓	✓
Eckerd College, FL	✓	✓	Stanford University, CA	✓	✓
Faulkner University, AL	✓		Stonehill College, MA	✓	✓
Florida A&M University, FL	✓	✓	Syracuse University, NY	✓	✓
Florida Institute of			Southern Methodist		
Technology, FL	✓	✓	University, TX	✓	✓
Georgetown University, DC	✓	✓	Southwest Missouri State		
Georgian Court College, NJ		✓	University, MO	✓	✓
Hampton University, VA	✓	✓	Towson State University, MD	✓	✓
Henderson State			Troy State University, AL	✓	✓
University, AR	✓	✓	Tuskegee University, AL	✓	✓
Howard University, DC	✓	✓	University of Alabama—		
Jacksonville State			Birmingham, AL	✓	✓
University, AL	✓	✓	University of Alabama—		
Lander University, SC	✓	✓	Tuscaloosa, AL	✓	
Loyola College, MD	✓	✓	University of Florida, FL	✓	✓
Lynn University, FL	✓	✓	University of Illinois at		
Michigan State			Urbana, IL	✓	✓
University, MI	✓	✓	University of Maryland—		
Mississippi University for			College Park, MD	✓	✓
Women, MS		✓	University of Miami, FL	✓	✓
Mississippi Valley State			University of Missouri—		
University, MS	✓	✓	Columbia, MO	✓	✓
Moorhead State			University of Northern		
University, MN	✓	✓	Colorado, CO	✓	✓
Morehouse College, GA	✓		University of North		
Morgan State University, MD	✓	✓	Dakota, ND	✓	✓
Murray State University, KS	✓	✓	University of Pittsburgh, PA	✓	✓
Northeast Missouri State			University of San Diego, CA	✓	✓
University, MO	✓	✓	University of Southern		
Northwest Nazarene			Indiana, IN	✓	✓
College, ID	✓	✓	University of Texas—		
Northwestern College, MN	✓	✓	Arlington, TX	✓	✓
Northwestern University, IL	✓	✓	Vanderbilt University, TN	✓	✓
Nova Southeastern			Virginia Polytechnic		
University, FL	✓		Institute, VA	✓	✓

Basketball

	Men's	Women's
Washington State University, WA	✓	✓
Wayne State College, NE	✓	✓
Western Illinois University, IL	✓	✓

	Men's	Women's
Winthrop University, SC	✓	✓
Xavier University, LA	✓	✓

Crew

	Men's	Women's
Boston College, MA	✓	✓
Florida Institute of Technology, FL	✓	✓

	Men's	Women's
Syracuse University, NY	✓	✓
Washington State University, WA	✓	✓

Cross-Country Running

	Men's	Women's
Alabama A&M University, AL	✓	✓
Appalachian State University, NC	✓	✓
Auburn University, AL	✓	✓
Austin Peay State University, TN	✓	✓
Barber-Scotia, NC	✓	
Boston College, MA		✓
Bowie State University, MD	✓	✓
California State Polytechnic Univ.—Pomona, CA	✓	✓
Campbellsville College, KY	✓	✓
Centenary, LA	✓	✓
Central Connecticut State University, CT	✓	✓
Clarion University, PA	✓	✓
Clemson University, SC	✓	✓
Colorado School of Mines, CO	✓	
East Carolina University, NC	✓	✓
Eckerd College, FL	✓	✓
Florida A&M University, FL	✓	✓
Georgetown University, DC	✓	✓
Georgian Court College, NJ	✓	✓
Hampton University, VA	✓	✓
Howard University, DC	✓	✓
Lander University, SC	✓	✓
Michigan State University, MI	✓	✓
Mississippi Valley State University, MS	✓	✓
Moorhead State University, MN	✓	✓
Morehouse College, GA	✓	
Morgan State University, MD	✓	✓

	Men's	Women's
Murray State University, KY	✓	✓
Northeast Missouri State University, MO	✓	✓
Oklahoma City University, OK	✓	✓
Northwestern College, MN	✓	✓
Nova Southeastern University, FL	✓	✓
Ouachita Baptist University, AR	✓	
Pittsburg State University, KS	✓	
Providence College, RI	✓	✓
Purdue University, IN	✓	✓
Samford University, AL	✓	✓
San Diego State University, CA	✓	✓
Southern Illinois University—Carbondale, IL	✓	✓
Southern Methodist University, TX	✓	✓
Southwest Missouri State University, MO	✓	✓
Syracuse University, NY	✓	✓
Towson State University, MD	✓	✓
Troy State University, AL	✓	
University of Alabama—Birmingham, AL	✓	✓
University of Alabama—Tuscaloosa, Al	✓	✓
University of Florida, FL	✓	✓
University of Idaho, ID	✓	✓
University of Illinois at Urbana, IL	✓	✓
University of Maryland—College Park, MD	✓	✓

Cross-Country

	Men's	Women's		Men's	Women's
University of Miami, FL	✓	✓	Virginia Polytechnic Institute, VA	✓	✓
University of Missouri—Columbia, MO	✓	✓	Washington State University, WA	✓	✓
University of Pittsburgh, PA	✓	✓	Wayne State College, NE	✓	✓
University of Southern Indiana, IN	✓	✓	Western Illinois University, IL		✓
University of Texas—Arlington, TX	✓	✓	Winthrop University, SC	✓	✓
University of Virginia, VA	✓	✓	Xavier University, LA	✓	✓
Vanderbilt University, TN	✓	✓			

Fencing

	Men's	Women's		Men's	Women's
Stanford University, CA	✓	✓	University of Illinois at Urbana, IL	✓	

Field Hockey

	Men's	Women's		Men's	Women's
Appalachian State University, NC		✓	Stanford University, CA		✓
Boston College, MA		✓	Syracuse University, NY		✓
Duke University, NC		✓	Towson State University, MD		✓
Michigan State University, MI		✓	University of Maryland—College Park, MD		✓

Football

	Men's	Women's		Men's	Women's
Alabama A&M University, AL	✓		Hampton University, VA	✓	
Appalachian State University, NC	✓		Henderson State University, AR	✓	
Ashland University, OH	✓		Howard University, DC	✓	
Auburn University, AL	✓		Jacksonville State University, AL	✓	
Austin Peay State University, TX	✓		Michigan State University, MI	✓	
Bemidji State University, MN	✓		Mississippi Valley State University, MS	✓	
Benedictine College, KS	✓		Morehouse College, GA	✓	
Boston College, MA	✓		Morgan State University, MD	✓	
Bowie State University, MD	✓		Murray State University, KY	✓	
Central Connecticut State University, CT	✓		Northeast Missouri State University, MO	✓	
Chadron State College, NE	✓		Northwestern College, MN	✓	
The Citadel, SC	✓		Ouachita Baptist University, AR	✓	
Colorado School of Mines, CO	✓		Pittsburg State University, KS	✓	
Duke University, NC	✓		Purdue University, IN	✓	
East Carolina University, NC	✓		Samford University, AL	✓	
Florida A&M University, FL	✓				

Football	Men's	Women's		Men's	Women's
San Diego State			University of Maryland—		
University, CA	✓		College Park, MD	✓	
Southern Illinois University—			University of Miami, FL	✓	
Carbondale, IL	✓		Univrsity of Missouri—		
Southern Methodist			Columbia, MO	✓	
University, TX	✓		University of Northern		
Southwest Missouri State			Colorado, CO	✓	
University, MO	✓		University of North		
Tuskegee University, AL	✓		Dakota, ND	✓	
Troy State University, AL	✓		University of Pittsburgh, PA	✓	
University of Alabama—			University of Virginia, VA	✓	
Tuscaloosa, AL	✓		Washington State		
University of Florida, FL	✓		University, WA	✓	
University of Idaho, ID	✓		Wayne State College, NE	✓	
University of Illinois at			Western Illinois		
Urbana, IL	✓		University, IL	✓	

Golf	Men's	Women's		Men's	Women's
Appalachian State			Northwestern University, IL	✓	✓
University, NC	✓	✓	Oklahoma City		
Ashland University, OH	✓		University, OK	✓	
Auburn University, AL	✓	✓	Providence College, RI	✓	
Austin Peay State			Purdue University, IN	✓	✓
University, TX	✓	✓	Samford University, AL	✓	✓
Bemidji State			San Diego State		
University, MN	✓		University, CA	✓	✓
Benedictine College, KS	✓	✓	Southern Illinois University—		
Campbellsville College, KY	✓		Carbondale, IL	✓	✓
Centenary College, LA	✓		Southern Methodist		
Central Connecticut State			University, TX	✓	✓
University, CT	✓		Troy State University, AL	✓	
The Citadel, SC	✓		University of Alabama—		
Clarion University, PA	✓		Birmingham, AL	✓	✓
Clemson University, SC	✓		University of Idaho, ID	✓	✓
Colorado School of			University of Illinois at		
Mines, CO	✓	✓	Urbana, IL	✓	✓
Columbia College, MN	✓	✓	University of Maryland—		
East Carolina			College Park, MD	✓	
University, NC	✓		University of Missouri—		
Jacksonville State			Columbia, MO	✓	✓
University, AL	✓		University of Missouri—		
Mississippi Valley State			St. Louis, MO	✓	
University, MS	✓		University of Southern		
Murray State			Indiana, IN	✓	
University, KY	✓	✓	University of Texas—		
Northeast Missouri State			Arlington, TX	✓	
University, MO	✓		University of Virginia, VA	✓	
Northwestern College, MN	✓		Vanderbilt University, TN	✓	✓

Golf

	Men's	Women's		Men's	Women's
Virginia Polytechnic Institute, VA	✓		Western Illinois University, IL	✓	
Washington State University, WA	✓		Winthrop University, SC	✓	✓
			Xavier University, LA	✓	✓

Gymnastics

	Men's	Women's		Men's	Women's
Auburn University, AL		✓	Syracuse University, NY	✓	
Centenary College, LA		✓	Towson State University, MD		✓
Eckerd College, FL	✓		University of Alabama—		
Florida A&M University, FL	✓	✓	Tuscaloosa, AL		✓
Lynn University, FL	✓	✓	University of Florida, FL	✓	✓
Nova Southeastern University, FL	✓		University of Illinois at Urbana, IL	✓	✓
San Diego State University, CA		✓	University of Maryland— College Park, MD		✓
Stanford University, CA	✓	✓	University of Miami, FL		✓

Ice Hockey

	Men's	Women's		Men's	Women's
Bemidji State University, MN	✓		Boston College, MA	✓	

Lacrosse

	Men's	Women's		Men's	Women's
Boston College, MA	✓		Georgetown University, DC	✓	
Colorado School of Mines, CO	✓		Towson State University, MD	✓	✓
Duke University, NC	✓		University of Maryland— College Park, MD	✓	✓

Skiing—Downhill

	Men's	Women's		Men's	Women's
Colorado School of Mines, CO	✓	✓	Seattle University, WA	✓	✓

Soccer

	Men's	Women's		Men's	Women's
Alabama A&M University, AL	✓		Centenary College, LA	✓	
Auburn University, AL		✓	Central Connecticut State University, CT	✓	
Auburn University at Montgomery, AL	✓		Clemson University, SC	✓	
Benedictine College, KS	✓	✓	The Citadel, SC	✓	
Birmingham— Southern College, AL	✓	✓	Colorado School of Mines, CO	✓	
Boston College, MA	✓	✓	Duke University, NC	✓	✓
California State Polytechnic Univ.—Pomona, CA	✓	✓	East Carolina University, NC	✓	✓
Campbellsville College, KY	✓		Eckerd College, FL	✓	
			Florida Institute of Technology, FL	✓	

Soccer

	Men's	Women's
Howard University, DC	✓	
Loyola College, MD	✓	✓
Lynn University, FL	✓	✓
Michigan State University, MI	✓	
Northeast Missouri State University, MO	✓	✓
Northwestern College, MN	✓	
Northwestern University, IL		✓
Northwest Nazarene College, ID	✓	
Nova Southeastern University, FL	✓	
Oklahoma City University, OK	✓	
Providence College, RI	✓	✓
San Diego State University, CA		✓
Seattle University, WA	✓	✓
Southern Methodist University, TX	✓	✓
Stanford University, CA	✓	

	Men's	Women's
Syracuse University, NY	✓	
Towson State University, MD	✓	✓
University of Alabama—Birmingham, AL	✓	
University of Maryland—College Park, MD	✓	✓
University of Missouri—St. Louis, MO	✓	✓
University of Northern Colorado, CO		✓
University of Pittsburgh, PA	✓	
University of Southern Indiana, IN	✓	
Vanderbilt University, TN	✓	✓
Virginia Polytechnic Institute, VA	✓	
Washington State University, WA		✓
Western Illinois University, IL	✓	
Winthrop University, SC	✓	
Xavier University, LA	✓	✓

Softball

	Men's	Women's
Ashland University, OH		✓
Barber-Scotia College, NC		✓
Benedictine College, KS		✓
Boston College, MA		✓
Bowie State University, MD	✓	
Campbellsville College, KY		✓
Centenary College, LA		✓
Central Connecticut State University, CT		✓
Clarion University, PA		✓
Colorado School of Mines, CO		✓
Columbia College, MO		✓
East Carolina University, NC		✓
Eckerd College, DL		✓
Faulkner University, AL		✓
Florida Institute of Technology, FL		✓
Georgian Court College, NJ		✓
Jacksonville State University, AL		✓
Lander University, SC		✓
Mississippi University for Women, MS		✓
Murray State University, KY		✓

	Men's	Women's
Northeast Missouri State University, MO		✓
Northwestern College, MN		✓
Northwestern Illinois University, IL		✓
Oklahoma City University, OK		✓
Pittsburg State University, KS		✓
Providence College, RI		✓
Purdue University, West Lafayette, IN		✓
Samford University, AL		✓
Southern Illinois University—Carbondale, IL		✓
Southwest Missouri State University, MO		✓
Towson State University, MD	✓	
University of Missouri—St. Louis, MO		✓
University of North Dakota, ND		✓
University of Texas—Arlington, TX		✓
University of Virginia, VA		✓
Wayne State College, NE		✓
Western Illinois University, IL		✓
Winthrop University, SC		✓

Swimming and Diving

	Men's	Women's
Ashland University, OH	✓	✓
Auburn University, AL	✓	✓
Boston College, MA		✓
Campbellsville College, KY	✓	✓
Central Connecticut State University, CT	✓	✓
Clarion University, PA	✓	✓
Clemson University, SC	✓	✓
Colorado School of Mines, CO	✓	✓
East Carolina University, NC	✓	✓
Florida A&M University, FL	✓	✓
Howard University, DC	✓	✓
Michigan State University, MI	✓	✓
Morehouse College, GA	✓	
Northwestern University, IL	✓	✓
Providence College, RI	✓	✓
Purdue University, IN	✓	✓
Southern Illinois University—Carbondale, IL	✓	✓
Southern Methodist University, TX	✓	✓
Stanford University, CA	✓	✓
Syracuse University, NY	✓	✓
Towson State University, MD	✓	✓
University of Alabama—Tuscaloosa, AL	✓	✓
University of Florida, FL	✓	✓
University of Illinois at Urbana, IL		✓
University of Maryland—College Park, MD	✓	✓
University of Miami, FL	✓	✓
University of Missouri—Columbia, MO	✓	✓
University of Missouri—St. Louis, MO	✓	✓
University of North Dakota, ND		✓
University of Northern Colorado, CO		✓
University of Pittsburgh, PA	✓	✓
University of San Diego, CA		
University of Virginia, VA	✓	✓
Virginia Polytechnic Institute, VA	✓	
Washington State University, WA	✓	✓
Western Illinois University, IL	✓	✓
Xavier University, LA	✓	✓

Tennis

	Men's	Women's
Alabama A&M University, AL	✓	✓
Appalachian State University, NC	✓	✓
Auburn University, AL	✓	✓
Auburn University at Montgomery, AL	✓	✓
Austin Peay State University, TN	✓	✓
Barber-Scotia College, NC	✓	
Bemidji State University, MN		✓
Birmingham-Southern College, AL	✓	✓
Boston College, MA		✓
California State Polytechnic Univ.—Pomona, CA	✓	✓
Campbellsville College, KY	✓	✓
Centenary College, LA	✓	✓
Central Connecticut State University, CT	✓	✓
The Citadel, SC	✓	
Clarion University, PA		✓
Clemson University, SC	✓	✓
Colorado School of Mines, CO	✓	✓
Duke University, NC	✓	✓
East Carolina University, NC	✓	✓
Eckerd College, FL	✓	✓
Florida A&M University, FL	✓	✓
Florida Institute of Technology, FL	✓	
Hampton University, VA	✓	
Howard University, DC	✓	✓
Jacksonville State University, AL	✓	✓
Lander University, SC	✓	✓
Lynn University, FL	✓	✓
Michigan State University, MI	✓	✓
Mississippi University for Women, MS		✓
Mississippi Valley State University, MS	✓	

Tennis

	Men's	Women's
Moorhead State University, MN	✓	
Morehouse College, GA	✓	
Morgan State University, MD	✓	✓
Murray State University, KY	✓	✓
Northeast Missouri State University, MO	✓	✓
Northwestern College, MN	✓	
Nova Southeastern University, FL		✓
Oklahoma City University, OK	✓	✓
Providence College, RI	✓	✓
Purdue University, IN	✓	✓
Samford University, AL	✓	✓
San Diego State University, CA	✓	✓
Southern Illinois University—Carbondale, IL	✓	✓
Southern Methodist University, TX	✓	✓
Southwest Missouri State University, MO	✓	✓
Towson State University, MD	✓	✓
Troy University, AL	✓	✓
Tuskegee University, AL	✓	✓
University of Alabama—Birmingham, AL	✓	✓
University of Alabama—Tuscaloosa, AL	✓	✓
University of Florida, FL	✓	✓
University of Idaho, ID	✓	✓
University of Illinois at Urbana, IL	✓	✓
University of Maryland—College Park, MD	✓	✓
University of Miami, FL	✓	✓
University of Northern Colorado, CO	✓	✓
University of Pittsburgh, PA	✓	✓
University of San Diego, CA	✓	✓
University of Southern Indiana, IN	✓	✓
University of Texas—Arlington, TX	✓	✓
University of Virginia, VA	✓	✓
Vanderbilt University, TN	✓	✓
Virginia Polytechnic Institute, VA	✓	✓
Washington State University, WA	✓	✓
Western Illinois University, IL	✓	✓
Winthrop University, SC	✓	✓
Xavier University, LA	✓	✓

Track and Field

	Men's	Women's
Alabama A&M University, AL	✓	✓
Appalachian State University, NC	✓	✓
Ashland University, OH	✓	✓
Auburn University, AL	✓	✓
Austin Peay State University, TX	✓	✓
Barber-Scotia, NC	✓	✓
Boston College, MA	✓	✓
Bowie State University, MD	✓	✓
California State Polytechnic Univ.—Pomona, CA	✓	✓
Central Connecticut State University, CT	✓	✓
Chadron State College, NE	✓	✓
The Citadel, SC	✓	
Clarion University, PA	✓	✓
Clemson University, SC	✓	✓
Colorado School of Mines, CO	✓	✓
East Carolina University	✓	✓
Florida A&M University, FL	✓	✓
Georgetown University, DC	✓	✓
Hampton University, VA	✓	✓
Howard University, DC	✓	✓
Michigan State University, MI	✓	✓
Mississippi Valley State University, MS	✓	✓
Moorhead State University, MN	✓	✓
Morehouse College, GA	✓	
Morgan State University, MD	✓	✓
Murray State University, KY	✓	✓
Northeast Missouri State University, MO	✓	✓
Northwestern College, MN	✓	✓

Track and Field

	Men's	Women's		Men's	Women's
Northwest Nazarene College, ID	✓	✓	University of Idaho, ID	✓	✓
Pittsburgh State University, PA	✓	✓	University of Illinois at Urbana, IL	✓	✓
Providence College, RI	✓	✓	University of Maryland— College Park, MD	✓	✓
Purdue University, West Lafayette, IN	✓	✓	University of Miami, FL	✓	✓
Samford University, AL	✓	✓	University of Missouri— Columbia, MO	✓	✓
San Diego State University, CA	✓	✓	University of North Dakota, ND	✓	✓
Southern Illinois University— Carbondale, IL	✓	✓	University of Northern Colorado, CO	✓	✓
Southern Methodist University, TX	✓	✓	University of Pittsburgh, PA	✓	✓
Southwest Missouri State University, MO	✓	✓	University of Southern Indiana, IN	✓	
Stanford University, CA	✓	✓	University of Texas— Arlington, TX	✓	✓
Syracuse University, NY	✓	✓	University of Virginia, VA	✓	✓
Towson State University, MD	✓	✓	Virginia Polytechnic Institute, VA	✓	✓
Troy State University, AL	✓		Washington State University, WA	✓	✓
Tuskegee University, Al	✓	✓	Wayne State College, NE	✓	✓
University of Alabama— Birmingham, AL		✓	Western Illinois University, IL	✓	✓
University of Alabama— Tuscaloosa, AL	✓	✓	Winthrop University, SC	✓	✓
University of Florida, FL	✓	✓			

Volleyball

	Men's	Women's		Men's	Women's
Alabama A&M University, AL		✓	Columbia College, MO		✓
Appalachian State University, NC		✓	Duke University, NC		✓
Auburn University, AL		✓	D'Youville College, NY		✓
Austin Peay State University, TX		✓	East Carolina University, NC		✓
Barber-Scotia, NC		✓	Eckerd College, FL		✓
Bemidji State University, MN		✓	Florida A&M University, FL		✓
Benedictine College, KS		✓	Florida Institute of Technology, FL		✓
Boston College, MA		✓	Georgetown University, DC		✓
Bowie State University, MD		✓	Hampton University, VA		✓
California State Polytechnic Univ.—Pomona, CA		✓	Henderson State University, AR		✓
Centenary College, LA		✓	Howard University, DC		✓
Central Connecticut State University, CT		✓	Jacksonville State University, AL		✓
Chadron State College, NE		✓	Loyola College, MD		✓
Clarion University, PA		✓	Michigan State University, MI		✓
Clemson University, SC		✓	Mississippi University for Women, MS		✓
Colorado School of Mines, CO		✓			

Volleyball

	Men's	Women's
Moorhead State University, MN		✓
Murray State University, KY		✓
Northeast Missouri State University, MO		✓
Northwestern College, MN		✓
Northwestern University, IL		✓
Northwest Nazarene College, ID		✓
Nova Southeastern University, FL		✓
Ouachita Baptist University, AR		✓
Pittsburg State University, KS		✓
Providence College, RI		✓
Purdue University, IN		✓
Samford University, AL		
San Diego State University, CA	✓	✓
Southern Illinois University—Carbondale, IL		✓
Southwest Missouri State University, MO		✓
Stanford University, CA	✓	✓
Syracuse University, NY		✓
Towson State University, MD	✓	✓
Troy State University, AL		✓
Tuskegee University, AL		✓
University of Alabama—Birmingham, AL	✓	
University of Alabama—Tuscaloosa, AL		✓
University of Florida, FL		✓
University of Idaho, ID		✓
University of Illinois at Urbana, IL		✓
University of Maryland—College Park, MD		✓
University of Missouri—Columbia, MO		✓
University of Missouri—St. Louis, MO		✓
University of North Dakota, ND		✓
University of Northern Colorado, CO		✓
University of Pittsburgh, PA		✓
University of San Diego, CA		✓
University of Southern Indiana, IN		✓
University of Virginia, VA		✓
Virginia Polytechnic Institute, VA		✓
Wayne State College, NE		✓
Western Illinois University, IL		✓
Winthrop University, SC		✓
Xavier University, LA		✓

Wrestling

	Men's	Women's
Appalachian State University, NC	✓	
Central Connecticut State University, CT	✓	
Chadron State College, NE	✓	
The Citadel, SC	✓	
Clarion University, PA	✓	
Clemson University, SC	✓	
Colorado School of Mines, CO	✓	
Duke University, NC	✓	
Howard University, DC	✓	
Michigan State University, MI	✓	
Moorhead State University, MN	✓	
Morgan State University, MD	✓	
Northeast Missouri State University, MO	✓	
Purdue University, IN	✓	
Southwest Missouri State University, MO	✓	
Stanford University, CA	✓	
Syracuse University, NY	✓	
University of Illinois—Urbana, IL	✓	
University of Maryland—College Park, MD	✓	
University of Missouri—Columbia, MO	✓	
University of North Dakota, ND	✓	
University of Pittsburgh, PA	✓	
Virginia Polytechnic Institute, VA	✓	

INDEX OF COLLEGE SCHOLARSHIPS
BY INSTITUTION

Adrian College, MI
General
Minority/Race-Specific
Agnes Scott College, GA
Academic
Academic—Religion
City/County/State
Creative/Visual/Performing Arts—
Music
Other
Alabama A&M University, AL
Academic
Allegheny College, PA
Academic
Minority/Race-Specific
Allentown College of St.Francis, PA
Academic
Antioch College, OH
Academic
Biological Sciences
City/County/State
Computer Science and Mathematics
General
Language/Literature/Humanities
Minority/Race-Specific
Social Science—Public Administration
Social Science—Social Work
Appalachian State University, NC
Academic
Business
City/County/State
General
Minority/Race-Specific
Ashland University, OH
Academic
Athletic
General
Minority/Race-Specific
Auburn University, AL
Academic
Engineering
Minority/Race-Specific

Austin Peay State University, TN
Academic
Athletic
Communications—Speech
Creative/Visual/Performing Arts
General
Language/Literature/Humanities—
Writing
Minority/Race-Specific
Other
Veterans/Military
Barber-Scotia College, NC
General
Bard College, NY
Academic
Biological Sciences
General
Physical Sciences
Bates College, ME
General
Minority/Race-Specific
Bemidji State University, MN
Communications—Journalism/Radio and
Television Broadcasting
Creative/Visual/Performing Arts—Music
Creative/Visual/Performing Arts—Theatre
General
Benedictine College, KS
Academic
Academic—Religion
City/County/State
Minority/Race-Specific
Berea College, KY
General
Bethany College, WV
Academic
General
Minority/Race-Specific
Birmingham-Southern College, AL
Academic
Creative/Visual/Performing Arts—
Fine Arts

INDEX OF PRIVATE SCHOLARSHIPS

Agriculture

ANIMAL SCIENCE
Alabama Cattlemen's Foundation
Dexter Hobbs Scholarship
FORESTRY
Alabama Farmers Federation

Biological Sciences

Association of Official Analytical Chemists,
    International
Clare Boothe Luce Scholarships in Science and
    Engineering

Business

ACCOUNTING
Alcoa Foundation
American Institute of Certified Public
    Accountants (AICPA) (Minority
    Scholarships)
American Society of Women Accountants,
    Chicago
American Society of Women Accountants,
    Montgomery, AL
National Association of Black Accountants, Inc.
ACTUARIAL SCIENCE
Society of Actuaries/Casualty Actuarial Society
    (Minority Scholarships)
BUSINESS ADMINISTRATION
Armco Insurance Group
Duracell/National Urban League Scholarship
Fukunaga Scholarship Foundation
General Electric Foundation Minority Student
    Scholarship
Golden State Minority Foundation
James S. Kemper Foundation
National Association of Plumbing-Heating-
    Cooling Contractors
National Electronic Distributor Association
    Education Foundation
National Urban League

Pepsi-Cola Company
Thomas A. Watson Scholarship
BUSINESS INFORMATION MANAGEMENT
Alcoa Foundation
BUSINESS MANAGEMENT
Alcoa Foundation
HOSPITALITY ADMINISTRATION
The Club Managers Association of America
MARKETING
Alcoa Foundation
Asbury Park Press Scholarships for Minority
    Students
J. Victor Herd Memorial Scholarship
REAL ESTATE
American Institute of Real Estate Appraisers
TRANSPORTATION MANAGEMENT
GMI Engineering and Management Institute

Communications

ADVERTISING/PUBLIC RELATIONS
American Association of Advertising Agencies
    Minority Internships
Asbury Park Press Scholarships for Minority
    Students
Black Communicators Scholarships
Gannett Foundation Scholarships
The Poynter Fund
JOURNALISM/RADIO AND TELEVISION
    BROADCASTING
Academy of Television Arts & Sciences
Asbury Park Press Scholarships for Minority
    Students
Aviation—Space Writers Association
Black Communicators Scholarships
Chicago Association of Black Journalists
    Scholarships
Chip Quinn Scholars Program
Concerned Media Professionals
    Scholarship
Cox Newspapers Minority Journalism
    Scholarship

The Foundation for Exceptional Children
The Franan Scholarship Fund for Black Women
Thomas A. Watson Scholarship
Thurgood Marshall Scholarship Fund

Other

A. G. Bell Association for the Deaf
American Society for Enology and Viticulture
American Meteorological Society
Carver Scholarship Program
Lonzie L. Jones, Jr., National Sickle Cell
    Scholarship
National Civil Community Corps

Radio Technical Commission for
    Aeronautics
The Foundation for Exceptional Children

Union/Club Affiliation

Agnes Jones Jackson Scholarship
Alpha Kappa Alpha Sorority, Inc.
Business and Professional Women's
    Foundation
Omega Psi Phi Fraternity, Inc.

Veterans/Military

Alabama Department of Veterans Affairs